ALT KID LIT

Children's Literature Association Series

ALT KID LIT

What Children's Literature Might Be

Edited by Kenneth B. Kidd and Derritt Mason

University Press of Mississippi / Jackson

The University Press of Mississippi is the scholarly publishing agency of the Mississippi Institutions of Higher Learning: Alcorn State University, Delta State University, Jackson State University, Mississippi State University, Mississippi University for Women, Mississippi Valley State University, University of Mississippi, and University of Southern Mississippi.

www.upress.state.ms.us

The University Press of Mississippi is a member of the Association of University Presses.

Copyright © 2024 by University Press of Mississippi
All rights reserved

∞

Library of Congress Cataloging-in-Publication Data

Names: Kidd, Kenneth B., editor. | Mason, Derritt, editor.
Title: Alt kid lit : what children's literature might be / Kenneth B. Kidd, Derritt Mason.
Other titles: Children's Literature Association series.
Description: Jackson : University Press of Mississippi, 2024. | Series: Children's literature association series | Includes bibliographical references and index.
Identifiers: LCCN 2023058471 (print) | LCCN 2023058472 (ebook) | ISBN 9781496851024 (hardback) | ISBN 9781496851031 (trade paperback) | ISBN 9781496851048 (epub) | ISBN 9781496851055 (epub) | ISBN 9781496851062 (pdf) | ISBN 9781496851079 (pdf)
Subjects: LCSH: Children's literature—History and criticism. | Young adult literature—History and criticism. | Gender identity in children—Juvenile literature. | Queer theory—Juvenile literature. | Identity (Philosophical concept)—Juvenile literature.
Classification: LCC PN1009.A1 A44 2024 (print) | LCC PN1009.A1 (ebook) | DDC 809.89282—dc23/eng/20240129
LC record available at https://lccn.loc.gov/2023058471
LC ebook record available at https://lccn.loc.gov/2023058472

British Library Cataloging-in-Publication Data available

CONTENTS

Acknowledgments ix

Introduction 3
Kenneth B. Kidd and Derritt Mason

PART I. ALT GENRE

Kid Lit from beyond the Grave: Spiritualism,
Child Mediums, and the Haunting Problem of Child Agency.......... 19
Victoria Ford Smith

Singing a "Sea Island Song": Alice Childress's
Responsive Black Theater 32
Katharine Capshaw

The Seductions of *Little Red Riding Hood*:
On the Thresholds of Children's Drawings........................ 44
Jakob Rosendal

Snanger Danger: SS/HG Fanfiction, Kinship, and an
Affinity Space Model of Children's and Young Adult Literature 65
Amanda K. Allen

Zine Ecoactivism and Pedagogies of Hope
in *World War 3 Illustrated* #46 79
Brianna Anderson

Emergency Children's Literature: Some Observations
on Pandemic Picture Books 99
Gabriel Duckels

The Case of *Jonny*'s Genre: An Interview
with Joshua Whitehead 114
Joshua Whitehead and Derritt Mason

PART II. ALT MEDIUM

YA Literature, *Plus Ultra*: A Case Study
of the Shōnen Anime *My Hero Academia*......................... 127
Brandon Murakami

From Melodrama to Kitschy Romance:
Alt Kid Media in India and Pakistan 141
Tehmina Pirzada

"Bizarre Creatures" and the Fans Who Love Them:
The Dark Crystal as Alternative Children's Culture 156
Paige Gray

Video Games and Young People's Digital Cultures:
A Panel Discussion 170
Kristopher Alexander, Negin Dahya, TreaAndrea M. Russworm,
Catherine Burwell, and Derritt Mason

PART III. ALT EPISTEMOLOGY

The Alt Within: Queerness, Psychoanalysis,
and Children's Literature as Enigmatic Signifier 187
Natasha Hurley

"We're Americans Too!": Contingencies and Contradictions
in Picture Books about Japanese American Incarceration 202
Gabrielle Atwood Halko

Retomando el Día de los Muertos: Death, Life,
and Latinx Epistemology in Children's Literature 217
Cristina Rhodes

Reimagining the "Alternative": Sustaining Representation
of Indigenous People and People of Color through
Speculative Fiction in *The Marrow Thieves* and *Mañanaland* 230
Erica Law-Montes and Cristina Rivera

Silkpunk and Agender Childhoods in
Neon Yang's *Tensorate* Universe 246
Shuyin Yu

Alt Publishing for Young People: An Interview with Vivek Shraya 260
Vivek Shraya and Derritt Mason

Contributors 273

Index 279

ACKNOWLEDGMENTS

We would like to offer our biggest thanks to our contributors for their work and dedication over a very challenging period of time. We're grateful to Vivek Shraya and Josh Whitehead for so generously sharing their time and experiences with us, and to Eden Middleton for their expert assistance with the transcription and editing of the interviews and roundtable.

We owe thanks to many of our (alt) kid lit friends and colleagues for their care and for encouraging this project (and its editors!), in particular: Kate Capshaw, Naomi Hamer, Pete Kunze, Angel Matos, Kate Slater, Beth Marshall, and Victoria Ford Smith. We appreciate the confidence and support of Katie Keene and her colleagues at University Press of Mississippi, as well as Roxanne Harde, editor for the Children's Literature Association Series with UPM.

Kenneth would like to thank Derritt, above all, for patience, humor, and social topping (and for his fantastic contributions to this volume); Derritt would like to thank Kenneth, his favorite cocounselor, for always making collaboration such a joy. Both Kenneth and Derritt are grateful to their broader networks of family, friends, and colleagues, for just the right balance of encouragement and distraction.

ALT KID LIT

INTRODUCTION

Kenneth B. Kidd and Derritt Mason

What we call children's and young adult literature (hereafter CYA) is simultaneously a body of imaginative work, a field of professional engagement, and a civic good. At the same time, CYA means different things in different contexts and is forever shifting in aims, practices, and boundaries. *Alt Kid Lit: What Children's Literature Might Be* attempts to focus on materials, methodologies, and epistemologies that are absent or underacknowledged in the field of CYA studies. On the materials side alone, CYA has long been populated with texts and genres that weren't intended for children but have been associated with them and thus recruited into the big tent. There are also many texts or traditions that might be considered CYA but are not (yet). In some cases, these texts and traditions exist outside the normative mechanisms of print culture or are ostensibly too ephemeral or lowbrow. Moreover, many narrative traditions beyond the hegemony of Anglo-European culture (especially Indigenous ones) aren't well known or haven't been included. Essays in this volume consider overlooked materials and also challenge conceptualizations of and approaches to CYA.

The "alt" in our title is less a theoretical term and more a working idea, even a provocation. It applies at once to the "kid" and the "lit"—meaning, we're interested in alt childhood as well as alt CYA. The *Oxford English Dictionary* offers this definition of "alt": "Alternative; spec. denoting a version of some cultural phenomenon (originally and esp. music) that is regarded as outside the mainstream of its genre." The alt prefix more specifically—historically alt-, a kind of hashtag—dates to the late 1980s when it was used by internet newsgroups to indicate that a topic of interest falls outside the mainstream. Newsgroups were similar to online discussion groups, and the Usenet was essentially a bulletin board system (BBS). Computer users involved in alt newsgroups sought alternatives to more mainstream discussions already available on Usenet, across a wide range of areas, from sports and politics to literature to sex. Alt designated not only the content but the channels themselves. As noted by David Barr, alt is not simply short for the word "alternative" in the apocryphal history of the term; it ostensibly also is an acronym for "anarchists, lunatics, and terrorists." The prefix functioned not merely alongside but also in oppositional critique to mainstream topics and channels. Alt newsgroups on the net valued free speech above all else. Some were linked with illegal activities while others were less provocative. In social media and gaming there are "alt accounts," additional accounts created on a platform by an existing user, usually for subversive purposes. Another alt usage with some social traction is alt-right, which has unfortunately escaped the Usenet context and gone mainstream. In the United States, the alt-right (later the radical right) is now just the Right. Another contemporary manifestation of alt is alt-ac, or alt academia, meaning career tracks for holders of graduate degrees that are in some way alternative to the painfully declining model of tenure-track positions.

As this terminology review suggests, the alt prefix carries some risk.[1] Its most obvious drawback is that referring to something as alternative can reinforce that status rather than interrogate it. If we use alt to designate minority or nonnormative or politically oppositional projects, we can't assume that it will function in an interrogative or deconstructive way. Moreover, some of the more negative connotations of alt might come into play. In her essay on Alice Childress and Black children's theater in this volume, Kate Capshaw speaks to this risk, writing that "categorizing Black CYA as an alternative form is deeply unnerving, since the formulation of 'alternative' replicates the othering that has shaped scholarship in children's and young adult literature. Alternative as a term summons the dominant form as a ghostly presence, makes us think about alternative to (. . . what?), calling up Whiteness even as it seeks to rectify its abuses and elisions." Other contributors to the volume express similar unease as they consider their topics. We take this concern seriously. We understand alt to be a term of contestation, useful but not without its drawbacks.

We suggest that a working notion of alt can help identify overlooked possibilities and dislodge more conventional ideas about what constitutes CYA. While it's risky, as we agree with Capshaw, to present non-white literature as alt, we must acknowledge that white privilege has been a defining feature (not a bug) of Anglophone CYA.[2] Readers are surely familiar with the grim statistics about the relative lack of materials for children by and about diverse authors and especially by and about BIPOC people. The widely circulated infographic put together by Sarah Park Dahlen and David Huyck and drawn from data provided by the Cooperative Children's Book Center in Wisconsin shows that in 2018, only 22 percent of the materials published for children in the United States depict characters from non-white backgrounds—vs. the 27 percent of books featuring animal or toy characters. The #WeNeedDiverseBooks campaign and other initiatives, which build on ongoing efforts, are helping make some headway in both publishing and general awareness, but suffice to say that (to echo Nancy Larrick's famous line) the world of CYA remains all-too white. Writing about Puerto Rican literature and culture, Marilisa Jiménez Garcia argues compellingly that the idea of "children's literature" is too saturated with white privilege and cultural racism to be usable; she introduces an alternative concept, "youth literature." Perhaps in time this alt formulation will become widely operational. White privilege, of course, is a structural reality not only in children's publishing but also in children's literature studies as a discipline, as recognized by the 2017 #WeNeedDiverseScholars special forum in *The Lion and the Unicorn* and the same journal's 2019 issue on "One Hundred Years of African American Children's Literature"; the founding of a new academic journal, *Research on Diversity in Youth Literature* (*RDYL*); and other initiatives. We have sought to give priority in this volume to the voices of BIPOC, queer, international, and early-career scholars.

We might describe CYA scholarship as alt to the degree that it pushes against received wisdom and offers new ways to think about texts and contexts. To take another example, Capshaw followed up her first book on Harlem Renaissance CYA with a spectacular long study of what she calls the African American "photobook," an amalgam of picture book and coffee table book and political tract and an important vehicle of Civil Rights activism. Alt scholarship can cast fresh light on less diverse and/or ideologically problematic materials, asking us to think anew about how they work and circulate. Such scholarship tends to spotlight the construction of childhood as much as the identity or role of CYA. Robin Bernstein's *Racial Innocence*, for instance, was groundbreaking in its central argument that only white kids get to be innocent in Anglo-American culture, and also in its emphasis on the performative life of "scriptive things," including books but also dolls, toys, and other artifacts of material culture.

Sometimes a shift in basic interpretive frame can expand the way we grasp a topic, as, for instance, when Joe Sutliff Sanders describes children's nonfiction as a literature of questions rather than a literature of answers, or when Marah Gubar and Victoria Ford Smith (in separate books) reframe CYA as child-adult collaboration. Gubar's subsequent notion of the "kinship model" of children's literature, formative for many contributors to this collection, is an alt theory of children's literature with growing traction. Gubar's model speaks back to probably the most infamous alt theory of children's literature, that of Jacqueline Rose concerning the "impossibility" of children's literature. Now available is a rich body of critical literature dealing in this question of child-adult articulation. Along those lines, Michelle Ann Abate has examined the substantial body of CYA written for and marketed to adults. Mandy Suhr-Sytsma draws on Indigenous literature to reframe the discussion on YA literature, underscoring that adolescent individuation occurs in dynamic relation to systems of power, while Julia Passanante Elman proposes that across the twentieth century and into our decidedly neoliberal moment, adolescence more broadly has been constructed as a kind of medical disability. Rachel Conrad, meanwhile, expands our understanding of children's poetry in terms of both material and our thinking about time, while Alison Waller examines the "lifelong reading act," which in her view collapses any easy child-adult distinction.

In accordance with these examples, we mean "alt" to align with the broad tradition of progressive critique and analysis as well as with materials not always granted literariness. There's extensive scholarship with alt tendencies on comparative CYA and translation; on the impacts of imperialism and colonialism and on postcolonial pushbacks; on leftist and socialist as well as right-wing CYA; on ableism and bodily variation (including neurodivergence); on queer energies and gender identities; on archives and libraries and book history; on new media, digital cultures, imagetexts, and fandoms; on trauma and the impacts of war and genocide; on climate change and childhood ecologies and youth activisms. In its alt explorations of child users and children's forms, and its positioning of childhood as a modern biopolitical formation, childhood studies increasingly dovetails with CYA studies, as does some recent work in philosophy and theory studies focused on children, beginners, and minors (Breslow, Kidd, Newland, Sainsbury).

Alt CYA studies might involve new or unexpected techniques of analysis. Those techniques, of course, can become familiar, even routine, as has happened with most theoretical and critical innovations in literary studies. Queer theory, to take one example, used to represent an alt lens not just on sexuality but social life more generally, and now queer frameworks have been seamlessly integrated into interpretive discourse (that's not to say that we can't queer queer theory!). The same may eventually happen for, say, macroanalysis or big data approaches to CYA. In some cases, alt theories or methodologies are introduced through innovative narrative frameworks, as with Elizabeth Wheeler's conceit of "Handiland" in her study of disability narratives and ableism. Alt theory may call for alt rhetoric or alt presentation.

The more we consider scholarship in the field, the more alt we see. And to be fair, most scholarship seeks to make an original contribution to a field or line of thinking, which is to say that most scholarship is alt aspirational. Innovation, however incremental, is the name of the humanities research game. In that sense, we are already living in an alt kid lit moment, if we mean an ongoing expansion of materials and methodologies beyond more traditional or familiar ones. At the same time, custodial or conservative understandings of CYA have not gone away, any more than have the ideologies with which they are entangled—most centrally, the idea of childhood innocence, asserted against sexuality and mobilized along racial lines. CYA remains a messy jumble of objects, ideas, and attitudes, the site of both cultural indoctrination and cultural resistance, of formal repetition alongside aesthetic innovation. Hence, we suggest that alt is good to think with, as a hedge against business as usual, as much for its risks and confusions as for its more positive associations.

This collection spotlights how CYA has been understood thus far, and also how it has not yet been imagined. We are interested in diverse, speculative, emergent, and alternative materials, methods, epistemologies, and theorizations. What kinds of texts, genres, and mediums might be studied as CYA, expansively construed? What interpretive frameworks are not yet employed or imagined? Already available to us, of course, are alternatives to "children's literature," such as "young people's texts and cultures," an alt formulation used by the Centre for Research in Young People's Texts and Cultures (CRYTC), or "youth literature," as suggested by Jiménez Garcia—in both cases, the emphasis on youth aligns with social science paradigms as well as social justice initiatives (and pushing against a perceived infantilization). Aware of these useful alt terms, we retain "kid lit" to spotlight the complications around it. In the States at least, CYA was long dismissed by gatekeepers as "kiddie lit," as Beverly Lyon Clark observes at length in her foundational study about the cultural and academic capital of CYA. We use "kid lit" in part because it invokes that history of dismissiveness toward youth and its materials. Ultimately, the alt in *Alt Kid Lit* gestures not so much to any specific content or viewpoint but rather to the structural discontents of CYA as a term of designation, institutionalization, and professionalization. *Alt Kid Lit* seeks to find alternative ways of doing CYA, so that we don't get too settled in our ideas and practices.

Recognizing that there are many alt arrangements for the book, we have organized our chapters into three categories: alt genre, alt medium, and alt epistemology. The contributions in Part I attend to materials that are either not usually considered CYA or are insufficiently consecrated as such. Chapters in Part II continue that theme but focus on child-attentive media other than forms of writing, especially visual and imagetext media. Part III meanwhile gives priority to alt epistemology in and around a range of materials and contexts; here the focus isn't necessarily on new forms but on new ways of understanding. Most chapters fit under all three categories in some measure, and there are thematic, theoretical, and other sorts of affinities across these categories. There's considerable overlap, for instance, between the chapters in Parts I and II, and it's sometimes hard to distinguish genre from medium.

That said, the first group of chapters in the volume makes use of diverse genres to explore the issue of child agency as well as to develop theoretical perspectives on CYA and children's forms that might help move our conversations forward. Victoria Ford Smith turns to the intriguing topic of child mediums during the American Spiritualist period of the nineteenth century, arguing that debates around the child medium's agency or lack thereof speak to concerns about child agency and adult manipulation central to CYA studies. The literature on child mediums includes both fiction and nonfiction, and the young subjects of these narratives, she shows, are at once active and passive, imagined as powerful instruments for communications from the dead and/or as particularly sensitive to spirit interference. The Spiritualist movement found ways to spotlight purported child mediums and their unusual abilities, interviewing them or putting them in dialogue with adult interlocutors. Smith finds in these accounts ample evidence that children could and did engage with adult scripts.

An understudied if more conventionally recognizable genre of CYA is children's drama, and we have even less scholarship on Black dramatic literature for young people. As Capshaw points out in her important chapter, "Black cultural production for youth before the twenty-first century can already be considered an 'alternative' story of CYA, one that privileges Black cultural contexts over White publishing power." Black creativity has been constant in Black culture, she stresses, but white archives have failed to document such, largely due to racism, white privilege, and lack of attention to ephemeral forms such as the pamphlet and the newspaper. Capshaw's essay on Alice Childress's musical play "Sea Island Song" (1977) not only spotlights this and other important compositions by Childress but also models the kind of scholarship we desperately need on material by and about underrepresented groups. Celebrating African diasporic culture and music, "Sea Island Song," Capshaw argues, stands for Black children's theater at-large as a "space for restorative pedagogy for Black children."

Jakob Rosendal reflects on an experiment with children's drawings he conducted with Danish kindergarten and school children in 2019–2020. Curious about how they would illustrate a popular narrative with marked gender and sexual content, he asked the children to draw the *Little Red Riding Hood* fairy tale, reading them a 1916 Danish translation of the Brothers Grimm version. Other than that, he gave them no directions as to what or how they should draw. In 2020, the resulting 184 drawings were exhibited at The Women's Museum in Denmark. Rosendal explores the interpretive as much as the imaginative power of the child artists, asking: "If we follow the lines of children's drawings engaging with the narrative lines of a fairy tale, where might they take us? What might CYA look like from the perspective of children's drawings?" Examining individual drawings while looking across the full archive, and leaning on psychoanalysis in particular, Rosendal proposes a "threshold model of childhood" (akin to Marah Gubar's affinity model of CYA) in which children variously accept, resist, and revise adult scripts about sexual and social life.

Amanda K. Allen also works with the notion of child-adult kinship in her analysis of a strain of Harry Potter fanfiction known as Severus Snape/Hermione Granger (SS/HG). Allen proposes that in fanfiction young people speak in tandem with as much as against adults, working collaboratively across categories of age and other identity markers to create meaning. Allen draws on Gubar's kinship model of CYA and also on James Paul Gee's notion of "affinity spaces," meaning spaces—often virtual—organized around a shared passion or concern. Through her case study of a novel-length SS/HG fic, which ran from 2000 to 2010, as one such affinity space, and one thematizing child-adult collaboration, Allen proposes a theory of CYA based not around age distinctions or even texts and genres but rather "shared passion." Catherine Tosenberger and Kimberley Reynolds had already proposed fanfiction as a form of CYA, since it is produced as well as consumed by young people, and Allen broadens that proposition by suggesting that "shared passion" matters more than age distinctions.

Brianna Anderson makes the case that child-produced material about environmental crises offers a more radical vision of young people as change agents than do more mainstream (adult-produced) texts, even those with progressive environmental messages. Through analyses of the text and illustrations of the anthology zine *World War 3 Illustrated #46: Young and Climate Change*, Anderson shows how this specific issue builds on the collaborative and activist tendencies of the zine series to which it belongs, by focusing on environmental complexities not typically addressed in more mainstream materials and by encouraging agency through DIY zine-making. Youth-produced materials such as this zine, Anderson points out, align with the reality of young climate activists such as Greta Thunberg, who are sounding alarms about environmental damage and climate change. In Anderson's reading, *World War 3 Illustrated* models what Paolo Freire calls a critical "pedagogy of hope" even in the face of daunting problems.

The COVID-19 pandemic has dramatically impacted the world, with accelerating sickness, death, and social isolation causing widespread anxiety and panic. Another consequence was the rapid development of picture books and other narratives for children about the pandemic, often in the form of downloadable pdfs or similar digital forms that could be rapidly disseminated. That material—ephemeral, openly didactic, and/or therapeutic—is the topic of Gabriel Duckels's chapter. Putting COVID-19 children's materials in conversation with earlier CYA materials about HIV and the AIDS crisis, Duckels raises questions about what he calls "emergency children's literature," meaning material generated in response to crisis and this crisis in particular. The emergency CYA produced in and around COVID-19, he shows, bears some resemblances to material about HIV/AIDS and reflects some of the same pressures of inequality and oppression, even as the divergences between the two genres are significant.

Part I closes with one of two original interviews conducted by Derritt Mason with creative writers whose compelling and provocative work is often located within and around the generic boundaries of CYA. Together, these interviews speak to how industry pressures, genre and form, local and national borders, and individual creative impulses and agendas have shaped storytelling. Mason's interview with Joshua Whitehead reveals how Whitehead initially imagined his award-winning novel, *Jonny Appleseed* (2018), as young adult literature, while his publisher had other ideas, largely due to the book's queer sexual content. Whitehead also details his own commitment, as a Two-Spirit Indigenous Oji-nêhiyaw storyteller, to decolonizing Eurocentric understandings of genre; narrative patterns often understood to be fundamental *Bildungsroman* conventions, he points out, appear in Indigenous oral storytelling; "magical" elements often labeled as "speculative" are in fact "the most real" dimensions of his work.

Chapters in Part II attend to imagetext and visual media, making the case for its inclusion in the CYA big tent. Urging, like other contributors, a more expansive understanding of what counts as children's materials, Brandon Murakami writes on the genre of shōnen anime, emphasizing how it resonates with both superhero comics and the narrative structures of CYA. Shōnen anime, he points out, is legible to Western consumers due to its reworkings and combinations of familiar themes and tropes. His case study is the popular series *My Hero Academia*, which in his view encodes the history of US–Japan political relations even as it offers a kind of transcultural superhero story. Murakami's essay is instructive both as a close reading of this popular production and as a discussion of the broader benefits of thinking about anime and manga as CYA.

Pirzada takes up what she calls "alt kid media" in India and Pakistan, discussing television programs for children designed to counter the influence of imported Western media and to emphasize aspects of national culture, language included. Pirzada's contribution is twofold: first, she makes the case that media texts such as these shows share much territory with children's literary texts and should be considered a form of CYA; second, she underscores that while these shows do fit the category of children's media, they also actively resist that category to the extent that "children's media" (like CYA) connotes Western themes and values. The innovative shows *Alif Laila* (India) and *Ainak Wala Jinn* (Pakistan) both are and are *not* children's media by Western standards, she holds. While she sees these shows as laudatory, Pirzada also discusses how they construct a particular sort of child audience, reflecting adult anxieties about children under the usual pressures of linguistic and national belonging.

Another curious text associated with children and children's culture in the US context is Jim Henson's cult classic *The Dark Crystal* (1982). In her chapter, Paige Gray reads the film as a queer, posthuman, existential engagement with childhood and its discontents, related to but pushing beyond Henson's more conventionally upbeat Muppet franchise. Gray links *The Dark Crystal* to Henson's interests in fairy tales and Lewis Carroll's *Alice* books, similarly full of bizarre and sometimes menacing creatures. Of interest to Gray is not only the film itself, with its unsettling cast of puppets, but also the ongoing fandom around the film, which has inspired websites, social media fan groups, a film prequel, and even a two-year museum exhibit on Henson's puppetry. In the *Dark Crystal* fandom, she writes, we see people of diverse ages and backgrounds "deliberately and deliciously confusing what it means to be young or old"—more evidence of the kinship and affinity culture observed by other contributors as well.

A rich and emerging site of critique is the intersection between CYA and video game studies. In her essay for the journal *Games and Culture*, "Kideogames," Emma Joy Reay points to potential strategic and thematic resonances between these two fields. In particular, she argues, both disciplines often find themselves occupying liminal academic spaces. Their shared marginalization, she suggests, opens the possibility for a strategic critical alliance where both disciplines would benefit from each other's critical tools. To continue fostering dialogue between these areas of study, Part II concludes with a panel discussion on "Video Games and Young People's Digital Cultures" that originally took place on May 13, 2022, as part of the Association for Research in Cultures of Young People (ARCYP)'s annual research symposium. This conversation features interdisciplinary scholars Kristopher Alexander, Negin Dahya, and TreaAndrea M. Russworm.

Russworm, who has published on racial empathy and dystopian Blackness in the context of the video game adaptation of *The Walking Dead* and its child protagonist, here outlines her work with "Radical Play," a "civic and community engagement program" that she developed for high school students. Russworm explains how this program shifted her view of the scope and audience of video game studies in and beyond academic contexts. Next, Dahya describes a study that saw her working with youth in juvenile rehabilitation in order to codesign concept art for a virtual reality (VR) program. Her team's research, Dahya explains, was influenced by carceral logic, the role of VR technology, and the institutional regulations that govern research and collaboration with young people. Finally, Alexander invites us to consider the pedagogical potential of games and digital technology when teaching and learning with students of all ages. The discussion that follows explores the relationship between academic disciplines, institutional barriers, and video game studies; the ethics and challenges of participatory research with youth; and the stakes of "gamifying" difficult topics including slavery, colonialism, and genocide.

Chapters in Part III spotlight alternative epistemologies or frameworks for understanding CYA, both more generally and with respect to particular genres. Natasha Hurley opens the section with her compelling meditation on the places CYA isn't yet allowed to go. Ironically, those non-places are often policed not so much by their repression as by their phantasmatic figuration and ridicule, as with, to mention one of her examples, the Robert Mapplethorpe Museum for Children. As Hurley observes, however, we shouldn't just counter censorship and ridicule with progressive materials; rather, we need to understand how our stories about youth sexuality, both sincere and satirical, work beyond their manifest content. Hurley draws upon Marc Augé and Jean Laplanche to explore CYA as a non-place (Augé) and an "enigmatic signifier" (Laplanche), which enacts not only what we *don't* want children to hear and see but also what we *do*. "If we proceed from the premise that addresses to children are fundamentally enigmatic, and that the enigmatic nature of the address is fundamentally sexual," Hurley writes, "then we can begin to understand how even the seemingly blandest of stories might shed some light on the erstwhile guilty forms of sexuality that we deem inappropriate for children." In this context, "there is no alternative children's lit; there is only the alt *within* children's lit."

Gabrielle Atwood Halko, meanwhile, analyzes nine picture books about Japanese American internment, reflecting on what the picture book can and cannot accomplish in the face of such realities. Other scholars have written on the challenges of depicting such traumatic events and topics for children, young children especially, and Halko finds that even the more successful of these titles still hang back in some ways and resist the unsettling lessons they seek to teach. While these materials successfully depict the travesties of internship and interrupt the self-congratulatory story of World War II America, they sometimes stop short of criticizing the xenophobia and exceptionalism that drove the practice of internment in the first place and that remain with us still. "Intentionally or not," she writes, "citizenship is modeled in these picture books as racialized, unequal status that is conferred conditionally and unequally," shoring up the exclusionary dynamics of white privilege and identity. Picture books, she holds, do important cultural work, including the work of alt citizenship cultivation.

The chapters by Cristina Rhodes, Erica Law-Montes and Cristina Rivera, and Shuyin Yu shift focus to contemporary speculative CYA and its potential for challenging normative epistemologies. Rhodes examines recent Latinx novels for young readers that present death not as the tragic endpoint of life (as in many white narratives) but rather as a natural and even positive part of the life cycle. Through readings of *Cemetery Boys* (2020) by Aiden Thomas and *Labyrinth Lost* by Zoraida Córdova (2016), novels in which gender and sexuality are dynamic rather than binary, Rhodes argues that for Latinx people death is "full of possibility and transformation." Rhodes offers a sobering context for that argument, noting ongoing racialized and ethnic violence in the United States. Rhodes proposes that Latinx epistemologies of death have long emphasized themes of empowerment and transformation, and that these themes play out intriguingly in these two titles, with death and proximity to death recast as a transition, a rite of passage, and a form of social power.

In their analysis of *The Marrow Thieves* (2017) and *Mañanaland* (2020), Law-Montes and Rivera remind us that speculative fiction has historically privileged white childhood and has only more recently been taken up by BIPOC authors seeking to decenter whiteness and dramatize the histories of racism and colonialism. Law-Montes and Rivera draw upon Ebony Elizabeth Thomas's account of the "dark fantastic" and Suhr-Sytsma's scholarship on Indigenous YA to show how these two speculative and rather dystopian novels offer a grim but necessary picture of social realities even as they imagine alternative ways of being and living in the world. Law-Montes and Rivera situate the work of these novels in the larger context of calls for a more diverse and equitable body of work for young people as well as for more diverse and equitable practices of book production and promotion. Like Capshaw, they reflect on the vexed and vexing notion of the "alternative" and the construction of such to mean anything not white.

In a similar vein, Yu emphasizes the possibilities of speculative fiction and the genre of silkpunk, which challenges Orientalism by prioritizing Eastern forms of knowledge and emphasizing biological or organic materials (unlike the more Western tradition of steampunk, she points out, which favors inorganics like steel and glass). She looks specifically at Neon Yang's silkpunk novella *The Black Tides of Heaven* (2017), the first in the *Tensorate* series, and its creative modeling of agender childhood. By refusing the usual binary of innocent vs. sexual child, Yu argues, Yang manages in this novel to affirm children's agency in the construction of their own subjectivity. Silkpunk worldbuilding stresses alternatives to the "realistic" status quo, recognizing without capitulating to social norms. As with other contributions to the volume, Yu's essay stresses the relevance of a presumptively adult genre or mode (here silkpunk) to CYA by emphasizing how that genre attends to childhood while pushing against normative scripts.

Part III concludes with Mason's interview with another Canadian writer, Vivek Shraya. While Whitehead encountered resistance from his publisher, Shraya's writing career began with a formative experience in alt publishing: her illustrated book of short stories, *God Loves Hair*—recently rereleased by Arsenal Pulp Press in a ten-year anniversary edition (2020)—was originally self-published. Based on Shraya's "experience growing up in Edmonton [Canada] as a gender nonconforming child of Hindu immigrants," *God Loves Hair* is a fascinating alt kid lit case study on many levels: from its unique publishing history to the object itself, an unusually-shaped object that is part picture book, part coming-of-age story—a text that signifies as CYA while dealing with complex and often controversial topics like masturbation, racism, suicidal ideation, religion, and gender identity. In addition to *God Loves Hair*, Shraya has published two more formally (if not thematically) "traditional" children's picture books—*The Boy & the Bindi* (2016) and *Revenge of the Raccoons* (2022)—and she speaks passionately about the importance of visual elements to her storytelling, as well as the joys, pleasures, and potential political impact of the picture book form and CYA more broadly.

We hope that *Alt Kid Lit* will be usefully suggestive. It offers a necessarily select take on the alt question, reflecting where the field is right now and also our particular processes of volume assembly. The same paper call would surely generate a different set of materials today—the today of our writing this introduction, and the today of your encounter with it. We see the volume's potential weakness—the sheer range of possibilities here, and the flexibility of alt—as also its potential strength. Like many edited volumes, it's a kind of experiment, playing with a concept to encourage and amplify innovative scholarship. We invite you to continue the experiment.

Notes

1. With a few exceptions, we omit the hyphen that typically follows "alt" as a prefix. We consider "alt" to be a signifier worthy of interrogation in and of itself.

2. In this introduction we follow the Associated Press practice of not capitalizing "white," but we recognize that the topic is complicated and defer to the preferences of contributors in the following chapters.

Works Cited

Baer, Elizabeth. "A New Algorithm in Evil: Children's Literature in a Post-Holocaustal World." *The Lion and the Unicorn*, vol. 24, no. 3, Sept. 2000, pp. 378–401.

Barr, David, and The Pennsylvania State University. "So You Want to Create an Alt Newsgroup." *FAQS.org: Internet FAQ Archives*, http://www.faqs.org/faqs/alt-creation-guide/. Accessed 25 Aug. 2022.

Bernstein, Robin. *Racial Innocence: Performing American Childhood from Slavery to Civil Rights*. New York UP, 2011.

Breslow, Jacob. *Ambivalent Childhoods: Speculative Futures and the Psychic Life of the Child*. U of Minnesota P, 2021.

Capshaw, Katharine. *Civil Rights Childhood: Picturing Liberation in African American Photobooks*. U of Minnesota P, 2014.

Conrad, Rachel. *Time for Childhoods: Young Poets and Questions of Agency*. U of Massachusetts P, 2020.

Elman, Julia Passanante. *Chronic Youth: Disability, Sexuality, and US Media Cultures of Rehabilitation*. New York UP, 2014.

Gee, James Paul. *Situated Language and Learning: A Critique of Traditional Schooling*. Routledge, 2004.

Gubar, Marah. *Artful Dodgers: Reconceiving the Golden Age of Children's Literature*. Oxford UP, 2009.

Gubar, Marah. "The Hermeneutics of Recuperation: What a Kinship-Model Approach to Children's Agency Could Do for Children's Literature and Childhood Studies." *Jeunesse: Young People, Texts, Cultures*, vol. 8, no. 1, summer 2016, pp. 291–310.

Gubar, Marah. "On Not Defining Children's Literature." *PMLA*, vol. 126, no. 1, 2011, pp. 209–16.

Huyck, David, and Sarah Park Dahlen. "Diversity in Children's Books 2018." Infographic. With Edith Campbell, Molly Beth Griffin, K. T. Horning, Debbie Reese, Ebony Elizabeth Thomas, and Madeline Tyner, with statistics by the Cooperative Children's Book Center, School of

Education, University of Wisconsin–Madison, http://ccbc.education.wisc.edu/books/pcstats.asp. Accessed 2 Apr. 2020.

Jiménez Garcia, Marilisa. *Side by Side: US Empire, Puerto Rico, and the Roots of American Youth Literature and Culture.* UP of Mississippi, 2021.

Kidd, Kenneth B. *Theory for Beginners: Children's Literature as Critical Thought.* Fordham UP, 2020.

Newland, Jane. *Deleuze in Children's Literature.* Edinburgh UP, 2021.

Reay, Emma Joy. "Kideogames: Reimagining the Fringe of Literary Studies as the Forefront." *Games and Culture*, vol. 15, no. 7, Nov. 2020, pp. 772–88.

Reynolds, Kimberley. *Radical Children's Literature: Future Visions and Aesthetic Transformations in Juvenile Fiction.* Palgrave, 2007.

Russworm, TreaAndrea M. "Dystopian Blackness and the Limits of Racial Empathy in *The Walking Dead* and *The Last of Us*." *Gaming Representation: Race, Gender, and Sexuality in Video Games*, edited by Jennifer Malkowski and TreaAndrea M. Russworm, Indiana UP, 2017, pp. 109–28.

Sainsbury, Lisa. *Ethics in British Children's Literature: Unexamined Life.* Bloomsbury, 2013.

Sainsbury, Lisa. *Metaphysics of Children's Literature: Climbing Fuzzy Mountains.* Bloomsbury, 2021.

Sanders, Joe Sutliff. *A Literature of Questions: Nonfiction for the Critical Child.* U of Minnesota P, 2018.

Shraya, Vivek. *The Boy & the Bindi.* Illustrated by Rajni Perera, Arsenal Pulp Press, 2016.

Shraya, Vivek. *God Loves Hair: 10th Anniversary Edition.* Illustrated by Juliana Neufeld, Arsenal Pulp Press, 2020.

Shraya, Vivek. *Revenge of the Raccoons.* Illustrated by Juliana Neufeld, OwlKids Books, 2022.

Smith, Katharine Capshaw. *Children's Literature of the Harlem Renaissance.* Indiana UP, 2004.

Smith, Victoria Ford. *Between Generations: Collaborative Authorship in the Golden Age of Children's Literature.* UP of Mississippi, 2017.

Suhr-Sytsma, Mandy. *Self-Determined Stories: The Indigenous Reinvention of Young Adult Literature.* Michigan State UP, 2019.

Thomas, Ebony Elizabeth. *The Dark Fantastic: Race and the Imagination from Harry Potter to the Hunger Games.* New York UP, 2019.

Tosenberger, Catherine. "Mature Poets Steal: Children's Literature and the Unpublishability of Fanfiction." *Children's Literature Association Quarterly*, vol. 39, no. 1, spring 2014, pp. 4–27.

Waller, Alison. *Rereading Childhood Books: A Poetics.* Bloomsbury, 2019.

Wheeler, Elizabeth A. *Handiland: The Crippest Place on Earth.* U of Michigan P, 2019.

Whitehead, Joshua. *Jonny Appleseed.* Arsenal Pulp Press, 2018.

Part I

ALT GENRE

KID LIT FROM BEYOND THE GRAVE
Spiritualism, Child Mediums, and the Haunting Problem of Child Agency

Victoria Ford Smith

In the heyday of American Spiritualism, many adults spoke in the voices of the dead, but child mediums held particular fascination. James G. Allbe, writing in 1865 for the popular Spiritualist periodical *Banner of Light*, argued that no form of mediumship "engrosses deeper or more startling interest than that . . . given to us through the media of little children," whom he describes as "*great* instrumentalities" (2). Similar periodicals offered more reverent accounts of child mediums—children such as Ferdy Fox, son of Spiritualist royalty Kate Fox Jencken, who could channel spirits before he could talk, and fourteen-year-old Nellie Temple, whose trances hushed vast audiences at radical revivals. Child mediums were joined by other young people vital to the Spiritualist movement. Deceased children communicated from beyond to Spiritualist devotees, including one-year-old Spirit Matie, who "edited" the children's department of the periodical *Carrier Dove* through her mother's mediumship. In Spiritualist fiction, child characters participated in séances and submitted to the possession of spirit guides. Young Spiritualists captured the attention of adults who, intent on securing the future of their faith, published children's literature, catechisms, and curricula designed for the lyceums being established across the country.

While Spiritualists seemed to agree children were important to the movement, their admiration for baby mediums, spirit guides in short pants, and lisping future leaders was rooted in a Romanticism that tempered children's influence with assumptions of innocence and passivity.[1] For example, in 1873, the *Religio-philosophical Journal* introduced two child mediums living in

New Orleans, thirteen-year-old Mabel and seven-year-old Carrie. The girls were purportedly clairaudient and clairvoyant and could communicate with spirits, and George W. Kendall, the vice president of the Spiritual Society in the city, christened them "angel instruments." That pet name crystallizes both a celebration of the girls' power and the stubborn straitjacket of Romantic childhood, suggesting both their agency and its opposite. They were instruments, a word that signals a fine intuition but also implies they are tools, obedient to the desires of both the spirits inhabiting them and the adults around them. Carrie, for example, would sit placidly under a table upon the request of adults attending her séances while spirits tied her hands, delivering their messages by moving a crumb of chalk across her school slate.

Like other real and imagined children in the Spiritualist archive, Mabel and Carrie are simultaneously passive vessels and formidable forces. This contradiction might be familiar to scholars of children's literature and childhood. In this chapter, I argue not only that our field is uniquely poised to parse the fraught figure of the Spiritualist child but also that doing so reveals generative, alternate understandings of the history of children's literature and a useful perspective on its critical tradition. I take this position not because the Spiritualist child transformed children's literary history, although this figure does introduce previously ignored texts and genres.[2] Instead, I contend that the Spiritualist child is an evocative figure because it acts as a limit case for one of the primary and persistent questions in our field: what is the relationship between the child as construct and the child as actor, between adult desire and child agency?

Many scholars have considered this question. James R. Kincaid, in *Child-Loving: The Erotic Child and Victorian Culture* (1992), argues that "what we think of as 'the child' has been assembled in reference to desire, built up in erotic manufactories"—that "[a] child is not, in itself, anything. Any image, body, or being we can hollow out, purify, exalt, abuse, and locate sneakily in a field of desire will do for us as a 'child'" (5).[3] The same year, in his landmark article "The Other: Orientalism, Colonialism, and Children's Literature," Perry Nodelman interrogated "the possible oppressiveness of our supposedly objective or even benevolent truths and assumptions about childhood," and he has followed that theme through the present, most memorably in *The Hidden Adult* (2008). There, he argues that children's books act as primers for children in "being appropriately childlike in terms of one common adult conception of desirable and rewardable childlikeness" (30); that childlikeness is imagined in opposition to adults and often as a seductive innocence steeped in unknowingness, emptiness, and dependency. His work builds on Jacqueline

Rose's now canonical contention that "there is no child behind the category 'children's fiction,' other than the one which the category itself sets in place, the one which it needs to believe is there for its own purposes" (10). The adult, from this critical perspective, always haunts the child and its literature, speaking for and even through the child, who is but a medium. Nina Christensen describes this child figure as "restricted, defined, denied by her structural predicament" and suggests that a critical approach centered on agency provides an alternative to this position (13). Explorations of child agency, active for decades in sociology and other disciplines, have been vital to recent work by scholars such as Marah Gubar, Richard Flynn, and Rachel Conrad. For example, Conrad acknowledges children as "active interpreters, makers, and participants" in culture, arguing that recognizing young people as such requires us to question prevalent developmental models of childhood that reinforce the assumption that "ideas and works that children create are of less value than words produced by adults, and are noted only for their precocity or insufficiency" (*Time* 3, 4).

The child-as-construct and the child-as-agent are often presented as oppositional figures, but Christensen is clear that "between these two positions, a range of variations coexist" (13)—and, indeed, a close examination of scholarship on either side of this debate reveals a complicated gray area. For instance, while Sarah Schwebel ultimately contends that "pursuing the question of children's agency may lead to dead ends, in particular for children's literature scholars," primarily due to the difficulty of locating traces of children's cultural participation in available historical resources, she "do[es] not deny that children past and present have influenced, contributed to, and at times even authored texts most critics would characterize as children's literature" and advocates for helping children understand "how the texts authored for them work" (287). Among champions of child agency, Conrad understands that recognizing children as cultural agents requires retooling our understanding of agency itself to account for adults' influence on children's lives and literary productions ("My" 199). She claims that definitions of agency as autonomy "likely interfere" with our understanding of child agency, as young people's participation in culture involves "adult mediation through prompting, transcribing, teaching, editing, or other scaffolding." Adult mediation, she writes, "rather than eroding children's autonomy, is part of the background against which children's literary productions"—and I would argue all their cultural productions—"take shape" (200). Gubar argues that all people, adults and children alike, exert agency amid discourses that often impact how we speak, behave, and understand ourselves ("Hermeneutics").

The Spiritualist child usefully inhabits the middle (medium?) ground, the range of variations that Christensen identifies, between these two schools of thought. She both speaks forth and is spoken for. She is, in Robin Bernstein's formulation, both subject to the scripts adults provide her and able to resist or manipulate those scripts (165). She could be appropriated as definitive evidence for the child both as inescapably subject to adult imagination and as cheekily resistant to adult desire. In other words, the Spiritualist child, like the child of children's literature and childhood studies, epitomizes *both* the child as defined adult ideology and the child as agentic subject, and she helps us understand how those two positions are inextricable.

"Mere Babes, and Wholly Passive Mediums"

Many trace the start of Spiritualism to Kate Fox and her sister Margaret, who later were joined by their sister Leah, twenty-three years their senior. In the late 1840s and 1850s, the younger girls gained substantial fame for interpreting "spirit rappings," which they first heard (or produced) in their home in Hydesville, New York. The sisters established themselves as celebrity mediums, traveling the country and performing at public and private séances, with Leah acting as manager. In 1888, the sisters confessed that the rappings were a hoax, although Margaret (likely for financial reasons) attempted to recant her confession the following year.

The Fox sisters' youth was manipulated by writers both credulous and skeptical of their second sight. Believing Spiritualists cited the sisters' youthful innocence to reinforce the trustworthiness of their mediumship. For example, in 1878 a writer for *The Medium and Daybreak* insisted that the Foxes, "instead of being grown up, as is ordinarily supposed," at the time of the rappings "were mere babes, and wholly passive mediums" ("Mediumship" 296). According to recent accounts, Margaret Fox likely was fourteen or fifteen years old while Kate was eleven or twelve, but nineteenth-century Spiritualist periodicals claim they were as young as six and four. Skeptics also called upon the sisters' youth to safeguard the girls' reputations while condemning the rappings and the subsequent growth of Spiritualism as a malignant fraud. For instance, in *The Death-Blow to Spiritualism* (1888), Reuben Briggs Davenport writes the girls "were but little children, innocent of the thought of wrong, ignorant of the world and the world's guile" (14). Adults turned to common scripts about children's innocence, then, to emphasize the child medium's trustworthiness, to protect her from accusations of fraud—and, I would suggest, to maintain comfortable power hierarchies between adult and child by reading the remarkable powers of a young person through an assumption of childhood passivity. Consider Isabella Smith, who in 1870 was nine years old and, according to *Spiritual Monthly*, proof that "invisible intelligences can manifest . . . through the organism of a mere child" ("Sittings" 120). Smith's spirit guides "promised her certain presents. The presents did not come, but the entrancement did" (120), and "[w]hen [she] was restored she said that she had been to Boston with a little friend of hers, and had been eating candy. There appeared not the slightest evidence that she was at all conscious of what she had been made to do" (121). A child such as Smith will never be the mistress of her powers; she will remain an "organism" subject to the "controlling power" of both the spirits and her caretakers.

This sense of the child as subject to adult control is embedded in the idea of the medium. Mediums of any age are often described as vulnerable to the whims or desires of their spirit guide, often called their "control," and therefore the medium can be understood as merely a conduit for another's voice. In the case of the child medium, that voice is typically (although not always) an adult's, and the passivity associated with mediumship is exaggerated by youth. Even in death, the adult thus speaks for the child. The oblivious child medium is a stock character in Spiritualist periodicals and fiction, a reassuring figure that suggests not only that a child's mediumistic powers *rely* on innocence but also that such innocence forecloses the possibility of deceit and therefore must be maintained through secrecy. For example, in *Nora Ray, the Child-Medium: A Spiritualistic Story* (1878), the title character is described as "a wee little bit of humanity" who nevertheless "possessed the wonderful powers of mediumship," a child whose "organism could be used by those who had gone on before" (42). Nora both *possesses powers* that confound the adults around her and *is possessed*, an organism "used" by spirits, including a "gruff old sailor," an enslaved nursemaid named Aunt Susie, and eventually Nora's own deceased father (51, 67, 88–89). For most of the novel, Nora is unaware of her mediumship, interpreting her visions as dreams, and her caretakers are vigilant in maintaining her ignorance: "They did not make any explanations or intimate to the little one anything which would give her any knowledge that she possessed mediumistic powers, fearing that it might have a retarding influence, and prevent her giving way to the controlling power" (43).

Few contemporary scholars have considered the assumptions that underpin the particular appeal of child mediums. Anne Braude argues that the appearance of youth "associated the medium with the innocence of childhood," "added to a medium's credibility and to the impression she made on her audience," and was "considered to reduce the motivation for fraud"

(86–87). Braude focuses on the intersection of mediumship and gender, and indeed the play between passivity and power I locate in accounts of child mediums finds its closest parallel in representations of female mediums, who have received more critical attention. While female mediums possessed not only supernatural power but also social and economic capital, mediumship required them to become an empty space a spirit can occupy.[4] Child mediums' role in Spiritualism was interpreted through both gendered and aged lenses. Their assumed innocence, ignorance, and passivity were flexible commodities dependent on popular constructions of childhood deployed by adults (and, as I will consider below, potentially by children themselves) that could frame child mediums as powerful, as weak, and sometimes as both simultaneously.

Not every Spiritualist child channeled the dead, but even those less sensitive to spirit controls were imagined by adults in the movement—in ways that Nodelman, Rose, and Kincaid would recognize—as mediums for adult desire. For example, in *The Lyceum Manual: A Compendium of Physical, Moral, and Spiritual Exercises for Use in Progressive Lyceums Connected with British Spiritualists' Societies*, Spiritualist leaders Emma Hardinge Britten, Alfred Kitson, and H. A. Kersey outlined the proper organization and curriculum of Sunday schools for young Spiritualists. The proper lyceum, they imply, is one largely structured by adult authority, demanding the obedience of children's minds and bodies. The majority of the manual is dedicated to instructions for organized weekly meetings—including marches and calisthenics, conducted in ordered lines and begun and ended with the chime of a bell—as well as texts for recitation and catechisms for group dialogue between the instructor and students called "golden recitations." Those catechisms take the familiar form of dialogues published in similar texts, such as the *New England Primer*:

> CONDUCTOR—Does the spirit body die?
> LYCEUM—No, it is only the physical body that dies.
> . . .
> CONDUCTOR—What is a medium?
> LYCEUM—A medium is a sensitive person, through whose nervous forces spirits communicate. The bridge that connects the two worlds, and o'er which the angels come and go. (73)

Referred to only in the collective, "Lyceum," the children are expected to dutifully repeat the tenets of the conductor's beliefs, so while they are not channeling spirits, they are, nevertheless, a conduit for the words of adults. These Spiritualist children are remarkable because they exaggerate the idea that children are ciphers available to be defined by, spoken for, and scripted by adults. We could consider Spiritualism and its discourses of childhood as Nodelman considers children's literature: "as an adult practice with intentions toward child readers" (*Hidden* 4). Doing so might mean that the child medium, the child reader of a Spiritualist periodical, or the child attending a Sunday meeting at a lyceum would "develop the knowledge of what one particular adult philosophy understands to be the meaning of their own existence as young human beings, and possibly they even learn to view themselves and their own actions as this philosophy understands them" (*Hidden* 13).

Evangelizing Children

While it is productive to point to ways that Spiritualists construct the child as passive—a conduit communicating others' voices, a puppet repeating the catechism—doing so obscures how the movement imagined childhood in more radical ways that emphasized young people as agentic subjects. As Braude explains, in addition to championing women's rights, abolition, and reforms in marriage, health, labor, and dress, Spiritualists advocated for children's rights (3). This advocacy appears in Spiritualist periodicals, where children are often represented as vocal, independent subjects worthy of attention and respect. For example, in 1895, the children's column in *Light of Truth* begins with an explanation of the origins of the National Spiritualists Association, noting that one of the founding members brought his ten-year-old son to the organization's first official meeting. The boy "attended all [the] sessions of the trustees," the editor explains, which "awakened in him a deep interest in the N.S.A." He attends the N.S.A.'s first convention (after "securing the consent of his papa"), where "he was furnished with a badge, and by the board jokingly named their 'walking delegate'" (Longley 2). While this young Spiritualist is made a pet or gentle joke, the column nevertheless interprets his participation as the beginning of a long career of leadership; as he leaves, he tells some of the trustees that "he was going to try and come every year; then when he grew to be an old man he would have plenty to tell about the early struggles of the N.S.A." (2).

Children were imagined as influential beyond the formal structures of the movement as well, recognized as members of their families and communities able to enact social change in line with Spiritualist values. Consider Mrs. Louisa Shepard's "A Dialogue Between Aunt Chloe and Her Nieces," published in 1869 in the *Religio-philosophical Journal*. The dialogue, in the form of a script, calls to mind the catechisms in *The Lyceum Manual*. However, here the roles are reversed: while Aunt Chloe initially is skeptical of "these reforms that are making such stir in the world"—not only Spiritualism but also temperance, women's rights, and school reform—and laments that "[t]he women have got so they know more than the men; wives more than their husbands; children more than their parents," she is persuaded by her nieces' earnest arguments, conceding "I will join you Heart and Hand" (5). An even more striking example appears in the serialized story "California," published in *The Present Age* in 1872. There, a young character named May—inspired by her mother, who "talks about children's rights and men's rights" on the lecture circuit—delivers her own speech on "little girls' rights," focusing on her need for sensible dress. May not only convinces her mother, who proclaims "You shall have your rights, May" before providing her daughter with a boys' cloth suit, but also inspires a later conversation between her aunt and mother in which the women devise an alternate wardrobe May can wear at home and abroad. "You see," the narrator emphasizes, "her speech did some good" (71).

These examples could be interpreted as evidence that children, with the help of adults—in this case, adult editors and authors, such as Shepard, or even adult characters, such as May's mother—can identify and engage with the scripts we typically write for children. The young "walking delegate" of the N.S.A. hears the gentle jibes of his elders that reduce his role into innocent (and perhaps ineffectual) make-believe, but he takes his position seriously. He aligns his youth with the infancy of the organization itself; the organization will grow past its "early struggles" just as he will mature into leadership. Chloe's nieces see they have been deemed antiauthoritarian upstarts, children who believe they know more than their parents, and gently guide their aunt toward the age-democratic tenets of Spiritualism. May finds herself hemmed in by restrictive ideas of youthful femininity and reimagines a girlhood that allows for liberatory, active play. These examples fictionalize what Nodelman considers the aspirational (if not fully realized) project of children's literature studies. Adults, Nodelman maintains, write texts that "represent adult voices speaking to and for young people," and therefore "operate often in ways that work to deprive children of their individual voices in the name of an acceptable childlikeness," but he supports adult readers "in the work of encouraging children to use their voices," helping them read the texts we provide to them in a critical way (267–68). Perhaps those writing for children in Spiritualist periodicals are trying to do just that.

However, there are moments when the Spiritualist child seems to challenge these narratives of vulnerability or passivity *despite* adult authority, rather than in collaboration with elders, often using the very constructs of innocence meant to secure the child in place to create space for their own power and voices. For example, Kate Fox's son Ferdy, famous as an infant for spirit writing, snatched a pencil and paper when she attempted to limit his mediumship due to concerns of exhaustion ("Return" 200). And child medium Nellie Temple, according to S. B. Nichols of the *Religio-philosophical Journal*, declared her intentions of developing as a medium at twelve years old after attending a lecture by a teenaged medium. "[A] circle was formed for mediumistic development," Nichols explains, "and Miss Nellie was entranced and gave a lecture that astounded her parents and the few friends present" (1). She reprised the performance at the 1858 Free Convention in Vermont:

> When the time came for her to speak . . . [s]he was found in the yard of a private residence near by, playing with the dolls of the little girls whose acquaintance she had made. My memory goes back thirty years to the scene in that large canvas tent filled with five thousand or more people. . . . Miss Nellie with her short dress and hair rough and uncombed, was brought in from her play and placed upon the platform, and as this child-medium began an invocation to the All Father, that vast and discordant audience was hushed, and the discourse given through her organism was listened to with wrapt attention. Many a sturdy son and daughter of Vermont can date their first wandering from the faith of their fathers to the time they listened to this child evangel in that three days' stormy convention. (1)

Temple was about fourteen years old at the convention—young, but certainly older than the short dress, doll play, and uncombed hair of this passage suggests. Her talent is both signified by and relies on this image of her; she can hush the "vast and discordant audience" of "sturdy" New Englanders because of the discrepancy between her status as a child and the purported power of her words. Other accounts of the convention in Spiritualist periodicals offer similarly girlish portraits of Temple. Andrew Jackson Davis, for example, called her "a spiritual-faced girl, her brow preternaturally beaming with a heavenly radiance," whose "hair hung in graceful ringlets about her neck and shoulders." Davis writes that she spoke "in a poetic and singularly enrapped strain," although he could not recall what she said—evidence, perhaps, that he found her girlishness more important than the content of her lecture (26–27).

But what if Temple, like the adults around her, *manipulated* the ideas of innocence that shaped her mediumship? What if she understood, as Braude notes, that youth is valuable currency? Her address is a fiery message channeled from the spirits that unfolds in a manner similar to Wordsworth's *Ode*, opposing tropes of innocent divinity and freedom to the bondage of experience. While Temple is a vessel for spirits, she intones that those listening to her trance have "dwelt so long in the shadow and in darkness, that the breath of God cannot reach [them] in its swift progress from the bowers of heavenly light" ("Addresses" 179). Temple's address draws upon Spiritualism's tenets, which, as Jennifer Bann has written, held that "[f]reedom from the physical body was linked inextricably to freedom of agency in a wider sense" (668). However, when these words emerge from the lips of a girl, they activate an image of the Romantic child widely embraced in the nineteenth century and by the Spiritualists in particular: a child allied with God and nature, still illuminated by the heavenly light. In her address, in other words, Temple could be capitalizing on the alignment between her own state of innocence—signified visually by the short frock, spiritual face, and hanging ringlets—and the enlightened state of the spirits speaking through her, calling upon her adult listeners to cast off the shades of the prison-house and attain spiritual freedom.

Conclusion

Proving that Temple could be playing on her audience's investment in childhood innocence is difficult because we have limited insight into her subjectivity free from the distortions of adult representation. The transcription of her address is likely the sort of document that Schwebel envisions in her meditation on child agency: her words follow a familiar pattern of mediumistic trance just as, for example, children's letters to authors often follow the classroom formula of the "friendly letter" (281). However, this uncertainty—the haunting suspicion that this portrait of a powerful child is potentially undermined by visions of Romantic childhood—is what makes the child medium a useful limit case for children's literature and childhood studies, fields that often struggle with theorizing children's voices. The child medium is an exaggerated example of the difficulty of access. We rarely hear the child medium's words in Spiritualism's archives, and when we do, that voice often is not the child's own but a dead person's. When the child medium's voice does emerge, it often is employed as evidence for adult claims about the truth or fraudulence of Spiritualism. For example, Epes Sargent, in *Proof Palpable of Immortality* (1876), publishes a letter from adolescent medium Florence Cook, famous for her manifestations of a spirit named Katie King, describing one of her materializations as evidence of "the intellectual calibre of the writer ... who was soon to become so famous as a medium" (50).[5] Other evidence of the child medium's perspective is autobiographical and attenuated through memory and the agenda of an adult reframing her childhood past. In her fifties, Margaret Fox wrote of her childhood mediumship in the *New York*

Herald—a confession in which she attempts to justify what has been revealed as her childhood deception: not spirit rappings, but toe crackings.

Beleaguered by such methodological challenges, we might conclude that the project of investigating the child medium as a subject independent of powerful constructions of childhood is futile. Instead, I suggest the child medium—freighted with adult expectations but, perhaps more than other young people, proffering the tantalizing possibility of a child whose abilities exceed adult understanding—reminds us that we should account for but refuse to grant all power to *ideas* of childhood at the expense of embodied children. We might indeed be able to locate evidence that some children achieved the types of critical reading and discourse manipulation that scholars such as Nodelman and Schwebel wish for them. As Clémentine Beauvais has noted, "adult agency, even when didactic, is not necessarily powerful; the child figure, even when turned into a projector-screen for adult desires, is not automatically deprived of power" (3).

There are many other, later children who offer similar conundrums of construction and agency, brought to the fore by their extraordinary visions. In the decades following the American boom in Spiritualism, modernists celebrated the child's "innocent eye," lamenting the moment young artists were trained into more professional practices; the drawings and paintings of child artists were read by adults as evidence of the child's Romantic inheritance, their closeness to God, their untrammeled imaginations, and yet these young artist's work was hung in museums, collected in archives, their influence undeniable and perhaps more canny than we imagine. Today, Greta Thunberg, whose youth visually signals childhood under threat by climate change, and the students of Parkland, who represent a generation traumatized by gun violence, exhibit a maturity that often infantilizes the adults they appeal to for change, and their activism is considered by turns remarkable and insightful, unreliable and indulgent, because of their youth. The child medium, then, anticipates the stubborn persistence of adult ambivalence about children's vision and the ideological acrobatics that shape it—the acknowledgment that children are powerful but the insistence that their authority arises from the very qualities that make them vulnerable.

Notes

1. For a brief consideration of Romantic childhood and Spiritualism, see Braude, p. 41.
2. What would happen, for example, if we read Alfred Kitson's *Outlines of Spiritualism for the Young* alongside the *New England Primer*, or considered Frances Hodgson Burnett's *In the Closed Room*, a tale of child haunting, with *The Secret Garden*?

3. Kincaid's description of the eroticized child is part of a larger project examining Anglophone culture's investment in the figure of the pedophile. Pedophilia "describes the response to the child we have made necessary," he writes. "If the child is desirable, then to desire it can hardly be freakish. To maintain otherwise is to put into operation pretty hefty engines of denial and self-deception. And that is what we have done" (5). While I do not use Kincaid's theorization of the pedophile as an organizing idea in this chapter, I do think that descriptions of the Spiritualist child and especially the child medium could be read productively through the lens of sexual desire for the child alongside frantic denial of that desire; child mediums were very much bodies on display, as my later account of Nellie Temple will make clear, and yet those writing about Spiritualist children not only insisted on their purity, innocence, and *dis*embodiedness but also performed an intense solicitousness about the physical well-being of children and repulsion at the idea that Spiritualism exploited or fetishized children's bodies. See endnote 5.

4. For more on gender and mediumship, see Bednarowski.

5. Sargent argues that Cook was nearly drained to death by Katie King—and no wonder, really, as Katie "scraped" Cook for her "influence," purportedly calling the beleaguered medium "nothing but a machine" (51). Many Spiritualists sought to "protect" children from their visions because mediumship was thought to physically exhaust the young. By 1924, tales of the overtaxed child medium had become so common that the periodical *Light* railed against "stories of immature boys and girls who are stated to have been trained to use their psychic powers to the permanent detriment of their minds and bodies" (Lieutenant-Colonel 508). *Light* insists that that these are false reports circulated by the Catholic church, but the threat of overextension justified many adults' decision to limit children's participation in séances.

Works Cited

"Addresses by Trance Speakers." *Proceedings of the Free Convention Held at Rutland, VT, July 25, 26, and 27, 1858*. J. B. Yerrington and Son, 1858, pp. 177–84.

Allbe, James G. "An Hour with a Child Medium." *Banner of Light*, 27 May 1865, pp. 2–3. IAPSOP.

Bann, Jennifer. "Ghostly Hands and Ghostly Agency: The Changing Figure of the Nineteenth-Century Specter." *Victorian Studies*, vol. 51, no. 4, summer 2009, pp. 663–86.

Beauvais, Clémentine. *The Mighty Child: Time and Power in Children's Literature*. John Benjamins, 2015.

Bednarowski, Mary. "Women in Occult America." *The Occult in America: New Historical Perspectives*, edited by Howard Kerr and Charles L. Crow, U of Illinois P, 1986.

Bernstein, Robin. "Toys Are Good for Us: Why We Should Embrace the Historical Integration of Children's Literature, Material Culture, and Play." *Children's Literature Association Quarterly*, vol. 38, no. 4, winter 2013, pp. 458–63.

Braude, Ann. *Radical Spirits: Spiritualism and Women's Rights in Nineteenth-Century America*. Beacon Press, 1989.

Britten, Emma Hardinge, Alfred Kitson, and H. A. Kersey. *The Lyceum Manual: A Compendium of Physical, Moral, and Spiritual Exercises for Use in Progressive Lyceums Connected with British Spiritualists' Societies*. 9th ed., British Spiritualists' Lyceum Union, 1909.

"California: Chapter 27." *The Present Age*, vol. 6, no. 9, 3 Feb. 1872, p. 71. IAPSOP.

Christensen, Nina. "Agency." *Keywords for Children's Literature*, 2nd ed., edited by Philip Nel et al., New York UP, 2021, pp. 10–13.

Conrad, Rachel. "'My Sole Desire Is to Move Someone through Poetry, and Allow for My Voice to Be Heard': Young Poets and Children's Rights." *The Lion and the Unicorn*, vol. 40, no. 2, Apr. 2016, pp. 196–214.

Conrad, Rachel. *Time for Childhoods: Young Poets and Questions of Agency*. U of Massachusetts P, 2020.
Davenport, Reuben Briggs. *The Death-Blow to Spiritualism: The True Story of the Fox Sisters, as Revealed by Authority of Margaret Fox Kane and Catherine Fox Jencken*. G. W. Dillingham, 1888.
Davis, Andrew Jackson. *Beyond the Valley, A Sequel to The Magic Staff, An Autobiography*. Colby and Rich, 1885.
Gubar, Marah. "The Hermeneutics of Recuperation: What a Kindship-Model Approach to Children's Agency Could Do for Children's Literature and Childhood Studies." *Jeunesse: Young People, Texts, Cultures*, vol. 8, no. 1, summer 2016, pp. 291–310.
Kincaid, James R. *Child-Loving: The Erotic Child and Victorian Culture*. Routledge, 1992.
Kitson, Alfred. *Outlines of Spiritualism for the Young, Designed for the Use of Lyceums in Particular and Spiritualists in General, to Which Is Added The Children's Progressive Lyceum: What Is It? A Discourse for Teachers and Parents*. 3rd ed., British Spiritualists' Lyceum Union, 1906.
Lieutenant-Colonel. "The A. B. C. Of Spiritualism. Guidance and Counsel for Inquirers. Child Mediums." *Light*, 9 Aug. 1924, p. 508.
Longley, M. T., editor. "Children's Column." *Light of Truth*, 26 Jan. 1895, p. 2. IAPSOP.
"The Mediumship of Children." *The Medium and Daybreak*, 10 May 1878, p. 296. IAPSOP.
Nichols, S. B. "Mediumship: The Subject Analyzed from Various Standpoints." *Religio-philosophical Journal*, 4 Sept. 1886, pp. 1, 8. IAPSOP.
Nodelman, Perry. *The Hidden Adult: Defining Children's Literature*. Johns Hopkins UP, 2008.
Nodelman, Perry. "The Hidden Child in *The Hidden Adult*." *Jeunesse: Young People, Texts, Cultures*, vol. 8, no. 1, summer 2016, pp. 266–77.
Nora Ray, The Child Medium. A Spiritualistic Story. Published by the Author, 1878.
"Return to England of Mrs. Kate Fox Jencken and Her Medial Children." *Religio-philosophical Journal*, 4 Sept. 1875, p. 200. IAPSOP.
Rose, Jacqueline. *The Case of Peter Pan; or, The Impossibility of Children's Fiction*. U of Pennsylvania P, 1984.
Sargent, Epes. *Proof Palpable of Immortality; Being an Account of the Materialization Phenomena of Modern Spiritualism, with Remarks on the Relations of the Facts to Theology, Morals, and Religion*. 2nd ed., Colby and Rich, 1876.
Schwebel, Sarah. "The Limits of Agency for Children's Literature Scholars." *Jeunesse: Young People, Texts, Cultures*, vol. 8, no. 1, summer 2016, pp. 278–90.
Shepard, Louisa. "A Dialogue between Aunt Chloe and Her Nieces.—Written for the Benefit of the Children's Lyceum." *Religio-philosophical Journal*, 6 Nov. 1869, p. 5. IAPSOP.
"Sittings with Mediums. Isabella Smith, the Child Medium Recently Developed." *Spiritual Monthly and Lyceum Record*, vol. 1, no. 3, Dec. 1870, pp. 120–21. IAPSOP.

SINGING A "SEA ISLAND SONG"
Alice Childress's Responsive Black Theater

Katharine Capshaw

In her essay celebrating *The Brownies' Book*'s one-hundredth anniversary, Karen Chandler reflects on the critical excitement about contemporary Black children's and young adult literature, noting that "Many books by important black authors, including some by Joyce Hansen, Mildred Pitts Walter, John Steptoe, Rosa Guy, and Joyce Carol Thomas are no longer in print. . . . This loss and suppression of books diminishes the tradition of writing for children, constituting a loss of cultural history" (172). As many of us who study noncontemporary Black children's literature have noted, commitment to creativity for the young runs deep in African American culture, and writers and illustrators from the nineteenth century to the nineteen nineties have produced an astonishing body of work, much of which has been sidelined in critical appraisals of our field. Black cultural production for youth before the twenty-first century can already be considered an "alternative" story of children's literature, one that privileges Black cultural contexts over white publishing power, one more attuned to the generative spaces that bear traces of creative production for the young than bestseller or prizing lists. That creativity has been a constant presence in Black culture, but we miss it because white archives fail: in general, they fail to value blackness; in particular, they fail to care enough about Black childhood to gather its literature; and they fail in vision by refusing to see Black writers for youth as creative forces worthy of institutional memory. As scholars, we fail continually, remaining unmindful of Black creative engagement with childhood because we do not value more ephemeral (but more accessible to creators) forms of production—the newspaper, the pamphlet, the mimeographed manuscript—as well as the stories created and shared in oral and performative contexts.

In truth, categorizing Black children's literature an alternative form is deeply unnerving, since the formulation of "alternative" replicates the othering that has shaped scholarship in children's and young adult literature. Alternative as a term summons the dominant form as a ghostly presence, makes us think about alternative to (. . . what?), calling up whiteness even as it seeks to rectify its abuses and elisions. In some sense, perhaps, the term reifies the idea that Black children's literature is secondary. And, of course, Black children's literature is not at the center of critical discussions in children's literature studies. It remains an alternate in our theorizations, which draw not from Black critical recognition of the permeability and mutability of forms and audiences but from a fixation on the divide between child and adult, between what is us and what is them. It remains an alternate on our syllabi and in our classrooms, in what we ask our students to value. The reason is plain and must be stated loudly and often: our field is grounded in white supremacy. Being "alternative" both implicitly acknowledges the structures that have sidelined Black children's literature and replicates them. I do not wish Black children's culture and literature to be alternative to any other figuration. I wish it to be central in any critical conversation that engages the relationship of art to youth.

Keeping in mind the Black creators who have prefaced the contemporary moment—those we know about, and those who have yet to be recovered—we must foreground the idea of responsiveness when reflecting on our construction of the field and its possibilities. Black writers and illustrators have been intensely aware of the exchange between authorship and youth, whether that be editors W. E. B. Du Bois and Jessie Fauset in *The Brownies' Book* giving space to readers for their stories, illustrations, games, and photographs, or civil rights worker Doris Derby in 1964 Mississippi publishing little books for her preschool students that reflect their experiences and images. Responsiveness to actual Black youth—not to the child as theorized or imagined abstractly—has been at the heart of the work of Black creators.

One cultural site that is particularly weighted in terms of this ethos of responsiveness is theater, in which playwrights (and actors) rise to the embodied presence of Black children as an audience that is continually engaging the drama's ideas. Theater has been erased almost entirely from our conversations about children's literature, and even more so in our configurations of Black youth literature. As La Donna Forsgren explains in her powerful book *In Search of Our Warrior Mothers: Women Dramatists of the Black Arts Movement*, Black feminist drama of the 1970s in general has been almost completely erased, even from the written record. She explains, "The devaluation of black women's writings has resulted in the exclusion of . . . works from publication and traditional archives" (111). For the past several years, I have visited libraries and archives, and interviewed artists, in search of elusive scripts of plays by Black writers for the young. I have learned of seventy-five distinct plays for young people (some by men, some by women) in the 1970s alone; I have been able to secure scripts for approximately half of those productions.

How do we preserve a cultural legacy that is ephemeral and predicated on responsiveness? In an interview with Brad Brewer, whose 1974 puppet performance "The Jackson 5 Meet Malcolm X" sold out the Apollo Theater, he told me that his family did not save the scripts for the shows, and even though his work was a "first" for children's puppetry and performance, the puppeteers were more concerned with the children in front of them than in preserving a legacy. In fact, many of the plays that survive in script form were written by authors who are better known for their other works, those for adults. In the case of literary stars like Amiri Baraka, Ed Bullins, and Sonia Sanchez, their body of work for adults survives and children's material appears in the archive as a kind of incidental inclusion, a gesture towards completeness rather than an effort intentionally to preserve work for the young. This is also the case for Alice Childress, who is best known for her plays for adults in the 1950s and 1960s, including *Wedding Band* (1966) and *Wine in the Wilderness* (1969), and whose *Trouble in Mind* (1955) was revived on Broadway in 2021–2022. Childress's work for children includes her acclaimed young adult novel *A Hero Ain't Nothin' But a Sandwich* (1973) and several plays for young people composed in the 1970s, such as the fanciful interracial *Let's Hear It for the Queen* (1976), based on the nursery rhyme about the Queen of Hearts, and the moving description of Harriet Tubman's work as a laundress, *When the Rattlesnake Sounds* (1975), which was derived from her leftist musical of the 1950s *Gold Through the Trees* (1952). These two children's plays were published by a major house (Coward, McCann, and Geoghegan) that issued her popular *A Hero*, and her archive at the Schomburg Center for Research in Black Culture contains several additional plays for the young, including "Young Martin Luther King/A King Remembered" (1968) and "Harriet Tubman/Glory by Starlight" (1975).

A striking example of the responsiveness of Black children's literature is Childress's musical play for the young, "Sea Island Song" (1977), which was scored by her jazz composer husband Nathan Woodard; it is available at the Schomburg library's archives. Like Alice Walker, Audre Lorde, and other black women writers of the 1970s who reclaimed stories as a means to cultural survival, Childress places black folk life at the center of new articulations of Black cultural identity, focusing "Sea Island Song" on the Gullah people of Johns Island off of South Carolina. Several factors that influenced this play point toward its acts of innovation and empathy.[1] Childress had moved from South Carolina as a very young child to New York and had rarely returned to the state, although she bore affection for it. As she explained in a newspaper interview, "I was raised in New York, but I was definitely born in Charleston, my mother was born in Charleston, my grandmother was born in Charleston, my great grandmother was a slave in Charleston. So I know Charleston people about as well as any and then my stepfather was buried on Edisto Island. He's from Edisto" (Sundstrom 6). Childress also spent time in New York City with communities drawn from the Sea Islands, and the "Teacher's Guide" to the play explains it as "drawn from her understanding of South Carolinians and stories of islanders told by her grandparents" (Atkinson 3) since Charleston is close to the islands. The Columbia, South Carolina, actor and director Jim Thighpen had seen Childress's *Wedding Band* in New York, and when the Arts Commission became interested in producing a play for its Stage South company's educational tour, Thighpen recommended Childress to create a play based on Sea Island communities.[2] Childress and Woodard began research for the play in the summer of 1977 and drew in part on a previous play Childress had drafted, "African Garden" (1967–1968), that included a song focused on Gullah culture. Childress discussed with a newspaper reporter her pleasure in writing for an audience of young people: "I wanted to do something for the state of South Carolina, especially the children. . . . I love the idea of the play being done for children" (Todd).

The actors in Stage South's interracial cast played multiple parts in the production, which was directed by Leonard Peters; the score, which is not extant, is described as involving "black African rhythms based on West African musical patterns. The play has one musician who plays guitar, African thumb piano, harmonica, tambourine, cowbells and African drums" (Frierson 12). In the fall of 1977, the play toured across the state to hundreds of schoolchildren, performing "in school auditoriums, cafetoriums, or gymnasiums" (Atkinson 13). It was staged in rural, poor, African American communities like Dillon, South Carolina, and in many schools that were recently integrated, like Bennettsville High School and Hopkins Junior High School, integrated in 1970. According to the "Weekly Schedule" for October 9–15, 1977, the play toured in junior high schools, high schools, a two-year college, and the Shaw Airforce Base.[3] On November 2, 1977, the play was staged on one of the Sea Islands, St. Helena, in a community center, and "[a] spirited discussion of the play and the lions on the islands followed the performance" (Spieler).[4] The record of the play's performances is incomplete, but what remains in the archive suggests an effort to reach Black child and community audiences as well as schools with large Black populations that had been recently integrated.

The fact that the company staged the play on the Sea Islands evokes the production's responsiveness to its audience and subject matter. In fact, Childress had a longtime interest in the cultural legacies of Africa, and she is the frequently uncredited first black woman playwright in the United States to stage African characters in a major play, *Gold Through the Trees* (1952). In addition to conducting extensive research on Gullah cultures, Childress and Woodard visited the site depicted in the play, Johns Island, in August 1977 to research the script and music. As the teacher's guide suggests, two crises faced the Sea Island community in the 1970s: "During the last few decades, historians, linguists, craftsmen, and students of human behavior have taken a deeper interest in the sea island residents in an effort to record, analyze, and understand the culture and background of the islanders. In recent years, people of the sea islands have faced another problem in their history as much of the land has been purchased for industrial and recreational purposes" (Atkinson 16). Childress's play takes on both of these crises expressly, including a character who has come to study the community, and depicting the threat of loss of the central couple's land and home. In fact, her time on Johns Island cemented her desire to use the play to engage both of these losses. In an interview she explains,

> Because we were talking to people on Johns Island who are concerned about losing property because the land is put up for sale for lack of taxes. The people don't sell their land for little or nothing because they are stupid, necessarily, but because they have no money and no place to work out there on the island and very often need a chunk of money. And of course the tragedy of that is the money is gone and so is the land, so now you are in the same position only landless. (Sundstrom 7)[5]

In terms of form, Childress typically uses the well-made realistic play, with traditional plotting, especially in her nonmusical plays, and as a result critics have been ambivalent about placing her within conversations about aesthetic innovations like the Black Arts Movement, though Mary Helen Washington argues that her "work was always informed by progressive thinking and radical activism" (198). By insisting on the continuance of history through embodied performance, her children's musical combines the plotting of traditional theater with more experimental modes of revolutionary theater;

and by responding to the Sea Island crises of objectification by white auditors and the dispossession of Black landowners, the play offers a groundbreaking statement of empathy and advocacy. Because these pressing threats to Gullah communities helped shape the content of the play, the ethic of responsiveness is present from the outset. As Childress explains, "I kept writing so that when this show is done on Johns Island I would like them to recognize or feel some kind of knowledge, since we selected it, Johns Island as the setting" (Sundstrom 7).

The play focuses on a married couple, Pete and Evalina Johnson, who meet a graduate student working on Gullah culture. Pete mocks the student, Maytag: "(Does a take-off on research students) 'Yall talk to me. Lemmie mark that down. Anh-hah. Now you sing for me. Uh-huh. Lemmie mark that in a notebook. What yall eat? Uh-huh, pinders, goober peas and ground-nuts.' Don't know it's all . . . PEANUTS! 'Mmmm, they live so quaint.' I ain't quaint!" (2.a).[6] The play thus begins by valuing the contemporary life of the community and resisting the objectification of an ethnographic perspective. Not only does the play reject the containment of Gullah people by academics and white audiences, but also the problems the characters endure represent the real economic and psychological challenges faced by islanders; the play links those challenges to a folkloric perspective in describing them as "Lions" that the characters have to battle. Pete tells a story to Maytag about hunting on the island with his dogs and claims that a lion raced after them, and when Maytag objects, "[N]o lions, man" (6), Pete says, "There's all kindsa lions in this world. Some walk the jungle . . . others through your mind, devour your very soul . . . that's the kind we got on Johns" (6). As corrupting ideas that the characters challenge, the "Lions" are also pragmatic, refocusing attention away from the supposed quaintness of the people to the urgent crises they face and making the folkloric invocation of lions live in the present moment. The lines about Lions recall the call and response of Black Arts Movement theater:

PETE: One time I work for a man and he cheat me outta half my pay. Ain't that a lion!?
THE DOGS: Thassa lion!
EVALINA: Some children could go to school when I was a child . . . I had to work in the field. Ain't that a lion?!
THE DOGS: Thassa lion!
MAYTAG: Yes, Mam!
PETE: I can't find a job!
MAYTAG: Baddest lion of all! (7)

Involving the kind of critique typical for Black radical theater, the text even moves expressly into invocation of an Afrocentric perspective, what the stage directions call an "African way" of counting out loud drum beats as Pete slays the lion. The play reshapes the Black Arts Movement trope of the male warrior in this scene, which ends with Pete killing the lion and Maytag changing into a supporter rather than student of Gullah culture, singing a song titled "The Sound of Drums for my Friend."

Though Pete can slay the "Lion" of inferiority, he and his wife still face the actual economic deprivation that islanders had been experiencing in the 1970s. Desperately poor, they ask a character called the Gate Spirit at the cemetery to accept their spirits. The Gate Spirit replies, "Never say die. Yall got one thing left. You can't come in until you've used it all up" (9). Waterfront property on Johns Island is what's left, and when Pete suddenly comes into an inheritance, his ego swells and he starts thinking about selling the land in order to travel and inflate his sense of self. He argues with Evalina, "Your mind is lock down on Johns Island . . . I'm interested in the world . . . atomic energy, algebra, space program . . African history . . . I got nobody to talk to round here" (17). At this juncture, the play shifts into an interrogation of Black American perspectives on African identity, posing the superficial, commercial, performative versions of Africa evoked by Pete against the genuine, unpretentious, lived experience of Africa in America that the Gullah people, like his wife Evalina, embody. In response to Pete's desire to study African history, Evalina explains, "City folk used to laugh at my old Affikan hair style . . . corn row and string tie . . . Now models and movie stars—copy after me" (17). At this point, a new character enters: Penny Candy, who wears "the largest Afro wig ever made . . . and in 'African' print dress which is thigh high . . . loopy earrings . . . she is very commercial, 'stock' looking African" (17). The funny, playful scene makes clear that the 1970s embrace of Africa, if shallow and commodified, becomes inauthentic and corrupt. Penny Candy enters carrying a sign with her African name, Panikandi, and sings a song, "African Bag," during which she jangles her jewelry and swings her earrings. This comic version of the African presence in Black culture evokes Alice Walker's short story "Everyday Use," which juxtaposes the falsity of commodified African identity embraced by supposedly sophisticated youth with the generative, familial identity of a less flashy woman.

Childress emphasizes the African origins of Gullah practices in the remainder of the play, which shifts tone to focus on Pete's possible redemption. Pete sells the land, then in a surge of excitement says he wants to hunt a lion to impress Penny Candy. The lion reappears, says as an aside to the audience, "Behold a miracle. A man become a jackass" (21), and eventually kills Pete. Evalina challenges Penny Candy and "dances her down in the old African-Island way which symbolizes a fight" (23); Evalina reclaims the deed to the land and then approaches the Gate Spirit to ask for the right to bury Pete in the cemetery. The stage directions state that the Gate Spirit is "dressed in croker-sack rags, tatters and ashes . . . an awe-inspiring mask . . . stern and noble countenance . . very colorful in contrast to his tattered, dull clothing. He wears some kind of hat or headdress . . . not comical" (25). The description adheres to language around the Haitian figure Papa Legba, the vodoun spirit of the crossroads or openings—the gate—who permits access to the loas, or spirits, on the side of the dead. Dressing the Gate Spirit in tatters fits the way Legba is often figured in rags, limping, with a cane, but is (in trickster mode) the powerful opener of a vodoun ceremony. There is also a tradition in Gullah culture of asking permission of the ancestors at the gate to enter the cemetery, and Childress is combining these customs and signaling their African origins through the costuming and masking.[7] In the play, the Gate Spirit rejects Pete's body because he has been too "ugly" (26) in life to others, and calls to Evalina, "[H]e's so ugly till only cunja will do. Yall go to cunja!" After a fruitless exchange with a "con artist" named Madame Tooroo (27), who is contrasted with the Gate Spirit just as Childress has juxtaposed the false African identity of Penny Candy against Evalina, ultimately Pete awakens. Because of Pete's materialism and betrayal of the community, the Gate Spirit wishes to condemn him to exist as a ghost who haunts the swamp for eternity.

The culmination of the play in Pete's redemption enacts and encourages responsiveness to Gullah culture and music, all of which is positioned as an extension of an African creative perspective. In truth, the characters weave Gullah terms and expressions across their dialogue, and from the start insist that the term "Gullah" is "talk, not people" (1). The teacher's guide offers a list of Gullah words included in the play "of probable African origin" (Atkinson 21). Even the costumes were indebted to the distinctive creativity of the islands, including those of the three actresses who, according to a review, were "delightfully cast as Pete's dogs, wearing appropriate masks of authentic Lowcountry woven baskets" (Spieler). Woodard and Childress were sure to include versions of the distinctive music of the Sea Islands, including a gospel song and another that turns into a ring shout,[8] placing them at the end of the play as part of the emphasis on the need for Pete to embrace the island folkways as a key to his redemption. Childress asked in an essay theorizing drama in the 1950s, "Where is truth? Where are the schools that will teach us Negro art forms?" ("Negro Theater" 63); we see in Childress's respect for Sea Island creative forms—music, crafts, storytelling, language—the theater becoming that space of restorative pedagogy for Black children, responding with deep empathy to the need for Black children to see themselves and their art validated in performance.

Pete's restoration comes through public commitment both to the Sea Islands and to ongoing education for the young. The Gate Spirit consults with the devil to ask two questions of Pete in order for him to return to life and escape being a ghost. The first is to name out loud one hundred Sea Islands: Pete and the other characters say the names of one hundred and three islands, an exciting way to demonstrate their vastness and range, and to create a sense of shared knowledge and value for the communities. The Gate Spirit then asks Pete to "name one great, shining, everlasting, magnificent deed of importance that you have done in your life" (37). A touching scene unfolds in which Pete and Evalina's adopted child talks about Pete teaching her to read, even though he was not educated. The Gate Spirit says: "That made the devil laugh. Pete can hardly read 'e-self! Do well to sign his name. Handwritin look like chicken scratch cross the paper . . . bad as his father before him . . . used to sign name with cross-mark and wouldn't know it if it was writ four foot high on side of a barn. Illiterate, that's what" (41). The girl then talks about Pete's gentleness and care in teaching her (in a sweet song, "A Reason to Read"); his deed becomes everlasting in that she grows into a teacher, whose students also teach others. The final lines of the play from Pete emphasize community support and are directed to the audience: "Look out for one another. We've tried everything else" (45). The play concludes with this embrace of responsiveness, collectivity, and collaboration that will sustain the audience.

Remembering that these closing words were spoken in school spaces that were largely Black, and in those that were newly integrated, we hear Childress's call for respect for the traditions and art forms of a culture that had been objectified by white popular culture as quaint, backwards, and endangered. Moreover, the entire play evidences what Fred Moten calls the "material reproductivity of black performance." According to Moten, this is "an ontological condition[,] . . . the story of how apparent nonvalue functions as a creator of value; it is also the story of how the value animates what appears as nonvalue" (Moten 18). Theater can create value from that which has been disregarded, can be responsive in the moment to the aesthetic and political needs of its audience, as "Sea Island Song" demonstrates with great insight and understanding. Childress realized what the play would mean to Black children; in the periodical *Black News*, she states, "Children . . . are people and they have very adult thoughts and pain. . . . I wanted to write something healing. The thought of children all over a southern state enjoying something together and leaving feeling whole and not ashamed—that was our aim. . . . We wanted to teach a little something about the islands and bring about more appreciation of the people who have been ridiculed and not understood" ("Alice Childress").

Childress published in the 1960s several essays theorizing drama; in one she argues, even before Rudine Sims Bishop's famous formulation, that "black communities have always had black theaters. . . . [W]e will continue to need them, even when, if ever, this land is free of racism. Theater serves as the mirror of life experience and reflects only what looks into it; everyone yearns to see his own image once in a while" ("My Thing" 9). In many ways Childress's play speaks to Julius B. Fleming's argument in "Staging Civil Rights: African American Literature, Performance, and Innovation" that as an act of *black performative revealing*" a play can depict ways "of being that the prescriptive and normalizing parameters of identity categorization are far too often reluctant to recognize" (22). In short, we have failed to envision the new identities our field could encompass should it attend to the illuminating innovation, courage, and brilliance of Black theater for children. As a field we might look with more care into the formulations that have been present in Black communities across the nineteenth and twentieth centuries and take them seriously in our theorizations, scholarship, and pedagogy. We might resist intentionally the erasure of more responsive forms of art for youth from the narratives we construct about the shape and possibilities of children's literature. The work of Childress and so many other Black playwrights for youth reveal a form of children's literature that should be central to our work, one that is culturally recuperative, politically and aesthetically responsive, and deeply joyful.

Notes

1. Since production histories for unpublished children's plays are scant, I include a sense of its origins and scope, taken from the newspaper interviews with Childress and coverage of "Sea Island Song."

2. A newspaper report describes Thighpen's influence: "In the early summer of this year, he discussed the Workshop Theatre plans with Myrna Rodriguez, director of development of the Arts Commission, and suggested Alice Childress as the author Stage South was looking for to write a musical play built around the people living on the sea islands off the S.C. coast" (Sundstrom 6).

3. The schedule notes performances at J. V. Martin Junior High School in Dillon on October 10 and 11, Hopkins Junior High School in Hopkins on October 12, Bennettsville High School in Bennettsville on October 13, Chesterfield Marlboro Technical College in Cheraw on October 14, and Shaw Air Force Base on October 15, with "Humanities discussion after show." According

to Elizabeth George in an undated newspaper piece, "It was presented for students Tuesday at Bryson Middle School in Fountain Inn. Public performances will be scheduled in Greenville before the year's end" ("Sea"). In an additional article, George notes that "[t]he troupe gave the musical for several hundred students of Bryson Middle and Elementary schools and League Middle School Tuesday. The cast members, many of whom have acted in New York, conducted acting and make-up workshops for students of a new drama program at Bryson Middle school following the performance" ("Actors").

4. "'Sea Island Song,' a musical based on Lowcountry life and traditions, was enthusiastically applauded by islanders and guests who filled the auditorium of the Frissell Community House at Penn Community Services on St. Helena Island Wednesday night" (Speiler). The Frissell Community House had hosted in the 1960s Martin Luther King Jr. and members of the Southern Christian Leadership Conference.

5. Childress also reveals her awareness of the particularly fraught condition of collective ownership of the land, and the way developers exploit that arrangement:

There are people who have sold their land before who still have land but no money and no work out there or anything to do, and they have a little group that is trying to pool their resources to buy the land to keep it in trust. It's hard to do because sometimes the land is in the name of someone who lived 90 years ago and the land belongs to all the heirs. And if you trace all the heirs, there might be a hundred of them. And you have to get all of them to sign . . . when one sells his share, the buyer can go to court and demand that the court divide the land and say what the share is. And if they all have equal shares, the buyer might say, well, I want the waterfront or whatever. Someone else might have swamp for theirs so they decide the best solution is to let (a developer or someone) buy all of it and they will divide the money. (Sundstrom 7).

6. Childress uses ellipses across the dialogue and stage directions in the play. I have retained them when quoting from the manuscript.

7. Unfortunately, no images of this figure appear in reviews or in the archives.

8. In the manuscript, Childress describes "Peter Walk on the Water" as "a Johns Island Gospel Song" (35.a) sung by Evelina, and "God Made Me" as a "Johns Island Gospel Song" sung by Pete that "[s]witches into faster timing from single to double, then triple hand claps, working up to gospel 'shout' movement until even The Gate Spirit is moved to join in" (34).

Works Cited

"Alice Childress, Visits Columbia." *Black News* [Columbia, SC], 22 Oct. 1977. Alice Childress Papers, The New York Public Library, Schomburg Center for Research in Black Culture, Manuscripts, Archives and Rare Books Division, Sc MG 649, Box 36, F 5.

Atkinson, Jennifer E. "'Sea Island Song': A Teacher's Guide." Stage South, The State Theatre of South Carolina, 1977. *South Carolina State Library Digital Collections*, https://dc.statelibrary.sc.gov/handle/10827/10420.

Capshaw, Katherine. Interview. Conducted by Brad Brewer, 29 Nov. 2018, Storrs, CT.

Chandler, Karen. "Uncertain Directions in Black Children's Literature." *The Lion and the Unicorn*, vol. 43, no. 2, 2019, pp. 172–81.

Childress, Alice. "But I Do My Thing." *The New York Times*, 2 Feb. 1969, p. 2.

Childress, Alice. "For a Negro Theater." *Masses and Mainstream*, vol. 4, no. 2, Feb. 1951, pp. 61–64.

Childress, Alice. "Sea Island Song." 1977. Alice Childress Papers, The New York Public Library, Schomburg Center for Research in Black Culture, Manuscripts, Archives and Rare Books Division, Sc MG 649, Box 36, F 1.

Fleming, Julius B. *Staging Civil Rights: African American Literature, Performance, and Innovation*. 2014. U Penn, PhD dissertation. *Publicly Accessible Penn Dissertations*, http://repository.upenn.edu/edissertations/1276.

Forsgren, La Donna. *In Search of Our Warrior Mothers: Women Dramatists of the Black Arts Movement*. Northwestern UP, 2018.

Frierson, Don. "Jazzman promotes 'Sea Island Song.'" *Black News* [Columbia, SC]. 22 Oct. 1977, pp. 12. Alice Childress Papers, The New York Public Library, Schomburg Center for Research in Black Culture, Manuscripts, Archives and Rare Books Division, Sc MG 649, Box 36, F 5.

George, Elizabeth. "Actors Cast Spell Over Students." Alice Childress Papers, The New York Public Library, Schomburg Center for Research in Black Culture, Manuscripts, Archives and Rare Books Division, Sc MG 649, Box 36, F 5.

George, Elizabeth. "'Sea Island Song' Rolls Gently Like Ocean Wave." Alice Childress Papers, The New York Public Library, Schomburg Center for Research in Black Culture, Manuscripts, Archives and Rare Books Division, Sc MG 649, Box 36, F 5.

Moten, Fred. *In the Break: The Aesthetics of the Black Radical Tradition*. U of Minnesota P, 2003.

Spieler, Gerhard. "'Sea Island Song' Pleasing in Debut." *The Beaufort Gazette*, 3 Nov. 1977. Alice Childress Papers, The New York Public Library, Schomburg Center for Research in Black Culture, Manuscripts, Archives and Rare Books Division, Sc MG 649, Box 36, F 5.

Sundstrom, Karen. "Osceola Interview: Playwright Alice Childress." *Osceola: South Carolina's Newsweekly*, 21 Oct. 1977, pp. 1, 6–8.

Todd, Sharon. "Playwright's 'Folk Story' Told in Native State." *The Greenville News*, 12 Oct. 1977. Alice Childress Papers, The New York Public Library, Schomburg Center for Research in Black Culture, Manuscripts, Archives and Rare Books Division, Sc MG 649, Box 36, F 5.

Washington, Mary Helen. "Alice Childress, Lorraine Hansberry, and Claudia Jones: Black Women Write the Popular Front." *Left of the Color Line: Race, Radicalism, and Twentieth-Century Literature of the United States*, edited by Bill V. Mullen and James Smethurst, U of North Carolina P, 2003, pp. 183–204.

"Weekly Schedule: October 9th–15th 1977." Alice Childress Papers, The New York Public Library, Schomburg Center for Research in Black Culture, Manuscripts, Archives and Rare Books Division, Sc MG 649, Box 36, F 4.

THE SEDUCTIONS OF
LITTLE RED RIDING HOOD
On the Thresholds of Children's Drawings

Jakob Rosendal

If we follow the lines of children's drawings, where will we end up? What kind of child can be traced from the movements of drawn lines? And what do such lines express about children's gender and sexuality? How might gender and sexuality be (dis)figured—appear or dissolve as forms—in children's drawings?

Pursuing such questions and with permission from both parents and institutions, I started collecting drawings from Danish kindergarten children and schoolchildren during the spring of 2019.[1] Due to its explicitly gendered and more symbolic sexual content and its continued widespread circulation, I asked the children to draw the *Little Red Riding Hood* (*LRRH*) fairy tale. I used the Danish translation found in *Den lille Rødhætte og 41 andre eventyr* (*The Little Red Riding Hood and 41 other Fairy Tales*) from 1916 (5–9), a translation of the seventh German edition from 1857.[2] In this version, LRRH is tricked and eventually eaten by the wolf and then saved by a hunter, unlike in the Perrault versions, which end with her demise (see Zipes, *Trials* 91–93), and certain oral versions in which she rescues herself by tricking the wolf and running home (see Delarue 373–74). Importantly, the popularity of this version of the fairy tale meant that all of the children already knew the story, and that adults have been repeating it in both severely desexualized and highly sexualizing versions.[3] This narrative of a girl's journey through the woods is thus one way that Western culture deals with and talks to children about gender and sexuality in a more or less explicit fashion.

I visited one class at a time, briefly introduced myself and the drawing assignment (without going into the specifics of my research project), and then read LRRH to the class. After hearing the story, the children were given a white A4 sheet and felt-tip pens in twelve different colors, and then had about an hour to draw the fairy tale. (They were asked to write their age and gender on the back of the drawings, and in this context all of the children identified as either boy or girl.)[4] In 2020 the resulting 184 drawings were displayed as part of the exhibition *Barnestreger—Køn og seksualitet i børns tegninger* (*Crossing Lines—Gender and Sexuality in Children's Drawings*), which I curated at The Women's Museum in Denmark (fig. 4.1–4.2).[5]

Looking at this collection of drawings raises further questions: If we follow the lines of children's drawings engaging with the narrative lines of a fairy tale, where might they take us? What might children's literature look like from the perspective of children's drawings? What if we, adults, allowed our interpretations of the literary works we narrate to children to be informed by how they, the children, process them in drawings? What reinterpretations of well-known texts might be generated? And more broadly, how might children's drawings further or challenge our understandings of childhood and of children's gender and sexuality?

This is of course not to say that we can dispense with (adult) theorizations regarding these issues. Even so, we can and should take children seriously as interpreters, as critics even, of the culture with which they engage; they are, as we shall see, capable of critical reinterpretation.[6] In the following, I will thus take my cue from the drawings, while also drawing inspiration from a few thinkers from childhood studies and psychoanalysis.[7] Between adult conceptualizations and child creativity, I will be pursuing the seductions of *LRRH* as they appear in adult narrative lines and children's drawn lines, and considering what these lines might reveal about gender and sexuality, and what I will call the threshold status of the child.

St(r)aying: Approaching a Threshold Model of Childhood

In preparing the exhibition, I proceeded from a working hypothesis about the child as a threshold being. To put this view of childhood in a single sentence: The child is both inside and outside the world of adults. Children are born into this world, and as such they are a part of it, but at the same time they are not yet fully a part of it. From this position, and this is obvious in everyday interactions with children, they will shift between assimilation and

Fig. 4.1–4.2. Exhibition views of the drawings showing specific scenes from *Little Red Riding Hood* displayed in the chronological order of the narrative. © Jakob Rosendal and KØN—Gender Museum Denmark.

opposition, either seeking to fit in or resisting their situation (their survival might very well depend on both). As an internal outsider or external insider the child both follows and diverts from the course set up by adults. The threshold child both stays on and strays from the path.

This threshold understanding of childhood, I believe, resonates with a certain tendency within children's literature studies perhaps best articulated in Marah Gubar's "kinship model of childhood." This model "is premised on the idea that children and adults are akin to one another, which means they are neither exactly the same nor radically dissimilar" ("Risky" 453). Seeing the child as both similar and dissimilar to adults, Gubar praises a "both-and approach" to childhood that she finds germinating in the work of Karen Sánchez-Eppler, who holds that children are both objects of adult socialization and makers of social meaning ("Recuperation" 305). Gubar's point is to acknowledge that while children are "shaped by a classification that preexists their arrival in the world," they also have some agency in the face of those classifications: Children are "simultaneously scripted and scripting" ("Recuperation" 295). They are st(r)aying. Positioned inside and outside the world of adults, as threshold beings, children will both seek out adult socialization and oppose it.

The kinship model serves as a critique of a predominant tendency within children's literature studies—what Gubar calls "Rose's paradigm" after Jacqueline Rose's influential work—to reduce the actual child to a passive recipient of adult-produced narratives (or socialization) and to put this child (as a participant) out of reach. Importantly, Gubar instead insists on the possibility of reaching actual children in their agency—as "coproducers and enactors of child-oriented texts" or "artistic agents" and thus as "participants in the production of culture" ("Risky" 452). She exemplifies this with children's drama and picture books composed by adults in collaboration with children ("Risky" 452–53). As I will explore further in the following, children's drawings are, of course, a big, albeit also underestimated, part of their cultural participation, considering the enthusiasm most children display when engaging in this activity.

In relation to Gubar's work, it is interesting to note how the history of the *LRRH* narrative reflects shifting negotiations of the child's agency in relation to adults. Depending on the version, it is either the girl's independence, her capacity to act on her own, or her dependence, her need for adult guidance and help, that is underscored. In an oral version known as *The Story of Grandmother* collected around 1885 in France, the girl, who is not wearing her characteristic red garment, initially does what the adults (her mother and the wolf) ask of her, but then saves herself by tricking the adult wolf and running home (Delarue 373–74).[8] By contrast, the Brothers Grimm's versions make the girl wholly dependent on adults, in terms of moral guidance (in the mother's sendoff), seduction (by the wolf), and rescue (by the hunter, but also by the grandmother in the appendicular story). Many of the more recent versions could be read as attempts to return agency to the girl. We thus see, through the vicissitudes of a particularly repeated narrative, how children's literature can itself be caught up in dealing with the agency of the child.

I maintain that all of the collected drawings of the fairy tale display some degree of agency and independence on the part of the children. I chose the particular fairy tale and the allowed drawing materials, but it was up to the children themselves to decide what to draw. For a few of them this was difficult and they would ask for further adult instruction, while others, on the contrary, would resist the limitations of the assignment and use other drawing materials. As they either sought out adult help in solving what an adult had asked of them or circumvented adult requirements, these children, at a collective level, thus already demonstrated their threshold existence.

Across all of the 184 drawings, something similar appears. On the one hand, the drawings follow the narrative and illustrate one particular scene (in 105 cases) or two or more particular scenes (18 cases), or zoom in on a particular motif or element from the story—e.g., the basket with gifts (11 cases). On the other hand, they divert from the narrative by mixing scenes, adding foreign elements, or otherwise making changes to the story (50 cases). The threshold child here appears through two strong tendencies to either stay on the narrative path or stray into the woods of alternative meanings and further narrative possibilities. This statistical or collective child shows us how the child as a threshold being appears to be caught between the adult narrative as it is and the possibility of using that narrative to tell a different story.

This tension should not be understood too simplistically, as if only those drawings that stray from the narrative path open up to something new and different, whereas the other drawings just confirm the status quo of the narrated version of the fairy tale. On the contrary, it is possible for the inside-outside threshold status of the child to appear in both types of drawings. The children who seem to stray from an adult narrative may just be influenced by other adult-produced narratives or cultural products; and the children who follow the narrative may, in fact, stress a difference or an externality in relation to adults, although not one immediately recognizable at the level of narrative scenes and motifs.

Fig. 4.3. An "x-ray" wolf is pulling out the intestines of LRRH. Boy, twelve years. © Jakob Rosendal and KØN—Gender Museum Denmark.

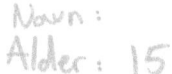

Fig. 4.4. The wolf stabs LRRH in the back. Boy, fifteen years. © Jakob Rosendal and KØN—Gender Museum Denmark.

Fig. 4.5. LRRH is the superhero "Super-Red" ("Superrøde"). Boy, fifteen years. © Jakob Rosendal and KØN—Gender Museum Denmark.

The possibility of such an alternative externality or difference will be explored in the following when we turn to the seductions of *LRRH*. While some children would add elements to the fairy tale from adult-produced toys, movies, or computer games or from adult-run activities that they had just been part of prior to hearing the fairy tale, others reworked the fairy tale so drastically that their work could not be so easily attributed to adult influences. It is, however, impossible to draw a clear dividing line, even if one should wish to do so, without more detailed knowledge of each of the children's lives. What we can say here is that these children are displaying at least some degree of agency in pitting one piece of adult meaning-making against another.

A striking example of this agency can be found in the drawings that seemed both to showcase a significant degree of creative independence and to lead to other versions of *LRRH* than the one by the Brothers Grimm the children had just heard. This was the case in a few drawings that would more or less explicitly depict strong or deadly violence against LRRH in retellings reminiscent of the protagonist's fatal ending in Perrault's 1697 version.[9] And it was the case, even more surprisingly, in drawings by two teenage boys that depicted LRRH as independent and capable of handling the wolf on her own either by declaring herself a superhero ("Super-Red") or by killing the wolf when she first meets it, which thus echoes, however inadvertently, the French oral version from 1885.

Fig. 4.6. LRRH leaves the dead wolf on the side of the path. Boy, fourteen years. © Jakob Rosendal and KØN—Gender Museum Denmark.

From inside the world of adult narratives these drawings insist on an aggression against LRRH (Perrault style) or on her independence and strength (like the oral French version). While these drawings can be placed on the spectrum of former adult versions, the drawings are still foreign and external to predominant adult versions of the fairy tale in Denmark in general and in particular to the Brothers Grimm's version that I read to them in class and they were asked to draw. These four drawings, as they demonstrate two ways of reworking one adult narrative with another, thus suggest the threshold status of the child. They display an externality based on an (inadvertent) internality.

The Two Seductions: Reinterpretation between Drawings and Psychoanalysis

There has been a strong tendency to read the LRRH-wolf relation as a girl-man or daughter-father relation and accordingly to interpret the seduction that unfolds within the fairy tale as a male or male-oriented seduction.[10] One consequence of this androcentric interpretive tendency is a suppression of possible feminine/maternal or less unequivocally gendered understandings of the fairy tale in general and of its theme of seduction in particular.[11]

In their drawings, none of the children actually attributed a distinct gender to the wolf. They might have perceived the wolf as masculine—as some of them certainly did, judging from their own written descriptions on the back of their drawings—but if they did, they did so without marking this masculinity visually.[12] One could of course argue that the absence of such a marker is a sign of the neutrality or unmarked character of masculinity in an androcentric culture. However, the absence of any signs of masculinity still holds open the possibility of reading the wolf's gender differently. This lack of gendering aligns with the Danish translation that I read to the children, in which the wolf is referred to with the gender-neutral pronoun "den" ("it") and not "han" ("he"). In the German text the wolf's pronouns are masculine in accordance with the German masculine noun "Wolf," but in referring to the noun these pronouns need not refer to the gender of the wolf, and it would therefore be better to use a neuter pronoun.[13] English translations, however, usually gender the wolf by way of masculine pronouns. The same goes for the illustration history of *LRRH* throughout which plenty of illustrations have gendered the wolf by way of masculine clothes or associations with phallic pictorial elements.[14] In line with the scholarly interpretation history's androcentric tendencies, these two types of adult meaning-making—unlike the children's drawings—thus create an unnecessary masculinization of the wolf.

Working with the children's drawings and interpreting them and the fairy tale itself from the vantage point of psychoanalytical theory made me realize the presence of not just one, but two scenes of seduction in the fairy tale. The first one, commonly described in terms of seduction, is the encounter with the wolf in the forest, whereas the other comes with the second encounter with the wolf (or wolf-like grandmother). The drawings furthermore made me reconsider the nature of the seduction these two scenes display in ways that have, to the best of my knowledge, not yet been explored in the scholarship.

Within the 105 drawings of a single scene from the fairy tale, the importance of the first seduction scene becomes evident from the fact that it is the most reproduced, appearing in 22 of the 105 drawings. The scenes immediately before and after this first encounter with the wolf—where LRRH is either alone on the path or picking flowers in the woods—make up the third and second most reproduced scenes, counting 18 and 21 instances, respectively. It is as if the seduction draws so much attention that it also affects the attention paid to the surrounding moments of the narrative.

This concentration of the drawings on these three scenes might not be that surprising, since the first seduction constitutes a narrative point of no return. And yet, is such a narratological explanation sufficient, considering that the

Fig. 4.7. Before the first seduction scene: LRRH in the woods before the first encounter with the wolf. Girl, nine years. © Jakob Rosendal and KØN—Gender Museum Denmark.

drawings of these three scenes make up almost 60 percent of the single-scene depictions? Furthermore, the children seem ambivalent in their individual and collective interpretation of this crucial moment of the fairy tale: Judging from the sheer number of drawings, the children are surely also seduced by the first encounter with the wolf—as a point of narrative intensity and transgression in relation to parental authority (the mother's sendoff); at the same time, though, their drawings of the two surrounding scenes also reveal a kind of avoidance of the first scene of seduction.

These drawings appear in many cases to function as *screen drawings* along the lines of what Freud called screen memories, as the children are both attracted to the seduction scene and try to repress it by displacing the memory of this scene with another related scene. The preceding scene serves to interject and insist on a prolonged moment in the woods prior to the wolf's presence, which is not really part of the fairy tale itself (fig. 4.7), and the following scene allows for a focus on the joyful picking of flowers, revealing nothing of the seduction and thus functioning as a screen against it, while also in several instances serving as a moment of identification with a stereotypical image of floral girlhood (fig. 4.8). The drawings of the first seduction also to varying degrees display a screening function, most clearly in those drawings in which LRRH and the wolf are shown as friends and the wolf as a

Fig. 4.8. After the first seduction scene: LRRH picking flowers in the woods. Girl, six years. © Jakob Rosendal and KØN—Gender Museum Denmark.

sweet teddy bear (fig. 4.9). With their screen drawings, the children are going against an adult-produced and adult-narrated fairy tale. However, they are also acting in accordance with certain popular adult-produced retellings of the fairy tale made for young children that serve a similar screening function and, in some cases, in accordance with adult-sanctioned images of friendship or girlhood. Again, the children's agency or independence is caught up in a dependence on adult culture—it is on the threshold.

The children's strong interest in the first seduction scene combined with their efforts to screen against it indicates, I believe, something more fundamentally troubling at work in this scene than the interpretation history usually acknowledges. Lacan might be helpful here. The first seduction scene is indicative of how "desire is the Other's desire" and how "desire is the flipside of the law" and is therefore "tied to prohibition" (Lacan 690, 665, 723): The wolf (as an other) succeeds in its seduction by pointing out what it finds desirable in the woods (pretty flowers and sweet singing birds) and by urging LRRH to disobey her mother (as another other). Where prior readings have stressed the oral, anal, or genital dimensions of this fairy tale type (see Róheim, Fromm, Bettelheim, Dundes), what is important here from a Lacanian perspective is the scopic dimension: In the beginning, the mother admonishes LRRH not to "peep" around when arriving at her grandmother's place, while the wolf seduces her with the question "Why do you not look round?" In this way, the wolf appears as the flipside of the mother (her desire and her prohibitions). The fairy tale thus already here links mother and wolf, thereby adding to the possibility of a maternal interpretation of the wolf.

Fig. 4.9. The first seduction scene: LRRH encounters the wolf. Girl, five years. © Jakob Rosendal and KØN—Gender Museum Denmark.

Moreover, the wolf's seduction works because it opens up toward the constitutive lack of desire, its fundamentally unfulfillable character: In LRRH's case picking one flower always leads to the next even prettier flower, which she then wants. Desire resulting in the desire for something else is what leads her "deeper and deeper into the woods." But this movement of desire also leads to the dimension of the drive. It leads beyond the Freudian pleasure principle, as it constitutes a repetition-induced "*dérive* [drift]" towards a certain limit, where an insistence on pleasure turns unpleasurable (Lacan 680; Freud, "Beyond"). LRRH's straying into the woods constitutes such a drift that only stops when she has "gathered so many [flowers] that she could carry no more," thus reaching a physical limit to her (scopic) pleasures. The seduction of LRRH is troubling not only in how it awakens her desire, opening up toward lack, but also in how it leads her towards a potential excessive enjoyment of the drive revealed by the limits of what her body can bear. That none of the children's drawings and no adult illustrations, as far as I know, have shown LRRH with an almost unbearable amount of flowers in her arms—an image akin to some of Yayoi Kusama's flower-obsessed works—is indicative of the usual screening functioning of this imagery.

As LRRH reaches her grandmother's house, the second seduction scene starts to unfold. Whereas the first seduction could more easily be read as perverse, the second scene could be interpreted along the lines of Laplanche's general theory of seduction. Importantly, this theory contributes to our threshold understanding of childhood, since it articulates a difference between (infant) child and adult that places them on either side of both communication (verbal and nonverbal) and the repression of infantile sexuality (*Foundations* 88–104; *Sexual* 27–51, 99–113). The adult has more or less mastered certain communication codes, unlike the child, but in doing so the (neurotic) adult has also repressed its now unconscious infantile sexuality, a sexuality which it shares with the child, who is currently living with this sexuality and only just beginning the unending process of coming to terms with it—through repression or otherwise. Seduction is what occurs when the child is confronted with and will have to try to make sense of adult messages that are disturbed by the noise of the adult's unconscious infantile sexuality. These messages contain what Laplanche calls *enigmatic signifiers*, that is, libidinally charged "designified signifiers," which, precisely for being without a clear signified, raise questions for the child: What does the other want from me? What am I to the other? (*Foundations* 126). It is through such questions induced by enigmatic signifiers that the child is seduced by the adult's unconscious infantile sexuality.

The beginning of the fairy tale, when LRRH's mother tells her to greet her grandmother upon arrival, already calls attention to potential difficulties in or disturbances of the intergenerational communication. This is confirmed when no one answers LRRH's "Good morning" and her "strange feeling" upon arrival leads to a "very strange [looking]" grandmother. Then comes the famous dialogue in which LRRH is in fact drawn closer and closer, moving from the remote senses of hearing and sight to the near senses of touch and taste, and from the scopic dimension that was part of the seduction of LRRH in the woods to the (perhaps more) infantile dimension of the oral drive. This underscores how repetition—here not through flower picking but by way of puzzled comments—again serves the straying movement of seduction. Furthermore, LRRH's remarks about her grandmother's strange appearance are similar to the kind of questions raised by the adult's enigmatic signifiers. It is as if LRRH is asking: "What do these ears, eyes, hands, and this mouth want? What does grandmother want with me? What am I to her?" By way of libidinally charged and enigmatic part-objects/signifiers, LRRH is seduced into the mouth (as part-object and locus of the wolf's desire). She is seduced by the sexuality and more specifically the oral drive of the maternal wolf.

The wolf could thus be read as a symbolic representation of the (grand)mother's unconscious infantile sexuality. The opening lines of the fairy tale indicate that it is a story about a maternal love that is greater than any other ("a ... girl who was loved ... most of all by her grandmother") and potentially

Fig. 4.10. The second seduction scene: LRRH anxiously meets the wolf. Girl, fourteen years. © Jakob Rosendal and KØN—Gender Museum Denmark.

excessive ("there was nothing that she would not have given to the child"), which has already marked the girl (the gift of the red garment). All of this speaks to the ordinariness or generality of seduction, especially since LRRH's attempts to comment on the adult's enigmatic appearance are answered by a symbolic realization of the clichéd expression of adults' (unconscious sexual) desire for children: "I could just eat you up."

Despite the fact that both the first and the second seduction scene are similar moments of narrative intensity, only three children drew the second encounter with the wolf-(grand)mother. Maybe the children's drawings of the first scene of seduction could be said to serve as screen drawings in relation to the second more explicitly maternal seduction scene. If so the three drawings of that later scene are all the more remarkable. In two of them, fourteen-year-old girls successfully convey the "strange feeling" LRRH experiences: One by drawing the red-hooded girl anxiously stiff—as expressed by her verticality, narrow mouth, and wide open eyes—while placing her in the white void space of the page on the threshold to the furnished space that frames the wolf-(grand)mother (fig. 4.10), and the other by placing the spectator in the position of LRRH in front of the maternal wolf, which, in perhaps yet another instance of ambivalent screening, appears cute with its rounded almost mouselike appearance, while its pointy nails are decidedly more threatening as they reach the edge of the paper, and thus the space of the spectator, and the eyes in different shades of red display an unfocused and enigmatic expression (fig. 4.11).

Fig. 4.11. The second seduction scene: The enigmatic gaze of the wolf. Girl, fourteen years. © Jakob Rosendal and KØN—Gender Museum Denmark.

Fig. 4.12. The second seduction scene: "There is something black at the top. Grandmother is the black eyes, and LRRH is above her. They are talking together." Boy, four years. © Jakob Rosendal and KØN—Gender Museum Denmark.

The third drawing, made by a four-year-old boy, is the only collected drawing that was not clearly figurative (fig. 4.12). But his description is revealing: "There is something black at the top. Grandmother is the black eyes, and Red Riding Hood is above her. They are talking together." From this the central black circular marks become readable as the grandmother—the wolf is not even mentioned—and the small more vertical red marks must be LRRH. Above that the back-and-forth of their dialogue appears to be represented by the red and black zig-zag lines gradually approaching each other from left to right, only to end in a dark patch where red is devoured by black. Tellingly, this drawing reduces the grandmother to her "black eyes" (the scopic dimension) and the devouring (the oral dimension), the endpoint of the seduction, to something more indefinable ("something black") and thus enigmatic.

These three drawings follow the adult-produced narrative, as they draw a specific scene; but they also allow for an interpretation—in terms of maternal seduction—that goes against the predominant masculine or androcentric focus of interpretations of the wolf and its seduction. On the level of interpretation the drawings thus show the threshold status of the child, which the narrative plays out in the figure of the girl who is both inside adult communication and external to its enigmatic messages, and both inside sexuality (the erogeneity of her body, her scopic pleasures) and outside it (outside adult sexuality).

It is interesting that *LRRH* has been retold in versions stretching from the desexualized to the hypersexualized, since this explicitly makes it a site where

Fig. 4.13. LRRH on the path and already moving into the woods: St(r)aying. Oliver, seven years. © Jakob Rosendal and KØN—Gender Museum Denmark.

adult culture negotiates its relation to sexuality through a fairy tale understood as a story for children. In this way, each adult telling of the story could entail—for adult and child participants both—a confrontation of the enigmatic dimensions of sexuality and, more broadly, of the cultural unconscious.

Sendoff: Growing Sideways inside a Fairy Tale

Another part of the exhibition of children's drawings showed more than a hundred images by Oliver, a sixteen-year-old transgender boy, starting with some of his earliest scribbles and ending with recent self-portraits. In a happy coincidence, the collection of Oliver's images, which contained more than eight hundred works, happened to have two drawings of *LRRH*.

These two drawings show how Oliver both followed and diverted from the adult narrative: In one drawing, Oliver stays on the narrative path and draws a specific scene (fig. 4.13), and in the other drawing, he strays from the narrative in significant ways (fig. 4.14). The drawing of the specific scene shows LRRH on the path prior to the encounter with the wolf. Interestingly, even though she is clearly on the path, she already appears to be moving into woods, as her hands and the top of her head have disappeared behind a

Fig. 4.14. LRRH off the path. The trans-wolf and the green-haired cyclops-girl straying and escaping the threats from above. Oliver, seven years. © Jakob Rosendal and KØN—Gender Museum Denmark.

bush. In a paradoxical way, she is thus both on the path and moving deeper into the woods. She is effectively st(r)aying.

The other drawing takes this straying much further: Here we see the wolf and the girl running, maybe further into the woods, but certainly away from three spaceships firing red beams at them. One beam sets a tree on fire, while a blue cloud placed in front of the sun in a way that repeats the shape of the spaceships fires a bolt of lightning that strikes the ground just in front of the girl. In this context, it is difficult not to read this depiction of an attack from above as an image of the symbolic violence that grown-ups afflict on children when assigning a gender and expecting certain normative behaviors, especially since both escaping figures display certain queer transformational capabilities: The wolf has kept the dress and has teamed up with the girl, who now appears as a green-haired cyclops—usually a male creature—in a rainbow-striped dress. At the time of these drawings, Oliver was seven years old and very much aware of the conventional gendering of colors, so it is most likely not a coincidence that the wolf's dress is bright blue with pink flowers, thus underscoring its gendered transformation and liminality. This partnership with the wolf—as a figure symbolic of polymorphous infantile sexuality—appears to be predicated on while also enabling further bodily transformations: The girl is transformed into a mythological creature, losing an eye in the process but gaining access to another kind of being. This highly creative drawing seems to allow Oliver to navigate the restricting violence of adult gender assignment and express another more open-ended and transformational relation to his body and gender. It allows him—to use Kathryn Bond Stockton's fitting metaphor—to grow sideways inside *LRRH*.

These two drawings give us a strong impression of the child as a threshold being. They show us how Oliver during his childhood was both growing up and growing to the side, resisting adult gender assignment with an adult narrative that he both follows and goes beyond. For better or for worse, adults must lay out some sort of a path for children, while children—as a matter of survival—will both stay on it and stray from it, in ways that play out their threshold existence.

Notes

1. The research for this text has been made possible by funding from The Velux Foundations for the research project *Gender Blender: Everyday Life, Activism, and Diversity* (project number 00021290), a collaboration between Aarhus University and KØN—Gender Museum Denmark. Permission was granted from parents and teachers to read the fairy tale and collect, analyze, and exhibit the drawings, with an agreement that no other information about the children than their age and gender would be made public or drawn upon for research and exhibition purposes.

The study of children's drawings is relatively young, yet quite extensive, with the earliest studies dating back to the 1880s (see Pierre Naville's bibliography, which covers the research up until 1949 with almost one hundred pages of references). Since then the growth of the field has not slowed down. The study of children's drawings appears, however, to be in need of more nuanced engagements with gender and sexuality, which could move the field beyond its cis-/heteronormative tendencies to focus solely on girl and boy drawings. Karen Vibeke Mortensen's overview of the field from 1991 confirms this impression (71–91). Not much has changed on this front since then. As far as I know, prior to my own work, only one anthropological study from 2018 has been devoted to the subject of transgender children's drawings (Galman).

2. This German edition exists in an English translation by Margaret Hunt from 1884, which I will rely on in this chapter. Hunt translates the title as "Little Red-Cap." I will, however, stick to the more commonly used title *Little Red Riding Hood*. For a sense of the widespread circulation of the fairy tale in textual form, see Zipes and Beckett, "World."

3. For more on the (de)sexualizing repetitions and interpretations of *LRRH*, see for instance Orenstein, Beckett ("Ages"), Dundes, and Zipes.

4. All participants described themselves as either girl or boy; however, they were free to write what they saw fit, either including or not including information about trans or nonbinary identities.

5. Almost all of the drawings are reproduced in the exhibition catalogue (Rosendal). Since the exhibition, the museum has changed its name to KØN—Gender Museum Denmark.

6. This point, as will be clear in the following, is inspired by the work of Marah Gubar. A similar idea can also be found in the work of Walter Benjamin and has been elaborated by Benjamin-inspired children's literature scholars. For an overview of Benjamin's influence on

children's literature see Kenneth B. Kidd's *Theory for Beginners* (95–99). As Kidd writes, "Benjamin modeled and encouraged the idea that childhood and its forms are resources for critical thinking and cultural refashioning" (99).

7. I shall not here enter into a discussion of the longstanding use of children's drawings within psychoanalytic treatment and theory. For a classic work in this regard see Melanie Klein's *Narrative of a Child Analysis*; and for a useful introduction to the analysis of children's drawings from a psychoanalytic perspective see Daniel Widlöcher's *L'interprétation des dessins d'enfants*. Nor shall I try to assess the possible influences between children's literature and psychoanalysis. See in this regard chapter four of *Freud in Oz* by Kenneth B. Kidd where he touches upon the significance of children's drawings to what he terms "picturebook psychology" (105); Kidd suggests seeing Klein's book as "a psychoanalytic picturebook" (111) and "the successful picturebook writer or illustrator" as "a lay child analyst" (112).

8. For an English translation, see Zipes, *Trials* 21–23.

9. For this version, see Zipes, *Trials* 91–93.

10. I am thinking here particularly of the psychoanalytical and sociohistorical work by Fromm, Bettelheim, Zipes, and Barzilai as well as feminist readings by Brownmiller and in various texts by Marshall. It seems indicative of the strength of the tendency to masculinize the wolf that Shuli Barzilai in her book *Lacan and the Matter of Origins* on the maternal in Lacan's thought never entertains the possibility of a feminine/maternal reading of the wolf even as she explores the *LRRH* fairy tale in the context of Lacan's statements about the mother as a ferocious animal (a crocodile or tigress) (199–217).

11. On the possibility of feminine interpretations of this fairy tale type, see Verdier, Crawford, and Dundes. Telling, Bettelheim draws on Crawford's article without mentioning her work, and he excludes her focus on the wolf as also feminine—thus doubly repressing the feminine. For more on Bettelheim's plagiarism see Kidd (*Freud in Oz* 21–23), which references the critical autobiographies of Sutton and Pollak.

12. Two exceptions seem to prove this rule: In one drawing by a six-year-old boy, the wolf has a line between its legs similar to that of a peeing alien in a UFO above the other protagonists; in the other drawing, a fifteen-year-old boy has endowed the wolf with a large penis in what appears—judging from the inscription on the paper—as a homophobic attempt to poke fun at a classmate.

13. This point about grammar, translation, and gender is inspired by Wentzel.

14. See Zipes, *Trials* 343–81.

Works Cited

Barzilai, Shuli. *Lacan and the Matter of Origins*. Stanford UP, 1999.
Beckett, Sandra L. *Red Riding Hood for All Ages: A Fairy-Tale Icon in Cross-Cultural Contexts*. Wayne State UP, 2008.
Beckett, Sandra L. *Revisioning Red Riding Hood around the World: An Anthology of International Retellings*. Wayne State UP, 2014.
Bettelheim, Bruno. *The Uses of Enchantment: The Meaning and Importance of Fairy Tales*. 1976. Vintage Books, 1977.
Brownmiller, Susan. *Against Our Will: Men, Women and Rape*. Secker and Warburg, 1975.
Crawford, Elizabeth. "The Wolf as Condensation." *American Imago*, vol. 12, no. 3, 1995, pp. 307–14.
Delarue, Paul. *Le conte populaire français*. Éditions Érasme, 1957.
Dundes, Alan. "Interpreting 'Little Red Riding Hood' Psychoanalytically." *Little Red Riding Hood—A Casebook*, edited by Alan Dundes, U of Wisconsin P, 1989, pp. 192–236.

Freud, Sigmund. "Beyond the Pleasure Principle." *The Standard Edition of the Complete Psychological Works of Sigmund Freud, Volume XVIII (1920-1922): Beyond the Pleasure Principle, Group Psychology and Other Works*. Translated by James Strachey, The Hogarth Press and the Institute of Psycho-Analysis, pp. 1–64.

Freud, Sigmund. "Screen Memories." *The Standard Edition of the Complete Psychological Works of Sigmund Freud, Volume III (1893-1899): Early Psycho-Analytic Publications*. Translated by James Strachey, The Hogarth Press and the Institute of Psycho-Analysis, pp. 299–322.

Fromm, Erich. *The Forgotten Language: An Introduction to the Understanding of Dreams, Fairy Tales and Myths*. Victor Gollancz, 1952.

Galman, Sally Campbell. "Enchanted Selves—Transgender Children's Persistent use of Mermaid Imagery in Self-Portraiture." *Shima*, vol. 12, no. 2, 2018, pp. 163–80.

Grimm, Jacob, and Wilhelm Grimm. *Den lille Rødhætte og 41 andre eventyr*. Translated by Carl Ewald, Nordisk forlag, 1916.

Grimm, Jacob, and Wilhelm Grimm. *Grimm's Household Tales*. Vol. 1. Translated and edited by Margaret Hunt, George Bell and Sons, 1884. https://archive.org/details/grimmshousehold t01grim/page/n3/mode/2up.

Gubar, Marah. "The Hermeneutics of Recuperation: What a Kinship-Model Approach to Children's Agency Could Do for Children's Literature and Childhood Studies." *Jeunesse: Young People, Texts, Cultures*, vol. 8, no. 1, 2016, pp. 291–310.

Gabar, Marah. "Risky Business: Talking about Children in Children's Literature Criticism." *Children's Literature Association Quarterly*, vol. 38, no. 4, winter 2013, pp. 450–57.

Kidd, Kenneth B. *Freud in Oz: At the Intersections of Psychoanalysis and Children's Literature*. U of Minnesota P, 2011.

Kidd, Kenneth B. *Theory for Beginners: Children's Literature as Critical Thought*, Fordham UP, 2020.

Klein, Melanie. *Narrative of a Child Analysis: The Conduct of the Psycho-Analysis of Children as Seen in the Treatment of a Ten-Year-Old Boy*. Vintage, 1998.

Lacan, Jacques. Écrits: *The First Complete Edition in English*. Translated by Bruce Fink with Héloïse Fink and Russell Grigg, W. W. Norton, 2006.

Laplanche, Jean. *Freud and the Sexual: Essays 2000-2006*. Translated by John Fletcher et al., International Psychoanalytical Books, 2011.

Laplanche, Jean. *New Foundations for Psychoanalysis*. Translated by David Macey, Basil Blackwell, 1989.

Marshall, Elizabeth. "Girlhood, Sexual Violence, and Agency in Francesca Lia Block's 'Wolf.'" *Children's Literature in Education*, vol. 40, no. 3, 2009, pp. 217–34.

Marshall, Elizabeth. "Picturing Rape Culture: Little Red Riding Hood and School Dress Codes." *Graphic Girlhoods: Visualizing Education and Violence*. Routledge, 2018.

Marshall, Elizabeth. "Stripping for the Wolf: Rethinking Representations of Gender in Children's Literature." *Reading Research Quarterly*, vol. 39, no. 3, 2004, pp. 256–70.

Mortensen, Karen Vibeke. *Form and Content in Children's Human Figure Drawings: Development, Sex Differences, and Body Experience*. New York UP, 1991.

Naville, Pierre. "Éléments d'une bibliographie critique relative au graphisme enfantin jusqu'en 1949." *Le dessin chez l'enfant*. Presses Universitaires de France, 1951, pp. 129–222.

Orenstein, Catherine. *Little Red Riding Hood Uncloaked: Sex, Morality, and the Evolution of a Fairy Tale*. Basic Books, 2002.

Pollak, Richard. *The Creation of Dr. B: A Biography of Bruno Bettelheim*. Touchstone Books, 1988.

Róheim, Géza. "Fairy Tale and Dream: 'Little Red Riding Hood.'" *Little Red Riding Hood—A Casebook*, edited by Alan Dundes, U of Wisconsin P, 1989, pp. 159–67.

Rose, Jacqueline: *The Case of Peter Pan; or, The Impossibility of Children's Fiction*. 1984. U of Pennsylvania P, 1992.

Rosendal, Jakob. *Barnestreger: Køn og seksualitet i tegninger af børn*. Kvindemuseet and Passepartout, 2020.

Sánchez-Eppler, Karen. *Dependent States: The Child's Part in Nineteenth-Century American Culture*. U of Chicago P, 2005.

Stockton, Kathryn Bond. *The Queer Child; or, Growing Sideways in the Twentieth Century*. Duke UP, 2009.

Sutton, Nina. *Bettelheim: A Life and a Legacy*. Translated by David Sharp, Westview, 1996.

Verdier, Yvonne. "'Grands-mères, si vous saviez . . .': Le Petit Chaperon Rouge dans la tradition orale." *Cahiers de Littérature Orale*, no. 4, 1978, pp. 17–55.

Wentzel, Knud. "En kulturbegivenhed. Villy Sørensens oversættelse af Grimms eventyr. En hyldest med halvanden indsigelse." *Bogens Verden*, no. 2, 1996, http://wayback-01.kb.dk/wayback/20101108104748/http://www2.kb.dk/guests/natl/db/bv/bv-96/2-96/villys.htm.

Widlöcher, Daniel. *L'interprétation des dessins d'enfants*. Charles Dessart, 1965.

Zipes, Jack. *The Trials and Tribulations of Little Red Riding Hood*. Routledge, 1993.

SNANGER DANGER
SS/HG Fanfiction, Kinship, and an Affinity Space Model of Children's and Young Adult Literature

Amanda K. Allen

On February 3, 2021, *Slate.com* posted a self-help article titled "My Teen Is Writing Erotic Fan Fiction. Should I Make Them Stop?" The article includes the following statement from a parent: "My 16-year-old is basically writing porn. . . . I found some other fan fiction they've also written, and it's very . . . mature. And adult. I don't know where they learned half of this stuff—it feels like a year ago they didn't even know what a condom was, and now they're writing explicit and age-inappropriate fan fiction" (Chung). This parent's dilemma underscores an ongoing debate (mostly among adults) regarding young people and fanfiction.[1] While young people's involvement in fanfiction is often positive, particularly as it relates to literacy development and to gender and sexual (and particularly queer) identity exploration, fanfiction itself—especially fanfiction written by authors of unknown ages—continues to exist in an uneasy relationship with the field of published children's and young adult literature.[2] Catherine Tosenberger suggests that fanfiction is crucial to the study of that field, because "[f]anworks based on texts for young people give us the actual responses of actual audience members for this genre of literature—a genre defined by its audience, but necessarily alienated from that very audience by established cultural and industry-related paradigms" (22). As she suggests, fanfiction allows young people to "speak for themselves: to talk back to the narratives given to them and develop aesthetic forms and traditions to suit themselves, outside of the direct control of adults" (22). I agree with Tosenberger wholeheartedly but offer a small revision: young people speak and talk back to adults, but do so *in tandem with them*. Examining novel-length Severus Snape/Hermione Granger fanfiction during its heyday (2000–2010), as I do in this essay, reveals the extent to which SS/HG fans, younger and older, collaborate in creating fic conventions that demonstrate a likeness between fans; this shared affinity is independent of age and recalls Marah Gubar's "kinship model." The kinship among SS/HG fans young and older gestures toward an alternative model of children's and young adult literature that manifests through what James Paul Gee calls "affinity spaces": accessible spatial configurations organized around a shared passion rather than around identity markers such as age. By using SS/HG fanfiction as a representative case study of such an affinity space, I suggest an expanded, anti-aetonormative concept of children's and young adult literature: one that reconceptualizes it not as a set of "texts" (broadly defined) but as a site of shared passion.

Known also by the portmanteaus Snanger, Snamione, or Sevmione, Snape/Hermione (SS/HG) fanfiction is fan-written stories (fics) that emphasize a relationship between loathed teacher Severus Snape and know-it-all student Hermione Granger.[3] Started in September 2000 by author Lupinlover, who was then twelve years old, SS/HG is one of the most popular "het" pairings within the Harry Potter fandom, encompassing tens of thousands of stories across multiple fanfiction archives. As one might expect, the tone, length, scope, and content of these many SS/HG fics showcase a wide-ranging corpus, from one-hundred-word "drabbles" in which Snape secretly watches a teenage Hermione from afar, to three-hundred-thousand-word novels in which an adult Hermione travels back in time to save Snape from Nagini's bite. Collectively, SS/HG fanfiction possesses its own periodization and tropes, with significant generic differences between, for example, a Gothic hero–style Snape of the "Classic Era" (fics written before *Order of the Phoenix* was released) versus the damaged, abused Snape of the "Half-Blood Prince Era." Writing in 2004, fan idlerat defines the genre's main tropes:

> Snape/Hermione is known as the subgenre of HP most allied with the traditional, bodice-ripper type romance, with an older, dark, mysterious, powerful, nasty and (in many stories) rich hero and a younger, idealistic heroine who steals his heart. But it's equally important to remember that this is the teacher/student ship *par excellance* [sic], since Hermione builds her identity around being a student so much more than any other of the young characters in the series.

Even with the significant reinterpretation of Snape following publication of *Half-Blood Prince* (which reduced the fanonical pure-blood Lord Snape and

Snape Manor to poor, half-blood Severus and Spinner's End), these conventions continued to define SS/HG through 2010.⁴

As these conventions might suggest, the mature nature of much SS/HG fanfiction clashes with adult notions of appropriate reading and writing for younger people, and non-SS/HG fans are often surprised to learn of the significant percentage of younger fans who participate in SS/HG (and in fanfiction generally).⁵ In 2010, for example, fandom researcher Charles Sendlor's analysis of large fanfiction repository *FanFiction.Net* demonstrated that 80 percent of users who revealed their age were between thirteen and seventeen years old.⁶ Of course, when it comes to understanding younger fans' participation in SS/HG, it matters that Rowling's books are the source texts since, as Tosenberger notes, the Harry Potter fandom was the "first major online participatory fandom based upon a text published for young people" (5). Of equal importance is the online venue of most SS/HG fanfiction; whereas participating in previous fandoms often meant attending conventions or making and circulating zines (both of which required disposable income not always accessible to younger people), the Harry Potter fandom emerged during the late 1990s/early 2000s moment of widening fandom access to younger people and is considered to be the "primary 'threshold fandom' of the Internet era" (9).

Although the idea of young people joining older fans in reading and writing the explicit content of SS/HG may feel wrong to many adults, recognizing this multigenerational participation in SS/HG fanfiction allows us to acknowledge a significant like-mindedness between fans. This like-mindedness, or affinity, foregrounds Clémentine Beauvais's observation that the differences between children and adults are "not in nature or status but contingent on the passing of time" (18). That is, "children and adults draw their imagined otherness relative to one another from the fact that they have overlapping but distinct temporalities" (18), not because they have fundamental differences in personality or even in power. Focusing on the affinity between younger and older SS/HG fans thus recalls Marah Gubar's "kinship model" of childhood, which emphasizes connection and similarity without implying homogeneity, and acknowledges the messiness of development. The kinship model "[maintains] that children and adults are fundamentally akin to one another, even if certain differences or deficiencies routinely attend certain parts of the aging process" ("Hermeneutics" 299).⁷ I suggest that SS/HG fans are akin to one another via their interest and investment in SS/HG, even if they may possess "differences or deficiencies" such as younger fans' reading and writing abilities, or their sexual inexperience. General fanfiction conventions such as ratings, minimum ages on fanfiction archives, and access to the internet similarly acknowledge age-related differences, as do fans' individual senses of what may or may not be appropriate content for younger fans. Ultimately, however, the SS/HG fandom is focused not around age but around shared affinity: fans' mutual love for narratives surrounding Snape and Hermione.

SS/HG fans demonstrate kinship through their collective enjoyment of creating, categorizing, and regularly using conventions that are specific to SS/HG fanfiction. For example, author Riley's extremely popular 2001 "Pawn to Queen" established three SS/HG tropes that became well used within the first years of the fandom and formed the basis for many early SS/HG fics: the "dark revels" trope, in which Death Eaters party by raping and torturing; the "rape to save" trope, in which Death Eater Snape is forced to claim (and sometimes rape) student Hermione as his slave in an effort to protect her from rape and torture performed by other Death Eaters; and the "time-turner aging" trope, in which Hermione's use of the time-turner in her third year physically ages her. These tropes provide the foundation for not only the narratives of physical/sexual abuse that run throughout much SS/HG fanfiction (particularly during the Classic Era) but also the forgiveness and/or acceptance of that abuse by Hermione, which is equally present in many SS/HG fics, and which spurred many paratextual conversations within the WIKTT (When I Kissed the Teacher) mailing list—an online list dedicated to the SS/HG fandom.[8]

The 2000–2010 heyday of SS/HG fanfiction is particularly helpful in revealing fans' multigenerational kinship because the fics provide examples of a dominant focus shared by SS/HG fans (even as they approach and judge said focus in multiple ways). That focus is on age-related taboos, specifically the taboos of teacher/student sexual relationships and adult/child sex.[9] Both taboos imply the possibility of danger, abuse, and trauma. The distressing nature of these taboos (as well as, for some, their titillation, which I will explore later) hinges on the eroticization of the binaries that form them, as well as on SS/HG fans' collective perception of danger in that eroticization. Notably, however, the taboos also reveal how fans' kinship extends past a general shared interest in SS/HG narratives to encompass shared morality, as fans create SS/HG-specific tropes that work to circumvent the taboos. Put simply, regardless of their individual ages, most SS/HG fans share an awareness and moral concern regarding the dangers of the taboos, and they collectively create tropes that seek to avoid the taboos either by normalizing a relationship between Snape and Hermione or by legitimizing it.

Examples of these normalizing or legitimizing attempts (and thus of SS/HG fans' shared morality) abound in SS/HG fanfiction. Fics that attempt to normalize the relationship usually do so by finding inventive ways to alter the ages of the characters. Thus, many fics age Hermione well into her twenties or thirties, where she inevitably meets a fanonical Snape in his forties or fifties while she is working at Hogwarts or in an obscure department within the Ministry of Magic, or is a lonely housewife trying to escape her ill-suited marriage to Ronald Weasley. Snape, similarly, is often de-aged as the result of a potions accident (usually caused by Neville Longbottom), becomes a teenager, and falls in love with Hermione over their mutual regard for books and potions. Authors who choose to maintain at least one of the characters' canonical ages frequently turn to the convention of the time-turner to allow them to normalize sex between Snape and Hermione. These fics allow Hermione to travel back in time to Snape's adolescence (known as the Marauders Era). True love follows each of these agings/de-agings/time travels—at least until Snape and Hermione return to their original age or time. Once their canonical age/times are reestablished, the normalization attempt often fails because the adult/child and teacher/student sex taboos can no longer be avoided, regardless of how much Snape and Hermione claim to love each other. SS/HG fans' normalization techniques, then, are successful in circumventing the dangers of the taboos for a while, but many of these fics are abandoned when their authors can no longer find a way to support a sexualized Snape/Hermione relationship set during the characters' canonical time periods and ages.

A second convention designed to circumvent the taboos involves legitimizing a relationship between Snape and Hermione through social or institutional authority. Examples of social authority include Dumbledore's sanctioning of a relationship between adult Snape and teenage Hermione (often starting with a twinkly-eyed Dumbledore ordering Snape to take on Hermione as an assistant), or Harry's and Ron's endorsement of the relationship as "natural" based on their authority as Hermione's best friends and predicated on Snape and Hermione's shared bookish interests. Institutional authority, conversely, may be real *or* fictional. While some writers provide a paratextual author's note that incorporates a UK-based legal definition of age of consent, emphasizing that Hermione is "of age," others insert age of consent laws directly into their narratives.[10] Most often, fictional institutional authority is provided by Hogwarts (which has a tendency to rearrange stairways and create new rooms to bring Snape and Hermione together), or by the Ministry of Magic.

In the "marriage law challenge"—the best-known SS/HG fanfiction convention, and an obvious example of how SS/HG authors use institutional authority to legitimize an otherwise tabooed relationship—the Ministry of Magic forces Snape and Hermione to marry. First created by Chelleybean in 2003 as a fanfiction challenge for the WIKTT mailing list, the challenge articulates the Ministry of Magic's requirement that all pure-bloods must marry Muggle-borns to produce magical offspring ("Marriage Law"). Many variations exist, but in most fics the Ministry forces Snape and Hermione to marry and copulate, or else give up their magic; or Snape marries Hermione to protect her from the abuse of a forced marriage to Death Eaters such as Lucius or Draco Malfoy. In either case, by marrying Hermione, Snape's protection of the student (and symbolic child—or real child, depending on how one positions adolescence) is expanded, in that the purpose of the marriage law—to repopulate the Wizarding World—ensures that the fics become fantasies of what Lee Edelman calls "reproductive futurism." The marriage law thus usually includes a clause stating either the number of times per week that Snape and Hermione must have sex or the number of children they must produce. At the end of these fics, when Hermione has fulfilled her mandated duty by producing at least one child, she is recognized as an adult, regardless of her age. The moment she gives birth often coincides with her NEWTS, enabling her to graduate from Hogwarts. The avoidance of the adult/child and teacher/student sex taboos through the Ministry of Magic's legitimization of Snape and Hermione's sexual relationship is thus no longer required; Hermione is now positioned as an adult and no longer a student. Ultimately, many SS/HG marriage law fics ensure that the figure of the child/student is both sacrificed *and* saved by the narrative; sacrificed in the sense of the symbolic—and sometimes physical—violence inherent in symbolic child Hermione's forced marriage and sexual activity with Snape, and saved in the new existence of baby Granger-Snapes, ensuring the reproductive futurism of both Snape and Hermione, as well as the Wizarding World.

As these examples demonstrate, in collectively revealing their moral judgements via their establishment of SS/HG tropes to circumvent age-based sexual taboos, young and older SS/HG fans establish shared community norms, including shared knowledge of the Harry Potter source texts, familiarity with earlier SS/HG fanfiction, and participation in paratextual elements such as fic comments, WIKTT posts, and SS/HG fic reviews. What they also share, however—and what feels particularly disturbing to adults—are the "desires" associated with textual kink, including perceiving the taboos as a source of titillation.[11] Kristina Busse analyzes such textual kink in the "Fictional Consents and the Ethical Enjoyment of Dark Desires" chapter of her book *Framing Fan Fiction*. Busse notes the prevalence of rape and "noncon" (nonconsensual sex) themes that operate as textual kink in much fanfiction. She establishes the important distinction that fans do not defend their use of these themes through realist arguments often employed by literary contexts—namely that "sexual violence is a part of our society and thus should not be a taboo topic in fiction" (210)—but instead explains that fans' defense focuses on rape fantasies, as well as on the eroticization of fictional rape. As Busse contends: "The argument is one of antirealism, where the appeal is directly dependent on the transgression of shared community norms and the eroticization of sexual acts that are clearly only acceptable within a fictional space. In other words, the very reason rape fiction can be eroticized safely within fan fiction spaces is that everyone agrees that rape and sexual violence are truly despicable crimes in need of punishment" (210). In a similar vein, one might argue that the teacher/student and adult/child sex taboos can be eroticized safely within SS/HG fanfiction because everyone agrees that the forms of violence inherent in these taboos are despicable crimes in need of punishment. Indeed, many SS/HG authors articulate this sense of the despicable directly in their fics, and "pedophile" and "pervert" are terms readily bandied about both within SS/HG fanfiction (in reference to Snape) and about SS/HG fanfiction. Busse's point, however, is of the unreality of the portrayal of taboo; thus, she emphasizes: "Here fiction is a tool to evoke emotion, allow escape, and enter a space that is not bound by the limits of reality. . . . It is safely ensconced within a fictional space that is framed (often repeatedly) as imaginary" (210).

Even accepting fanfiction textual kink as a safely-ensconced, fictional space, acknowledging young people's participation in such kink upsets our binary-based need to perceive youth as empty and asexual, which James Kincaid perceives as an act of adult-driven othering (*Erotic* 175). In *Child-Loving: The Erotic Child and Victorian Culture*, Kincaid calls attention to such reductive binary oppositions as "innocence and experience, ignorance and knowledge, incapacity and competence, empty and full, low and high, weak and powerful" (7), among others.[12] He emphasizes the dichotomy that "has been at least for the past two hundred years heavily eroticized: the child is that species which is free of sexual feeling or response; the adult is that species which has crossed over into sexuality" (6–7). Kincaid thus observes that our culture has constructed the child as nonsexual, innocent, and empty, while simultaneously positioning that nonsexuality, innocence, and emptiness as sexually arousing.[13] While I find Kincaid's binary-based model to be problematic, placing Kincaid's theories in conversation with SS/HG fanfiction underscores how young people's participation in SS/HG fics' violent and sexual content may be seen as a symbol of their own agency within the "child/adult imbalance" (Nikolajeva 8) of what Maria Nikolajeva might term an aetonormative culture.[14] Acknowledging young SS/HG fans' participation as shared with adult SS/HG fans' participation, regardless or perhaps *because* of the sexualized and violent content they create/consume within SS/HG fics, challenges adult normativity over such content. Thus, at stake in recognizing SS/HG fans through the lens of the kinship model is the possibility for a perspectival flip in our aetonormative culture. Gubar defines this flip: "instead of presuming that adults represent the norm and then investigating how children deviate from that norm, kinship-model adherents test out what happens if we regard the position that children generally inhabit as standard or shared" ("Hermeneutics" 300). In the case of SS/HG fans, that shared position may be sexual and violent, and that is a difficult and disturbing reality for many adults. Still, recognizing such kinship is important, because doing so undermines reductive binaries in traditional models of childhood that support an aetonormative culture.

Emphasizing the kinship between SS/HG fans allows us to become anti-aetonormative by acknowledging younger fans' position as "standard or shared" while also suggesting an alternative model of children's and young adult literature—one that is explicitly based on younger SS/HG fans' kinship with older fans. To explain this model, I borrow James Paul Gee's concept of affinity spaces. Gee reconceptualizes social configurations by shifting away from models of community (which carry problematic notions of "belongingness" and ambiguous membership) to a model of spaces (whether they be physical, virtual, or some blended combination) where people interact around a common activity or interest. He makes clear that "what people have an affinity with (or for) in an affinity space is not first and foremost the other people using the space, but the endeavor or interest around which the space is organized" (77). As Rebecca Black explains, because affinity spaces are organized around a shared passion (rather than spatial or temporal proximity), "they are often able to span differences in gender, race, class, *age*, ability, and education level" (389, my italics). Referring specifically to fanfiction, she notes that "[p]articipants in FanFiction.net are clear examples of this sort of heterogeneity, as they come from countries from across the globe, post fictions, comments, and reader reviews in many different languages, and range in life areas from small children in school to housewives, to university professors" (389).

Gee lists several additional defining aspects of affinity spaces, but I am particularly interested in his declaration that "[n]ewbies and masters and everyone else share common space" (77), meaning that no one is forced to the periphery of activity because of their novice positioning; instead, everyone has access to the same forms of participation, although they may possess different forms of knowledge and experience in regard to their shared passion. Fan gatekeeping and "fantagonisms" may still exist, of course, but they are based primarily on fan factions rather than on individual identity.[15] Black explains an additional defining aspect, that "there is a wide range of expertise and many forms of knowledge that are valued; thus, the roles of 'expert' and 'novice' are highly variable and contingent on activity and context at any given moment" (389). In their emphasis on shared participation and multiple knowledges, both of these aspects speak directly to Gubar's kinship model, particularly to her acknowledgement that "development is a messy and variable process" ("Hermeneutics" 299), and to her suggestion that "[e]ven as the concept of kinship highlights likeness and relatedness, however, it also makes room for difference and variation" (300).

I suggest that SS/HG fanfiction—and, by extension, multigenerational fanfiction generally—constitutes an affinity space. Accessed through portals such as fanfiction archives or the WIKTT list, SS/HG fanfiction is organized around fans' affinity for stories featuring a relationship between Snape and Hermione rather than around the identities of those fans (including age identity). It possesses few constraints that prevent younger fans from participating in the same venues as older ones, and it acknowledges multiple forms of expertise and knowledge that undermine aetonormativity. SS/HG fanfiction thus expands children's and YA literature by offering an alternative model: one that changes the focus from "children's and YA literature as texts" to "children's and YA literature as social configuration," and, more specifically, as affinity space. This shift allows us to reconceptualize young people's literature via the lens of kinship, thereby emphasizing the common participation of younger *and* older readers/writers, and refusing traditional models and binaries of adult producer/distributor versus young person consumer. It also opens up the possibility to include nontraditional forms of children's and young adult literature, such as fanfiction, but also any "texts" (literature, games, performances, social media, among others) with which "younger people, like older ones, are involved in various and complex ways" (Gubar 306). As such, it draws out, encourages, and perhaps even authorizes many of the adult/young person collaborative tendencies that already circulate within children's and young adult literature and culture. These collaborations are not necessarily examples of specific adult/youth cooperation in creating a single text (although they can be, as is the case with texts written jointly by a child and an adult, or dictated by a child and mediated by an adult), but rather they emphasize shared, communal interest in and responsibility for creating texts/forms/genres together, as spaces of affinity.

The affinity model, then, offers an alternative to the usual accounts of who holds and wields power in adult-child relations and in children's literature.

The model avoids extreme claims of power imbalances between children and adults, such as Karín Lesnik-Oberstein's assertion that "the 'child' has no 'voice' within the hierarchies of our society, because 'adults' either silence or create that power" (187). Other critics have pushed back against that claim. As David Rudd points out, the assertion that young people have no power further disempowers them and "helps construct the child as a helpless, powerless being, and contributes to the culturally hegemonic norm" (17). Commenting on the history of children's literature theory, Clémentine Beauvais observes that "there has been an increasingly frequent theoretical short-cut from the notion of necessary adult normativity to that of necessary adult domination. This slippage . . . is controversial, because the theoretical finding that children's literature represents and perpetuates adult power over children is becoming a definition of this type of text. Children's literature theory appears en route to being another power theory" (17). In my view, an affinity space model of young people's literature is not a power theory. Because it is a spatial model organized by affinities—not a social model organized by identity—it does not reinscribe an adult/child binary nor cast younger and older voices in opposition. Instead, it supports young and older voices in tandem while acknowledging and accepting differences.

I understand that this affinity space model of young people's literature may be unpopular with some, at least when it opens the possibility of including elements such as the taboos, violence, and rape scenes represented by 2000–2010 SS/HG fanfiction. Of course, such "adult" tropes are already present in young people's literature; from *Struwwelpeter* to *The Hunger Games*, violence has long been a key component in much literature for younger readers, and Eric Tribunella points out that "the pervasiveness of sexuality in kiddie lit is . . . widely accepted at this point, at least among scholars of children's literature" (140). Nevertheless, there remain general societal boundaries regarding what is and is not appropriate for younger readers, and perhaps rightly so. What an affinity space model might provide, however, is what Nat Hurley calls the "possibilities of perversion" (124), those possibilities that, following queer theory, "can thus take us an even greater distance toward thinking impossible things and for refusing the demands of normativity in theorizing young people and their texts" (120). I like to think that this affinity space model seeks to expand rather than to limit; to refuse fixed boundaries; and ultimately to embrace unstable, often-changing meaning in adults, young people, and whatever might encompass their "literature."

In doing so, perhaps it participates in Gubar's advice that "in order to expand our knowledge of children's literature as a whole, the best approach we can take is to proceed piecemeal, focusing our attention on different subareas and continually striving to characterize our subject in ways that acknowledge its messiness and diversity" ("On Not" 212). While children's and young adult literature may traditionally be perceived (à la Jacqueline Rose) to have derived from adult needs and desires, SS/HG fanfiction and the perverse possibilities of an anti-aetonormative affinity space model ask that we focus on kinship and affinity rather than difference. Perhaps the unacknowledged taboo at the heart of SS/HG fanfiction, or young people's literature more generally, is not young people reading and writing about graphic sexual acts or violence; perhaps it is that young people read and write for themselves, on their own terms, yes, but not necessarily against or separate from adults.

Notes

1. Thanks to Kenneth and Derritt for outstanding feedback. I would also like to thank Jill Coste, Sara K. Day, and Sonya Sawyer Fritz for their thoughts, suggestions, and support as I worked through the ideas presented here.

A note on terms: although I refer to "younger" and "older" fans throughout this chapter, I recognize that such categorizations are ever-changing and amorphous, particularly as young fans age into older fans. More generally, of course, "youth" and "adulthood" are unstable, culturally-generated constructs.

2. As Cecilia Aragon and Katie Davis explain, "[W]e believe that encounters with fanfiction, contrary to popular negative beliefs, inspire and support young people today—particularly members of marginalized groups—to develop literacy, to support one another in positive ways, and to teach and learn through new types of informal learning and mentoring" (21).

3. I follow the fan convention of using "Snape" and "Hermione" to refer to the characters. Doing so emphasizes the power imbalance between them and replicates typical fan discourse. Although "SS" has unfortunate echoes of the Schutzstaffel, within fandom conventions it represents the initials of Severus Snape, just as "HG" refers to Hermione Granger.

4. As a play on the word "canon," which refers to characters, information, or events in the source text, "fanon" denotes "information or characterization that has never been confirmed in canon but is accepted as such by fans" (Fanfiction Glossary, qtd. in Black 390).

5. It is important to note that while not all SS/HG fanfiction includes "adult" themes, Rebecca Moore observes that sometimes teenagers "crave more explicit fantasies. This is fanfiction's slipperiest slope, as overt sexuality pervades a huge portion of the genre.... Sexual content ranges from innocent handholding to hardcore kink, and writing of both types often inhabits the same sites or even the same stories" (17). Such is the case with SS/HG fanfiction, which can include sweet stories of friendship between Snape and Hermione, but far more often focuses on graphic narratives of sex and violence, the sort of narratives about which adults express concern.

6. Sendlor notes an overall average age of 15.8, median age of 15, and mode of 14. While there are children under thirteen (the minimum age allowed by *FanFiction.Net*), "they make up a very small portion of the community, and seem to have an understanding that they should not make their age public. Eleven-year-olds appear to be the most knowledgeable in this respect" (Sendlor). While Sendlor's analysis relies solely on members' self-disclosure of their

age, and thus may not match actual ages, it certainly suggests that, in 2010 at least, the 6.6 million members on *FanFiction.Net* skewed decidedly young and female.

Aragon and Davis suggest that one reason for the younger audience's use of that site is its status as a "gateway" archive: "readers in their teens may find Fanfiction.net first and begin reading, posting, learning, and mentoring there" (20). Indeed, although there are SS/HG-specific fan sites, the sheer size of *FanFiction.Net* continues to make it an important archive of SS/HG, currently listing over twelve thousand fics tagged "Severus S." and "Hermione G." since June 2001 and suggesting that although we may not know specific ages, young people are certainly active in SS/HG participation.

7. The model focuses on people as people, regardless of age, but also "assumes that young people have enough commonalities with each other—and differences from adults—to justify some form of adult paternalism and our continued use of the category 'child'" (300).

8. In "Domesticating Hermione: The Emergence of Genre and Community from WIKTT's Feminist Romance Debates," Anne Kustritz examines over fifty thousand messages posted to the WIKTT list (from 2001 to roughly 2015), observing that "[t]his forum became the site of heated debates about what women can and should be, the purpose of art in life, and the responsibility of authors to their readers, conversations that together shape a dynamic and heterogeneous community and communicative ethics" (445).

9. Many of us (including myself) would typically perceive adult/child sex to be rape.

10. Although there are suggestions within Rowling's texts that the age of majority in the Wizarding World is seventeen, there is no specified age of consent. Thus, most SS/HG authors use UK law to determine age of consent but occasionally refer to the laws of their own nations. The age of consent in the UK is sixteen but raises to eighteen if sexual activity involves a person in a position of trust (such as a teacher). Many SS/HG authors do not know this additional regulation or choose not to reference it.

11. For example, throughout "Out of the Depths" (2009), author laurielove includes passages establishing that Snape's and Hermione's mutual arousal stems specifically from the erotic stimulation of the teacher/student sexual taboo. During a quiet moment when she and Snape reminisce over the development of their relationship, Hermione observes "We had some . . . interesting . . . moments early on," before pointing out, "There seemed to be a certain control issue," and listing examples:

> "the denial of eye-contact, the insistence on student-teacher protocol, taking away house points, setting essays . . ."
> He did not respond.
> "Did that turn you on?" she dared ask.
> She waited for an answer. At length, she got one.
> "Yes."
> His response could have raised her anger, but his candour instead confirmed entirely her own feelings on his treatment of her early on. Why deny it?
> "As it did me."
> "I know." (laurielove)

Laurielove has given permission to quote from her fic.

12. I call these binary oppositions "reductive" because, as Zohar Shavit notes, they position "the understanding of childhood purely in terms of its opposition to, lack of, and subordination to maturity" (67). Recent scholarship—particularly coming from queer readings—by scholars such as Lee Edelman, Stephen Bruhm and Nat Hurley, and Kathryn Bond Stockton, has sought to challenge these traditional binaries, particularly as they relate to the notion of the child as the innocent, empty tabula rasa.

13. As Kincaid states, "[T]his hollowing out of children by way of purifying them of any stains (or any substance) also makes them radically different, other. In this empty state, they present themselves as candidates for being filled with, among other things, desire. The asexual child is not . . . any the less erotic but rather more" (*Child-Loving* 175).

14. Nikolajeva defines aetonormativity as "adult normativity that governs the way children's literature has been patterned from its emergence until the present day" (8). Interestingly, within SS/HG fanfiction in which Hermione is of canonical age, many authors choose to provide her with a similar agency in shunning binary-based categorizations that place her as "child."

15. Derek Johnson describes "fantagonisms" as "ongoing, competitive struggles between both internal [fan] factions and external institutions to discursively codify the fan-text-producer relationship according to their competitive interests" ("Fan-tagonism" 287). In regard to fan gatekeeping, Johnson explains that "fan positions in relation to media industries are nearly always positions taken in opposition to other fan factions with their own positions in relation to industry" ("Fan-tagonism" 397).

Works Cited

Aragon, Cecilia, and Katie Davis. *Writers in the Secret Garden: Fanfiction, Youth, and New Forms of Mentoring*. MIT P, 2019.

Beauvais, Clémentine. *The Mighty Child: Time and Power in Children's Literature*. John Benjamins, 2015.

Black, Rebecca W. "Fanfiction Writing and the Construction of Space." *E-Learning and Digital Media*, vol. 4, no. 4, Dec. 2007, pp. 384–97.

Busse, Kristina. *Framing Fan Fiction: Literary and Social Practices in Fan Fiction Communities*. U of Iowa P, 2017.

Chung, Nicole. "My Teen Is Writing Erotic Fanfiction. Should I Make Them Stop?" *Slate*, 3 Feb. 2021, slate.com/human-interest/2021/02/teen-fanfiction-discovery-care-and-feeding.html.

Edelman, Lee. *No Future: Queer Theory and the Death Drive*. Duke UP, 2004.

Gee, James Paul. *Situated Language and Learning: A Critique of Traditional Schooling*. Taylor and Francis, 2004.

Gubar, Marah. "The Hermeneutics of Recuperation: What a Kinship-Model Approach to Children's Agency Could Do for Children's Literature and Childhood Studies." *Jeunesse: Young People, Texts, Cultures*, vol. 8, no. 1, summer 2016, pp. 291–310.

Gubar, Marah. "On Not Defining Children's Literature." *PMLA*, vol. 126, no. 1, Jan. 2011, pp. 209–16.

Hurley, Nat. "The Perversions of Children's Literature." *Jeunesse: Young People, Texts, Cultures*, vol. 3, no. 2, winter 2011, pp. 118–32.

idlerat. "The Buried Life." *The Shipper's Manifesto*, 2 Oct. 2004. ship-manifesto.livejournal.com/27376.html. Accessed 15 Jan. 2021.

Johnson, Derek. "Fan-tagonism: Factions, Institutions, and Constitutive Hegemonies of Fandom." *Fandom: Identities and Communities in a Mediated World*, edited by Jonathan Gray et al., New York UP, 2007, pp. 285–300.

Johnson, Derek. "Fantagonism, Franchising, and Industry Management of Fan Privilege." *Routledge Companion to Media Fandom*, edited by M. A. Click and S. Scott, Routledge, 2018, pp. 395–405.

Kincaid, James R. *Child-Loving: The Erotic Child and Victorian Culture*. Routledge, 1992.

Kincaid, James R. *Erotic Innocence: The Culture of Child Molesting*. Duke UP, 1998.

Kustritz, Anne. "Domesticating Hermione: The Emergence of Genre and Community from WIKTT's Feminist Romance Debates." *Feminist Media Studies*, vol. 15, no. 3, 2015, pp. 444–59.

Laurielove. "Out of the Depths." *Harry Potter* fanfiction. Snape/Hermione ship. *FanFiction.Net*, 5 May 2009, www.fanfiction.net/s/5041998/1/Out-of-the-Depths.

Lesnik-Oberstein, Karín. *Children in Culture: Approaches to Childhood*, Macmillan, 1998.

"Marriage Law Challenge." *Fanlore*, 31 Aug. 2020, fanlore.org/wiki/Marriage_Law_Challenge. Accessed 15 Jan. 2021.

Moore, Rebecca C. "All Shapes of Hunger: Teenagers and Fanfiction." *Voice of Youth Advocates*, vol. 28, no. 1, Apr. 2005, pp. 15–19.

Nikolajeva, Maria. *Power, Voice and Subjectivity in Literature for Young Readers*. Routledge, 2009.

Red Hen Publications. "On the Good 'Ship Granger/Snape." *The Commentary Collection*, http://www.redhen-publications.com/granger-snape.html. Accessed 15 October, 2020.

Rudd, David. "Theorising and Theories: How Does Children's Literature Exist?" *Understanding Children's Literature*, edited by Peter Hunt, Routledge, 2005, pp. 15–29.

Sendlor, Charles. "Fan Fiction Demographics in 2010: Age, Sex, Country." *Fan Fiction Statistics—FFN Research*. 18 Mar. 2011, ffnresearch.blogspot.com/2011/03/fan-fiction-demographics-in-2010-age.html. Accessed 14 Jan. 2021.

Shavit, Zohar. *The Poetics of Children's Literature*. U of Georgia P, 1986.

Tosenberger, Catherine. "Mature Poets Steal: Children's Literature and the Unpublishability of Fanfiction." *Children's Literature Association Quarterly*, vol. 39, no. 1, spring 2014, pp. 4–27.

Tribunella, Eric L. "From Kiddie Lit to Kiddie Porn: The Sexualization of Children's Literature." *Children's Literature Association Quarterly*, vol. 33, no. 2, summer 2008, pp. 135–55.

ZINE ECOACTIVISM AND PEDAGOGIES OF HOPE IN *WORLD WAR 3 ILLUSTRATED* #46

Brianna Anderson

"The adults have failed us," then-fifteen-year-old Swedish climate activist Greta Thunberg wrote in a 2018 *The Guardian* opinion piece about the global school strikes for climate movement. She concludes, "And since most of them, including the press and the politicians, keep ignoring the situation, we must take action into our own hands, starting today" ("I'm Striking"). Thunberg's remarks reflect many contemporary young people's feelings of frustration and panic as adults fail to enact substantial measures to curb the escalating climate emergency. Determined to "take action" in the face of pervasive adult disinterest and ineptitude, vocal youth activists have assumed prominent roles in the twenty-first-century climate movement. Teenage advocates such as Thunberg, Brazilian indigenous rights activist Artemisa Xakriabá, and Zero Hour–cofounders Jamie Margolin and Nadia Nazar have garnered widespread media attention (and, frequently, controversy) for their activist work. Their participation in high-profile, organized, and primarily youth-powered environmental activism demonstrates young people's capacity to exert agency, which Allison James and Adrian James define as "children's ability not only to have some control over the direction their own lives take but also, importantly, to play some part in the changes that take place in society more widely" (4). In other words, these young ecoactivists challenge adults not only to fight climate change but also to reconceive popular conceptions about children as passive and powerless victims incapable of grappling with environmental and social challenges.

Meanwhile, many adult authors and illustrators have produced children's comics, picture books, and other visual narratives that seek to educate young readers about environmental issues and inspire them to engage in small-scale activism. These texts, however, frequently fail to foster or even recognize the same political agency demonstrated by real-world youth ecoactivists. As Clare Echterling observes, environmental children's literature overwhelmingly "positions the child or young adult as apolitical, capable of activism and change only within the boundaries of the private sphere and their own lives, and perhaps even incapable of grasping the temporal, geographical, political, economic, and cultural complexities wrapped up in climate change" (285–86). Brendan Wenzel's picture book *Hello Hello* (2018), for example, draws attention to the plight of endangered species but concludes by merely encouraging the audience to write letters to conservationists. Similarly, Rachel Hope Allison's graphic novel *I'm Not a Plastic Bag* (2013) instructs young readers to engage in limited, consumerism-centered actions like recycling and buying in bulk. While a handful of texts, such as Jess French's picture book *What a Waste!* (2019), do acknowledge children's intellectual and political capabilities by educating readers about the systemic issues underlying environmental challenges, these adult-produced books are not the only effective literary facilitators of youth ecoactivism. In this essay, I argue that visual narratives created by young people themselves in response to environmental crisis do a far better job of positioning young people as activists and change agents. This material, unfortunately, has largely been overlooked by scholars thus far.

The anthology zine *World War 3 Illustrated #46: Youth and Climate Change* (2015) reveals how alternative children's literature produced *by* (though not necessarily *for*) children can empower young people to engage in ecoactivism. First published in 1979 in annual or biannual installments, each anthology of *World War 3 Illustrated* (*WW3I*) centers on a different political issue and features zines from a large cast of activist creators. With a reported print run of 2,000 to 6,000 copies per issue, *WW3I* circulates to a larger audience than many zines, but the anthology's content still embodies the DIY ethic and inclusion of nonprofessional voices that define the medium (Burton 109). Margaret Galvan notes that the zine has consistently included diverse perspectives, "not only including and centering populations we often think of when we evoke diversity—people of color, LGBTQ folks, and, when it comes to comix, women—but also incorporating other marginalized voices like incarcerated and homeless people" (99). For the first time in the zine's history, *WW3I* #46 officially grants a voice to another, often overlooked marginalized group "with the most at stake" when it comes to environmental issues: children and teenagers (Allison et al. 1). The issue prominently features zines produced by young people—often in collaboration with parents, teachers, and other youth—alongside the work of seasoned adult zinesters, such as Peter Kuper and Kevin Pyle. These multigenerational contributions explore "two overlapping themes: our planet's growing climate crisis and how young people are confronting the 'climates' they have inherited—social, political, cultural, and especially, environmental" (Allison et al. 1).

By centering on children and teenagers' responses to climate change, the issue's youth-created zines operate as political activism on two levels. First, the zinesters blend images and text to educate the implied adult audience of *WW3I* about pressing environmental and social issues from youth perspectives often still overlooked or dismissed in mainstream political discussions, despite the growing number of young activists. Second, the creative process of making a zine—regardless of the zine's content—allows youth to exercise agency in productive and often subversive ways. Focusing particularly on the Riot grrrl movement, zine scholars such as Stephen Duncombe and Trina Robbins contend that creating handmade zines can serve as a powerful political act for young people, especially those who belong to marginalized groups. Analyzing youth grrrl zines, Alison Piepmeier argues that these texts offer what Paolo Freire terms a "pedagogy of hope." She writes, "These hopeful interventions are not identical to traditional modes of doing politics, but they are political nonetheless, because they are drawing attention to what's wrong with the world, awakening their readers' outrage, and providing tools for challenging existing power structures" (161). Granted, several of the youth-produced zines included in *WW3I* #46 seem nearly to model a pedagogy of hope*lessness* in their acknowledgement of the severity of environmental crisis, even as they tackle environmental and social wrongdoings. Analyzing the anthology's youth contributions, I extend and complicate Piepmeier's analysis by examining how the zinesters use a range of narrative and political strategies to disrupt cultural norms, promote youth activism, and call attention to formidable, sometimes seemingly insurmountable environmental and social problems. Together, these examples reveal how zines created by and in collaboration with young people can empower children and teenagers to advocate against climate change and other large-scale problems while acknowledging the practical and emotional difficulties involved.

Two contributions created by John V. Lindsay Wildcat Academy high school students provide the direst representations of climate change but also most clearly demonstrate how zines can empower young creators to advocate on behalf of the environment. Colored in the same black-and-white palette used throughout the issue, Muntu Jahju's one-page zine "Global Disaster" depicts four hand-drawn figures: Uncle Sam, whose signature striped hat has been transformed into a cage imprisoning a tiny planet Earth and bearing the words "Global Warming" on the brim; a businessman labeled "Government Control" who wears a suit and dangles a small Earth impaled with a leaking oil pipe; an anthropomorphic, sweating planet Earth covered with manmade smokestacks emitting pollutants; and a leering, scarred clown labeled "Governe [sic]" (Allison et al. 53) (fig. 6.1). Beneath each of these drawings, a typeset caption or thought bubble expresses the characters' views on the impending "Global Disaster" heralded by the zine's title. For instance, Uncle Sam thinks, "Who cares about the Earth anymore? These days money is more important," while the forlorn Earth reflects, "The only time people think of me is on Earth Day" (53). Together, the zine's images and text portray American society as corrupt and greedy, with each of its familiar yet distorted archetypes—the Earth-imprisoning Uncle Sam, the businessman, and the clown, who declares himself the "real face of the government"—abusing the environment for profit (53). Placed alongside Jahju's illustration of the battered, neglected Earth, these caricatures offer a scathing critique of capitalism, oil extraction, and even democracy itself as inherently destructive and antienvironmentalist. The zine's emphasis on these larger economic and political factors, rather than on the behavior of individuals, frames climate change as a "super wicked problem," which Kelly Levin and colleagues define as a complex issue "for which time is running out, for which there is no central authority; those seeking the solution are also creating it, and policies discount the future irrationally" (124). Unlike many apolitical environmental children's texts that encourage readers to engage in small acts like recycling and taking public transportation, "Global Disaster" doesn't provide any potential solutions for this super wicked problem, because no easy or obvious solutions exist. Instead, the zine calls attention to the ways that capitalism and the American government "discount the future irrationally" by prioritizing short-term economic gain over the long-term consequences that unsustainable human actions inflict on the environment.

The zine's overt challenge to the status quo demonstrates the medium's revolutionary potential, particularly for young creators who may have fewer avenues to advocate for the environment than adults. As Duncombe observes, "First and foremost, zines are a tool for consciousness raising. . . . Reading the range of opinions and lifestyles, the probing search for authenticity, and the depth of the rage against society in zines encourages readers to think about who they are and what they believe in" (190–91). By expressing Jahju's "rage"—or, at the very least, his clear dissatisfaction with the treatment of the planet by corporations and the government—"Global Disaster" challenges

Fig. 6.1. "Global Disaster" by Muntu Jahju.

the audience to consider how dominant ideologies and structures, including capitalism and "government control," directly cause or exacerbate environmental issues. At first glance, the zine's bitter portrayal of these institutions and systems may seem likely to induce feelings of powerless in readers; after all, individuals, particularly children, have little hope of combatting capitalism and greedy governments. However, Karen Nairn suggests that negative emotions like anger and hopelessness can paradoxically inspire future-focused youth environmental advocacy. In her study of young climate activists in New Zealand, she observes, "Despair at the thought of a climate-altered future, and the desire to intervene in and change predicted trajectories, galvanized participants to take action in their individual daily lives and as part of collectives" (446). Likewise, many youth environmental activists have cited children and teenagers' negative emotions about climate change as a source of empowerment, with Thunberg remarking, "People are underestimating the force of angry kids" and "If they want us to stop being angry, maybe they should stop making us angry" (Rincon). By providing a decidedly unhopeful vision of environmental disaster, "Global Disaster" reflects this mounting dissatisfaction and provides an unsparing representation of the daunting obstacles that youth activists must overcome if they want to stem the effects of climate change. Moreover, Jahju's angry and hopeless portrayal of climate change as a complex, systemic problem with no obvious solution offers a counternarrative to the partial or superficial representations of environmental issues frequently found in mainstream children's literature produced by adults. "Global Disaster" deviates from this established apolitical literary tradition by demonstrating young people's capacity to grapple with climate change as a collective, intricate, and potentially solutionless issue amplified by intersecting systems of power.

Similarly, Kuilan's "The Wasteland" borrows familiar images from popular culture to confront readers with their own complicity in climate change and provide an ominous warning about the potential consequences of environmental destruction. The zine consists of a single, sprawling, double-spread illustration centered on a leafless tree, its bark studded with lightbulbs and electric sockets that sprout wires attached to a butterfly and a sickly bird (fig. 6.2). On the left side of the illustration, a train car marked with a radioactive symbol travels along a railway covered with littered food wrappers, with the splintered rail ties on the track just ahead of the wheels suggesting that additional ruin will soon follow. In the upper right-hand corner, industrial smokestacks pump dark clouds into the sky, and a pipe spews oil onto the ground. Accompanying this jumble of dystopian imagery, a one-sentence poem with accompanying paratext appears at the bottom right-hand side of the spread:

Fig. 6.1. "Global Disaster" by Muntu Jahju.

the audience to consider how dominant ideologies and structures, including capitalism and "government control," directly cause or exacerbate environmental issues. At first glance, the zine's bitter portrayal of these institutions and systems may seem likely to induce feelings of powerless in readers; after all, individuals, particularly children, have little hope of combatting capitalism and greedy governments. However, Karen Nairn suggests that negative emotions like anger and hopelessness can paradoxically inspire future-focused youth environmental advocacy. In her study of young climate activists in New Zealand, she observes, "Despair at the thought of a climate-altered future, and the desire to intervene in and change predicted trajectories, galvanized participants to take action in their individual daily lives and as part of collectives" (446). Likewise, many youth environmental activists have cited children and teenagers' negative emotions about climate change as a source of empowerment, with Thunberg remarking, "People are underestimating the force of angry kids" and "If they want us to stop being angry, maybe they should stop making us angry" (Rincon). By providing a decidedly unhopeful vision of environmental disaster, "Global Disaster" reflects this mounting dissatisfaction and provides an unsparing representation of the daunting obstacles that youth activists must overcome if they want to stem the effects of climate change. Moreover, Jahju's angry and hopeless portrayal of climate change as a complex, systemic problem with no obvious solution offers a counternarrative to the partial or superficial representations of environmental issues frequently found in mainstream children's literature produced by adults. "Global Disaster" deviates from this established apolitical literary tradition by demonstrating young people's capacity to grapple with climate change as a collective, intricate, and potentially solutionless issue amplified by intersecting systems of power.

Similarly, Kuilan's "The Wasteland" borrows familiar images from popular culture to confront readers with their own complicity in climate change and provide an ominous warning about the potential consequences of environmental destruction. The zine consists of a single, sprawling, double-spread illustration centered on a leafless tree, its bark studded with lightbulbs and electric sockets that sprout wires attached to a butterfly and a sickly bird (fig. 6.2). On the left side of the illustration, a train car marked with a radioactive symbol travels along a railway covered with littered food wrappers, with the splintered rail ties on the track just ahead of the wheels suggesting that additional ruin will soon follow. In the upper right-hand corner, industrial smokestacks pump dark clouds into the sky, and a pipe spews oil onto the ground. Accompanying this jumble of dystopian imagery, a one-sentence poem with accompanying paratext appears at the bottom right-hand side of the spread:

The Wasteland
The world is either dying
before it can achieve its dream,
or it has lived long enough
to see that it was never attainable
in the first place.
Alejandro Kuilan
inspired by Batman (Allison et al. 54)

As the paratextual note included below the author's name indicates, the poem alludes to a well-known line of dialogue spoken by Harvey Dent in *The Dark Knight* Batman film: "You either die a hero or you live long enough to see yourself become the villain." Neither the illustration nor the poem provides any hint as to what, precisely, the Earth may have dreamed of. However, the prominent placement of humanmade machines and materials in the illustration strongly suggests that humanity has caused the world's death or, at the very least, its disillusionment with its dream.

By reformulating to the *Batman* quote in a visual narrative that casts blame on humans for environmental ruin, Kuilan employs a zine-making strategy that Janice Radway, in her analysis of girls' zines, terms "insubordinate creativity": the use of "ready to hand" cultural materials to "explode, fragment, and recreate traditional forms of mass culture" (199). In other words, Kuilan appropriates and remixes icons of mass culture—the *Batman* quote, the radioactivity symbol, packages of junk food, and so on—to confront readers with the villainy of everyday human actions and industrialization, rather than of the supervillains figured in American popular culture. Moreover, the absence of a traditional heroic counterpoint to the villainy represented in the zine also implicitly invites readers to consider how they can fill this role and help to stem the rampant environmental destruction represented in the illustration. On the surface, this reinvention of the *Batman* narrative may appear derivative or uninspired rather than radical. However, as Piepmeier observes, young zine makers' use of insubordinate creativity "calls into question dominant cultural norms" and "may be so disruptive that it is invisible or unintelligible from mainstream vantage points, misread as comical, trivial, or insignificant" (11). As a result, "The Wasteland" demonstrates how young activists can use zines to critique consumer society and resist dominant ideologies by transforming familiar cultural symbols into alternative narratives that convey environmentalist messages.

While "Global Disaster" and "The Wasteland" feature bleak representations of climate change, several zines featured in "The Future," a subcollection

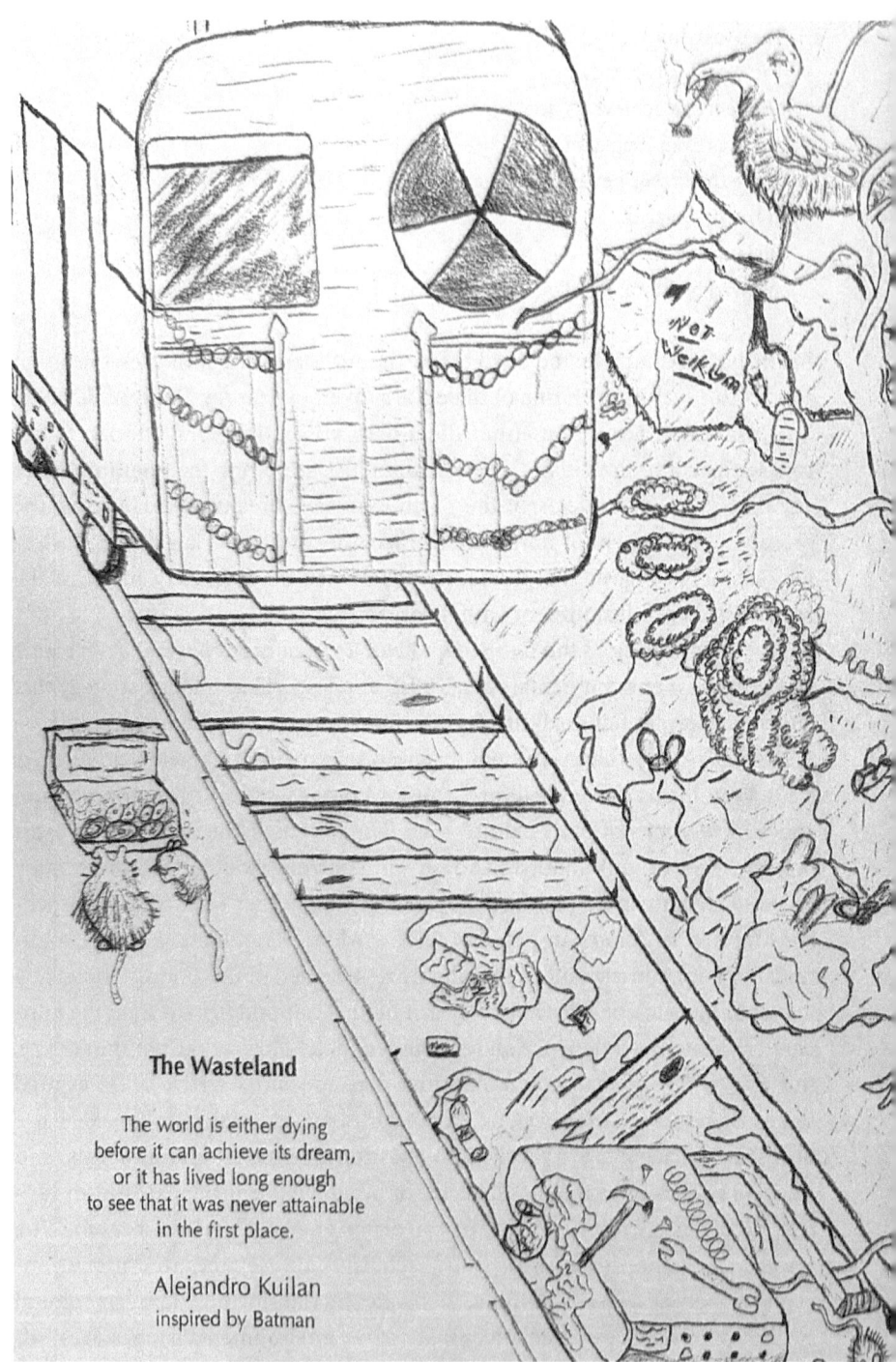

Fig. 6.2. "The Wasteland" by Alejandro Kuilan.

produced by child participants during a workshop hosted by *WW3I*, provide more optimistic portrayals of the future. "Untitled," a two-page zine created by eleven-year-old Isabella Ulfelder, centers on a teenage girl who visits the surface of the Earth before returning to her home under the ocean, a living situation enabled by a bubble-like machine that she wears over her head (Allison et al. 118–19). Similarly, sixteen-year-old Rebecca Goldin's "Untitled" depicts an "extreme farmer" who lives in a community-centered, hive-like biome dome inhabited by both bees and humans (hilariously referred to as "beevians") (124–25) (fig. 6.3). Instead of fixating on images of environmental destruction, both zines imagine futuristic worlds where humans have adapted to their changing climate in innovative and seemingly more sustainable ways. Notably, Goldin frames her characters' new lifestyle positively. In the zine's final panel, the smiling extreme farmer alludes to L. Frank Baum's *The Wizard of Oz*, declaring, "Personal space is tight and community work is tough, but there's no place like home" (Allison et al. 125). Like the *Batman*-inspired Kuilan, Goldin uses insubordinate creativity to transform elements of popular culture into a progressive environmental message, even if the final rehash of Dorothy's catchphrase potentially reflects a conservative impulse to prioritize the domestic sphere. Overall, though, Goldin and Ulfelder's utopian texts exhibit what Kimberley Reynolds describes as the "transformative power" of children's literature. These texts, she contends, have the "ability to envision and engage young readers with possibilities for new worlds and new world orders . . . in recognition of the fact that children will not just inherit the future, but need to participate in shaping it" (14). By portraying new, more environmentally friendly ways of inhabiting the world—no matter how fantastic or unrealistic—Ulfeder and Goldin provide a hopeful counterpoint to the dystopian imagery often evoked in representations of climate change and show how young people can help imagine alternative futures.

Moreover, the various youth-made zines featured in *WW3I* #46 promote a pedagogy of hope by implicitly inviting readers to participate in zine-making and, by extension, political activism. As a medium, zines embody a countercultural mindset that spurns commercialization and mass production. Duncombe writes, "Defining themselves against a society predicated on consumption, zinesters privilege the ethic of DIY, do-it-yourself: make your own culture and stop consuming that which is made for you" (7). Following this DIY tradition, the young zinesters of *WW3I* #46 made their visual narratives by hand using a limited range of materials easily accessible to most children at home or school: paper, pencils, markers, and, in some cases, a computer to type text that the creators combined with the handmade illustrations. While

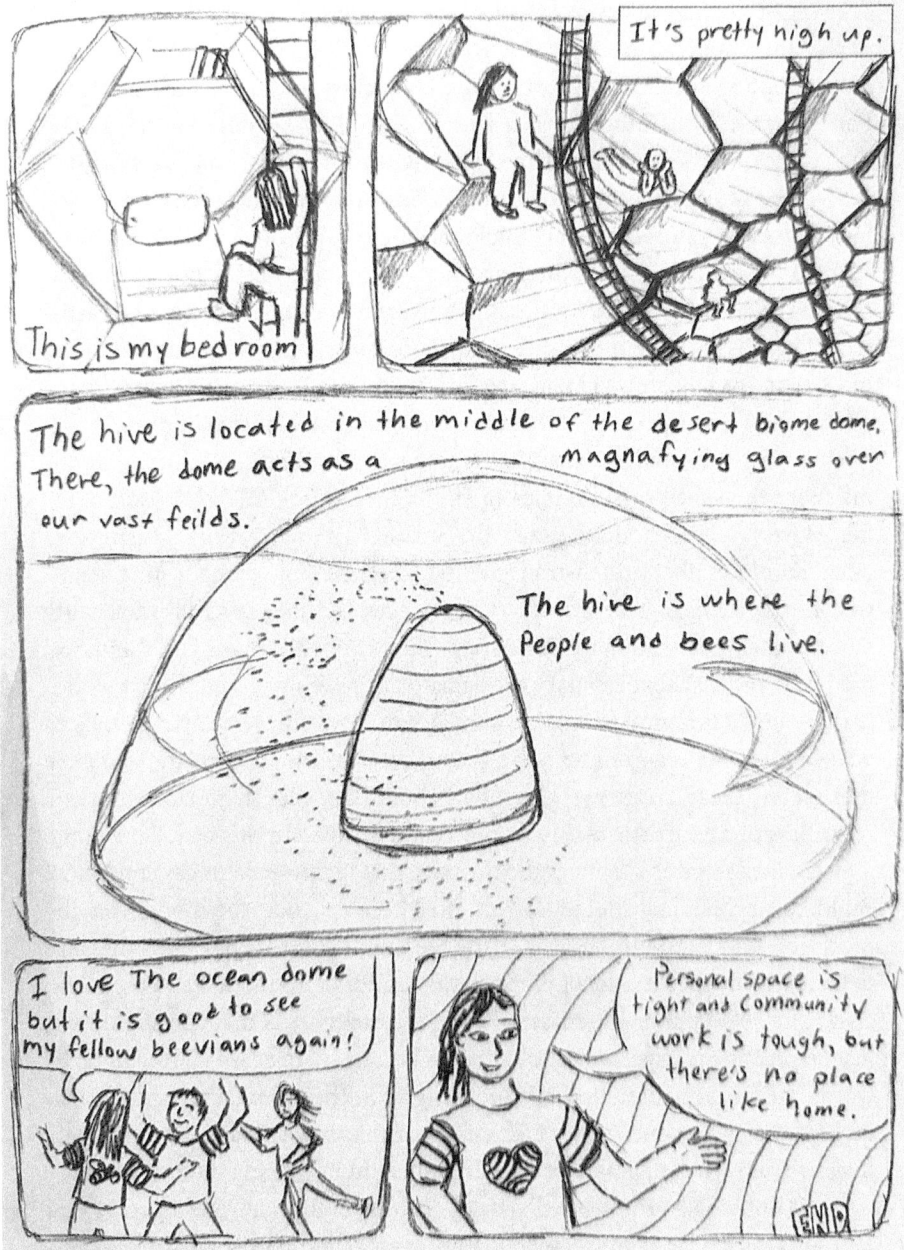

Fig. 6.3. "Untitled" by Rebecca Goldin.

drawing styles and levels of artistry vary between the young creators, most of the illustrations use simple shapes, lack complex backgrounds, and make no attempt to realistically portray the characters and their environments. For instance, "The Thingabobs," a zine produced by Jasmine Posner during the comics workshop and perhaps inspired by Dr. Seuss's *The Lorax* (1971), depicts the titular creatures as cartoonish, anthropomorphic blobs threatened by a factory composed only of simple rectangles (Allison et al. 121). Likewise, Jemima Eastwood's "The Future," another workshop zine, includes two illustrations of crowds of stick figures, the universal symbol of the amateur artist (112). Unpolished and uncommodified, these contributions resemble doodles more than the colorful, sophisticated artwork typically found in mainstream, adult-produced environmental picture books and comics for children.

At first glance, readers may be tempted to dismiss these zines as nothing more than the crude doodles of children who lack formal artistic training. However, as Piepmeier notes, the amateurish and disposable nature of zines amplifies their often-transgressive messages by complicating traditional understandings of "good" art. She writes, "[Z]ines revel in informality and threaten conventional boundaries. They explicitly reject the standards, methods, and visual vocabulary of mainstream publishing and the art world" (73). By using nonprofessional artwork produced with everyday materials to advocate for the environment, the young creators' zines teach the audience that everyone can create meaningful art about the issues that matter to them, regardless of age, artistic ability, or physical resources. In this way, Duncombe argues, zines serve as a democratic medium that tacitly encourages emulation. Building on Marshall McLuhan's oft-cited concept that "the medium is the message," Duncombe argues that "[t]he medium of zines is not just a message to be received, but a model of participatory cultural production and organization to be acted upon. The message you get from zines is that you should not just be getting messages, you should be producing them as well" (135). In other words, the zines featured in *WW3I* not only allow their youth creators to advocate for the environment, they also empower readers of all ages to participate in activism by rejecting passive consumption and producing their own zines.

As a (potentially unintended) side effect of the DIY nature of zines, *WW3I* #46 also serves as a more sustainable counterpoint to mainstream children's environmental literature. Like most zines, the *WW3I* series does not seek financial gain, but operates instead as "a collectively produced, irregularly published, not-for-profit anthology" (Worcester x). *WW3I* #46 retails for a mere $7 cover price, and the paperback anthology is printed in economical black and white ink on inexpensive, uncoated papers, which, the environmental organization *Conservatree* reports, "are a more environmental choice [than coated paper] because they yield a higher percentage of fiber for recycling" ("Choose"). As a material product, the zine collection stands out from the brightly colored, glossy-paged, and often more expensive picture books and graphic novels that have dominated recent environmental children's literature produced by adults. These mainstream texts, Nathalie op de Beeck contends, present a paradox, because publishers often print them with non–environmentally friendly materials (metal-infused inks, nonrecyclable paper, etc.) and use harmful production methods that run counter to the environmental messages preached within the pages of the books. As a result, these texts highlight "a telling disconnect between a commonsense save-the-forest narrative and the material actualities of mass production and everyday shopping" (op de Beeck 266). Of course, *WW3I* #46, like all physical texts, cannot completely avoid the production issues op de Beeck identifies—its producers must still print the zine on paper created from trees, use petroleum to ship copies from the small print run to consumers, and so on. However, the issue's DIY ethic and materiality do model how environmental children's literature can utilize (at least somewhat) more sustainable production practices that reinforce rather than undermine their ecofriendly messages. In these ways, then, the environmentally focused contributions to *WW3I* #46 demonstrate how youth zines and popular culture references can form as an alternative children's literature that empowers kids and teens to advocate against climate change and critique systems of power.

While most of the texts contained in *WW3I* #46 focus on climate change from a strictly environmental perspective, the five-page zine "Ops on the Block: An ELM Comic" uses collaborative zine-making and an intersectional approach to educate readers about a different kind of changing climate: an urban landscape undergoing gentrification. Created as "an experiment in non-hierarchical intergenerational exchange and popular education," the zine centers on a group of fictional Brooklyn teenagers as they walk through the city, discussing the "hipsters" who have invaded their neighborhood and recounting their personal experiences with an increasingly large, hostile police force (Allison et al. 31). By focusing on the perspectives of urban youth, the zine seeks to educate readers about its youth cocreators' "everyday experiences with both aggressive gentrification and frequent profiling by police." The zine makers' personal encounters with these two social issues, the explanatory paratext notes, "were heightened by the birth of the #BlackLivesMatter Movement" (31). Analyzing the zine's framing paratext, materiality, and portrayal of social issues from a collective youth perspective, I argue that "Ops on the Block" serves as an example of what Clemencia Rodriguez terms "citizen's media," in which "first . . . a collectivity is *enacting* its citizenship by actively intervening and transforming the established mediascape; second, that these media are contesting social codes, legitimized identities, and institutionalized social relations; and third, that these communication practices are empowering the community involved" (20). Consequently, "Ops" reveals how zines can serve as powerful tools of community-building and resistance for young activists, particularly those who occupy other marginalized identities in addition to their age.

Immediately preceding the first panel, a paratextual list of contributors provides the first indication of the zine's status as a work of citizens' media. The lengthy list details the names and roles of nine collaborators who participated in the creation of the short zine: "Written by: Josh Rolon, Rolando Nellis, Keyshawn Lawson, Esteban Estevez, Ruthie Lopez, Ariel Gomez; Illustrated by: Josh Rolon; Backgrounds by: Bianca Perez and Très; Design by: Mensen; Organized by: Mensen + Très" (Allison et al. 26). A paratextual note included at the end of the comic identifies the six cowriters and one illustrator as youth members of Educated Little Monsters (ELM), a local grassroots arts organization that aims to "provid[e] an artistic outlet for Brooklyn youth of color while empowering them to become socially responsible and aware of the changes affecting them in their communities" ("Home"). Three additional adult collaborators played supporting roles in the creation of the comic by drafting a preliminary script based on the young writers' ideas, drawing abstract backgrounds for some of the panels, and combining the youth's illustrations, photographs, and text into the final comic. By blending youth and adult creative contributions within the space of a community organization, "Ops on the Block" serves as an example of alternative children's literature produced in what Brent Wilson has dubbed the "third site" of children's visual cultural spaces, an area "between school classrooms and kids' self-initiated cultural spaces—a site where adults and kids collaborate in making connections and interpreting webs of relationships among the images that kids make for themselves and the images that adults ask them to make" (18). Significantly, as a third site of children's art production, ELM lacks the intergenerational power structures that traditionally characterize relationships between adults and children within formal classroom spaces: the youths voluntarily participated in ELM and the zine project rather than producing art for a compulsory class; the three adults served as supporting collaborators rather than as instructors and evaluators; and the youths chose the comic's topic and content, rather than complying with assignment requirements or adult directives.

Thus, "Ops on the Block" demonstrates how the process of creating collaborative, youth-centered zines can help young people renegotiate conventional power hierarchies, as well as foster community between children and between children and adults.

The comic's materiality also reveals how the zine-making process enables the young cocreators to exercise agency and convey political messages to the audience. The narrative begins as teenager Deshawn arrives late to a meeting with his friend Miguel after he was stopped and frisked "for the 4th time this week" by the police officers "always posted up by my school" (Allison et al. 27). Outraged by this latest injustice, the two boys walk together through the Brooklyn streets, discussing the heightened police presence in their neighborhood and the "new people"—presumably upper-class, primarily white gentrifiers—who have recently moved in (29). The creators use collage to illustrate this conversation, overlaying primarily white line drawings of the characters on a mixture of abstract, line-drawn backgrounds and black-and-white photographs of buildings and streets taken by the youth ELM members in their own gentrifying neighborhoods. Police cars feature prominently in three of these photographs, emphasizing the oppressive presence of law enforcement in the teenagers' environment (fig. 6.4). By blending hand-drawn illustrations, text, and photographs within the space of the panels, the young zinesters use everyday, easily accessible materials—pencils, photographs, paper, and so on—to resist singular, dominant narratives. As Marjorie Perloff contends, "[E]ach element in the collage has a dual function: it refers to an external reality even as its compositional thrust is to undercut the very referentiality it seems to assert" (49). In other words, by literally pasting their own stories over the photographic evidence of gentrification and police surveillance, the creators juxtapose symbols of the invading dominant culture with a collective, youth-centered perspective typically relegated to the margins. Their physical insertion of alternative viewpoints disrupts the authority exerted by these symbols and asks readers to consider how these spaces seek to erase the narratives and groups represented in the comic. Significantly, these collaged panels only include textual narration from the teenage characters, not from the featureless police officers driving the cars or the unseen "hipsters" who have transformed the boys' favorite corner shop into an upscale café. As a result, the comic's visual narrative enables the cartoonists to challenge stereotypical power dynamics between law enforcement, gentrifiers, and urban teenagers by granting primacy to the youth voices superimposed over the one-sided "external reality" captured in the photographs.

Fig. 6.4. "Ops on the Block" by Josh Rolon, Rolando Nellis, Keyshawn Lawson, Esteban Estevez, Ruthie Lopez, Ariel Gomez, Bianca Perez, Très, and Mensen.

In the comic's written narration, these youth voices consistently draw attention to the injustices perpetrated against the fictional teenage characters and real-world young people, forming a spoken collage of different youth perspectives to accompany the visual patchwork. In addition to Deshawn's encounter with the police outside of his school, Miguel recounts anecdotes about police officers beating his cousin's teenage friends outside of the former neighborhood corner store and about the deportation of a local undocumented immigrant. He recalls, "I remember Manuel's dad got stopped by the cops and they found out he ain't have his papers. He got deported that summer and Manuel's family got kicked out that fall. Now it's a condo where all them rich white people stay" (Allison et al. 29). These narratives explicitly attribute the injustices suffered by male teenagers of color and undocumented immigrants and their families to the influx of law enforcement in their gentrifying neighborhood, highlighting how these issues impact multiple marginalized groups. Later in the comic, the boys' teenage friend Tanya offers an additional, female- and LGBTQ-oriented perspective by narrating her own experience being frisked by a police officer. She tells the boys, "I didn't know male cops could do that to a girl. When he was patting me down, he saw my bracelet and asked me 'what are these, @#?& dyke beads?' Cause I was wearing the rainbow joins my girl got me" (Allison et al. 30). Accompanied by an illustration of a male police officer grabbing her waist and leering down at her rear, Tanya's experience extends Deshawn's opening story about his fourth frisking of the week by demonstrating how invasive body searches can also sexually victimize vulnerable people, especially women and LGBTQ individuals. By providing stories from a range of youth perspectives, the comic models an intersectional approach and educates the audience about the multifaceted ways that gentrification and police abuse harm marginalized groups.

Alongside each of the three characters' textual narratives of their traumatic experiences, the creators include a single, smaller panel depicting police officers frisking and assaulting teenagers. These accompanying panels contain no text, and they color the police and their victims with the same drab gray used for these frames' backgrounds. This lack of identifying textual or background details, as well as the monotone color scheme, gives the panels a sense of hazy nonspecificity and placelessness that deviates sharply from the photographed, recognizably Brooklyn setting of the collaged panels. As a result, these small gray panels do not merely illustrate Deshawn, Miguel, and Tanya's fictionalized stories but instead serve as a visual shorthand for countless instances of police brutality and racial profiling against young people that have taken place across time and space. The characters also underscore the pervasiveness of these issues by referencing the highly publicized fatal police shooting of eighteen-year-old black man Michael Brown in Ferguson, Missouri, in 2014 (Allison et al. 27), as well as the lesser-known brutal beating of twenty-year-old black man Donovan Lawson by a police officer at the Brooklyn Myrtle–Broadway subway station in 2014 (28). While the characters do not explicitly name Brown and Lawson, instead only alluding to them by the locations where the incidents took place, these real-world examples supplement the characters' fictional anecdotes and make it clear that these issues extend beyond the teenagers' own Brooklyn neighborhood. Additionally, these nonfictional cases provide interested readers with two starting points to further research police brutality. Together, this collection of fictional and true anecdotes and their accompanying illustrations channel an intersectional, collective youth voice to educate readers about the ways that changing urban environments and everyday interactions between police and urban youth can inflict harm, often in less sensationalized ways that do not attain the widespread media and public attention garnered by police shootings.

Given the daunting obstacles presented by climate change and systemic social issues like police brutality, my analysis of these case studies raises an obvious question: What, exactly, do youth activist zines accomplish? To be sure, the activism taking place in the pages of *WW3I* #46 does not resemble the large-scale youth-centered environmental advocacy figured in the media, and the anthology's small print run and relative obscurity limit its ability to have a tangible impact on the public and lawmakers. As of July 2021, the issue had received only a single review on *Goodreads.com* and no reviews on *Amazon.com*, likely due to its low circulation. Galvan's digital project "*World War 3 Illustrated* and Its Network Visualization" does include the issue's contributors as part of a network analysis map of the anthology series' creators; otherwise, *WW3I* #46 had garnered virtually no scholarly attention or reviews.

Due to this lack of tangible impact, a skeptical reader may be tempted to dismiss child-produced environmental zines as ineffective tools or easily ignored curiosities. As Piepmeier writes, "If we want a form of expression and activism that will cause large-scale social change, something equivalent to the social justice movements of the 1960s and 1970s, then we'll be disappointed in zines" (160). However, as small-scale acts of resistance, the zines showcased in *WW3I* #46 demonstrate how the comics medium can amplify the voices of children and teenagers by providing both hopeful and despairing youth-centered perspectives on the environmental and social issues that impact their lives, both now and in the future. Additionally, these progressive texts model and promote everyday and easily enacted forms of activism, such as educating others about the dangers of climate change and sharing personal stories about racial profiling, that allow youth to contribute to larger societal conversations that may eventually lead to collective shifts in attitudes towards climate change and other environmental problems. In this way, *WW3I #46* offers important counternarratives to mainstream environmental texts and demonstrates the pressing need for alternative children's texts—created by both children and adults—that acknowledge and foster the political agency already exercised by real-world youth activists.

Works Cited

Allison, Hillary, et al., editors. *World War 3 Illustrated #46: Youth, Activism, and Climate Change*. Top Shelf Productions, 2015.

Allison, Rachel Hope. *I'm Not a Plastic Bag*. Archaia, 2012.

Burton, Nicole Marie. "Thirty-Five Years of *WW3*." *Peter Kuper: Conversations*, edited by Kent Worcester, UP of Mississippi, 2016, pp. 104–11.

"Choose the Right Paper for Your Project." *Conservatree.org*, http://www.conservatree.org/paper/Choose/Paper4Project.shtml. Accessed 2 Jan. 2021.

The Dark Knight. Directed by Christopher Nolan, Warner Bros. Pictures, 2008.

Duncombe, Stephen. *Notes from the Underground: Zines and the Politics of Alternative Culture*. Microcosm Publishing, 2014.

Echterling, Clare. "How to Save the World and Other Lessons from Children's Environmental Literature." *Children's Literature in Education*, vol. 47, no. 4, Dec. 2016, pp. 283–99.

French, Jess. *What a Waste!: Trash, Recycling, and Protecting Our Planet*. DK Children, 2019.

Galvan, Margaret. "Adjacent Genealogies, Alternate Geographies: The Outliers of Underground Comix and *World War 3 Illustrated*." *Inks: The Journal of the Comics Studies Society*, vol. 3, no. 1, spring 2019, pp. 92–113.

Galvan, Margaret "*World War 3 Illustrated* and Its Network Visualization." *Margaret Galvan*, http://margaretgalvan.org/ww3-illustrated/. Accessed 7 July 2021.

Geisel, Theodor Seuss. *The Lorax*. Random House Books for Young Readers, 1971.

"Home." *Educated Little Monsters*, http://www.educatedlittlemonsters.org/. Accessed 4 Jan. 2021.

James, Allison, and Adrian James. *Key Concepts in Childhood Studies*. SAGE Publications, 2012.

Levin, Kelly, et al. "Overcoming the Tragedy of Super Wicked Problems: Constraining our Future Selves to Ameliorate Global Climate Change." *Policy Sci*, vol. 45, 2012, pp. 123–52.

McLuhan, Marshall. *Understanding Media: The Extensions of Man*. McGraw Hill Education, 1964.

Nairn, Karen. "Learning from Young People Engaged in Climate Activism: The Potential of Collectivizing Despair and Hope." *YOUNG*, vol. 27, no. 5, Nov. 2019, pp. 435–50.

op de Beeck, Nathalie. "Speaking for the Trees: Environmental Ethics in the Rhetoric and Production of Picture Books." *Children's Literature Association Quarterly*, fall 2005, vol. 30, no. 3, pp. 265–87.

Perloff, Marjorie. *The Futurist Moment: Avant-Garde, Avant Guerre, and the Language of Rupture*. U of Chicago P, 1986.

Piepmeier, Alison. *Girl Zines: Making Media, Doing Feminism*. New York UP, 2009.

Radway, Janice. "Girls, Reading, and Narrative Gleaning: Crafting Repertoires for Self-Fashioning within Everyday Life." *Narrative Impact: Social and Cognitive Foundations*, edited by Melanie C. Green et al., Psychology Press, 2013, pp. 183–204.

Reynolds, Kimberley. *Radical Children's Literature: Future Visions and Aesthetic Transformations in Juvenile Fiction*. Palgrave Macmillan, 2007.

Ricon, Paul. "Greta Thunberg: People Underestimate 'Angry Kids.'" *BBC News*, 3 Dec. 2019, https://www.bbc.com/news/science-environment-50644395.

Robbins, Trina. *From Girls to Grrlz: A History of Women's Comics from Teens to Zines*. Chronicle Books, 1999.

Rodriguez, Clemencia. *Fissures in the Mediascape: An International Study of Citizens' Media*. Hampton Press, 2001.

Thunberg, Greta. "I'm Striking from School to Protest Inaction on Climate Change—You Should Too." *The Guardian*, 26 Nov. 2018, https://www.theguardian.com/commentisfree/2018/nov/26/im-striking-from-school-for-climate-change-too-save-the-world-australians-students-should-too.

Wenzel, Brendan. *Hello Hello*. Chronicle Books, 2018.

Wilson, Brent. "More Lessons from the Superheroes of J. C. Holz: The Visual Culture of Childhood and the Third Pedagogical Site." *Art Education*, Nov. 2005, pp. 18–34.

Worcester, Kent. Introduction. *Peter Kuper: Conversations*, edited by Kent Worcester, UP of Mississippi, 2016, pp. ix–xviii.

EMERGENCY CHILDREN'S LITERATURE
Some Observations on Pandemic Picture Books

Gabriel Duckels

One of the most compelling responses to the COVID-19 pandemic has been the deluge of stories and picture books that amassed during its first months. While children's literature's role in negotiating crises and disasters is obviously not a new phenomenon, the primarily digital and often viral circulation of these first texts about COVID-19 signifies a renewed and amplified context for such. In this chapter, I frame this ad hoc archive of artefacts as an "emergency children's literature." My analysis draws on earlier children's picture books made in response to emergencies, such as natural disasters, but primarily focuses on picture books created about the impact of AIDS. Health crises such as COVID-19 or HIV/AIDS signify—in markedly different ways—levels of affect and experiences of the world that jar with the purported coziness of children's literature as an arena of cultural production. That is to say, when we think about books written for children, we tend not to think about experiences of COVID-19 and HIV/AIDS. Yet both pandemics separately and simultaneously demand representation, demonstrating the bibliotherapeutic and didactic possibilities of texts for young people, as well as framing the cultural politics of each pandemic and its relation to mythologies of the child. To examine the representation of either is to recognize underexamined forms and genres often disregarded as less important or interesting (because more ephemeral and immediately useful) than more traditional instances of "children's literature."[1]

I adapt "emergency children's literature" from Helen Patuck's description of her freely downloadable picture book, *My Hero Is You* (2020), which was commissioned by the Inter-Agency Standing Committee of the United Nations as the COVID-19 pandemic began in spring 2020.[2] *My Hero Is You* developed out of emergency education—"education in situations where children lack access to their national education systems, due to man-made crises or natural disasters" (Sinclair 4). Emergency education calls to mind the urgent needs of young people in conflict zones around the world but includes what Mary Joy Pigozzi describes as "silent, chronic emergencies" (1) such as youth homelessness and HIV/AIDS. To consider the production of children's literature about emergencies might seem to prioritize the utilitarian facets of a text above its aesthetic dimensions, and to thus pick a side in the "pedagogical/aesthetic divide" (Nordenstam and Widhe) among scholars working on texts for young people. And yet emergency children's literature exposes this divide as a false dichotomy that relies upon the notion that a text's pedagogical, ideological, and aesthetic contexts are separable, rather than interwoven and mutually negotiated.

One might ask: What text for a young person does *not* arise out of an emergency of some kind, even just the anxiety that circulates around the cultivation of a young person's successful development, or interpellation, into young adulthood? How can we know in advance what constitutes an emergency situation or an emergency children's text? Even so, calling more everyday material emergency children's literature would make the term less useful for thinking about material that registers and responds to larger-scale traumas and disasters. Hence, this chapter gestures toward a larger definition by focusing on the representation of the specific biopolitical contexts of COVID-19 and HIV/AIDS in the United States and the United Kingdom. This chapter uses children's literature to contemplate the cultural politics of each pandemic in young people's lives in the Global North and, in turn, uses COVID-19 and HIV/AIDS to explore children's literature as an aesthetic and political project. I draw from two specific digital archival contexts: Siân Cook's *HIV Graphic Communication*, in which I came across *It's Clinic Day* (Stevens; 1992), and the New York City School Libraries' database of COVID-19-related stories and picture books.

Despite their differences, COVID-19 and HIV/AIDS are alike as ongoing global health crises that emerge from and reproduce oppression and inequality, interlocking in different ways around the figure of the child. Ted Kerr noted at the start of the COVID-19 pandemic that people made comparisons because there were so few points of reference available for modern experiences of disease. Comparisons between the two pandemics at first felt inescapable, but the stakes have always been contentious. We need to discuss the fear and ignorance that HIV/AIDS continues to signify in the Global North without implying that the pandemic ended in the mid-1990s with the arrival of antiretroviral medication, or neglecting its ongoing epidemic status, particularly in marginalized communities. By contrast, COVID-19 is more infectious, less lethal, and emphatically visible across society; as David Craig argues, while "coronavirus is figured as a global blight afflicting all of humanity, the media discourses at the peak of the AIDS crisis signified the opposite" (1026). With this in mind, the vaccination of billions of people around the world is constitutive of governmental will to dehystericize COVID-19 and resignify it as an endemic illness, a commitment of resignification that has never been made with HIV. HIV/AIDS was first framed as oppositional to mainstream ideological constructions of childhood due to its association with death, sexuality, and drug use, even though HIV/AIDS has always been relevant to the lives of children and young people in the United States and elsewhere. HIV/AIDS is associated with Othered subjects, a stigma exacerbated in children's literature by the heterosexist, disability-phobic, and white supremacist framework of writing for young people in mainstream contexts. The different epidemiology of COVID-19—or to be exact SARS-CoV-2, the virus which causes COVID-19—means that its effects are so public as to become universal and national experiences, as waves of mass contagion and national lockdowns around the world and across the Global North demonstrated. If the moral panic of HIV/AIDS in the mass media often cast the white, innocent, soon-to-be heterosexual child as under attack from the deviant Other, then decades later, the first years of COVID-19 cast that child into a new ambivalence. In the early 2020s, the innocent child carries a virus that might kill its teachers or caretakers (grandparents especially). Here again, the family is under threat, but this time from inside, as it were. Finally, the disruption of education brought about by school closures and shelter-in-place mandates speaks to preexisting fears of the uncivilized child: uneducated, unsocialized, a child not being made docile in the Foucauldian sense.

AIDS Picture Books as Scriptive Things

Perhaps the most obviously unusual aspect of the development of an emergency children's literature about COVID-19 is the means of its circulation, which primarily occurred online in response to a locked-down, socially distanced new world. These texts are often a simulacrum of the traditional codex or printed book, which remains normative not in spite of the abundance of alternative digital media but because of it. To understand the material context of emergency children's literature and the questions that it raises, I turn to the work of Robin Bernstein, whose concept of the scriptive thing—as "a heuristic tool for dealing with incomplete evidence . . . to make responsible, limited inferences about the past" (*Dances* 76)—provides a powerful means to think about the material effects of children's texts about COVID-19 and HIV/AIDS.

In her study of the relationship between anti-Black racism and American histories of childhood, Bernstein shows how material culture, including children's books, contains certain scripts that offer insights into the lives of young people and the engagements that those artefacts invite. Understanding works of children's literature as scriptive things establishes a connection between the textual discourse of a children's book—what the pages say and show—and its extratextual, material uses. That is, analyzing the book as both discursive construction and material artefact highlights its embodied use and the meanings it encodes into young people's lives. The ideological work of a children's text thus comes about through the combination of "narrative with materiality" (Bernstein, *Racial Innocence* 77). Bernstein calls this synergy of textuality and materiality a process of "enscription" while noting that the scripts that children's books reveal are not all obeyed or interpreted the same way. Enscription is a powerful concept with which to comprehend representations of COVID-19 or HIV/AIDS because these texts explicitly advocate—or rather, enscript—discursively constituted actions and gestures like routes of HIV transmission, mask-wearing, and feelings of compassion. As scriptive things, these works of emergency children's literature seek to prompt certain behaviors and emotions according to social codes within changing ideological frameworks, and they therefore illuminate these codes and these frameworks for the children's historian and literary scholar. Examining the scripts that can be gleaned from picture books about the AIDS crisis provides not only a primer on Bernstein's concept but also a point of comparison for contemporary scripts at work in children's literature's responses to COVID-19.

Megan Blumenreich and Marjorie Siegel examine twenty-six picture books for children about HIV/AIDS published between 1989 and 1999—the most visible period of AIDS in the Global North—and argue that "lack of access to books about HIV/AIDS may reinforce the legacy of silence about HIV/AIDS that persists in schools" (106). Writing in the late 1990s, Robert McRuer critiques several children's picture books published about the AIDS-related deaths of gay men. As he notes, these picture books were obviously created to reflect the impact of HIV/AIDS on the gay community, yet that impact is veiled for younger readers, with the sexuality of the HIV+ characters pushed into subtext. In other words, McRuer's study shows how emergency children's literature needs to be queried by what is *not* represented as much as by what *is* represented. The representation of health crises is structured by omission and inaccuracy—which is to say, these texts are not only bound up in larger profound social and political discourses but actively produce and sustain them.

In this light, consider how three different AIDS picture books about the experiences of HIV+ and HIV-affected children in the Global North undergo shifting reception over time and with cultural change: *Alex, the Kid with AIDS* (Girard; 1991), *It's Clinic Day* (Stevens; 1992), and *Melissa's Story* (Glynne; 2017). Writing in the early 2000s, Blumenreich and Siegel applaud *Alex* for its empowering depiction of a young white boy living with HIV/AIDS. Blumenreich and Siegel argue that the book transcends "the typical ways of speaking about people with HIV" by representing a "funny, mischievous" HIV+ child "whose teacher realizes she has been letting him get away with misbehavior because of his HIV status" (105). *Alex* affirms the rights of HIV+ children and transcends the stereotypical trope of victim-pariah, as does another and otherwise rather different picture book, *You Can Call Me Willy* (Verniero; 1996), which offers an empowering portrait of a young HIV+ Black girl. *You Can Call Me Willy* remains a respected text, however, while *Alex* is now sometimes met with ridicule.

Three decades after its publication, *Alex* was submitted to *Awful Library Books*, a website that gathers outdated books found in public library catalogues. These titles range from humorously outdated to outright offensive. The description for *Alex* reads: "This book was shelved in the children's fiction area of a public library. There has to be better books on this subject now, especially targeted towards this age group. . . . And our head of Materials Management immediately called for it to be weeded [destroyed]." Certainly this picture book is outdated in various ways: to come across the brightly colored front cover with its title emblazoned in incongruously cheerful lettering is to be confronted by a crude-looking and tragic past. If these books are scriptive things that invite actions to shape public behavior, then *Alex* becomes an awful thing through its survival on open library shelves and the afterlife that it represents. Indeed, the outrage regarding the text is more to do with its paratext than the contents of the book; the latter goes unseen by the website's editor and so has no role in its eligibility on *Awful Library Books*. But despite the shock of the cover, the paratext affirms the author's bibliotherapeutic intention and its basis in a real-life incident: the endpapers acknowledge "Central School in Wilmette, Illinois, whose staff and board carried out an inspiring model of community education when a student was diagnosed as having AIDS." As with the character of Alex in the text, the outcome of that spectral, real-life student's diagnosis goes unstated. The contemporary awfulness of the picture book is thus called into question by the ways in which its paratext declares it as an example of justice-oriented best practice. Its conceptualization as an awful thing underlines the ephemerality and sheer volatility of children's literature in general, and of emergency children's literature specifically. When it comes to scriptive things, a good thing can become a bad thing as the world changes around it.

While *Alex* is intended to be used by children attending school with an HIV+ child, *It's Clinic Day* is about the children of HIV+ women in Edinburgh, at a time when the city was crudely known as "the AIDS capital of Europe," in part due to a high number of heroin users and drug policy that restricted access to clean needles ("Choose Life"). The picture book was commissioned by the Women's Committee of Edinburgh District Council, created by an HIV+ mother named Ruth Stevens, and subsequently printed by the Lothian Health Education Department to be used alongside the Take Care campaign to raise awareness of HIV/AIDS in Scotland. The author's dedication to "all positive parents past and present" nods to the high stakes at the time of publication in the early 1990s, recognizing the high rates of death for HIV+ people and drug users in Edinburgh at that time. As a regional Scottish title, the picture book is not listed among Blumenreich and Siegel's findings and finds its textual afterlife today through Cook's *HIV Graphic Communication* archive. The artefact exists today as an example of AIDS ephemera in the archive, but it was published with an ISBN and so also constitutes a conventional picture book, despite lacking recognition or posterity as such.

With its combination of simple text and bright, friendly illustrations—recalling Matthew P. McAllister's assertion that visual narratives help spread knowledge among drug-users as well as children—*It's Clinic Day* depicts an HIV+ mother and child visiting the local clinic to see an HIV/AIDS specialist. While the mother undertakes a checkup with the doctor, the child meets other children who have HIV+ parents and speaks with a doctor, who provides information to the character and therefore reader about HIV in neutral language. The formulaic story and straight-forward composition concludes with a sudden example of mise en abyme. The doctor offers the child a picture book as a gift, which in the final double-spread is revealed to be the child's own copy of *It's Clinic Day*. This metafictive device nods to the picture book's intended use in clinical settings with children, presenting those real-life children with a mirror-image of their own identity and experiences, constructing the reader it intends to represent. The picture book's enscription—the intersection between what is represented on the page and the material means by which those pages came to be read in young people lives—is thus a textual trace of HIV+ and HIV-affected children in Edinburgh in the early 1990s, but one that tends to go unremembered within scholarly conceptualizations of HIV/AIDS in children's literature studies.

For contrast and continuity both, consider a more contemporary example of HIV/AIDS-related children's literature, *Melissa's Story*, a picture book version of a YouTube animation about a young Black girl living with HIV in a Western country (in the animation, the London skyline is visible, but not in the picture book version). The paratext provides an insight to the changed script that HIV today denotes, as a condition no longer synonymous with death. The synopsis invites the reader to find out "what it means to grow up being HIV positive" and refers to other books in the "Living with Illness" series, which explores chronic and terminal illnesses in children's lives. By juxtaposing HIV/AIDS with serious but less moralized conditions such as leukemia and epilepsy, the paratext creates distance between the moral panic that first shaped HIV/AIDS and its comparative normalization in contemporary culture. According to the back cover, *Melissa's Story* reveals "the impact an illness has on a child's daily life, how they cope," and then crucially "how they *enjoy* their life" (my emphasis). Emphasizing Melissa's struggle to take her medication and then to disclose her condition to her friends, the picture book moves from the cliché of "dying with" to "living with" and even "thriving despite" HIV/AIDS (Watkins-Hayes)—a rhetorical shift that remains integral to the ethics of mediating HIV/AIDS. Indeed, this representational imperative shares common ground with the earliest AIDS picture books, such as *Alex*, despite their alleged awfulness.

Digital Enscription and the Construction of COVID-19

If AIDS narratives illustrate various modes of enscription that emphasize certain material contexts, then the challenge to represent COVID-19 in texts for young people demanded different and drastic scripts for different and drastic times. Hundreds of primarily digital stories and picture books were created in response to the first waves of the pandemic to address its impact on young people, materials now gathered and available on the New York City School Libraries website. Working with Amy Ryder, I recently undertook a critical content analysis of British examples from this archive (Duckels and Ryder, in press). In this research, we argue that the rapid production of a new emergency children's literature about COVID-19 took place online and evidences a definitive period of the cultural politics of the pandemic. One might conceptualize the upheaval provoked by COVID-19 as what Michael Rustin—drawing on Antonio Gramsci and Stuart Hall—calls a *conjuncture*, "a specific historical moment in which different contradictions and conflicts within a social order become unexpectedly juxtaposed[,] . . . sometimes giving rise to situations of great uncertainty and unpredictability." In this conjuncture, rapid and radical change come into possibility, insofar as the juxtaposition of new events and realities undermines dominant systems of power. The first children's literature about COVID-19 spontaneously emerged to address the vacuum in children's educational needs created by the pandemic, constituting a provisional, unstable field of representation. That field was made viable by a combination of mass digital literacy and unprecedented national lockdowns that created time and space for nonprofessional authors and illustrators to produce their texts.

The combination of this rapid digital circulation and the precarious biopolitics of the pandemic has generated an archive of texts that became quickly anachronistic. In retrospect, these texts are a representation of the "crip time" that COVID-19 brought about as a universal experience. Crip time is a concept used in disability studies to describe how "disability and illness have the power to extract us from linear, progressive time with its normative life stages and cast us into a wormhole of backward and forward acceleration, jerky stops and starts, tedious intervals and abrupt endings" (Samuels). The emergency children's literature created by Meredith Polsky is a useful symbol of crip time as a collective experience, including in education. Her series of simple digital picture books became a record of the pandemic's social-temporal contingency: *My School Is Closed Today* was posted online on the thirteenth of March 2020, quickly followed by *Can We Play Now?* and *My School Is Still Closed* a few weeks later. As spring became summer, Polsky released *My School Will Stay Closed* and *My Camp Is Closed* before concluding the series in summer 2020 with *Time for In-Person School*, which prepares children for returning to physical educational environments. While the first titles in the series imply that the pandemic would soon be over, the final entry is more ambiguous, instead offering hope that "some things are different, and lots of things are the same." Polsky's texts demonstrate the relationship between ephemeral utility and anachronism in the creation of health promotional texts for young people, and they encapsulate the shift towards crip time—or something like it—that COVID-19 brought about as a mass experience. This parallel kind of crip time did not encourage solidarity between able-bodied people and people with disabilities, unfortunately; rather, it underscores how the lives of the latter have often been disregarded in what Henry Giroux calls "capitalism's ruthless logic of disposability in a time of crisis" (209).

In our content analysis, Ryder and I argue that this ad hoc archive spans a wide range of quality and a diverse pool of creators: nonprofessional and professional writers and illustrators; creators working in education and medical professions; organizational authors such as literacy charities and state bodies. Key themes across these texts include health promotion, social distancing, experiences of quarantine, and managing difficult feelings such as loneliness and fear. Building on existing research (Caldwell and Falcus; Moruzi et al.), we note that these themes are often constructed using anthropomorphic and microbial characters, as well as through heroification narratives in which children and frontline workers are emphasized as especially virtuous, future-facing figures. While visual depictions of multicultural-coded children and families are fairly common, scarcely any of these new texts foreground children of color as central characters—a trend which seems at odds with the broader global corpus as captured through the New York City School Libraries database, although I have not conducted sufficient macroanalysis to draw such a conclusion definitively. Half of the representations we surveyed were self-published texts, signifying spontaneous production, while the remainder were created by mainstream children's publishers or other literacy and state organizations. A common paratextual element is the regional news article that celebrates texts created by members of local communities who are also working in medical environments. While admirable in some respects, this valorization of the frontline worker obscures that a disproportionate number of these workers were non-white people who died from the caretaking of COVID-19 patients. Foregrounding this context of authorship provides a symbol of the workers' commitment to ending the pandemic, while the authors' subsequent viral context demonstrates the importance of "networked publics" (Varnelis) to sustaining this field of production.

Given this context, what are the implications for how we might understand pandemic material as children's literature? The initial dominance of nonprofessional texts and authors in this new and urgent field of COVID-19 representation functions as a *disruption* of mainstream models of children's literature. The circulation of downloadable multimodal visual narratives (to be read on smartphones or printed at home) was geared toward a moment in which schools, libraries, and booksellers were abruptly closed in many countries around the world. Conventional modes of circulation and consumption had to be bypassed. As scriptive things, these texts not only reflect the biopolitical context of COVID-19 but actively construct it through their digital format. As such, these texts upend preconceived notions of children's literature and children's literacy, but at the same time, they do reaffirm the value of both during a period of global educational emergency.

Giroux rejects the neoliberal response to the pandemic, which he sees as immorally affirming the individual over the community, while Charles

Rosenberg and Priscilla Wald have famously theorized the fear and prejudice that new outbreaks of disease drum up in the social body. Tedder's *A Message from Corona* offers an example of how these anxious attitudes of xenophobia can be drawn out from the mediation of the pandemic for young people through the personification of the virus. The picture book opens with a cartoony germ figure—"My name is COVID-19, my friends like to call me Corona"—who explains its desire to leave "a little town in a faraway land." The faraway land is depicted as Asian, with Orientalist overtones. The personified virus describes its determination to see the world: because "humans would not let me on board their ships or planes," the virus decided to "get into a human" and jump "from person to person" to enter new countries, drawing attention to the role of human borders and even alluding to the fears and dangers that surround the migrant crisis. The travelogue turns into a lament as the virus realizes the harm it is causing to humans by invading their bodies and begs to be restricted in a direct address to the reader: "WE NEED TO BE STOPPED!" Passport motifs are used visually throughout to further emphasize the association between disease and the national border. This patronizing personification of the virus is resonant of the preexisting panic icon of the migrant figure and even evokes racist Chinese stereotypes. While these aspects of the book are troubling, it's worth recalling that Tedder created this text as a student in the first British lockdown and distributed it for free. As this example shows, the charitable and bibliotherapeutic connotations of emergency children's literature do not sever it from the broader systems of power that structure the realities and emotions that the pandemic both brought about and compounded.

If the outbreak of COVID-19 inspired a good deal of anxiety, it also generated optimism about the pandemic's potential for generating a better world. For example, *The Great Realisation* by Tomfoolery is a print picture book version of a poem he penned that went viral on YouTube at the start of the pandemic. Written as though in the future, the poem and picture book remember 2020 as a watershed year that brought about massive social change, implicitly anticapitalist and explicitly environmentalist. The early viral success of the poem encapsulates Rustin's point that crisis "can create the conditions for more sudden changes . . . from which rapid changes in the distribution of power can result." It became a print picture book a few months later in September 2020, demonstrating how the pandemic made progressive politics suddenly and particularly visible in the mainstream. Arguably, *The Great Realisation* idealizes the pandemic by overlooking the lives of people who were not able to stay at home reconnecting to nature, as well as the millions of deaths that COVID-19 has since caused. To preempt this critique, the picture book's paratext acknowledges the one-off context of the chaotic first months of COVID-19. The poem performs a future in which the pandemic brought about mass change and pastoral renewal, even as the print version is perhaps doomed to gather dust in children's libraries as an increasingly anachronistic record—even a eulogy—of an anxious but also hopeful moment.

I do not mean to downplay the progressive, worldbuilding potential of politically motivated children's literature. If many of the first texts about COVID-19 are the work of adults grappling with their own fears and anxieties during a time of great upheaval and change, we can trace what Giroux sees as the potential pedagogy of the pandemic: "a radical vision of the future coupled with the courage to struggle collectively to bring into being a new society" (208). With this in mind, I want to consider two picture books created by organizations that were *already* deploying children's literature in emergency education contexts. For example, Helen Patuck, the author of *My Hero Is You*, is a cofounder of Kitabna, a charity that uses storytelling in conflict zones to support children's wellbeing. Kitabna publishes digital and print versions of picture books told in dual languages, such as the Arabic and English title *Once Upon a Time in Zaatari and Azraq*, themed around the experiences of children in the eponymous refugee camps in Jordan founded through the impact of the Syrian Civil War. Illustrated by Patuck and coauthored by Syrian teachers who live and work in the camps, the digital versions of the stories replicate the codex format of the conventional print picture book, accompanied by optional audio versions in both languages. The dual-language format, then, signifies a dialogic exchange between Arabic and English and the cultural and political contexts each denotes. Another example of the pedagogical power of pandemic material is Piplo Productions's *Trinka and Sam* series, first created as a response to Hurricane Katrina with the National Child Traumatic Stress Network in the United States, described as coloring books that "help young children and families after disasters, with specific versions for hurricanes, tornadoes, earthquakes, wildfires, and COVID-19" ("Our Stories"). The first title, *Trinka and Sam: The Rainy Windy Day*, was developed in response to Hurricane Katrina and published online in 2008. Making use of the accessibility that a digital format provides, the text has since been translated into Spanish, Haitian Creole, Cebuano, Waray, and Vietnamese versions, demonstrating the disproportionate impact of such disasters on these communities in the United States. Piplo Productions's and Kitabna's preexisting focus on emergencies such as conflict, displacement, and natural disasters points to the reality of COVID-19 as a similarly severe—but more universal and less avoidable—event in children's lives in the Global North.

Patuck's *My Hero Is You* is a prominent early example of emergency children's literature about COVID-19, inspired by children's and families' responses to a survey about dealing with the pandemic. Published at the end of March 2020 in connection with the United Nations, the picture book begins with a young dark-skinned girl named Sara discussing COVID-19 with her mother, a scientist. That evening, Sara is visited by Ario, a flying magical creature, after Sara wishes for "a way to tell all the children in the world how to protect themselves so they can protect everyone else." Sara and Ario travel around the world to exchange solidarity and information with other children in diverse international contexts, including an implied reference to a refugee camp. *My Hero Is You* is available for download in more than 144 languages and has also yielded an animated version, which circulates on YouTube. The global focus continues in *My Hero Is You 2021*, published in September 2021, in which Ario returns to visit Sara before transporting all the children from the first title to be reunited on a satellite floating above the earth to discuss the ongoing impact of COVID-19 in their lives. Ario asks the children "to write down what gives you hope, and share it with the world. . . . Take a piece of paper and write what is in your heart" (21)—scripting a restorative educational exercise for real-life children as they engage with the title. On the final page, the messages from the children fall to the earth, with Ario taking the children to watch as other children return to school in different countries across the world, as though to signify the end of the pandemic and postpandemic futures built around a pedagogy of international solidarity and compassion.

The prompt to write down a hopeful thought draws attention to an important part of the digital production of these texts. Although predominantly digital, many of the first examples of emergency children's literature about COVID-19 make use of the haptic and interactive affordances provided by a printable format. Piplo Productions's *Trinka and Sam Fighting the Big Virus: Trinka, Sam and Littletown Work Together* provides a compelling example of these material implications. As with other examples from the *Trinka and Sam* series, the endpapers of this freely downloadable title note that any reader is permitted to print, copy, and share the story so long as they do not profit from it. The coloring-book format of the series is cost effective because it requires black-and-white rather than full-color printing, therefore aiding the creation of physical copies to be distributed in emergency settings. One can imagine piles being printed in schools in areas impacted by hurricanes or wildfires as well as by the COVID-19 pandemic. Of course, as Bernstein notes, the script of an artefact from children's material culture is always dependent upon the physical engagement of the child, whose agency in the reading process is crucial. If the coloring book is a tool for assisting traumatized children in emergency situations, then the child-reader makes a choice to affirm that enscription (by coloring the illustrations) or to resist it (by refusing the task or by scribbling over the pages instead).

In *Trinka, Sam, and Littletown Work Together*, the COVID-19 pandemic is the latest emergency to impact the eponymous characters' cartoon town. As with *My Hero Is You*, the picture book drums up themes of solidarity and community, focusing on the microcosm of a small town rather than phantasmagorical global visions of humanity. The narrative depicts Trinka and Sam's confusion as an unprecedented virus impacts Littletown, making them unable to see one another due to quarantine rules. The mice and their families model the newly normal abnormal experiences, such as discovering empty supermarkets during periods of panic-buying, becoming irritated with family members while staying at home, missing friends, and worrying about family members who work in the hospital with people who are suffering from a serious case of COVID-19. The picture book includes a mask insert that guides children to draw masks onto each character "if people in your area are wearing masks." The reader is invited to "cut out paper masks and tape them to their faces when they go outside," becoming an active "player-reader" (Reid-Walsh), encouraged by the text to use the paper dimensions of the reading experience to normalise mask use and contemplate the difference between home and not-home in a quarantine context. Along with Patuck's picture books, Piplo Productions's examples of emergency children's literature about COVID-19 demonstrate how these texts sought to encourage better, safer worlds.

Conclusion

This chapter has proposed the concept of "emergency children's literature" to define the production of texts for young people in times of crisis. In the unfolding and ongoing crises of COVID-19 and HIV/AIDS, children's picture books work to shape young people's behavior, self-understanding, and feelings towards others. My emphasis on the emergency children's book as a scriptive thing provides a way to approach the digital mediation of COVID-19: its initially primarily digital format reflected the aspiration to a suddenly socially distanced and physically isolated world. This context spotlights how the material (or indeed, antimaterial) dimensions of children's texts not only portray but in fact actively produce the social experience of new disease. On one hand, the rapid accumulation of emergency children's literature about

COVID-19 in the first six months of 2020 was prompted largely by the fear and ignorance that the pandemic provoked. And yet the emergency children's book about COVID-19 also had radical cultural as well as pedagogical potential, even when that potential was not fully realized. The *My Hero Is You* and *Trinka and Sam* series incorporate important ideas about community and solidarity. Tellingly, COVID-19 texts often emerged from publishers whose earlier publications negotiate prior, ongoing emergencies in the lives of children, underscoring that the pandemic, while specific in some ways, cannot and should not be isolated from other experiences of challenge and difficulty.

Notes

Thank you to Hannah J. Elizabeth, Helen Patuck, Meredith Polsky, and Amy Ryder.

1. I use quotation marks here to agree with Marilisa Jiménez Garcia's skepticism toward the term, the incorporation of which into the academy she sees as an allegiance to an already white supremacist Victorian-centric canon.

2. Patuck described *My Hero Is You* as an "emergency children's book" during a panel at the conference *Rainbow in Windows: Childhood in the Time of Corona*, hosted on Zoom by the University of Warwick in July 2020. The term "emergency children's literature" is my own.

Works Cited

"Alex, the Kid with AIDS." *Awful Library Books*, http://awfullibrarybooks.net/alex-the-kid-with-aids/. Accessed 14 Oct. 2021.

Bernstein, Robin. "Dances with Things: Material Culture and the Performance of Race." *Social Text*, vol. 27, no. 4, 2009, pp. 67–94.

Bernstein, Robin. *Racial Innocence*. New York UP, 2011.

Blumenreich, Megan, and Marjorie Siegel. "Innocent Victims, Fighter Cells, and White Uncles: A Discourse Analysis of Children's Books about AIDS." *Children's Literature in Education*, vol. 37, 2006, pp. 81–110.

Caldwell, Elizabeth, and Sarah Falcus. "Little Bugs and Wicked Viruses: Communicating the COVID-19 Pandemic through Picturebooks for Children." *Journal of Science and Popular Culture*, vol. 4, no. 1, 2021, pp. 3–19.

"Choose Life." *Waverly Care*, https://www.waverleycare.org/news/choose-life. Accessed 14 Oct. 2021.

Craig, Daniel. "Pandemic and Its Metaphors: Sontag Revisited in the COVID-19 Era." *European Journal of Cultural Studies*, vol. 23, no. 6, 2020, pp. 1025–36.

Duckels, Gabriel, and Amy Ryder. "Emergency Children's Literature: Rapidly Representing COVID-19 in Digital Texts for Young People in the United Kingdom." *COVID-19 and Education in the Global North: Storytelling as Alternative Pedagogies*, edited by Ruby Turok-Squire, Palgrave, in press.

Girard, Linda. *Alex, the Kid with AIDS*. Albert Whitman, 1991.

Giroux, Henry. *Race, Politics, and Pandemic Pedagogy*. Bloomsbury, 2021.

Jiménez Garcia, Marilisa. *Side by Side: US Empire, Puerto Rico, and the Roots of American Youth Literature and Culture*. UP of Mississippi, 2021.

Kerr, Ted. "How to Live with a Virus." *Poz*, 23 Mar. 2020. https://www.poz.com/article/live-virus. Accessed 14 Oct. 2021.

McAllister, Matthew P. "Comic Books and AIDS." *The Journal of Popular Culture*, vol. 26, no. 2, 1992, pp. 1–24.

McRuer, Robert. "Reading and Writing 'Immunity': Children and the Anti-Body." *Over The Rainbow: Queer Children's and Young Adult Literature*, edited by Michelle Ann Abate and Kenneth B. Kidd. U of Michigan P, 2011, pp. 183–200.

Moruzi, Kristine, et al. "Public Health, Polio, and Pandemics: Fear and Anxiety about Health in Children's Literature." *Children's Literature in Education*, vol. 53, no. 1, 2022, pp. 97–111.

Nordenstam, Anna, and Olle Widhe. "The Uses of Children's Literature in Political Contexts: Bridging the Pedagogical/Aesthetic Divide." *Children's Literature*, vol. 49, 2021, pp. 1–7, 10.1353/chl.2021.0001.

Patuck, Helen. *My Hero Is You*. E-book, Inter-Agency Standing Committee, 2020. https://interagencystandingcommittee.org/iasc-reference-group-mental-health-and-psychosocial-support-emergency-settings/my-hero-you-storybook-children-covid-19. Accessed 16 Oct. 2021.

Patuck, Helen. *My Hero Is You 2021*. E-book, Inter-Agency Standing Committee, 2021. Retrieved from: https://interagencystandingcommittee.org/my-hero-is-you-2021.

Pigozzi, Mary Joy. *Education in Emergencies and for Reconstruction: A Developmental Approach*. UNICEF, 1999.

Piplo Productions. *Fighting the Big Virus: Trinka, Sam, and Littletown Work Together*. E-book, https://piploproductions.com/trinka-and-sam-virus. Accessed 14 Oct. 2021.

Polsky, Meredith. *Can We Play Now?* E-book, https://www.meredithpolsky.com/picture-stories. Accessed 17 Oct. 2021.

Polsky, Meredith. *My Camp Is Closed*. E-book, https://www.meredithpolsky.com/picture-stories. Accessed 17 Oct. 2021.

Polsky, Meredith. *My School Is Closed Today*. E-book, https://www.meredithpolsky.com/picture-stories. Accessed 17 Oct. 2021.

Polsky, Meredith. *My School Is Still Closed*. E-book, https://www.meredithpolsky.com/picture-stories. Accessed 17 Oct. 2021.

Polsky, Meredith. *My School Will Stay Closed*. E-book, https://www.meredithpolsky.com/picture-stories. Accessed 17 Oct. 2021.

Polsky, Meredith. *Time for In-Person School*. E-book, https://www.meredithpolsky.com/picture-stories. Accessed 17 Oct. 2021.

Reid-Walsh, Jacqueline. *Interactive Books: Playful Media before Pop-Ups*. Routledge, 2018.

Rosenberg, Charles. "What Is an Epidemic? AIDS in Historical Perspective." *Daedalus*, vol. 118, no. 2, 1989, pp. 1–17.

Rustin, Michael. "The Coronavirus Pandemic and Its Meanings." *Stuart Hall Foundation*, 11 Oct. 2020, https://www.stuarthallfoundation.org/resource/the-coronavirus-pandemic-and-its-meanings/. Accessed 14 Oct. 2021.

Samuels, Ellen. "Six Ways of Looking at Crip Time." *Disability Studies Quarterly*, vol. 37, no. 3, 2017, https://dsq-sds.org/article/view/5824.

Sinclair, Margaret. "Education in Emergencies." *Learning for a Future: Refugee Education in Developing Countries*, edited by Jeff Crisp et al., United Nations High Commissioner for Refugees, 2001, pp. 1–83.

Stevens, Ruth. *It's Clinic Day*. Edinburgh District Council Women's Committee, 1992.

Tedder, Charity. *A Message from Corona*. E-book, https://drive.google.com/file/d/1FevOhksly48LpUo6slikMd1CowArYyrF/view.

Tomfoolery. *The Great Realisation*. Egmont, 2020.

Varnelis, Kazys, editor. *Networked Publics*. MIT P, 2008.

Verniero, Joan C. *You Can Call Me Willy*. Magination Press, 1996.

Wald, Priscilla. *Contagious*. Duke UP, 2007.

Watkins-Hayes, Celeste. *Remaking a Life: How Women Living with HIV/AIDS Confront Inequality*. U of California P, 2019.

THE CASE OF *JONNY*'S GENRE
An Interview with Joshua Whitehead

Joshua Whitehead and Derritt Mason

Joshua Whitehead is among the most exciting and important young storytellers currently working on Turtle Island. A Two-Spirit, Oji-nêhiyaw member of Peguis First Nation (Treaty One), Whitehead published his debut book of poetry, *Full-Metal Indigiqueer*, in 2017 to widespread acclaim. In 2018, Whitehead released his novel *Jonny Appleseed*, which earned nominations from Canada's most prestigious literary awards—including the Giller Prize and the Governor General's Literary Award—and went on to win the Lambda Literary Award for Gay Fiction and the Canadian Broadcasting Corporation's *Canada Reads* competition. Whitehead has since published an edited collection, *Love after the End: An Anthology of Two-Spirit and Indigiqueer Speculative Fiction* (2020), and *Making Love with the Land* (2022), a book of personal essays. In the interview that follows, Whitehead discusses *Jonny Appleseed*'s YA influences; the importance of queer, Indigenous, and Two-Spirit representation in texts for young people; the limits of genre; and his sense of the differences between the Canadian and American publishing landscapes.

Derritt Mason: Can you briefly summarize *Jonny Appleseed* for our readers?

Joshua Whitehead: *Jonny Appleseed*'s titular character is a cybersex worker who lives in the Exchange District of Winnipeg, Manitoba, and is from Peguis First Nation, both of which are Treaty One territory.

Jonny's returning home to his reservation for the wake of his stepfather, Roger, who has passed away. He has a week to earn enough money to get there. That's the base plot, but the story is really about Jonny's life, his memories, loves, traumas, and triumphs. It's a whole smorgasbord, a collection of memories. I think of it more as a photo album than a novel, really, but the base plot is a returning home narrative.

DM: I know from our previous conversations that you originally imagined *Jonny* as a young adult novel. Why was this the case? Did it have anything to do with the "home-away-home" plot structure?

JW: Yes—I wrote *Jonny* as young adult and pitched it to Arsenal Pulp Press. Eventually it became a quote unquote "adult novel," whatever that means. The differentiations between age and genre are interesting to me. When I was writing *Jonny*, I was writing it for a youth or youthful audience. I wanted to create representation of what we might call queer Indigeneity, or Indigiqueerness and, more specifically, a Two-Spirit narrative that wasn't written by a white, appropriative writer. Immediately *The Miseducation of Cameron Post* comes to mind, but also contemporary Indigenous lit like *Fire Song* by Adam Garnet Jones, which also includes queer Indigeneity, but in this really pained valence, which is not something that I wanted to do. When I was conceptualizing *Jonny* it came to me from the remnants of *Full Metal Indigiqueer*, my book of poetry that preceded it. They're kind of sibling stories in that sense. But Jonny was a character that I've had in me for a long time.

Regarding the home-away-home narrative—yes, when thinking about youth, youth culture, and Indigeneity and queerness in both urban and reservation spaces, I think the fundamental question that came to me was: what is home, really? Is home the space that one is birthed in, is home the space where one has found family, is home transportable or transformational, or really is home the self, an embodiment? I wrestle with those questions in *Jonny*.

I think a lot of these themes come from my experience working with youth, but also—and I've come to avoid this language—what I used to call my "guilty pleasure" of reading YA novels. I think home and its definitions, its morphology, its grammatology—that is really the animating motor in almost any form of literature or storytelling. I think "home" begs the fundamental question of being human, and also of being Indigenous or BIPOC or queer or any other intersection that may be disempowered under the nation state, that is, Canada and Western and Global North powers right now. Where is "home" when home is continually stolen, when home is occupied and when home is an imperial force?

This question came to me with *Jonny*, *Full Metal*, my edited anthology *Love after the End*, and *Making Love with the Land*, which is my nonfiction book. I think it's something that will haunt me as a writer until my last book.

DM: These are some quintessential *Bildungsroman* or coming-of-age themes that you're wrestling with, that Jonny is wrestling with as a protagonist.

I think you're also really pushing at the limits of these generic categories. As you know, the *Bildungsroman* is very much a Eurocentric category, but you're looking at how colonialism and racism affect how Jonny conceives of family and home. Regardless, these are some foundational young adult themes, so what was it about *Jonny* that made your publisher say: actually, this isn't a young adult book, this is something else?

JW: Just to back up slightly: when thinking about the *Bildungsroman* and these Eurocentric notions of quintessential story arcs, there are ways in which these are also quite quintessential, I would say, to Indigenous oral storytelling. Home-away-home narratives, specifically in the prairies and in Treaty One—which is a mix of prairie and woodlands—are often about a kind of nomadic movement for hunting and trapping. These stories are about the literal formation of home, but also the Trickster stories are all about returning to home, which is here on earth, but also in spaces like the fourth world, or sky world as some people might call it. Home is also found in dreams and in ceremony and sweat lodges and visions.

As I've become more fluent in Cree, I've become more of what I call a genre outlaw. I need to be as decolonial on the page as I am on the land, and I think *Jonny* was what started that for me, as well as the YA-related concepts of the *Bildungsroman* and its home-away-home structure.

Jonny was very much inspired by Raziel Reid's *When Everything Like the Movies*, which I was introduced to years ago at the Thin Air Festival, a Winnipeg writer's festival, which is run by the amazing Charlene Diehl. I was very infatuated with the book, and I went to Raziel's talk and became even more infatuated, even though there are some issues around [racial] identity and character in the book.[1] Regardless, something sparked, and the kind of character I wanted Jonny to be was starting to unearth itself creatively for me.

At the time, I was writing *Full-Metal Indigiqueer*, and I started to see Jonny as the human counterpart to Zoa [*Full-Metal*'s protagonist]—kind of like the human behind this avatar who uploads the virus, the protozoa. Fast-forward a bit, and Raziel was winning many awards for his book, including the Governor General's Award for Children's Literature, but also getting brutal criticism from the likes of Barbara Kay in the *National Post*. So, I was watching this national dialogue around what constitutes children's literature and what is appropriate for children: What is a young adult novel? Should something that features queerness and queer characters and queer sex be winning awards like this? That might quote-unquote "corrupt" children, right? I immediately hear Mrs. Lovejoy from *The Simpsons*: "think about the children!" What some people might call indecency, I just call livelihood.

I was reading and watching all this, and also seeing what Arsenal Pulp Press was doing. Brian Lam, who runs Arsenal Pulp, was staunchly and proudly defending this book for winning the Governor General's Award amidst the backlash. I immediately knew that I wanted Arsenal Pulp to be *Jonny*'s home. Arsenal has a long history of publishing queer and/or BIPOC writers and stories, and they don't just publish these for the sake of diversity quota. They actively invest financially and in terms of the feedback and support they offer their authors. So, Arsenal picked it up, Brian read it and said it was amazing, and that they want to take it. I said, lovely, it's going to fit so well in your YA repertoire. And he said they might have to rethink that, and I reminded him of *When Everything Feels Like the Movies*. The controversy around Reid's book had just happened, and I think Arsenal might have been a little burned out from the barricade they had to uphold. So they took *Jonny* and made it fiction, rather than young adult fiction. Erasing two words, I guess, completely shifts a book. I can see the reason why—it is a little more PG-13, a little more risqué than *When Everything Feels Like the Movies*. There's no rimming or bear topping scene in [Reid's] book.

Jonny doesn't have an age in the book. There are indicators through pop culture references, and certain historical moments point toward his age. I see him in the range of about seventeen to twenty years old, maybe twenty-one, so he's quite youthful, but he's older than Reid's protagonist Jude. As a result, he's undergoing and doing different things. So, I agreed to publish the book as general fiction, but I want readers to know that I wrote it for youth, so they can see themselves represented powerfully in ways that aren't trauma porn, but instead work through trauma and exist beyond and above that.

Aesthetically, however, I wanted to keep it close to YA, so I wrote shorter chapters that would have the kinetic energy of a YA novel, a quote-unquote "quick read." I numbered each chapter with a roman numeral to reflect time in short bursts, which I think approximate the reading styles of millennials and Gen Z now: quick access and short readings. That's how social media trains us to read, I wanted to kind of be in that realm. The font choice also approaches a YA aesthetic. It may be designated an adult novel, but when you pick it up and look through it and feel a tangible connection with it, it looks, reads, and feels like YA. There's also an alternate cover on the inside of the book, which I think looks like a young adult cover. It was originally made on birchbark by the amazing Erin Konsmo. The image is a headless torso with eggplant purple boxers on and a ptarmigan syllabic printed on the boxers, which I thought was very fitting. I can see why maybe that was just too YA, but I was adamant that we keep it in, so it's on the book's first inside page.

DM: When your publisher said, okay, you're writing an "adult" novel now and not a young adult novel, it sounds like you still went on to write what you imagined to be a young adult novel. Did the publisher's official change in genre alter the way you wrote and edited the book from that point on?

JW: I don't think it changed much. Actually, I don't think it changed a thing. Obviously, publishing designations of genre are for publicity, to sell books. Certain genres will sell better than others. As a poet I'm very aware of the minimal royalties I get. As a novelist, yeah, there's more money to be made. I said: just call it what you want. By the end, I was like well, maybe it's YA, maybe it's adult fiction. People call my prose poetic, my poetry prosaic, my essays theoretical. Regardless, I'm going to tell the story as the story ought to be told. It leans on multiple genres; it's a kind of cascading of genres. It's YA, it's fiction, I use poetic devices throughout. I apply many forms from different genres to tell the story as it needs to be told.

People can classify it however they want. But for me—I think it's a novel, but also I started by describing it as a photo album. It is all those things, and nothing, and if I had to pick a single genre I would call it YA. I think it is both identifiable but also unidentifiable by English literature standards, so that excites me too.

DM: I really like your image of the book as a photo album, because it does read like a series of snapshots in time of this this young character's life.

JW: It got more complex after being featured on Canada Reads, especially in terms of how older cis-het white folks read the book. During book events, I often want to talk about Jonny, but audiences are really attached to his grandma and his mom. They focus on Jonny's relationship with his grandma, how accepting she is, how beautiful the relationship is, and I wonder: Are you not seeing the violence happening around him and the unabashed queer sex he's having? I've had to return to Jonny and [his friend/lover] Tias a little bit because Canada Reads took it on a different path. Canada Reads exacerbated this idea that the book is more so about relationships across generations, rather than Jonny's relationship with his own generation.

DM: Returning to *When Everything Feels Like the Movies* as inspiration for *Jonny Appleseed*: you mentioned the controversy surrounding that novel winning the Governor General's Award for Children's Literature because it contains what some critics call "explicit" sex. Young adult literature, as you know, has represented sex for decades and decades, but maybe not the kind of queer sex that we see in that book. I was curious if you have any thoughts on the role of sex and sexuality in young adult literature. Why was it important for you to write sex into your book?

JW: It was very important for me from a personal and political standpoint to represent the beauty, and the occasional violence and messiness, and also the copious fluids often involved in queer sex. As someone who was born in the late eighties, I was inundated with heterosexuality and heteronormativity and hypermasculinity. I also live within the nation state of Canada, am Indigenous, and exist in the aftermath of residential schools and their intergenerational traumas. I had to critique both settler colonialism and whiteness in all of their imperial forms, heteropatriarchy included, and then I also had to critique my own community. I had to look at the ways in which heteropatriarchy and normativity and masculinity become so toxic because they're mimicked by "the master," to use Audre Lorde's words. Given that, I'm trying to trace a lot of this homophobia, transphobia, and femmephobia within Indigenous communities back to residential schools.

In my communities, we're not always discussing how same-sex sexual assault has impacted and continues to impact what we might call queerness within Indigenous communities. This comes from very personal conversations with my father, who was a sixties scoop survivor and was abused in foster care. When I came to terms with myself as Two-Spirit, this was a difficult topic and it took me years and years to unpack everything. A lot of it revolved around my dad, and I would say a lot of Indigenous men and Indigenous communities at large. Queerness is often demonized because of unresolved large-scale historical trauma that involved the targeted killing of Two-Spirit people since the docking of colonial powers—George Catlin is a prime reference. Also, same-sex sexual assault is something that primarily Indigenous men do not want to discuss and has traumatized these communities to the point that they commit extreme lateral violence.

So, I would say my desire to write queer sex into *Jonny* came from all this. I wanted to be inclusive of queer sex for young readers because of the epidemic of Indigenous youth suicides across Turtle Island. Something that's not talked about enough is that many of these youth are identifying as queer or trans or Two-Spirit as well, and are dying in spaces where lateral violence is being enacted. A culture of toxic masculinity is actively killing Indigenous youth and Indigenous folks across this island.

We also see that in practices like MMIWG [Missing and Murdered Indigenous Women and Girls], including red dress day and all the online posts—I see many people who do not include the 2S [Two-Spirit] at the end of the acronym. So it's inclusive of women and girls, but it's not inclusive of queer youth, many of whom are trans. There's this large-scale invisibility, which is so ironic to me. It was obviously brought about by settler colonial powers, but also by Indigenous communities that have been and are continuing to fight the erasure of Indigeneity but also continue to perpetuate it against Two-Spirit, queer and trans Indigenous folks.

For all these reasons it was important for me to include queerness, queer sex, and queer acts in this book to show that Two-Spirit people are not completely relegated to the past. We're not a "was," as I always say, we're an "is" and a "coming." I also wanted to show that we can succeed and thrive and find love and kinship, and we can define and make definitions and break English, and make homes that are translatable, undefinable, that are for the self and of the self.

A lot of that was encapsulated within Jonny's unabashed queerness and his willingness to strip, both literally and literarily, inside and outside the book as a character for youth to see themselves in. It was also a way for me personally and politically to stamp my voice and body and existence into a contemporary moment and just kind of watch how Jonny unfolds.

It's so empowering and hopeful to me, particularly when I go home to Peguis, or to Fisher River, a Cree Nation which is right beside Peguis. The youth would come out and say how much they love Jonny, and thank me for making this window or mirror for them, for having this representation. Winning Canada Reads and other awards is fine and dandy, but connecting with these youth is the most important thing driving my storytelling.

DM: Hearing you speak about the hopeful impulses in *Jonny* is reminding me of *Love after the End*, your anthology of Two-Spirit and Indigiqueer speculative fiction that was your first project to follow *Jonny*. Was there something about *Jonny* that brought you to *Love after the End* specifically, or to speculative fiction more generally?

JW: Every project leads me to another. *Full-Metal* led me to *Jonny*. I was working on editing *Love after the End* when I was finishing and touring with *Jonny*. Jonny is becoming a TV show now so we're working on the screenplay for that, which is also different. It's funny to revisit him now in 2022 versus 2018.

But I have to say, again, that I don't see the differentiation between speculative fiction or young adult fiction or prose or poetry. When I was writing *Jonny* I received a lot of editorial critiques asking me to remove the quote-unquote "magical realism." And maybe if *Jonny* belongs to another genre, it's magical realism. There are bears that top him, flying eagles, tricksters, and doomsday narratives. So, the critiques that were asking me to remove these magical elements, keep this a real novel, keep it realist fiction: I have no idea what the fuck that means. I do fundamentally, but politically it didn't make sense to me to remove so many limbs from this book, to completely neuter it to the point of following the exact standard of canonical and contemporary Canadian fiction. Not something I wanted to do.

For example, there's a scene in which Jonny is kind of taking on the role of Nanabush. He's on the back of this thunderbird and they basically ride off into the apocalypse. There are many other dream sequences throughout Jonny, too. The bear scene in Banff is the number one most-requested scene at readings. A lot of these quote-unquote "dream sequences" or fantastical elements might fall in line with what Daniel Heath Justice calls "wonderworking." When people asked me to remove these real, fantastical parts—those are the most real elements in this book. I've been taught that dreams are very fundamental parts of learning and being in relation. To remove these dreams, or to classify them as fantasy or magical—that shows the limitations of what Western writing validates and sees as worthy.

Love after the End relates to Jonny in that they both represent the work that a lot of Indigenous youth, and a lot of Indigenous emerging writers who are queer, trans, or Two-Spirit, are really trying to accomplish, specifically in this global pandemic. This pandemic is also a link in the long chain of bioweaponry that's been used against Indigenous peoples. What they're doing, and what I see myself doing, is using stories to propel us towards some type of future that is unhinged from the linear timeline through which the colonial nation-state understands itself, especially as we move towards economic and ecological destruction.

DM: *Jonny* was published with Arsenal Pulp Press, an independent Canadian publisher. *Making Love with the Land*, your new book of essays, is published in the US by the University of Minnesota Press. Can you speak to your experience working with Canadian versus American presses, and if there are any major differences in the publishing landscapes between the two countries?

JW: I think it's easier for me to be seen as doing something transgressive or transformative in Canada, because our racial divides are more Indigenous versus settler, whereas in America it's more of a Black/white divide. As a writer and speaker in the United States, I've noticed that Indigeneity is more peripheral. I don't think I would have had the same impact if I were to be writing in the United States.

There are amazing queer Indigenous writers like Tommy Pico and Natalie Diaz in the US who are doing great things. But it's not in the same register, I would say, as what folks in what we now call Canada are doing, like Billy-Ray Belcourt or Arielle Twist or jaye simpson. If I were to have published in the US, I don't think *Jonny* would have had been so relevant. I feel like Indigeneity in an American context, because of the kind of political divisions, is not seen as inherently threatening and is not as visible a population. This isn't to say that this labor is not being done by Indigenous folks in the US, but I think there's more political precedent for it in Canada. As a result, with *Jonny* and *Making Love with the Land*, I think I was able to have a little bit more import, a stronger paradigm, and a more acute rhetoric around critique in Canada. And obviously that comes from the social capital that I've accumulated from these books and through kinship and relation-making and networking that I've done here in Canada. I do think I have more agency in Canada than I would have had in the US.

DM: Place is very important to *Jonny*—it's set on Treaty One territory, including urban Winnipeg and Peguis First Nation. As a quote-unquote "Canadian" writer, have you ever experienced editorial pressure to de-Canadianize or delocalize your writing? I know, too, from speaking with you as a teacher of creative writing, you often encounter students who write stories about places in the US, simply because that's what we're often exposed to in a Canadian context. What do you make of this?

JW: I'm from Manitoba originally, and now I live in Alberta—there is a large body of Canadian Prairie literature that tends to work within a specific palette. I think that was consolidated and solidified by folks like Lorna Crozier, and Margaret Laurence, who wrote *The Diviners* and *The Stone Angel*. When I was studying in Winnipeg, there was a strong push in academic and creative circles to move beyond the traditional prairie aesthetic and lexicon: the prairies all look the same, it's flatland, wheat, silos, trains, maybe there's a pond, the magpies are out. A lot of folks think it's exhausted. These are conversations that came up on two literary juries I've served over the last year.

To a lot of writers, the prairies are beautiful. There's a reason Saskatchewan is called "Land of the Living Skies." Manitoba's just known as "Friendly Manitoba," but it's true. The prairies are beautiful, grand, and also terrifying. When a lot of readers picture "prairie literature" they're likely going to imagine a little square box of a field. I felt a strong push to write about different spaces: What about the ocean, what about the mountains, or what about the woodlands? At that point I hadn't seen the ocean, I'd only seen the mountains once, and I don't fundamentally know the woodlands. I was pretty adamant about maintaining myself and my stories in the prairies. Politically, too, I want to keep Indigiqueerness visible in the prairies. I want to avoid the popular trope of queer flight—I see a lot of writers, specifically queer writers, moving to and locating their stories in Toronto or Vancouver or San Francisco or New York or Paris. To me, it's important to be queer in the prairies, to make space for myself and others who are queer and Indigenous and from the prairies. Because we've always been here, and we always will be here. It's important that we not place stakes in the colonial standard, but kiss the earth and say, "we will always be here."

DM: As a final question, are there any recommendations you might make for the children's and young adult literature fans and scholars who might be reading?

JW: I just got a wonderful picture book from Second Story Press, which I'm loving: *Phoenix Gets Greater* by Marty Wilson-Trudeau and Phoenix Wilson. It has a Two-Spirit protagonist. It's adorable; I'm excited to give it to my niece and my nephew. Billy-Ray Belcourt's *A History of My Brief Body* is a book I've been giving to a lot of youth who have been finding it quite validating. Arielle Twist's book of poetry *Disintegrate/Dissociate* also lends itself towards young adults. It has a few problems, but I would still suggest Adam Garnet Jones's *Fire Song*.

But something I believe to be the most important cultural text for Indigenous youth is [the television series] *Reservation Dogs*. I've been showing it to everyone like I'm spreading the Gospel. [Series star] Devery Jacobs is the Rezziest girl, the queerest girl ever.

DM: Thank you so much for your time and thoughtful, generous comments, Josh!

Note

1. For more on *When Everything Feels Like the Movies*, including the controversy discussed later in this interview, see Mason and Whitehead (2019).

Works Cited

Belcourt, Billy-Ray. *A History of My Brief Body*. Penguin Random House Canada, 2021.
Jones, Adam Garnet. *Fire Song*. Annick Press, 2018.
Justice, Daniel Heath. *Why Indigenous Literatures Matter*. Wilfrid Laurier UP, 2018.
Harjo, Sterlin, and Taika Waititi, creators. *Reservation Dogs*. Piki Films and Film Rites, 2021.
Kay, Barbara. "Wasted Tax Dollars on a Values-Void Novel." *The National Post*, 21 Jan. 2015, nationalpost.com/opinion/barbara-kay-wasted-tax-dollars-on-a-values-void-novel.
Mason, Derritt, and Joshua Whitehead. "When Everything Feels Like the Horror Movies: The Ghostliness of Queer Youth Futurity." *Research on Diversity in Youth Literature*, vol. 2, no. 1, 2019, article 3, http://sophia.stkate.edu/rdyl/vol2/iss1/3.
Reid, Raziel. *When Everything Feels Like the Movies*. Arsenal Pulp Press, 2014.
Twist, Arielle. *Disintegrate/Dissociate*. Arsenal Pulp Press, 2019.
Whitehead, Joshua. *Full-Metal Indigiqueer*. Talonbooks, 2017.
Whitehead, Joshua. *Jonny Appleseed*. Arsenal Pulp Press, 2018.

Whitehead, Joshua, editor. *Love after the End: An Anthology of Two-Spirit and Indigiqueer Speculative Fiction*. Arsenal Pulp Press, 2020.

Whitehead, Joshua. *Making Love with the Land*. Knopf Canada, 2022.

Wilson-Trudeau, Marty, and Phoenix Wilson. *Phoenix Gets Greater*. Illustrated by Megan Kyak-Monteith. Second Story Press, 2022.

Part II
ALT MEDIUM

YA LITERATURE, *PLUS ULTRA*
A Case Study of the Shōnen Anime *My Hero Academia*

Brandon Murakami

A quick glance for the term "anime" in the major journals for children's literature is telling: only six results appear despite the medium's undeniable staying power among young audiences since the early 2000s and the emergence of Japan's "Cool" culture.[1] Among these articles are Lisa Hager's "'Saving the World Before Bedtime'" (2007), Katarzyna Wasylak's "Need for Speed" (2010), Katharine Kittredge's "Lethal Girls Drawn for Boys" (2014), and Gwen Athene Tarbox's "Young Adult Comics and the Critics" (2017), all published in *Children's Literature Association Quarterly*, plus Catherine Butler's "Shoujo Versus Seinen?: Address and Reception in *Puella Magi Madoka Magica* (2011)" (2019) and "Japan Reads the Cotswolds" (2020) in *Children's Literature in Education* and *Children's Literature*, respectively. Of these, the essays by Wasylak, Kittredge, and Butler analyze specific series while Hager and Tarbox reference the medium of anime more in passing. And though each scholar makes significant contributions to incorporating the study of anime into the fold of children's literature,[2] their work has only scratched the surface of how anime fits into the study of children's literature and culture. This chapter suggests how the field of children's literature might benefit from greater engagement with anime by looking at an instructive example of the latter's most dominant genre: shōnen.

Granted, scholars unfamiliar with anime might be nervous about studying this medium given its apparent linguistic and cultural differences from a traditional text. But manga and anime's ever-growing presence, in both American and global media, warrants greater scholarly attention from those interested in children's and youth media, and especially as texts increasingly experienced through digital platforms and access points. For instance, Sony has recently purchased the streaming service Crunchyroll for $1.2 billion ("Sony's") while the past decade has seen other platforms (Netflix, Amazon, Hulu) not only adopt licenses but also produce anime adaptations. In another recent example, Disney commissioned several Japanese anime studios for an original anthology for one of their biggest intellectual properties: *Star Wars*. The highly anticipated project has met much acclaim, with Jake Kleinman calling it a "revelation" for its fresh reimagining of a Western franchise ("Lucasfilm's"). Shortly after the anthology's debut and numerous rave reviews, Disney also announced additional original anime projects in production for its streaming platform ("Disney Plus"). These developments underscore the accelerating appeal of one of Japan's most notable—and profitable—cultural exports of the late twentieth and early twenty-first centuries.

In what follows, I examine the anime adaptation of Horikoshi Kohei's[3] popular series, *My Hero Academia* (2014–), to showcase how the genre of shōnen can be approached as adjacent to Anglophone young adult literature especially, given the resonance in themes, tropes, and narrative conventions between the two enterprises and despite the specifics of their histories and circulation. Analyzing the richness of a singular anime series suggests how the field of children's literature might embrace the motto of *My Hero Academia* and go "*plus ultra*" with its typical objects of study. I use Horikoshi's series because the superhero trope is the most legible to an Anglophone audience.[4] The trope makes it a unique text for Japanese audiences as well (superpowers abound in shōnen stories but superheroes in the manner of the *Marvel* and *DC* tradition, less so). I address how *My Hero Academia*, if best understood within the context of the historical ebb-and-flow of Japan's and the United States' postwar relations, is nonetheless legible and enjoyable as a YA-adjacent enterprise even to audiences unfamiliar with that history. I will discuss said history while also sketching the narrative's more generic features and appeal. Put another way, this chapter affirms what Susan Napier suggests: "What is visible through anime . . . is an uncanny and fragmented collection of conditions and identities. For the Japanese viewer, these fragments may have culturally specific resonance, but they are also fragments with which any . . . viewer may empathize on a variety of levels" (293).[5]

I argue that the hero "All Might" functions as a metaphor illustrating the shifting terrain of cultural authority between the United States and Japan, and offers a critique against and solution for American-imported social policies. Thus, it is possible to read All Might's "fall" and subsequent retirement as a "professional hero" and the rise of his protégé, "Deku," as Horikoshi's own prescription for how Japan's young(er) generations should move forward amid a time of seemingly endless crises, a prescription underscoring the futurity-orientation of the shōnen genre as a whole. At the same time, the vein of social precarity—palpable in Japanese society and cultural productions, particularly since the 1990s—reveals long-lasting tensions of Japan's postwar modernity as well as the cracks of its Westernization via wholehearted embrace of postwar capitalism.

Before I turn to *My Hero Academia*, some comments about anime and shōnen more generally might be useful. The Japanese word "anime" is the shortened form of the word for animation ("animēshōn") and is applied to any form of animated medium such as television series, OVAs (original video animation), and film anime (like much of Miyazaki Hayao's oeuvre). Often, though not always, anime are adapted from successful manga ("comic," though sometimes likened to "graphic novel") series, with the anime tending to revive interest in the manga, spurring an increase in sales and attracting new fans. The most recognizable series are undoubtedly shōnen ("young boy" or "male youth"), which are intended for an audience of boys, aged twelve to eighteen. However, as Frederik L. Schodt notes, it finds wide acceptance with all ages and genders, both in and outside of Japan (14). Shōnen is not only the most voluminous of genres, outpacing sales of the other major genres of shōjo ("young girls," aged twelve to eighteen), seinen ("young men," eighteen to roughly thirty), and josei ("young women," eighteen to roughly thirty) in sales and number of ongoing and new serializations, but its characters have undoubtedly become the "face" of anime itself. For example, consider Goku from Toriyama Akira's *Dragon Ball* series (1984–), Monkey D. Luffy from Oda Eiichirō's long-running *One Piece* (1997–), the ubiquitous Pikachu from the *Pokémon* franchise (1996–), or the eponymous ninja hero from Kishimoto Masashi's *Naruto* series (1999–), just a handful of familiar names—and faces—that signal shōnen and signify the medium from which they hail.

Shōnen, I propose, is best conceived as a "genre" that extends beyond just the mediums of anime and manga and participates heavily in the "media mix." Tackling the latter term first, the media mix is, by Marc Steinberg's definition, the "cross-media serialization and circulation of entertainment franchises," which we can readily observe in the constant adaptation of series into multiple mediums—such as from manga into anime or from anime into video game—and which, he argues, emerged from the moment television anime appeared in Japan during the 1960s (viii). It is because of the media mix that anime adaptations will often reinvigorate sales of manga or light novel volumes (though the reverse is also most certainly true); the media mix keeps the most popular series constantly circulating in the "ecology" of Japan's popular culture. As for genre, Stephen Neale describes genre as a "set of expectations" (51), and John

Corner adds that genre is the "principal factor in directing of audience choice and of audience expectations" (276). That is, audiences consume certain genres *because* of the expected tropes. In the case of shōnen, then, this would partially be the reason the majority of series tend to feature action-oriented and rather formulaic plots.[6] While both scholars are writing from very different perspectives, their positions are still useful and applicable to the study of shōnen (in its various forms—anime, manga, literature, etc.), particularly because combined they help explain the historical development of shōnen's "genericity" from two interconnected sides: the industry and the audience.

Weekly Shōnen Jump (1968–) is now the largest and most widely consumed manga magazine in the industry, though this wasn't always the case. Under the direction of Nagano Tadashi, the magazine's first editor in chief, *Weekly Shōnen Jump* concretized what would become shōnen's "core aesthetic values" amidst a shifting landscape of influences both inside and outside the industry. These values[7] are yūjō ("friendship"), doryuko ("perseverance" or "effort"), and shōri ("victory") (Ōgi 80). As Jason Thompson recounts, under Nagano's direction, the magazine prioritized not only the hiring of "fresh" mangaka ("manga artists/authors") over already-established ones but also promoted series that would "give the readers what they want" and fostered the "most individualistic art styles and the most formulaic stories" at the time (338). In other words, by catering to their demographic—the young and predominately male audience—*Weekly Shōnen Jump* devised a strategy for capturing market share away from more established competitors. Over time, the dominance of its sales and popularity of its artists and series would then go on to transform shōnen into the action-packed genre we are most familiar with today. At the same time, these younger authors also incorporated trends from other, related genres: shōjo and gekiga ("dramatic pictures"). While not every shōnen series adheres to the three values, the vast majority—and of course, the most popular, financially successful, and recognizable—reflexively do.

Thus, as a result of shōnen's "genericity," narrative arcs and character development are formulaic at worst whereas novelty comes by way of the blending of multiple subgenres, which then leads to diverse and unique worlds and worldbuilding. Although the action/adventure is one of the most dominant and recognizable subgenres that resonates strongly with shōnen's core aesthetic values, the most popular series tend to mix additional subgenres with it. For example, Kishimoto Masashi's long-running *Naruto* (1999–2014) series and spin-off *Boruto: Naruto Next Generations* (2016–) mix fantasy, adventure, and (ninja) martial arts while Oda Eiichirō's even longer-running series *One Piece* (1997–) likewise mixes adventure and (pirate) fantasy. Demonstrating much more complicated mixing of subgenres are Kawahara Reki's *Sword Art Online* (2002–), which predominantly features adventure within a video game–themed isekai ("other world") as well as the slice-of-life, harem, and action, and Isayama Hajime's *Attack on Titan* (2009–2021), which is a mix of action, dark fantasy, drama, thriller, and mystery. Although audiences can readily predict how the plots tend to go based on shōnen's core values (that is, the narrative skeleton remains more or less the same), the worldbuilding via its subgenres creates the conditions for the seemingly endless novel combinations of fictional worlds and compelling stories with, admittedly, the tendency for sometimes contrived or convoluted plots.

The three core aesthetic values of shōnen formulated by *Weekly Shōnen Jump*—friendship, perseverance, and victory—resonate deeply with the futurity embedded within the genre. I refer here to Lee Edelman's conception of the "child as the obligatory token of futurity," which, given Japan's own militaristic history, echoes the promise of continuity—and thus, progress and "normativity"—both within and beyond the next generation (12). Thus, the genericity and formulaicness of shōnen make it easily "readable" as a comparative medium and genre for scholars already working with narratives targeted at/for youths—albeit in Anglocentric contexts—despite the perceived linguistic and cultural barriers. For example, consider the headstrong protagonists, the journeys of personal growth, the emphasis on friendship, and the importance of hard work and determination (or "ganbare" for the Japanese) that are all common aspects of shōnen titles. These features, while not necessarily universal, are nonetheless observable across national and linguistic contexts.

Given the prevalence of Japanese popular culture globally and the financial power of Japan's largest merchandising franchises—and indeed its varied impact on the United States' own cultural productions[8]—it follows that even a passing knowledge of anime's and shōnen's cultural contexts and formations is sufficient for analysis. In turn, this presents enormous potential for the field especially if one considers that the unintended (read: non-Japanese) audience may be just as oblivious to more specific histories and contexts. And though there is an underlying logic of perpetual self-development tied to the notion of "progress" implicated in the average shōnen series, the lesson at hand—particularly in the top-selling series—is still a relatively positive message: cherish the bonds you make with others; and if you can dream it, you can achieve it. Put another way, what encapsulates the stereotypical shōnen narrative, apart from the prolific output of innovative and engaging storylines as well as wildly imaginative worlds, is a relatively universal experience for adolescents: what it means to grow up into the world and future set before you. I now turn to *My Hero Academia* as an example for what the study of shōnen and anime—and, more specifically, shōnen anime—can bring to the field of children's and young adult literature during the twenty-first century's moment of shifting cultural and technological flows, or as Emer O'Sullivan would phrase it, the "real international world market for children's literature, media, and other products" (128).

Horikoshi's *My Hero Academia* follows the protagonist, Midoriya "Deku" Izuku, a young teenaged boy who was born into a world where 80 percent of the population has some form of superpower called a "Quirk" (though not all of them are useful). Although he is obsessed with heroes and desires to become one himself, Deku is Quirkless—that is, "normal." Despite this, Deku vows to attend the prestigious superhero course at UA high school (a play on the Japanese word for hero, "eiyū") and become Japan's number one ranked hero like his role model, Yagi "All Might" Toshinori. A chance meeting with All Might in the first episode changes Deku's destiny as he learns about the pro hero's secrets: a past encounter with a villain has severely impacted All Might's ability to use his Quirk, "One For All," and thus foreshadows the hero's imminent retirement in the near future ("What" 5:37–7:41). That same day, Deku risks his life to save his childhood-friend-turned-bully Bakugō Katsuki, despite being weak. Witnessing Deku's selfless act of heroism, particularly in contrast to others' relative inaction, convinces All Might to reveal to Deku another of his secrets: One For All is *transferable*. Thus, inspired by Deku's actions to save his friend despite being "powerless," All Might then asks Deku if he truly wants to become a professional hero, saying he will help guide the young man if so. Expectedly, Deku, overwhelmed with emotion, replies: yes.

One heavily implied meaning of All Might's character is as a metaphor for an "Americanized" Japan. That is, the hero is a metaphor for the American influence on Japanese social and economic policy, which until the 1990s did indeed "save" the nation in the postwar era from the ruins of its aggressive imperial ambitions. However, All Might's downfall—or retirement—then, is also a metaphor, if only now ironic: the "Americanization" of Japanese policies that led to a level of enviable industrial and economic prosperity also led to the bubble and burst of Japan's economy, leaving the nation in a precarious position. Although the current moment sees State policy continuing to cling on the "American" (read: neoliberal) way of doing things albeit with a Japanese slant, the suggestion Horikoshi makes with All Might as metaphor is countered with the rise of Deku as his successor, a metaphor for a "new" Japan.

Standing at a towering seven feet two inches in his "muscle form" and decked out in a red, white, and blue bodysuit and golden bracers, belts, and boots, All Might's hero costume and persona are distinctly and generically "American." Readers and audiences rarely see All Might's complete face or eyes while he is in his muscle form, as heavy shadows and lines obscure his face, which is potentially an artistic nod to the heavy shading art style of American superhero comics. As if All Might's bombastic and boisterous personality and occasional use of English ("hey," "okay," "yes," "damn it") weren't clear enough signifiers of how his time spent in the United States has shaped All Might, all his "super moves" are named for American states and cities. For instance, viewers see All Might's "Texas Smash," a punch that creates a massive amount of wind pressure forward; another punch-based attack, "Detroit Smash," is powerful enough to change the weather in the sky above. Amusingly though not unexpectedly, All Might's "ultimate move" and final move as a hero is "United States of Smash," forceful enough to create a tornado capable of carrying rubble and nearby buildings skyward. Even All Might's self-proclaimed rival, the number two ranked hero, "Endeavor," mocks All Might behind his back by calling him "that American," as a knock to All Might's tendency of being overly exuberant . . . like an American in Japan ("All for One," 13:33). Horikoshi's depiction of All Might and his over-the-top, cartoonish behavior makes it easy to read All Might as a stand-in for an American-influenced Japan while also perhaps poking fun at the American superhero tradition. At the same time, Horikoshi's caricature of an Americanesque All Might opens the way for the characteristically *more* Japanese superhero in Deku.

This possibility is made even more explicit when one considers All Might spent time in America specifically to become stronger to avenge the death of his mentor and previous holder of One For All, Shimura Nana. Conveyed in one of their early exchanges, and part of the reason Shimura selects All Might as her successor, is his understanding of the average person's anxiety despite the presence of professional heroes. The then middle-school-aged All Might explains, "The reason crime in this country isn't decreasing is that the citizens have no support," and he proclaims he will "become that pillar" of justice despite being Quirkless himself ("One," 0:17–0:28). Part of All Might's modus operandi is to create "a world where everyone can smile and live together ("One" 0:08–09), which is not possible when everyone "looked uneasy. No matter how many heroes there were, the number of crimes never went down. . . . [E]veryone was afraid" ("Win" 17:31–44). Here, perhaps, is a comment on the state of Japan's citizens in the immediate aftermath of World War II—dispirited and impoverished, the future grim and seemingly hopeless without the "intervention" of the United States.

Thus, it is telling All Might can effect change in society only after returning from America and donning a heavily America-motifed hero persona and costume, establishing both an era of peace and himself as its personification. Reading this moment between Shimura and All Might with the influence of American policy and culture on a postwar Japan in mind, Horikoshi's figuring of All Might as *the* American-influenced Japanese citizen nods toward the role of the United States in Japan's "miraculous" recovery and "reintegration." It also reifies the futurity of youth between generations—Shimura's and All Might's and All Might's and Deku's. Progress moves ever forward.

Yet, this is not a whole-hearted and uncritical embrace Japan's Americanization. All Might's retirement is inevitable, necessitated, and expected given the narrative's focus on Deku and its critique of the damage Americanesque economic and sociopolitical policies have inadvertently caused to Japanese society. Additionally, the rise of villain organizations and crime following the end of All Might's career ironically mirrors the social anxieties of real-world Japan although the issues at heart are never addressed directly: Why, we might wonder, would people (ab)use their Quirks and turn to a life of crime? And how do Japan's social insecurities and precarities—at once contemporary and ongoing—register, however subtly, in Horikoshi's worldbuilding?

Writing on economic and social precarity in contemporary Japan, Anne Allison notes how "hopelessness and futurelessness are buzzwords of the time" (346). This is ultimately tied to the paring away of Japan's social safety net policies (via neoliberalism of the 1970s and 1980s) and the prioritization of the older generations' employment over freshly graduated students and young workers in the aftermath of Japan's asset price bubble burst in 1992, which resulted in the first—but certainly not the last—"Lost Generation" (Itoh 247). Despite the growth of Japan's cultural industries abroad during this time, economic insecurity continued to rock the nation with the Asian Financial Crisis of 1997, the global "Great Recession" of 2008, and the 3/11 disasters, all of which exasperated Japan's citizens' general sense of security. Moreover, the larger impact of the COVID-19 pandemic remains to be seen. Yet rather than shifting away from these policies of precarity, curiously, as Suzuki Takaaki finds, Japan has further entrenched itself in pursuing and enacting them at both state and local levels, endangering the oldest as well as upcoming generations (151). Thus, if All Might represents an American-influenced Japan, then All Might's inevitable failure to continue as a hero can be read as evidencing how the adoption of Americanesque social and economic policies fueled both Japan's miraculous recovery and its now decades-long period of precarity.[9]

This reading is also supported by the commentary made by two (unnamed) police officials following All Might's public retirement and his victory over his archnemesis, the supervillain "All For One." The first notes that with "All Might's weakened body [being] exposed to the world . . . there is no longer a Symbol of Peace that will never be defeated. Not for the citizens, or for the villains," to which the other comments, "That's what happens when we rely on one person," and concludes, "Something must change" ("End" 2:30–3:38). On one level, this barb at relying on All Might alone to uphold the mantle of Japan's Symbol of Peace can be read as a critique of both the rampant individualism of American culture and neoliberal policy in Japan: "jiko sekinin," quite literally, "self-responsibility" (Allison 346). On another level, what this "change" might look like is unprecedented given All Might's impact on transforming Japan into a nation of justice and peace, if only during his tenure as the number one superhero. The hesitancy and uncertainty of what *must* change for the police officials in *My Hero Academia* mirrors—perhaps unintentionally—the entrenchment of neoliberal policies even now, despite its long-noted negative and quite palpable impact on real-world Japan's own future.

Although the current government continues to struggle with staving off the literal decaying of Japan's futurity, most pressingly in the continuously falling birth rates, Horikoshi's series invokes a potential embodying UA's school motto, "*plus ultra.*" Invoked numerous times throughout the series as a catchphrase to remind everyone—pro heroes, students, and even the public alike—to extend themselves beyond their limits, we can read the transformation of Deku's character from the timid and Quirkless "crybaby" to someone who becomes Horikoshi's model for Japan's next generation. In other words, Japan must acknowledge and must also go "further beyond" the limits of the current "adult" generation. Deku himself goes from ordinary citizen to extraordinary hero and is the idealized model for a new kind of Japanese citizen by learning from the mistakes of his predecessors and still paving his own path even though Deku is quite literally unable to succeed without the power granted to him by All Might in the first place. Thus, Deku becomes quite an explicit metaphor for the futurity of the next generation just as much as we might read All Might as the *then*-future generation of youth in the aftermath of World War II. But the significance here is that Deku both grows into this inherited strength and also appropriates it in ways more fitting his body's capabilities.

This appropriation goes hand in hand with Deku's own realizations and with the careful nurturing by his mentors and teachers, most notably, All Might. Even in the earliest episodes, All Might recognizes what Deku physically can and cannot do and encourages the teen to find the answer for himself. In doing so, Deku realizes it is his admiration for All Might—to be "just like" his hero/role model—that ironically limits his ability to control and use One For All. His need to emulate All Might (beyond just copying attacks) acts as a "shackle" ("Bizarre!" 7:32). Faced with the challenge of developing his own special move, All Might chides his student, "You're still trying to imitate me" ("Create" 10:21–24) until Deku understands his own flaw: "Since I inherited One For All, I thought I should also do the same and decided that without realizing it" ("Create," 21:20–28). With this insight, Deku develops his own fighting style and is able to own One For All's power in a novel manner. Deku's development from student to burgeoning student-hero does two things. First, it humanizes All Might (who, indeed, is quite the approachable hero to his fans). Secondly, with the metaphor of All Might as an "Americanized Japan," it acknowledges the necessity of that influence—historically—but also affirms that it is time to move forward and appropriate only what is necessary for the future rather than accepting things as they are. In the case of Deku's early usage of One For All, then, we might read this as a metaphor for how truly damaging the Americanized policies have been to the (social) body given how the Quirk, quite literally, destroys his body upon use.

In later seasons, Deku is also able to tap into even greater powers—the Quirks of previous holders of One For All—which were unavailable to All Might. This development also suggests how the Quirk's return to a more Japanese-minded character (Deku) unlocks the fullest potential of One For All rather than solely the "brute force" of (the appropriately named) All Might. Thus, Deku's ability to control his Quirk in ways that differ from All Might's usage reinforces the weight of responsibility he now bears and marks a distinct shift as holder of One For All. Deku's inheritance is multiple: the Quirk itself, but also the world of peace and justice that is slowly eroding sans the pro hero All Might. In turn, Deku diverges from doing things like All Might not only in Quirk usage but also in relying more heavily on teamwork—something the series, as a whole, increasingly emphasizes in later seasons among both the student heroes and the pros. Fitting, then, are Deku's words in the closing scene of the fourth season. Watching Endeavor's victory over a bioengineered monster-villain known as "Nomu," Deku reinforces with his closing line the inevitable futurity awaiting his generation: "heroes cannot stop moving forward" ("His," 20:07–20:24).[10]

Even if the future belongs to—or is thrust into the laps of—Deku's generation, this does not mean that they face it alone and without support or guidance from the older generations. Indeed, while All Might's retirement signaled a shift in the battle between "good and evil," the other pro heroes have (to varying extents) stepped out of All Might's shadow to ensure some sense of social stability, despite the public's growing mistrust in the system. At the same time, these professional heroes continue to guide and shape the next generation through internship and work studies programs as part of their education at UA. Endeavor is perhaps the best representative of this ethic, taking on a much larger role in the later seasons of *My Hero Academia*, and thus providing an interesting Japanese counterpoint to All Might's "American" hero. Although this juxtaposition goes beyond the scope of this chapter, Endeavor's redemption arc (for his past emotional and physical abuse of his family) acknowledges how Japan's current adults still have the power to both rectify past mistakes and enact positive change for the future. (As an aside, Endeavor very much fits into the "career-obsessed" and "neglectful" father figure common in shōnen narratives.) In a real-world sense, this positive change might come in more progressive social policies and policy reform to counter the deeply embedded neoliberalism and meritocracy of twenty-first-century Japan.

My Hero Academia is like many of the most acclaimed and popular shōnen series for its emotional complexity and themes that resonate universally with its young(er) audiences. While I have suggested one reading of Horikoshi's series that maps onto a longer historical-cultural phenomenon, even without this background knowledge of Japan's social crisis, *My Hero Academia* can still be appreciated as a powerful story of an underdog determined to make the world a better place. While I advocate for the inclusion of the anime medium and the shōnen genre in the category of children's literature, I also extend this call-to-attention to the closely related medium of manga and the genre of shōjo. It is my hope that the field of children's and young adult literature becomes more invested in studying the mediums as well as narratives that have increasingly captivated the hearts and minds of young people today, regardless of origin country. What might children's literature look like once it includes anime and shōnen series in its range? How might such forms and mediums be embraced in the future and even *as* the future for the field? I hope this chapter inspires children's literature scholars to go *plus ultra*.

Notes

1. The term, "Cool Japan," can be attributed to Douglas McGray in his 2002 article, "Japan's Gross National Cool."

2. Admittedly, manga has had more success. Bettina Kümmerling-Meibauer's 2013 chapter "Manga/Comics Hybrids in Picturebooks" is one notable example of interdisciplinary work, although she admits that such scholarship is "in its early stages" (116).

3. I follow the typical naming conventions for Japanese authors within this chapter: family name, given name.

4. The scholarship in English on *My Hero Academia* is limited to an article by Ronald Lorenzo about how blood and hair are "sacred objects" and linked to superpowers, and a master's thesis and bachelor's thesis taking thematic approaches (Waller and Suvanto respectively). Published during this collection's production, Alek Sigley's 2021 *Mechademia* article, "Next It's Japan's Turn," offers a similar reading of seeing the United States and Japan embodied within the characters I examine here, though Sigley's focus is more on nation and gender in the manga than the anime.

5. In contrast, Jaqueline Berndt and Bettina Kümmerling-Meibauer emphasize that to "approach manga in a truly scholarly way" a multitude of things are needed, such as "knowledge about Japan . . . comics theory . . . [and] interdisciplinary methodological adeptness" (2). Yet, as I show in this chapter and within the context of the *lack* of scholarship on shōnen narratives and on anime within the fields and intersections of children's literature and anime studies, perhaps what is needed is less an encyclopedic knowledge and more a willingness to explore the vast world of shōnen manga and anime.

6. Curiously, it has received relatively little attention despite its ubiquity, unlike the shōjo genre or boys' love manga.

7. The origins of these values with Japan's social context are debated by scholars. Jean-Marie Bouissou argues that Japan's specific historical-cultural "trauma of defeat" (25) after World War II has dramatically impacted the manga tradition—and relatedly, all Japanese media, while Richard Reitan traces the rise of neoliberalism and cultural neoconservatism in Japan and its impact on the contemporary Japanese culture broadly, especially in the nation's recovery of its "traditional" values for a modern, postwar society (43; 55).

8. For example, consider Kathryn Hemmann's *Manga Cultures and the Female Gaze* (2020), which notes the impact of shōjo on American cartoons.

9. Recent developments in the manga reveal a new hero, "Star and Stripe," that consciously plays on aggressive American geopolitical policy in the form of her appropriately named Quirk, "New Order."

10. At time of writing the sixth season had yet to air.

Works Cited

Allison, Anne. "Ordinary Refugees: Social Precarity and Soul in 21st Century Japan." *Anthropological Quarterly*, vol. 85, no. 2, spring 2012, pp. 345–70.
Berndt, Jacqueline, and Bettina Kümmerling-Meibauer. "Introduction: Studying Manga Across Cultures." *Manga's Cultural Crossroads*, edited by Berndt and Kümmerling-Meibauer, Routledge, 2013, pp. 1–15.
Bouissou, Jean-Marie. "Manga: A Historical Overview." *Manga: An Anthology of Global and Cultural Perspectives*, edited by Toni Johnson-Woods, Continuum International Publishing Group, 2010, pp. 17–33.
Butler, Catherine. "Japan Reads the Cotswolds: Children's Literature, Tourism, and the Japanese Imagination." *Children's Literature*, vol. 48, 2020, pp. 198–233.
Butler, Catherine. "Shoujo versus Seinen? Address and Reception in *Puella Magi Madoka Magica* (2011)." *Children's Literature in Education*, vol. 50, 2019, pp. 400–416.
Corner, John. "Meaning, Genre and Context: The Problematics of 'Public Knowledge' in the New Audience Studies." *Mass Media and* Society, edited by James Curran and Michael Gurevitch, Edward Arnold, 1991, pp. 267–84.
Edelman, Lee. *No Future: Queer Theory and the Death Drive*. Duke UP, 2004.
Hager, Lisa. "'Saving the World Before Bedtime': The Powerpuff Girls, Citizenship, and the Little Girl Superhero." *Children's Literature Association Quarterly*, vol. 33, no. 1, spring 2008, pp. 62–78.

Hemmann, Kathryn. *Manga Cultures and the Female Gaze*. Palgrave Macmillan, 2020.
Horikoshi Kōhei. "All For One." *My Hero Academia*, season 3, episode 9, TBS, 2 June 2018.
Horikoshi Kōhei. "Bizarre! Gran Torino Appears." *My Hero Academia*, season 2, episode 14, TBS, 8 July 2017.
Horikoshi Kōhei. "Create Those Ultimate Moves." *My Hero Academia*, season 3, episode 14, TBS, 14 July 2018.
Horikoshi Kōhei. "End of the Beginning, Beginning of the End." *My Hero Academia*, season 3, episode 12, TBS, 23 June 2017.
Horikoshi Kōhei. "His Start." *My Hero Academia*, season 4, episode 25, TBS, 4 Apr. 2020
Horikoshi Kōhei. *My Hero Academia*. Weekly Shōnen Jump, 7 July 2014–.
Horikoshi Kōhei. "One For All." *My Hero Academia*, season 3, episode 11, TBS, 16 June 2018.
Horikoshi Kōhei. "What It Takes to Be a Hero." *My Hero Academia*, season 1, episode 2, TBS, 10 Apr. 2016.
Horikoshi Kōhei. "Win Those Kids' Hearts." *My Hero Academia*, season 4, episode 16, TBS, 1 Feb. 2020.
I. A., Alexander. "Disney Plus Announces Four Anime Projects Coming to Its Platform—Including Twisted Wonderland." *OmniGeekEmpire*, 14 Oct. 2021, omnigeekempire.com/2021/10/14/disney-plus-announces-four-anime-projects-coming-to-its-platform-including-twisted-wonderland. Accessed 20 Nov. 2021.
Itoh, Makoto. "Assessing Neoliberalism in Japan." *Neoliberalism: A Critical Reader*, edited by Alfredo Saad-Filho and Deborah Johnston, Pluto Press, 2005, pp. 244–50.
Kittredge, Katharine. "Lethal Girls Drawn for Boys: Girl Assassins in Manga/Anime and Comics/Film." *Children's Literature Association Quarterly*, vol. 39, no. 4, Winter 2014, pp. 506–32.
Kleinman, Jake. "*Star Wars: Visions* Is Lucasfilm's Best New Story Since the Original Trilogy." *Inverse*, 21 Sept. 2021, inverse.com/entertainment/star-wars-visions-review. Accessed 19 Oct. 2021.
Kümmerling-Meibauer, Bettina. "Manga/Comics Hybrids in Picturebooks." *Manga's Cultural Crossroads*, edited by Jaqueline Berndt and Kümmerling-Meibauer, Routledge, 2013, pp. 100–120.
Lorenzo, Ronald. "*My Hero Academia* and Durkheim: A Case Study of Blood and Hair as 'Sacred' Objects in a Japanese Anime Television Series." *The Phoenix Papers*, vol. 4, no. 1, Aug. 2018, pp. 93–101.
McGray, Douglas. "Japan's Gross National Cool." *Foreign Policy*, no. 130, May–June 2002, pp. 44–54.
Napier, Susan. *Anime from Akira to Howl's Moving Castle*. 2nd ed., Palgrave Macmillan, 2005.
Neale, Stephen. *Genre*. British Film Institute, 1980.
Ōgi, Fusami. "*Barefoot Gen* and *Maus*: Performing the Masculine, Reconstructing the Mother." *Reading Manga: Local and Global Perceptions of Japanese Comics*, edited by Jaqueline Berndt and Steffi Richter, Leipziger Universitätsverlag, 2006, pp. 80–91.
O'Sullivan, Emer. *Comparative Children's Literature*. Routledge, 2005.
Reitan, Richard. "Narratives of 'Equivalence': Neoliberalism in Contemporary Japan." *Radical History Review*, no. 112, winter 2012, pp. 43–64.
Schodt, Frederik L. *Dreamland Japan: Writings on Modern Manga*. Stone Bridge, 2007.
Sigley, Alek. "Next It's Japan's Turn: Nation and Otaku Masculinity in *My Hero Academia*." *Mechademia*, vol. 14, no. 2, spring 2022, pp. 77–98.
"Sony's Funimation Global Group Completes Acquisition of Crunchyroll from AT&T." Press Release. *Sony Pictures*, 9 Aug. 2021.
Steinberg, Marc. *Anime's Media Mix: Franchising Toys and Characters in Japan*. U of Minnesota P, 2012.
Suvanto, Marttaleena. *Applying MBTI to Analyzing Shōnen Manga Characters*. 2021. Dalarna U, Bachelor's thesis.

Suzuki, Takaaki. "After Neoliberalism? The Curious Non-Death of Neoliberalism in Japan." *Asian Journal of Social Science*, vol. 43, no. 1/2, 2015, pp. 151–77.

Tarbox, Gwen Athene. "Young Adult Comics and the Critics: A Call for New Modes of Interdisciplinary Close Reading." *Children's Literature Association Quarterly*, vol. 42, no. 2, summer 2017, pp. 231–43.

Thompson, Jason. *Manga: The Complete Guide*. Del Rey Books, 2007.

Waller, Jerry. *The World's Greatest Hero: An Examination of Superhero Tropes in* My Hero Academia. 2020. U of San Francisco, master's thesis.

Wasylak, Katarzyna. "Need for Speed: Anime, the Cinematic, and the Philosophical." *Children's Literature Association Quarterly*, vol. 35, no. 4, winter 2010, pp. 427–34.

FROM MELODRAMA TO KITSCHY ROMANCE
Alt Kid Media in India and Pakistan

Tehmina Pirzada

The limited programming for children in the Indian subcontinent in the 1970s changed considerably in the 1980s and 1990s as children became viable consumers and participants in the nation-building project. The Indian Doordarshan introduced a range of television shows— *Malgudi Days* (1986), *Vikraam Aur Betaal* (1985), *Ghayab Aaya* (1986), *Shaktimaan* (1997), and *Hum Paanch* (1995)—that were either dramatic adaptations of Anglo-American programs such as *Superman* (1952) and *Casper* (1996) or social dramas centering the lives of children in the Indian household. The purpose of these shows was to counter the foreign televisual content and to offer alternatives to shows such as *Dennis the Menace* (1959), *Sesame Street* (1969), *Pumpkin Patch* (1988), and *Rimba's Island* (1994) that catered principally to children with exposure to English, thereby reiterating the language divide(s) that haunt postcolonial India and Pakistan to this day.[1]

This language divide also draws attention to the trajectory of children's media in the Indian subcontinent, which tends to fall into one of two paradigms. The first, a stridently protectionist view, sees most "Western" media products as dangerous and negatively affecting "Indian" ethics and culture and hence children. The second views all developments as good because they somehow make India feel more "modern" and economically competitive, thus giving advertisers or ideologues a larger market (Banaji, *South Asian Media Cultures* 15). Though India's children's media output superseded Pakistan's, the desire to produce national content for children was a challenge for both countries. To offer children's televisual content in Hindi and other local languages, in the 1980s and '90s, India's Doordarshan channel also broadcast singing competitions, dance shows, and quiz shows—formulaic imitations of successful adult content recreated for children—valued primarily for the revenue they generated through advertising. Following India's example, Pakistan's well-known puppeteer Farooq Qaiser created the long-running *Kaliyaan* (1976), starring the beloved puppet Uncle Sargam, with the goal of introducing Pakistani children to the "correct" Urdu diction along with street humor, famous quotes, and informal moral training (Iftikhar). However, what boosted children's media in the Indian subcontinent were conceptually ambitious shows such as *Alif Laila* (1993), based on *One Thousand and One Nights*, and the ingenious Pakistani *Ainak Wala Jinn* (*The Genie with Spectacles*; 1993), created with the aim of providing children distinctly local content.

My chapter examines these two pioneering media texts as alt kid media with respect to their televisual histories, generic conventions, and use of indigenous tropes. These shows offer an alternative to Western children's media even as they provide insight into their respective national contexts and shared situation in postcolonial South Asia. Their handling of gender, sexuality, and other "adult" topics situate *Alif Laila* and *Ainak Wala Jinn* as both children's media and *not* children's media. *Alif Laila* and *Ainak Wala Jinn* resist adult-child stratification, and that resistance is rooted within the socioeconomic contexts in which the shows were initially broadcast.

Ramanand Sagar's *Alif Laila* was released by Doordarshan at a time when the economic liberalization of India had just begun, resulting in the privatization of government institutions and assets (including TV channels), followed by an unprecedented desire in the common public to participate in a globalized economy through consumption. This gradual "opening up" of the Indian economy not only paved the way for the subsequent privatization of TV channels but also brought an end to the monopoly of the state-run Doordarshan. However, at the time of *Alif Laila*'s release, the new profit-driven media had just started recognizing the child as a strong consumer, moving away from the pedagogically focused children's media output of the 1970s (Kini). As a result, there was a lot of experimentation with TV shows to see what forms of media would resonate with Indian children and subsequently garner more viewership. *Alif Laila* was therefore an attempt to solicit this presumed child viewer through the *Alif Laila* stories that were already well-known within India's oral culture. However, broadcasting these stories for children was unique in the 1990s because until 2003 only 5 percent of the programming in India directly addressed children (Sibii 401). In fact, children mostly watched the programs enjoyed by their adult family members. In addition, Indian programming often underplayed parental advisory warnings or enforced them inconsistently, further reinforcing the alt kid status of children's media in India.

Shakuntala Banaji contends that "so little has been made of the child audience in India [that] there is no known body with oversight of—or responsibility for rating—output available to children on television" (*Children and Media* 52). As a result, the child TV audience in India emerged as a culturally constructed phenomenon, a consequence of adult anxieties about how content for children should be curated, managed, and distributed.

In Pakistan, *Ainak Wala Jinn* was broadcast to counter the Indian "cultural invasion" by offering the child viewer a distinctly Pakistani show (Kazi 37). Shot mostly in Lahore, one of the largest cities of Punjab, *Ainak Wala Jinn* focused on an array of landmarks (both geographical and ideological) to emphasize the philosophy of Pakistan, rooted in the historic struggle and desire of South Asian Muslims for a separate homeland. This philosophy is reiterated through the show's cultural allusions and references to the country's founding fathers, patriotic songs, and celebrations as well as through filming locations such as Minar-e-Pakistan, reinforcing Pakistan's separate identity from India for the benefit of the child-viewer. However, the show also implicitly acknowledges the staggering economic and political challenges that Pakistan faced in the early nineties and its geopolitical precarity in the aftermath of the Cold War. As a result, *Ainak Wala Jinn* does not eschew discussions of poverty, unemployment, street theft, and injustice, repeatedly foregrounding the difficulty of leading an upstanding life in a fragile democracy. In fact, *Ainak Wala Jinn's* social concerns resonate with the apprehensions of the show's writer, Abdul Hameed, a romantic author disillusioned with the postpartition reality of Pakistan.

The generic ambiguity of *Alif Laila* and *Ainak Wala Jinn* also indicates the adult anxieties surrounding a rapidly transitioning Indian subcontinent in which globalization, economic liberalization, Western hegemony, and ethnoreligious polarity were transforming the social fabric as well as spotlighting the role of women, children, and minorities. Derritt Mason argues that "adult anxieties" about identity, power, and control are edging out childhood fantasies in contemporary young adult literature, replacing them with a moral perfectionism that persistently reimagines the "ideal" young person (11). This adult anxiety similarly manifests itself in the shows I consider, through conventionally celebrated representations of gender, sexuality, and community and through critique of deeply held religious, gender, and communal beliefs. Those elements contribute to the shows' "alt" sensibility. So, too, do the genres to which they belong and in which they operate—melodrama in *Alif Laila* and kitschy romance in *Ainak Wala Jinn*. In effect, these shows became established children's media through their many dimensions of alterity.

Televisual Histories

Alif Laila aired from 1993 to 1997 and was directed by the maestro Ramanand Sagar, introducing a brand-new cast of several hundred using Sagar's trademark style of elaborate costumes, numerous characters, supporting extras, and special effect teams (Munshi 284). The show told the story of the vengeful King Shahryār, who was committed to punishing women for their infidelity through daily executions. Enter Scheherazade, the pious but shrewd daughter of the wise Vizier. Scheherazade has the novel idea to tell the King (and by proxy the audience) magical tales every night to deter violence. As a result, Scheherazade and her entertaining *qissas* (short vignettes) become odes to the lasting power of storytelling. By drawing on Arabo-Islamic mythology executed through larger-than-life characters, prosthetics, and special effects, *Alif Laila*'s visual repertoire formulaically imitated the success of Sagar's earlier blockbuster *Ramayan*. Based on its namesake Sanskrit epic, *Ramayan* the show claimed a viewership of seventy-seven million—the largest viewership to date in the history of Indian television (Pathak). The "core" story of the *Ramayan* and its adaptations through comics, picture books, and graphic novels continues to dominate the Indian children's literature market, which reworks it both as religious pedagogy and also globalized entertainment.[2] With *Alif Laila*, Sagar's goal was to recreate a similar saga, with a focus on godly royal courts, rich costumes, lush forests, ferocious battle scenes, and universal morality imparted through saints and sages, but for a younger audience. However, unlike *Ramayan*, which was framed as "mythological," *Alif Laila* was based on Muslim subjects and labeled "historical" or "quasi-historical" to distinguish it from Hindu mythological shows, thereby creating two distinct/contested repositories for Indian popular culture (Rajagopal 95). Through these shows, Indian children were encouraged to develop a penchant for morally upstanding adult characters and cultivate "family values" celebrated through virtues of obedience, respect, and tradition (Banaji, *Children and Media* 85).

Released in the same year as *Alif Laila* was Pakistan's *Ainak Wala Jinn*. Like its Indian counterpart, it attained a massive viewership in a short time, airing on Pakistan's state-run television channel (PTV) from 1993 to 1996 for a total of 151 episodes. Created with a much smaller budget and a little-known cast, *Ainak Wala Jinn* attained a fan following propagated further by its theatrical adaptations and reenactments at children's fairs and high-profile charity functions and by its use as a form of trauma therapy for the 2005 earthquake victims in Kashmir (Alam). Written by the renowned Urdu writer Abdul Hameed and directed by veteran director Hafeez Tahir, *Ainak Wala Jinn* tells the story of the *jinn* Nastoor, who is exiled from Koh-i-Qaf (a mysterious Middle Eastern Mountain that is home to the *jinns*) and ends up in Pakistan. As repeatedly alluded to in the show, the mountains are considered part of Islamic mythology. Though they are not explicitly mentioned in the Qur'an, these mountains are often described in hadiths and in numerous tales of the pre-Islamic prophets (Lebling 95). Exiled after being harassed in Koh-i-Qaf because of his visual disability, Nastoor befriends the compassionate and intelligent Imran, who saves Nastoor by taking him to an eye doctor and getting him fitted with eyeglasses. Thus begins a series of adventures wherein Imran and Nastoor, along with Zakoota *jinn* and Sona Pari (the golden fairy), fight magicians, robbers, aliens, and other evil forces to protect Pakistanis.

Through its engaging dialogue and perfect comic timing, *Ainak Wala Jinn* celebrated Pakistani cultures and languages, thereby aligning itself with the linguistic goals of the creators and writers of Pakistani children's literature and their commitment to forge a Pakistani identity through their writings. Raees Ahmed Mughal contends that the 1990s was an era for the "reconstruction of [Pakistani] children's literature" (13): pro-Islamic messaging endorsed by magazines such as *Aankh Micholy* (*Hide and Seek*), *Taleem o Tarbiat* (*Education and Enrichment*), *Phool* (*Flower*), and others had become seriously committed to "providing quality content in the Urdu language" and the need to engage with scientific, ethical, and philosophical concepts in a conservative Muslim society (Mughal 14). Therefore, Abdul Hameed's script of *Ainak Wala Jinn* aligned with the goal of inculcating strong moral and religious values in young children to ensure the show's visibility and commercial success.

Both *Alif Laila* and *Ainak Wala Jinn* were marketed as children's shows and remain quite popular, with fans celebrating the shows through dedicated fan pages that include photos, interviews with cast members, and viewers' comments as well as fan-created adaptations of the shows. As a matter of fact, during the 2020 COVID-19 lockdown, *Alif Laila* was telecast on repeat on Doordarshan and procured a record viewership within a span of days (Bharati), while *Ainak Wala Jinn* has repeatedly returned to Pakistani TV channels on special occasions such as Eid because of fervent public demand (Ahmad). Despite their fan following, no academic scholarship on the televisual histories of the Indian subcontinent examines their positionality as (alt) children's media with lasting appeal.

Generic Conventions

Sagar's rendition of *Alif Laila* features "melodrama as a significant purveyor of changing attitudes and cultural norms" that within the context of Indian media emerges through a "tragic construction of emotion" (Ang 61), thereby defying easy categorization. In fact, in *Alif Laila* the stirred-up emotions generate empathy for Scheherazade's precarious position but also enable her to tell stories with viable lessons about justice, identity, love, infidelity, and tolerance.

In the case of *Alif Laila*, the genre of melodrama aligns with the construction of a highly charged emotional situation caused by the unjust actions of an otherwise bold and just leader, Shahryār, and the creative virtuosity of Scheherazade in deterring the violence against young women and girls by risking her own life. As a result, Scheherazade's story makes a sensational appeal to its young viewers in addition to creating a space for the display of intense emotions, which is considered a defining characteristic of melodrama. Moreover, as Jostein Gripsrud contends, the overt display of emotions in melodrama is often accentuated through pan shots, loud music, and the symbolic usage of sounds such as those of thunder, rain, and howling winds that relate to the internal strife of the character (84), thereby employing the stirred-up emotions to generate creative "disorder . . . without solving or finishing anything" (Barthes 76). This unfinished quality in *Alif Laila* is reasserted through loud drums and cymbals along with full face shots when the characters, particularly Scheherazade, are in any danger, which in turn enables both adults and young children to engage with the show and empathize with the characters aurally as well as visually.

It is worth noting that the contentious categorization of *Alif Laila* as children's media raises questions about its history, content, and viewership. Some opinions affirm that *Alif Laila* is of Arab origin, other scholars say that many of the tales are of Indian origin, and some maintain it is Persian. As a result, the origins of these stories remain a field of argument and contention (Wazzan 62). However, *Alif Laila* began circulation as "oriental tales for didactic purposes" in the late eighteenth century in Europe, after its translation by Antoine Galland was deemed "more suitable for European tastes," deconstructing for the West "the mysteries of the East" (Wazzan 64). The tales were also recommended by Alexander Pope as suitable for children. Subsequently, Richard Johnson published a children's anthology including tales such as "Aladdin," "Sindbad the Sailor," "The Merchant and his Wife," and a few others, which became very popular with children (Marzolph and Leeuwen 521). Though these abridged renditions were heavily sanitized and censored, their content was "calculated to both amuse and improve the minds of the youth," resulting in their increased circulation (521). From Great Britain, the *Alif Laila* tales once again returned to India, with Naval Kishore Press offering popular Hindi translations of *Alif Laila* in 1876 (Stark 269). This generic and linguistic fluidity of the tales informs Sagar's adaptation, highlighting the creative but uneasy position of *Alif Laila* within world literatures.

Since a children's show the scale of *Alif Laila* with its adult-centric format was a novelty on the state-run Doordarshan, *Alif Laila* opens with a parental preface that establishes its suitability and legitimacy through a direct address to the audience. The powerful male voice of an omniscient narrator alludes to the show's relevance for children, and the musical score features an interesting interplay of Indian musical instruments such as tabla, sitar, and sarangi, mixed with the Arabic oud. This creates an atmosphere of magic and whimsicality, supporting the "timelessness" of the *Alif Laila* as declared by the narrator:

> *Alif Laila*, written in Arabic, is a classic. Its appeal lies in its timelessness as the stories never get old. In fact, the lessons that the stories offer are universal, emphasizing that behind the curtain of fantasy is the philosophy of life. *Alif Laila* teaches how humans should live in different circumstances . . . how they should love other humans and believe in Allah and Bhagvan. . . . While the tales encourage children to immerse themselves in creativity through flying horses and bottled genies, they also teach emotions such as bravery to prove that mankind is indeed God's greatest creation. (my trans.; "Episode 1")

This didactic prelude then segues into King Shahryār's melodramatic frame story with its interplay of sexual desire, revenge, and heightened emotion that may seem misplaced in a children's show. In fact, the prelude features the beheading of a young woman ordered by Shahryār, evoking pathos and distress for the viewers. While the scene does not explicitly show blood and gore, the scene's presence in a children's TV show (without any parental advisory label or warning) may seem shocking, especially to non-Western audiences. The show's engagement with femicide, sexual desire, and sexual identity is radical as it directly engages children, highlighting the crucial need to normalize discussions of sexuality in a conservative society as well as cautioning against gender-based violence. This candid engagement is particularly interesting in the context of India, where no formal sex education is offered in schools, and it is often difficult to articulate the difference between formal and structured sex education and nonformal, informal, and incidental sex learning. While discussing sexuality in relation to Indian media, Banaji contends that "as sex education for children in formal schooling as well as speaking seriously about the subject in front of adults remains a serious taboo it forces children to acquire knowledge about sex and sexuality through older peers, television, magazines, or selectively through the internet with their access [chiefly related] . . . to their social class" (*South Asian Media Cultures* 65). Furthermore, many of the children's stories adapted from oral narratives focus on procreation as well as pleasure, revealing how oral literatures such as *Alif Laila* are deployed to share sexual knowledge.

Though *Alif Laila's* focus on sexuality is adult-centric and unabashed, it is also deeply gendered and mostly prescribes traditional gender roles—girls as good daughters and homemakers and boys as breadwinners, travelers, and adventurers. Purnima Mankekar points out that, in Doordarshan dramas, the good daughters always defer to the expectations of the patriarchal household (118). Scheherazade and her sister Dunyazad are portrayed as powerful young girls, but it is their primary role as dutiful daughters and wives that is repeatedly celebrated. Within the confines of this domestic existence, these girls are sexual and sexually desirable as iterated through Scheherazade's assertion of her "rights in the conjugal bed," her desire "to please and entertain the King" (my trans.; Episode 1), and the visual eroticism that she exudes through her visual and haptic performances: lounging in silken wear, massaging the King's feet, cradling his head, and soothing the King. Interestingly, the show's reviewers rarely question this performance of heteronormative sexuality though the primary audience is presumably children. In fact, the focus on compliant female sexuality in a children's show iterates that "sexuality in children's texts is both specific and diffuse, at once a physical reality and a polyvalent social form [that is] to a degree an adult construction/projection" (Kidd v).

Though female sexuality in *Alif Laila* is framed as caregiving extended to boys and men, the show builds empathy for its female characters by recognizing the endemic violence against them. The show does not refrain from portraying Scheherazade's repeated encounters with the executioner, her dignity in the face of imminent death, and her poignant celebration of women's intellect and courage. Scheherazade's portrayal ties to the depiction of the long-suffering daughters triumphing over their trials and tribulations in the domestic sphere—a persistent trope in Ramanand's televisual oeuvre—and celebrates the heroic agency that some of his female characters selectively exercise (Shoma 298). Therefore, the reliance in the genre of melodrama elicits a visceral response, creating empathy for women. As a result, melodrama not only generates intense emotion in *Alif Laila* but also emphasizes the need to create solidarity between the child viewers and the suffering female subject through strong responses to gender and sexual norms and the need to collectively examine these norms regardless of age.

In contrast to *Alif Laila*, whose liminal positionality stems from the show's adult-centric themes and excessive emotion, *Ainak Wala Jinn* attains a boundary-crossing status through its fusion of romance and kitsch. The show's Urdu romance harkens back to the sixteenth-century *dastaan* tradition with its tales of battles and elegant gatherings, as well as enchantments and trickery, enjoyed by both the aristocrats and commoners, and recited by professional *dastaan-go's* (Hussain, qtd. in Parekh). However, by the 1920s, oral *dastaan-go'i* had become outmoded, giving way to more Western-style novels and short stories, compelling the Urdu romance movement to reinvent itself in the twentieth century as *Adab-i-lateef*, or Light Literature, enthusiastically incorporating supernatural elements, enchantments, spells, and archetypal characters but in a compact narrative style. The new movement also embraced writers such as Abdul Hameed, who considered writing to be a "lyrical outpouring of romantic minds" (Hussain, qtd. in Parekh) and incorporated the themes of travel, quest, and adventure in their writings.

Furthermore, Hameed's reimagining of the Urdu dastaan as a televised entity disconnected the Urdu romance tradition from its elevated status and ornamental language, transforming it into entertainment through formula, familiarity, and shared cultural sensibilities. Hameed's *Ainak Wala Jinn* deployed the *dastaan's* oft employed tropes—*jinns*, kings, demons, magicians, divine emissaries, trickster figures (*ayyars*), beautiful princesses, and fairies—but also reinvented these tropes through its kitschy mise-en-scene speckled with garish costumes, cheap sets, lowbrow Punjabi humor, stock footage of Pakistani landmarks, and tacky special effects, which won the show critical acclaim and a niche fan following. Not only did the show's slapdash production value and commercial appeal defy easy categorization; the show also revealed how—especially in the context of a postcolonial society such as Pakistan—kitsch enables the coexistence of folk culture, in all its ethnic and regional vibrancy, with more urban and semiurban life (Dar). This uneasy blend further problematizes the status of *Ainak Wala Jinn* as a pioneer children's show with a presumed audience of Pakistan's urban children (with access to education and television sets), as contrary to expectation, the show also enjoyed popularity amongst the working poor who watched it in workshops, roadside restaurants, and poor neighborhoods.

Though *Ainak Wala Jinn*'s viewership is tethered to its staid Urdu, the show also incorporates vernacular languages such as Punjabi to generate humor through the logic of poetic refrain, thereby contributing to its genre-crossing status. Trafficking in what could be termed an aesthetic hyperbole, the so-called lyricism of *Ainak Wala Jinn* was relayed through its songs, jingles, and bad puns, entertaining audiences, especially from the lower socioeconomic strata. The mixing of Urdu, Punjabi, and English also played a significant role in the show's kitsch atmosphere, enabling it to emerge as a popular cultural artifact that mixed the more aesthete Urdu *dastaan* tradition with the folkloric *Bhānd* of comedy. Known for their abrasive humor, offensive jokes, and hypersexualized innuendoes, the *Bhānd* comedians have often been dismissed or discriminated against for their crassness within and outside the acting fraternity but continue to enjoy a viable presence despite their subaltern status (Pamment 133). In *Ainak Wala Jinn*, though the actors could not be regarded as professional *Bhānds*, many cast members such as Munna Lahori, Nusrat Ara, and Haseeb Pasha had experience with theater and came from working-class backgrounds. As a result, their performances imitated the Pakistani *Bhānd* tradition as they (usually in pairs) would engage in playful banter for conspiracy, comedy, or resistance, which is like the comedic form employed by the *Bhānds*. This comedic call-and-response was what made the show popular with children as they could easily mimic and recycle the dialogues of the show in streets, schools, and playgrounds.

The focus on witty ripostes, a hallmark of the *Bhānd* tradition, was fully incorporated in *Ainak Wala Jinn* though that focus was not the intent of the show's creators. Often employed to disrupt and challenge the respectability politics of the bourgeoisie, *Bhānd* comedy questions the adults' authority through humor. With its triviality, repetitiveness, and banality, *Bhānd* humor, promoted through the Punjabi jingles, became the hallmark of *Ainak Wala Jinn*, with some of its dialogues attaining canonical status. Moreover, the show's unstinting use of Punjabi defied the stereotype of Punjabi as an uncouth language and the widespread shame about the language that resulted in its outright rejection by the Pakistani urban elites (Rahman 88). Keeping Punjabi's fraught status in mind, as well as its complete absence from school curricula, *Ainak Wala Jinn* centered the Punjabi language to address children while glorifying the abundance of locutions, puns, and witty jokes that the language offered, promoting a language that has never been celebrated or taught in Pakistan's curricula despite being the native language of Pakistan's largest province.

What remains celebrated in popular imagination is the Punjabi banter between the clumsy villain Hamoon and the witch Bil Batori.[3] Their invocation "*Bil batori, naasa chauri, aadhi meethi, aadhi kori. I am sorry, I am sorry . . .*" ("Bil Batori, the wide nostril hag, sweet and sour, all in a bag"; my trans.; Episode 2) is the show's punchline. In return, Hamoon thanks Bil Batori through the oft repeated, "*Churail nahi tu dayn hai, meri pyari behn hai*" ("You are a witch but a witch with great powers, you are my loving sister"; my trans.; Episode 2) followed by Bil Batori's invisibility mantra, "*Assi chaar so bees, assi nou do giyara*" ("We are the fraudulent 420, we are the Escapist 9211"; my trans.; Episode 2). Though the code-mixing and linguistic pastiche is included primarily as entertainment, it draws repeated attention to the relatively lower status of the Punjabi language as compared to Urdu and English in Pakistan.

Though *Ainak Wala Jinn*'s celebration of Punjabi deserves recognition, it also highlights the gender and ethnic bifurcations endemic to Pakistan's sociocultural fabric. Ayesha Jalal contends that Pakistan, with its artificially demarcated frontiers and desperate quest for an officially sanctioned Islamic identity, lends itself remarkably well to an examination of the nexus between ideational power and bigotry often filtered through its creative cultural imaginings (74). These creative reimaginings also include gender stereotypes imposed on young girls and women by situating them simply as primary caregivers destined to toil in domestic spaces for the upkeep of the family along with dogmatic portrayals of ethnic and cultural differences. Although *Ainak Wala Jinn* shows young women and girls as viable friends and team players through the role of Mohatar and the witch Bil Batori, the show's primary focus is nonetheless the morally upright child-hero Imran and the jinn Nastoor, while the other supporting characters simply function as trivialized stereotypes to elicit laughter. These include the Hinduized Hamoon Jadoogar with a snake aigrette, the expat Uncle Charlie with a fake American accent, and Zakoota, derided by the audiences for his horns and desire for cannibalism (iterated through the rhyming, "Mujhe kaam batao. Mein kia karoon? Mein kisko khaoon." ["Give me a task. What should I do? Who should I eat?"; my trans.]). Though the depictions of these oddly eccentric characters are not explicitly nefarious, the show's villain Hamoon Jadugar is a Hindu character and practitioner of dark magic and thus disliked by many of the audience members. Therefore, the viewers of the show are implicitly cautioned against these non-Pakistani and non-Muslim characters, while the show's lead character Nastoor is well-loved by the children as he participates in nationalistic and religious celebrations. As a result, *Ainak Wala Jinn* reproduces certain societal dynamics that in turn shape the ideological and political views of its juvenile viewers.

Ainak Wala Jinn and *Alif Laila* frame gender and ethnic differences as contentious but also acknowledge the inevitability of sociocultural change through stock characters such as the Jinn, a cosmopolitan and hybrid figure, inherent to the storytelling traditions of India, Persia, and the Middle East. In Islamic mythology, *jinns* are depicted as complex and ambiguous figures, powerful spirits who, while themselves subject to God, can nonetheless intervene in human affairs for good or ill. In certain situations, they also serve as a moral barometer for adults, thereby acquiring a spiritual significance. In addition, with the Disneyfication of the *jinn* figure and its global recognition through the story of *Aladdin*, the *jinn* have become a symbol of material prosperity and modern consumption, subsequently returning to the Middle East via Western media.

The Boundary-Crossing Jinn

Ainak Wala Jinn reinterprets these culturally situated knowledges of the *jinn* through the exchange between Imran and Moatar, where Moatar is startled by the sudden appearance of the *jinn* on screen, compelling her to ask the question: "Do *jinns* actually exist?" (my trans.; Episode 1). Moatar's question evokes a collective cultural memory of the *jinn* from the ancient past. However, her curiosity entails a certain fear that contrasts sharply with Imran's reaction. Excited at the prospect of meeting a *jinn*, he candidly remarks, "There is nothing to be afraid of. In fact, I would love to have a *jinn* as a pet. I could even fly with him!" (my trans.; Episode 1). Imran's understanding of the *jinn* as a pet or a creature to be harnessed and controlled transforms the *jinn* into a suitable companion. Moreover, Nastoor's awe at the miracles of modern technology—cars, computers, gadgets, and modern medicine—emphasizes that he is also desirous of material prosperity and modern mobility. Nastoor is keen to explore new technology in exchange for his magical abilities, which in turn supports Imran's desire to venture into the modern world. Subsequently, the friendship between Nastoor and Imran is sealed when Imran arranges for Nastoor's ophthalmological treatment, thereby introducing the *jinn* to the miracles of modern medicine. As a result, Nastoor, forever indebted to Imran, becomes a beloved figure keen to support Imran in his struggle for success in the honor-bound Pakistani culture, situating him as an ideal role model for the children.

In contrast to *Ainak Wala Jinn*, in *Alif Leila* the *jinn* functions as a premonitory figure, punishing and rebuking humans for their reckless behavior and follies. He is often portrayed as dangerous and volatile as he punishes people for breaking the law, transgressing accepted social behaviors, and committing crimes against other living creatures (both intentional as well as unintentional). However, unlike *Ainak Wala Jinn*, where Nastoor functions as a symbol of entertainment and a selective social parity, the *jinn* in *Alif Leila* are a disciplinary force emphasizing the necessity of following both state-sanctioned and "godly" rules. Furthermore, the show situates the *jinn* as specifically a figure of Islamic mythology, which orientalizes him while distancing him from the composite Hindu-Muslim cultures of India. While part of this orientalizing stems from the original source materials of the *Alif Laila*, the show vehemently denies *Alif Laila*'s Indian roots, repeatedly situating the *jinn* and other characters as creations of the far-off lands of Arabia. The presumed child-viewer is implicitly encouraged to situate the *jinn* as a figure of Islamic mythology and therefore an "outsider" to the Indian subcontinent. Though the *jinn* advocates discipline, duty to community, and obedience—qualities that should be admired—the *jinn*'s existence is merely a threat within the narrative.

Furthermore, in *Alif Laila* the encounters with the *jinn* are often narrativized through Muslim poets such as Iqbal, Hairat Allahabadi, and others with a focus on the universal themes of life, death, love, and a devotion to the one true God, implicitly asserting the separate belief system of the Muslims from the Hindus and the positionality of the *jinn* as a figure of Islamic mythology only. This is particularly problematic in view of the show's implied viewers (who are supposedly Indian children belonging to diverse religious and social demographics), resulting not only in a blatant exoticization of Muslims but also functioning as an assertion of their separate identity within the Indian subcontinent. In fact, the delinking of the *jinn* figure from the mythologies of South Asia and his exclusive portrayal as a figure of Arabo-Islamic mythology exacerbates the ethnocentric consciousness of Indian children. By enabling non-Muslim children to perceive Muslims as outsiders, the show unwittingly contributes to the endemic ethnoreligious prejudices in the Indian subcontinent and the current cultural anxieties surrounding it.

In conclusion, *Alif Laila* and *Ainak Wala Jinn* are children's media texts that have attained renewed relevance because of their boundary-crossing status and their continued distribution through the Internet, leading to nostalgic memorialization by viewers. This chapter establishes that the alt kid status of these shows stems from a defiance of genre conventions and the affirmation of local storytelling techniques such as the *dastaan* as well as the use of comedic conventions such as the *Bhānd*. In addition, the chapter elucidates how these shows negotiate with these mythic traditions through local languages as well as the figure of the *jinn*, further highlighting the complexities of how these shows are produced and experienced. A further examination of these and related shows in the context of virtual cultures could enrich studies on children's literature, children's media, childhood studies, and digital storytelling in the context of South Asia and beyond, expanding our understanding of what registers as children's media locally, regionally, and globally.

Notes

1. The persistent tension between English and the myriad official and unofficial languages spoken in South Asia remains a contentious topic, as does the consequences of that tension on the instruction of children. Those concerns are beyond the scope of this paper. For discussion

of the language divide in India and Pakistan, see Vaidehi Ramanathan (51–61) and Fauzia Shamim (235–49).

2. The Ramayana continue to be a treasure trove for Indian children's literature, with current adaptations of the tales appearing in the forms of toys, comic books, digital illustrations, and video games. For more on the Ramayana graphic narratives for children, see Bhat ("Sita-centric Revisionism in *Sita's Ramayana*"), Singh ("Epics as Cultural Commodities"), and Gamzou and Fromm (*Comics and Sacred Texts*).

3. There is no consensus amongst native speakers of Urdu or Punjabi about the meaning of Bil Batori. A discussion conducted about Bil Batori in two public Facebook groups, *Bookay* and *Joy of Urdu*, yielded a range of meanings including ugly witch, smelly wort, mongoose, chatter box, green-eyed devil, and more. This linguistic plasticity invites exciting responses from both the adult and child viewers contributing to the lasting popularity of the chant.

Works Cited

Ang, Ien. *Watching* Dallas: *Soap Opera and the Melodramatic Imagination*. Routledge, 1985.
Alam, Nawaz. ". . . Mein Kis Ko Khaaon." *The Nation*, 26 Mar. 2015, https://nation.com.pk/26-Mar-2015/mein-kis-ko-khaaon.
Banaji, Shakuntala. *Children and Media in India: Narratives of Class, Agency and Social Change*. Routledge, 2016.
Banaji, Shakuntala. *South Asian Media Cultures: Audiences, Representations, Contexts*. Anthem P, 2011.
Barthes, Roland. *The Pleasure of the Text*. Éditions du Seuil, 1975.
Bharati, Ananta Ram. "Amidst Lockdown DD Makes a Return to People's Hearts." *Indus Scrolls*, 3 Apr. 2020, https://indusscrolls.com/amidst-lockdown-dd-makes-a-return-to-peoples-hearts/.
Bhat, Shilpa Daithota. "Sita-Centric Revisionism in *Sita's Ramayana*, Androcentric Encoding and Conceptualizing the Diasporic Abla Nari." *Journal of Graphic Novels and Comics*, vol. 13, no. 2, Feb. 2021, pp. 1–18. https://doi.org/10.1080/21504857.2021.1885459.
Dar, Saira. "Pop Art: Thoughtful Kitsch." *Dawn*, 20 Dec. 2015, http://www.dawn.com/news/1227212.
Gamzou, Assaf, and Ken Koltun-Fromm, editors. *Comics and Sacred Texts: Reimagining Religion and Graphic Narratives*. 1st ed., UP of Mississippi, 2018.
Gripsrud, Jostein. "Tabloidization, Popular Journalism and Democracy." *Tabloid Tales: Global Debates Over Media Standards*, edited by Colin Sparks and John Tulloch, Roman and Littlefield Publishers, 2000, pp. 285–300.
Iftikhar, Mohammed Omar. "The Magic of Uncle Sargam." *Daily Times* [Lahore], 21 May 2021, dailytimes.com.pk/758672/the-magic-of-uncle-sargam/.
Jalal, Ayesha. "Conjuring Pakistan: History as Official Imagining." *International Journal of Middle East Studies*, vol. 27, no. 1, 1995, pp. 73–89.
Kazi, Taha. *Religious Television and Pious Authority in Pakistan*. Indiana UP, 2021.
Kidd, Kenneth B. "Editor's Introduction." *The Lion and the Unicorn*, vol. 23, no. 3, 1999, pp. v–viii.
Kini, Sashank. "*Magic Lamp*—Doordarshan's Star Programme for Children in the 70s." *Sahapedia*, 4 Sept. 2018, www.sahapedia.org/magic-lamp-%E2%80%93-doordarshan%E2%80%99s-star-programme-children-the-70s. Accessed 12 Aug. 2021.
Lebling, Robert. *Legends of the Fire Spirits: Jinn and Genies from Arabia to Zanzibar*. IB Tauris, 2010.

Mankekar, Purnima. *Screening Culture, Viewing Politics: An Ethnography of Television, Womanhood, and Nation in Postcolonial India*. Duke UP, 1999.

Marzolph, Ulrich, and Richard van Leeuwen. *The Arabian Nights: An Encyclopedia*. ABC-CLIO, 2004.

Mason, Derritt. *Queer Anxieties of Young Adult Literature and Culture*. UP of Mississippi, 2021.

Mughal, Raees Ahmed. "Five Decades of Children's Literature in Pakistan." *Bookbird*, vol. 38, no. 4, 2000, pp. 10–15.

Munshi, Shoma. *Prime Time Soap Operas on Indian Television*. Routledge, 2020.

Pamment, Claire. *Comic Performance in Pakistan: The Bhānd*. Palgrave Macmillan, 2017. doi:10.1057/978-1-137-56631-7.

Parekh, Rauf. "Literary Notes: Romanticism in Urdu Literature and Mehdi Ifadi." *Dawn*, 26 Nov. 2019, www.dawn.com/news/1518797.

Pathak, Ankur. "*Ramayana* Cast Responds to DD's False Claim of 'Record-Breaking' Viewership," *Huffington Post*, 12 May 2020, https://www.huffpost.com/archive/in/entry/ramayana-breaks-tv-records-fact-check_in_5eba61bec5b69011a5737521.

Rahman, Tariq. *Language, Education, and Culture*. Sustainable Development Policy Institute, 1999.

Rajagopal, Arvind. *Politics after Television: Hindu Nationalism and the Reshaping of the Public in India*. Cambridge UP, 2001.

Ramanathan, Vaidehi. "A Critical Discussion of the English-Vernacular Divide in India." *International Handbook of English Language Teaching*, edited by Jim Cummins and Chris Davison, Springer, 2007, pp. 51–61.

Sagar, Ramanand, director. *Alif Laila*. Sagar Arts, 1993.

Shamim, Fauzia. "Trends, Issues and Challenges in English Language Education in Pakistan." *Asia Pacific Journal of Education*, vol. 28, no. 3, 2008, pp. 235–49.

Sibii, Razvan. "India, Media Use in." *Encyclopedia of Children, Adolescents, and the Media*, edited by Jeffrey Jensen Arnett, vol. 1, Sage Publications, 2006, p. 401.

Singh, Varsha. "Epics as Cultural Commodities: Comics Books of the *Ramayana* and the *Mahabharata*." *The Journal of Commonwealth Literature*, Nov. 2019. SAGE, doi.org/10.1177/0021989419881231.

Stark, Ulrike. "Hindi Publishing in the Heart of an Indo-Persian Cultural Metropolis." *India's Literary History: Essays on the Nineteenth Century*, edited by Stuart H. Blackburn and Vasudha Dalmia, Orient Blackswan, 2004, pp. 251–79.

Tahir, Hafeez, director. *Ainak Wala Jinn*. PTV Lahore, 1993.

Wazzan, Adnan M. "The Arabian Nights in Western Literature: A Discourse Analysis." *Islamic Studies*, vol. 32, no. 1, 1993, pp. 61–71.

"BIZARRE CREATURES" AND THE FANS WHO LOVE THEM
The Dark Crystal as Alternative Children's Culture

Paige Gray

As a kid, millennial Jennifer Clifton would routinely watch her VHS copy of Jim Henson's fantasy *The Dark Crystal* (1982). She loved immersing herself in the wondrous world of Thra—the film's fictional universe completely removed from Earthly reality and humanity, with all characters brought to life through puppets. "I loved the vivid atmosphere of the movie and the unique characters," Clifton told me by email. "I couldn't get enough of the . . . languages of Thra and would try to speak like Kira all the time," she explained, adding that "nothing [was] scarier than the Garthim—especially when they would snatch up podlings." For some of you reading this, Clifton's references spark no recognition and may as well be written in one of Thra's languages. For others, however, her words may awaken a long-dormant childhood thrill, one elicited by the horror and enchantment, weirdness and wonder of Henson's singular cinematic creation.

I found Clifton through a *Dark Crystal* fan group on Facebook. The group, created for fans "to connect, share[,] and expand the world of *The Dark Crystal*" as well as to "swap, trade[,] and discus[s] the film's history and impact" (The Dark Crystal–Fan Group), has about nine thousand members who regularly post artwork inspired by the film, as well as memorabilia and commercial products, new and old. Members also post links to articles and goods that likely appeal the those captivated by *The Dark Crystal* mythos. For example, a member, Michelle Rhiannon, posted a product link to "wearable iridescent faerie wings" from her friend's Etsy shop, WildFaeArts. Rhiannon let the community know that WildFaeArts makes "earrings, 2D art, and best of all faerie wings." (The aforementioned Kira boasts a pair of fairylike wings.) Using the Harry Potter–universe term for nonmagical people, Rhiannon notes that her friend "just got laid off from their muggle job" and asks the group to "please give their shop a gander."

Something about *The Dark Crystal* world and its adjacent folklore has provided an emotional or existential truth for Clifton, Rhiannon, and members of the Facebook group, as well as countless others over the years. The film, a more-or-less box-office disappointment, has built a steady, dedicated following and produced an array of adaptive works in various media, most notably the 2019 Netflix prequel series *The Dark Crystal: The Age of Resistance*, which won an Emmy for Outstanding Children's Program. Despite what many people in the entertainment industry thought after its 1982 premiere, *The Dark Crystal* endured; over the last four decades, young people (and those not-so-young) who've encountered it have seemingly claimed it as a canonical text of childhood—or, at least, of their own childhoods. What's more, as the Facebook group's description states, devoted fans also assert a kind of authorship, or even ownership, through their pursuit to "expand the world of *The Dark Crystal*." *The Dark Crystal*, I suggest, invites such ownership and expansion through its wholly puppet cast ensemble, complicating our understanding of what counts as children's media and culture, especially across generations.

The notion that puppetry was "always a vehicle for kids" baffled Henson, and Henson seemed to baffle critics with *The Dark Crystal*, a somber, sober, and very expensive film (Freeman 126). Given its near $25 million budget—an outrageous amount for 1982—*The Dark Crystal* performed only modestly at the box office. (The year's biggest film, *E.T. the Extra-Terrestrial*, had a reported budget of $10.5 million.) Rex Reed, a longtime New York film critic, wrote in his *New York Daily Post* review that it "seems almost obscene to spend" that much "on a movie for children" (Reed 43). While Reed found "the most expensive kiddie movie ever made" a visual triumph, he deemed the film too frightening for children. "The technology is impressive," Reed wrote at the time, "but the monsters and bizarre creatures that utilize it are so horrifying that they just might give impressionable tots nightmares for days" (43). Reed's review reinforces my belief that children should never be referred to as tots, but it also makes me curious about the phrase "bizarre creatures," which, in this instance, seemingly yokes together children, puppets, and otherness or strangeness. Perhaps the "horrifying" notion here is that children could identify with these "bizarre"—queer—"creatures."

Indeed, *The Dark Crystal* opens up new ways for us to think about childhood, ways that open up queer possibilities—it enables "sideways" thinking about childhood, to borrow from Kathryn Bond Stockton (3). In aligning *The Dark Crystal* with queerness, I refer to the term's circulations and manifestations within the historical trajectory of children's texts. Michelle Ann Abate and Kenneth B. Kidd note that "[i]n children's titles of the late nineteenth and early twentieth centuries, the term 'queer' appears not infrequently and has a range of associations, among them, the strange, the fantastic, the animal, the aristocratic" (3). Moreover, Abate and Kidd point out that in many of these stories, young people "are often linked to the assorted queer creatures they love" (4). We see precisely this sort of child-creature bond or linkage in Henson's "bizarre creatures," as Reed more anxiously recognizes.

Since queerness challenges binary views of gender and sexuality, it disrupts the basic ideological underpinnings of individual and social identity in Western heteronormative culture "Het culture thinks of itself as the elemental form of human association, as the very model of intergender relations, as the indivisible basis of all community, and as the means of reproduction without which society wouldn't exist," Michael Warner wrote nearly thirty ago in *Fear of a Queer Planet* (xxi). "Het culture" allows for the continuation of basic existence via sexual reproduction. But what if existence were considered beyond such reproductive human existence? And what if "reproduction" encompasses various means of *creative*, artistic reproduction? With its puppet "creatures" and its extensive, multigenerational fandom, *The Dark Crystal* enables us to think about how children's narrative can queer textual and human authority, and even fixed notions of truth. *The Dark Crystal* is a queer as well as posthuman text, one that resists normative plots and invites alternative identifications.

While *The Dark Crystal* (codirected with Frank Oz) is a remarkable film, I should admit that my childhood touchstone was *Labyrinth* (1986). (This admission may be scandalous to some members of *The Dark Crystal* Facebook fan group.) For *Labyrinth*'s enchanted journey, Henson included those elements that helped make the Muppet franchise so beloved, namely humor and original songs. The other critical addition to *Labyrinth* was human actors—one being iconic musician David Bowie—who function as the audience's guides in the transition between reality and Henson's dreamscape. The lack of human avatars in *The Dark Crystal* makes it something, perhaps, more than the sum of its parts given how it so openly invites questions of posthumanism into the realm of mainstream children's entertainment. As Zoe Jaques explains, the posthuman "provides a model for understanding the universe not from the perspective of a human-centered order that sets 'us' apart from a great many 'thems' but through connecting humanity to a wider ecosystem of bodies, both organic and mechanistic" ("Posthuman" 156).

The disturbing, even terrifying allure of *The Dark Crystal* derives from its deliberate artificiality and otherness. We're transfixed by this wholly creative realm, but we're also alienated by the lack of humanity. The film's absence of such calls attention to its artifice. For young people especially—but not exclusively—the unsettling, uncanny artificiality of the puppet is what gives *The Dark Crystal* power. So, while it may not be a "great" film—however greatness is understood—it does something much more significant. *The Dark Crystal* revels in its otherness, its specific queerness that questions the contours and connotations of reproduction. Indeed, it challenges not only the constitutive ideas of human centrality but also authorial centrality, thus forcing wider consideration of a text's fandom in regard to its creative legacy.

Play Things

The Dark Crystal poses the basic question of existence: How do we survive the threats of neglect and oppression—the threat of darkness? But who *or what* is that "we"? The film opens with a grim panorama of a bleak, ostensibly barren landscape. The dark blues and grays of a thunderous cloud mass unspool over a desolate stretch of rocky terrain, empty except for the phallic fortress in the center of the frame. An ominous nondiegetic narration lays bare the apocalyptic conditions that set Henson's story in motion:

> Another world, another time. In the age of wonder. A thousand years ago, this land was green, until the crystal cracked. A single piece was lost, a shard of the crystal. Then strife began, and two new races appeared. The cruel Skeksis, the gentle Mystics. Here in the Castle of the Crystal, the Skeksis took control. . . . For a thousand years they have ruled. Yet now there are only ten. A dying race, ruled by a dying emperor. Imprisoned within themselves in a dying land. (*The Dark Crystal*)

This opening scene distills the film's thematic, epic concerns, which can be read through any number of critical lenses. But I'm most fascinated by the narration's emphasis on the crystal object and nonhuman life. The Skeksis, truly bizarre creatures that feel more akin to technological objects than organic animals, and the sloth-like Mystics (also known as the urRu) exist by means outside biological reproduction and death, as far as humans understand this— "dying" for the Skeksis and the Mystics correlates not to physical age but to the crystal. So just from these first few minutes, the film unapologetically tells us that through its story and its chosen mode of storytelling—puppetry—it wants to wrestle with the very idea of life itself. The film, via its puppet creations, seeks to explore the limited nature of life as defined by mere humans.

Puppetry suggests the superseding condition of the human experience is that of creative invention—to be human is to create. The artifice of the puppet makes this notion inescapable, an exhilarating, liberating concept. Scholar, director, and dramaturg Claudia Orenstein argues that "puppetry redeploys objects to express the complexities of contemporary life; creates, questions, or strengthens communities; reforms relationships with technology and nature; balances tradition and modernity; and delves into metaphysical questions of existence" (3). Looking back to the form's cultural origins and endurance, theater historian Eileen Blumenthal describes puppets as "powerful conservators of social values, but also political subversives" (11). These objects, Blumenthal poetically explains, grant a "visible form to the vastness of the cosmos but also have shown the intimate interior of a human psyche" (11). Similarly, renowned puppeteer Bil Baird remarks on the unique reality forged in puppet creation: "When the puppet performs before an audience," Baird writes, "he begins to create a kind of life" (15). And John Bell, noted director of the Ballard Institute and Museum of Puppetry at the University of Connecticut, asserts "that to understand puppetry is to understand the nature of the material world in performance," and moreover, "the material world in performance is the dominant means by which we now communicate" (2). That "material world in performance" enacted through puppetry defines part of the human experience while simultaneously reifying nonhuman life; the "material world in performance" ignites a posthumanism discourse that, as Jaques sees it, "both exposes and ironically establishes boundaries between the human and non-human, to facilitate a dialogue as to how those very borders might become more fluid" (*Children's Literature* 2–3).

So why is puppetry often uncritically and derisively categorized as children's entertainment? And how have young people coopted this categorization as a call to creative agency? "It's something I've always faced, this slight condescension toward puppets," Henson said in a 1979 *Saturday Evening Post* interview (Freeman 126). It's not that Henson objected to his work being labeled as art for children so much as the supercilious attitude that puppets are only for children, a notion demeaning to both children and puppetry. And as Blumenthal, Bell, and others have shown, the American imagination's automatic association between children and puppets ignores centuries-old global puppetry traditions. But the condescension that Henson references can be found, sadly, in most critical commentary regarding children's literature and media. Though critical and academic approaches to youth culture and texts have made tremendous gains in the last forty years thanks to university departments and scholarship dedicated to children's literature and childhood studies, the condescension Henson mentions still exists. But in his work, most starkly in *The Dark Crystal*, Henson challenges the ideological boundaries between child and adult by way of some very bizarre creatures, situated at the border of human and nonhuman, even the organic and the inorganic.

A "Solemn Fairy Tale"?

Rex Reed's aloof appraisal of *The Dark Crystal* upon its 1982 premiere aligned with a not-uncommon response to the film, namely ambivalence and confusion. What was the Muppet guy doing with this strange, serious, scary film that had no humans? Contemporaneous reviewers found *The Dark Crystal* admirable in its aesthetic achievements but failed to see the significance of this feat beyond compelling visuals. The *New York Times* said that while "a lot of obvious effort has gone into this solemn fairy tale," it has all "been devoted to the complicated technical problems" resulting in a movie "without charm or interest" (Canby). Even before its release, many of those in the industry believed that "*The Dark Crystal* had become Henson's Folly—a project that was not only taking up too much of Jim's time and money, but was also squandering the global success of the Muppets on a project that no one but Jim seemed to fully understand or appreciate," according to Henson biographer Brian Jay Jones (323).

This "solemn fairy tale," a description that's rather a misnomer, also incorporates the tropes of the basic quest story or of the so-called hero's journey. Many a reviewer compared Henson's ambitious project to Tolkien's *Lord of the Rings*. And indeed, at one time, Henson did think about taking on Tolkien, "but eventually passed on the project after deciding Tolkien's sweeping epic was 'too big to handle' in a single film," Jones writes (304). As a review from the *New York Daily News* of *The Dark Crystal* plainly states, "The idea is old. It's the technology of the retelling that's impressively new" (18). The "retelling" itself began as a concept, not a narrative. "Instead of starting with a story treatment," explains Christopher Finch in *The Making of The Dark Crystal*, Henson "assembled a group of people with the capacity to invent a world, visualize it, and make it palpable. Only when that world began to exist as a self-contained entity did they consider plot and the detailed development of characters" (18). In fact, the genesis of *The Dark Crystal* comes from the place that so many things originate from in world of children's literature and culture—the work of Lewis Carroll. And yet, while the popular imagination and, certainly, many scholars see *Alice in Wonderland* as a quintessential text of children's literature, it, like *The Dark Crystal*, runs afoul of more traditional children's narratives. "*Alice* refuses to settle down sensibly in the realm of children's literature," Kenneth B. Kidd argues (74). "Carroll's *Alice* books are at least partly adult in tone and concern, containing not only fantastical creatures but also mathematical puzzles, educational satires, and not a little narratorial joking at Alice's expense" (Kidd 74). Though *Alice* and *The Dark Crystal* are wildly different texts, they each work to destabilize accepted cultural truths surrounding childhood, the bizarre, and creaturedom. And just as the *New York Times*'s reviewer inaccurately categorized *The Dark Crystal* as a fairy tale, some also incorrectly label *Alice* as such. While *Alice* and *The Dark Crystal* are decidedly not fairy tales (each has an identifiable creator, for one thing, and did not originate through oral storytelling), they both possess subversive qualities that exist in many (if not all) folk and fairy tales. And just as *The Dark Crystal* has its "bizarre creatures," *Alice* has its "queer-looking" and "queer-shaped" creatures (24, 55). In fact, Alice notices "[h]ow queer *everything* is to-day!" (17, emphasis mine). These two texts underscore a broader tradition of alternative children's literature and media that grapple with and seemingly embrace the bizarre through their normalized depictions of nonhuman life.

Henson happened upon an illustrated version of Carroll's poem "The Pig-Tale" in 1975. In particular, a drawing of a crocodile caught Henson's attention. "'It was the juxtaposition of this reptilian thing in this fine atmosphere that intrigued me,'" Henson recalled later about the illustration (qtd. in Jones 304). Biographer Jones details that soon after seeing this crocodile, Henson "began writing a treatment for a fantasy film called Mithra, a dry run of the various plot elements that would eventually coalesce as *The Dark Crystal*" (304). This early outline centered on "the two warring factions—the villainous Reptus and the wizardlike Bada," the first incarnations of the Skeksis and the Mystics, which Henson saw as creatures "split from a single species, through the influence of a mystical source of power" (Jones 305). In other words, an epic battle between good and evil in a fantastical universe.

Although I'm more concerned with *The Dark Crystal*'s use of puppetry and how it opens up ideas of the posthuman and creative production, this is not to say that we can't take other productive critical approaches to the film. For example, children's literature scholar Roxanne Harde examines the character of Aughra, the Keeper of Secrets, to show an ecological undercurrent in the film, arguing that Thra's maternal figure "functions as the earthy matrix of the film's environmentalist politics" (89). Harde sees Aughra as "an ethical force who is both eye and voice for the natural world" (89). Gideon Haberkorn, meanwhile, looks at the movie through a postcolonial lens, considering the positions of "Gelfling" characters Jen and Kira within Thra's power matrix (Gelfling are a sapient species who live close to nature): "These Gelflings are caught between the ethnic and racial context they have grown up in, and the image of Gelfling identity transmitted to them by their environment" (75). Perhaps closer to my take is that of art historian Catriona McAra, who, in her study of Froud's production design, notes the "imaginative investment and level of craft and detail devoted to the background and landscaping of this magical world," observing that "the quest narrative is fairly straightforward and the characterization is often stock" (101–2). This "stock" frame of *The Dark Crystal*, as McAra suggests, provides Henson an experimental space in which to test the bounds of posthuman storytelling. Amid this process, the division between real and unreal, living and nonliving, dissolves.

In creating the nonhuman universe of *The Dark Crystal*, Henson anticipates the later work of posthumanist scholars, including that of Donna Haraway. The puppet aligns with Donna Haraway's account of the cyborg, which she calls "a hybrid of machine and organism, a creature of social reality as well as a creature of fiction" (149). The cyborg, like the puppet and other automata, makes manifest the overlapping worlds of the material and the imaginary, and serves as reminder that social reality is itself an idea—something created in our imaginations. "Social reality is lived social relations, our most important political *construction*, a world-changing fiction," Haraway contends (149, emphasis mine). Henson explains that "'[w]e made a collective decision not to use humans in makeup or costume'" (qtd. in Gaines 37). To realize his vision, "'[w]e had to break free of the human form. . . . I wanted to be totally submerged in another world'" (qtd. in Gaines 37).

The Dark Crystal's complete absence of humans is, perhaps, what most estranges some viewers. Arguably, this lack put extra focus on Jen and Kira, the most humanlike of the movie's characters and the puppets that presented the greatest challenge for Henson, who performed the Jen puppet. Henson said in a 1983 interview that he is "'most strongly self-conscious about my own performance,'" underscoring that "Jen was a difficult character to make believable" (Shoemaker 9). Henson remarked that the Gelflings "'were the hardest of the characters to design'" because "'[t]hey're kind of our bridge characters. The characters through which the audience enters this world'" (qtd. in Gaines 65). Because of their proximity to human likeness, the Gelflings stood most vulnerable to criticism. In contextualizing the matter, Cheryl Henson says, "Now the phrase 'uncanny valley' is very popular, the idea that the human brain reacts negatively when something closely resembles a human but isn't one. . . . But when this film was being made, that wasn't a concept that people actively talked about" (qtd. in Gaines 176–77). The "uncanny valley" to which Cheryl Henson refers derives from Freud's notion of the "uncanny," or "that class of the terrifying which leads back to something long known to us, once very familiar." This idea is often used when thinking about our relationship to human representations—dolls, puppets, computer-generated imagery—to help explain why we find them creepy. Queer studies theorist Jack Halberstam, in discussing the "spooky and uncanny quality" of stop-motion animation, shrewdly observes that "it conveys life where we expect stillness, and stillness where we expect liveliness" (178). While some may be alienated by *The Dark Crystal* and other puppetry texts because of the unfamiliarized familiar, the film's fans welcome it. Its bizarre creatures and their intertwining associations with queerness and posthumanism signal a desire for alternative stories and opportunities for investment. "Through a negotiation of alterity within self and an address to oppressed entities," posits Patricia MacCormack, "queer theory and the posthuman mobilise and radicalise the here and now through desire, pleasure and pure potentiality" (112).

(Re)making Myth and Magic

The "pure potentiality" of Thra realized through the efforts of the film's designers and puppeteers reveals, or at least suggests, one path of agency for young viewers through creativity and artistic invention. Artist Brian Froud, known for his illustrations of fairies and fantasy landscapes, and one of the key minds behind the aesthetics of *The Dark Crystal*, remarked upon the appreciative reactions he often gets from fans who pursued creative careers because of the film:

> It is always gratifying to discover how many people have been affected by its beauty and strangeness. Over the past three decades, in almost every situation that we've found ourselves, people have asked the question, "What was it like to work on *The Dark Crystal*?" They want to know how it felt to be a part of the film that touched them in so many ways. . . . Many tell us that *The Dark Crystal* was the one film that made them decide on a career in the arts or in the film industry—informing how they approached their own contributions to the fantasy genre. (10)

While the movie, through its promotion of artifice, likely influenced a generation of artists, puppeteers, and filmmakers, it also speaks to a broader sense of creativity—the ability to create new realities of hope. At the very least, the film encourages active, participatory viewers through its mythology. More than a single narrative, Henson established a milieu in which viewers could engage further through their own imagination and creative careers, or through creative play—in fan communities, cosplay, and fanfiction.

The Dark Crystal's dedicated fans helped it achieve a cultlike status, leading to the production of the 2019 Netflix prequel, as well as a two-year exhibit, "Jim Henson's *The Dark Crystal*: World of Myth and Magic" at Atlanta's Center for Puppetry Arts, which ran from early fall 2018 to late 2020, showcasing more than fifty pieces from the film (Emerson). (The exhibit was then succeeded by "Masterpiece of Puppetry: *Jim Henson's The Dark Crystal: Age of Resistance*," which opened in June 2021.) The nonprofit, established in 1978, is the largest organization focused on puppetry. In addition to its museum collection (which brings in more than 100,000 visitors a year), it produces more than six hundred performances annually and offers more than fifty educational programs that reach students across the country (Wells; *Center for Puppetry Arts*). "There is only one Center for Puppetry Arts in the United States," Cheryl Henson, president of the Jim Henson Foundation, told *Atlanta* magazine. "We are so lucky that it exists" (Wells). The exhibit, as well as the Netflix series, inevitably introduced *The Dark Crystal* to new audiences. One of my students at the Savannah College of Art and Design in Atlanta wrote about the exhibit in detail for the school's online publication. Notably, he most enjoyed watching the engagement of young visitors:

> Easily the best part of the exhibit [is] seeing children[,] who are given nothing to watch nowadays but CGI garbage like "Minions," gasp in awe at the living breathing world made of latex, foam and beads. It goes to show that "The Dark Crystal"—even 35 years after its release—still has the power to captivate and inspire generations to push their imaginations to heights they never thought possible. (Trench)

This is important, particularly in showing the influence of *The Dark Crystal*'s bizarre creatures on children. While fans and critics marveled at the film's innovation in 1982, that technology has now become outmoded. What does the movie hold for contemporary children? Apparently, a lot. It still effectively presents a completely realized alternative universe that engenders creativity rather than passivity.

The extensive mythologies underwriting many fantasy epics do, indeed, beget fervent fan cultures and stories, be they new narratives set within those fantasy worlds or cosplay adventures. Some of these mythologies even provide an ontological or religious framework for fans to create new identities, according to religious studies scholar Joseph Laycock, who details individuals who understand themselves as nonhuman or "Otherkin." "Hundreds, perhaps thousands, of people throughout the English-speaking Western world define themselves as fundamentally different from the rest of humanity," Laycock writes. He reports that "in the mid-1990s, these individuals formed a nebulous identity group that adopted the label 'Otherkin'" (65–66). Laycock's specific interest lies with whether the Otherkin identity constitutes a religion, a notion that those who identify as Otherkin "have consistently denied" (66). What caught my attention was that many Otherkin "have taken the sacralization of fictional narratives to an unprecedented degree, in some cases espousing metaphysical frameworks in which fantasy narratives are taken to have a literal corresponding reality," and Laycock names *The Dark Crystal* as a narrative sacralized by some Otherkin (76). On the one hand, the phenomenon of Otherkin may feel strange or "wrong" given its rejection of human embodiment. But, on the other, how is this so terribly different from Haraway's belief that we live in "a mythic time" in which "we are all chimeras, theorized and fabricated hybrids of machine and organism; in short, we are cyborgs" (150)?

There may not be an adequate answer to this question—at least, not in the scope of my undertaking here. But perhaps we can find a little guidance by returning to Atlanta's Center for Puppetry Arts and its *Dark Crystal* exhibit. Notably, the Center celebrates puppetry not only through the museum but also through its theater and educational programs. We find meaning through puppetry, the Center suggests, in the "great conjunction" (to borrow from *The Dark Crystal*) between display, performance, and creative activity. We can understand what it means to be human through this life cycle of the puppet. And through its erosion of the divide between human and puppet, *The Dark Crystal* makes us question other ideological divides, such as the divide between child and adult. That's what we see in the space of *Dark Crystal* fandom—people of all ages (and gender identities and races and socioeconomic backgrounds) deliberately and deliciously confusing what it means to be young or old.

Websites and online publications not based in Atlanta (including *Mentalfloss.com*, *tor.com*, *Patch.com*, *Trial by Stone: The Dark Crystal Podcast*, and *Syfy.com*) posted news of *The Dark Crystal* exhibit's opening, which helped bring museum visitors from outside Georgia. (For example, my brother and his wife were quite excited to see it when they visited me from Ohio.) In a visitor survey from fall 2019, guests were asked about their reasons for touring the museum. Many cited being a "Henson fan," with several naming *The Dark*

Crystal specifically. Interestingly, some remarked that *The Dark Crystal* items were "too scary" ("Visitor Experience Survey"). Others indicated they'd like to see more adult programs.

These museum visitors, along with Clifton, members of the Facebook fan group, *The Dark Crystal* devotees mentioned by Froud who pursued creative careers, as well as others, show how *The Dark Crystal* encourages continued imaginative engagement. This engagement may take the form of a professional life in media or storytelling, or may be a fulfilling role in a fan community that promotes creative production through art and writing. Indeed, in the feed of *The Dark Crystal*'s Facebook group at the moment are posts featuring a member's beautiful illustrations of *Age of Resistance* characters; a YouTube interview that a member facilitated with *Age of Resistance* creators; a photo of a member's elaborate *Dark Crystal* tattoo; and a fan-made music video that renders *The Dark Crystal* into a 3-D experience. What I see as crucial here are the ways in which Henson's exquisite ecosystem functions as just that—a space where ideas can grow. But this ecosystem is not organic or biological. The "growing," the creative reproduction, occurs in fans' textual remakings that unsettle claims of a work's static state.

The Dark Crystal continues to defy—mystify—categorization. In its refusal to condescend or to project the myth of childhood innocence, it challenges the foundational binary of child and adult and thus forces other assumptions into question, in ways that disrupt the notion of human life as the fulcrum of knowledge and experience. In her history of puppets, Blumenthal says that since the earliest days of humankind, we've had an inclination to create replicas of ourselves through material means—to, more or less, give life to alternative human forms. The "bizarre creatures" of *The Dark Crystal* fascinate and endure not only because they challenge narrow definitions of childhood and children's culture but also because they imagine existence beyond human control—even beyond human life.

Works Cited

Abate, Michelle Ann, and Kenneth B. Kidd. Introduction. *Over the Rainbow: Queer Children's and Young Adult Literature*, edited by Abate and Kidd, U of Michigan P, 2011, pp. 1–14.

Baird, Bil. *The Art of the Puppet*. Bonanza Books, 1972.

Bell, John. *American Puppet Modernism: Essays on the Material World in Performance*. Palgrave Macmillan, 2008.

Blumenthal, Eileen. *Puppetry: A World History*. Harry N. Abrams, 2005.

Canby, Vincent. "Henson's Crystal." *The New York Times*, 17 Dec. 1982, https://www.nytimes.com/1982/12/17/movies/henson-s-crystal.html.

Carroll, Lewis. *Alice's Adventures in Wonderland and Through the Looking-Glass*, edited by Hugh Haughton, Penguin Books, 1998.
Center for Puppetry Arts. Center for Puppetry Arts. www.puppet.org. Accessed 20 Sept. 2020.
The Dark Crystal. Directed by Jim Henson and Frank Oz, The Jim Henson Company, 1982.
The Dark Crystal–Fan Group. *Facebook*. https://www.facebook.com/groups/590770974353530. Accessed 31 Dec. 2020.
Emerson, Bo. "'Dark Crystal' Exhibit Brings Scarier Henson to Puppetry Center." *The Atlanta Journal-Constitution*, 29 Aug. 2018. https://www.ajc.com/entertainment/arts—theater/dark-crystal-exhibit-brings-scarier-henson-puppetry-center/9JRLehUmYPGD3SiFFhygyL/.
Finch, Christopher. *The Making of* The Dark Crystal: *Creating a Unique Film*. Henry Holt, 1983.
Freeman, Don. "Muppets on His Hands." *The Saturday Evening Post*, Nov. 1979, pp. 50–53, 126. Nancy Staub Puppetry Research Library, The Center for Puppetry Arts, Atlanta, GA. Film and Television Box #2, "The Muppets 1979–1990" folder.
Froud, Brian, and Wendy Froud. Introduction. The Dark Crystal: *The Ultimate Visual History*, by Caseen Gaines, Insight Editions, 2017, pp. 10–11.
Gaines, Caseen. The Dark Crystal: *The Ultimate Visual History*, Insight Editions, 2017.
Haberkorn, Gideon. "Interpreting the Various Species of *Fraggle Rock* and *The Dark Crystal*." *The Wider Worlds of Jim Henson: Essays on His Work and Legacy beyond the Muppets and* Sesame Street, edited by Jennifer C. Garlen and Anissa M. Graham, McFarland, 2013, pp. 73–87.
Halberstam, Jack. *The Queer Art of Failure*. Duke UP, 2011.
Haraway, Donna. *Simians, Cyborgs and Women: The Reinvention of Nature*, Routledge, 1991.
Harde, Roxanne. "'What Was Sundered and Undone Shall Be Whole': Union, Nature and Aughra in *The Dark Crystal*." *The Wider Worlds of Jim Henson: Essays on His Work and Legacy beyond the Muppets and* Sesame Street, edited by Jennifer C. Garlen and Anissa M. Graham, McFarland, 2013, pp. 88–100.
Hunt, Peter. "Children's Literature." *Keywords for Children's Literature*. 2nd ed., edited by Philip Nel et al., New York UP, 2021, pp. 41–44.
Jaques, Zoe. *Children's Literature and the Posthuman: Animal, Environment, Cyborg*. Routledge, 2015.
Jaques, Zoe. "Posthuman." *Keywords for Children's Literature*. 2nd ed., edited by Philip Nel et al., New York UP, 2021, pp. 154–56.
Jones, Brian Jay. *Jim Henson: The Biography*. Ballantine Books, 2013.
Kidd, Kenneth B. *Freud in Oz: At the Intersections of Psychoanalysis and Children's Literature*. U of Minnesota P, 2011.
Laycock, Joseph P. "'We Are Spirits of Another Sort': Ontological Rebellion and Religious Dimensions of the Otherkin Community." *Nova Religio: The Journal of Alternative and Emergent Religions*, vol. 15, no. 3, 2012, pp. 65–90.
Leogrande, Ernest. "A Fantasy of Puppets." *New York Daily News*, 17 Dec. 1982, Friday section, p. 18. Nancy Staub Puppetry Research Library, The Center for Puppetry Arts, Atlanta, GA. Film and Television Box #1, "The Dark Crystal 1982–1984" folder.
MacCormack, Patricia. "Queer Posthumanism: Cyborgs, Animals, Monsters, and Perverts." *The Ashgate Research Companion to Queer Theory*, edited by Noreen Giffney and Michael O'Rourke, Routledge, 2009, pp. 111–28.
McAra, Catriona. "A Natural History of *The Dark Crystal*: The Conceptual Design of Brian Froud." *The Wider Worlds of Jim Henson: Essays on His Work and Legacy beyond the Muppets and* Sesame Street, edited by Jennifer C. Garlen and Anissa M. Graham, McFarland, 2013, pp. 101–16.

Orenstein, Claudia. Introduction. *The Routledge Companion to Puppetry and Material Performance,* edited by Dassia N. Posner et al., Routledge, 2014, pp. 1–4.
Reed, Rex. "Crystal-Clear Thrills and Chills for Lots of Tots." *New York Daily Post,* 17 Dec. 1982, p. 43. Nancy Staub Puppetry Research Library, The Center for Puppetry Arts. Atlanta, GA. Film and Television Box #1, "The Dark Crystal 1982–1984" folder.
Rhiannon, Michelle. "Wearable Iridescent Faerie Wings." The Dark Crystal–Fan Group. *Facebook,* 31 Dec. 2020, https://www.facebook.com/groups/590770974353530. Accessed 31 Dec. 2020.
Stockton, Kathryn Bond. *The Queer Child; or, Growing Sideways in the Twentieth Century.* Duke UP, 2009.
Trench, Mikael. "Step Back in Time with 'Jim Henson's *The Dark Crystal*: World of Myth and Magic.'" *SCADConnector,* 26 Jan. 2019. https://scadconnector.com/2019/01/26/step-back-in-time-with-jim-hensons-the-dark-crystal-world-of-myth-and-magic-exhibit/.
"Visitor Experience Survey." Center for Puppetry Arts, 2019. Accessed via email 30 Jan. 2021.
Warner, Michael. Introduction. *Fear of a Queer Planet: Queer Politics and Social Theory,* edited by Michael Warner. Minnesota UP, 1993, vii–xxxi.
Wells, Myrydd. "Peace, Love, and Puppets: Why Adults May Need the Center for Puppetry Arts More Than Kids Do." *Atlanta Magazine,* Sept. 2018, https://www.atlantamagazine.com/great-reads/peace-love-puppets-center-puppetry-arts-atlanta.

VIDEO GAMES AND YOUNG PEOPLE'S DIGITAL CULTURES
A Panel Discussion

Kristopher Alexander, Negin Dahya,
TreaAndrea M. Russworm, Catherine Burwell, and Derritt Mason

This roundtable originally took place online on May 13, 2022, as part of the Association for Research in Cultures of Young People (ARCYP)'s annual research symposium.

TreaAndrea M. Russworm: I'll give a bit of an introduction that helps situate me in terms of youth, digital culture, and games. I come to game studies as a media studies scholar. I've published works on Black popular culture and I'm also coeditor of the book *Gaming Representation*. I mostly write about representation in video games. When it comes to youth culture, the cover of our *Gaming Representation* book has an image from *The Last of Us*; you see in the foreground a young black character named Riley and then the protagonist of that game, Ellie. In *Gaming Representation*, I write about character representation or the social context in which we come to meet these characters. I mention how Black characters exist to help contrast the relationships between the non-Black characters and to create a sense of empathy that always dissipates. You create empathy through suffering, so Riley, for example, gets bitten by the Infected and dies, but that experience teaches Ellie that she's immune. There is a sacrificial agenda when it comes to marginalized characters in games.

I also look at the *Walking Dead* series in *Gaming Representation*. When it comes to youth representations, suffice to say that in mainstream games, we're not getting very full or dynamic stories that emphasize the agency of the minority characters, especially of the Black or Latinx characters. I think we have seen some differences in smaller games and in games by independent studios. And in the academic game space, we see some pushback against these kinds of tropes and conventions. So that's how I enter the space when it comes to studying games, and thinking about games, and playing games.

In my bio, I always say I'm an AfroGeek, and that means to me that I love all these things. I've loved games for as long as I can remember, and so I approach this work both as a fan and a critic. And my academic work has mostly been in this vein, writing about the cultural context of games.

I'm going to fast forward to the creation of Radical Play, which is a civic and community engagement program that I developed for high school students. So, I am shifting from my theoretical territory of the English professor who writes about games and audiences to work with high school students, ninth graders and up. The first year of Radical Play was 2016. This experience kind of shifted gears for me. I was thinking less about the theoretical landscape of what's happening in games to who's playing games and what games are teaching us as a wider public. Part of what we do in the Radical Play program is help students who love games, but maybe are not college-bound, to think about how their love of games tells them something about themselves. This work is with mostly BIPOC youth, Black and Latinx youth in Springfield, Massachusetts, and in Holyoke, Massachusetts.

We emphasize four pillars. First, we have Criticality, which is the analytical part—how we analyze the games that we're playing, whether it's *Call of Duty*, *Minecraft*, *Fortnite*, or whatever. How do we come to understand them and really think about them as text? Then there's Creativity: we always produce media in the program. Another pillar is Consciousness, which is about how we understand ourselves. If you like racing games, tactical games, or a particular genre of games, that probably tells you a lot about your own skill set and what you bring to the table as a player of interactive media. The final component to radical play is Community. We get students to think about how our love for games can connect us to the work that is being done or needs to be done in our communities. Radical Play students have done prototypes of serious or educational games they would like to see, thinking about things like racism, school shootings, and violence in schools.

Radical Play pushed me in another direction. I'm a professor who teaches video games to college students, but I had to ask: who do I really want to reach beyond that audience? That's an awesome audience to work with, but there are so many more people who play games who are not in that audience. Radical Play became so important to me because it was another way to engage with players across a wider spectrum.

The third and final iteration of the youth culture work that I do is running the Radical Play Game Studio. This was born out of the work with the Radical Play Community Engagement Program and the students' desire to do more than conceptual game design. I tell them all the time I'm not a game designer; I'm a scholar, I'm a reader, I'm a writer. I don't animate, I don't program. However, whether or not they were college bound, the students increasingly wanted to make games in the future. They wanted to be able to take their prototypes to another stage and to see their storyboarding and writing digitally realized. That led me and a bunch of undergraduate and graduate students to create the Radical Play lab.

The first year of this program running as a game lab was this year. The students created a game called *The Tides That Bind*. In doing that work, I think we started to develop a definition or an understanding or maybe an aspiration of what we're calling equitable game design. Some of the same principles that guided the Radical Play Community Engagement Program go into our desire to make games that challenge dominant norms. They're small games, they're games that have a serious slant to them, but through their representation and mechanics these are the kinds of games that still challenge dominant norms in the industry that, as I said before, can be pretty exclusionary without a lot of diversity in terms of characters, context, and story.

So that's the final iteration of what Radical Play has become and where my interests as a scholar are shifting. I feel most comfortable writing about youth culture from the standpoint of representation, but now design and other imperatives are definitely in view.

Negin Dahya: I think my remarks will resonate with TreaAndrea's comments about participation, representation, and design. I'm going to focus on methods and some of my recent youth media education research work: what has become possible and what has been limited based on institutional structures. These aren't necessarily bad structures, but they do frame and shape what is possible.

I'll start with a study that took place in Washington State when I was a faculty member at the University of Washington and working in a juvenile rehabilitation center there. We were working closely for several years with the state library, which has libraries within prisons and sites of incarceration for young people. We were looking to find ways to intervene in what were very poor conditions for a lot of these young people. They didn't have access to technology or to the burgeoning developments that were happening around them in the city of Seattle, which is a major tech hub. Virtual reality was one of these initiatives that was being deployed in public library systems and schools. Technology companies were donating tools and trying to create a mechanism of uptake for their products, but also looking for ways to get young people involved in these digital industries, which are potentially interesting and lucrative pathways.

This project was called "Co-Creating Concept Art and Stories for Virtual Reality." It was a partnership between the University of Toronto, University of Washington, school districts, public libraries, and the state library, so it was a large endeavor. Our research questions were: How can you codesign? How can codesign be used to create concept art and stories for virtual reality? And what does it look like to codesign concept art for a VR program with youth in juvenile rehabilitation? Working with these different partners, we wanted to create collaborative, cooperative, and design-based efforts for young people to participate in this project.

Often, we don't hear about all the things that bring us to this moment, and that's what I want to focus on. Carceral logics influenced our work and how we got to this point of being able to do what we did in this environment. By carceral logics, I mean the idea of imprisonment as a way of shaping our behaviors, our beliefs, and our social structures. This notion, this fear, this punitive system that we live within causes tensions and creates structures and rigidities at different moments in our movement through these research worlds and education environments. These are not new ideas; these are very widely discussed. People like Ruha Benjamin talk about the carceral logics of society and technology. You could also go back to Foucault's *Discipline and Punish* and discuss the ways in which education systems are structured with these carceral logics in place.

We endeavored to do codesign work, and yet we had many limits with regards to how and how often we could interact with the young people. We had limits on what kind of materials we could use and what kind of design choices we had to make to engage them in this process. There's also an important moment in media education research where you are facilitating educational programs and conducting participatory research at the same time.

Because we were researchers coming in with an academic agenda, we had to follow the protocols and institutional expectations of the university—and in this case, also the state. The Washington State Institutional Review Board had its own system that we had to go through to get ethical approval to enter the school for research purposes. The process took eight months. Our grant lasted a year, which could be extended for another year, but we didn't have a ton of time to engage in an ethical review process that takes almost a year to move through.

Within that there are important nuances. For example, we set out to create a coalition and spent many months working with community members, engaging with different organizations and local tech companies, and identifying people who wanted to support this work. We all wanted to create a network so that these young people could meet and interact with us, and then afterwards, when they were released, have pathways to continue pursuing their interests in the digital arts.

We were given very firm instructions that there was to be no exchange of information, including us giving our full names and information to the young people. Of course, it makes sense that they were not to give that information to us. But something that seems like a simple rule about security becomes a barrier to constructing community engagement with people who are already living with very strict regulations within a system of incarceration.

Similarly, the research design choices forced us to use only certain programs that could be run without the Internet, programs that would not induce trauma and would not be violent. This generated a lot of creativity in the team to develop a curriculum that was well suited to the restrictions in place for this particular group. We ran a successful program from an educational standpoint. We had twenty-four participants who attended regularly over about a month, and they created a lot of art, engaged with ideas about VR, and got to play and experience VR. But they couldn't have their views, contributions, and perspectives documented to their full capacity. TreaAndrea talked about not getting full representation of characters in mainstream video games. That resonated with me in thinking about not getting full representational participation in this restrictive setting because as researchers we had so many limits on our outputs. Even in presenting this work there are mental structures in place where I have to stop short of expressing something because of the rules of the institution. And yet as a researcher it is my commitment to share as much as I can, so that we can learn and create systems and programs for young people to move out of deeply oppressive environments like this.

A lot of my youth media education work has involved thinking about these processes. How do we do meaningful participatory research design and education? How do we work with young people in ways that allow them to really inform and participate in some of our newest and most exciting technologies? In this case, one of the major barriers that came down the line from the Washington State Institutional Review Board was that we needed written consent from parents for participants who are under the age of eighteen. We had asked for verbal consent or proxy consent between the parents and the staff who are the custodial guardians of the young people when they are inside this institution. But that was denied and what was required was written consent from the parents. Young people in this institution come from all over the state, and their parents don't come to visit them very often. So that became a barrier to what we could do. We had choices: we could say, "Okay, we'll wait. We'll do this the following year and just spend more time waiting for those parents to visit to get their documentation."

But that also pushed up against two other structural problems. One was that most of the people who were incarcerated in this juvenile rehabilitation center were not necessarily there for that long. A few people would be there for one, two, or three years but many folks are there for three months, six months, nine months, and then they're gone. The other more pressing reality was that our work was meant to help fill a gap in the curriculum. The institution didn't have a media arts teacher, and they needed media arts education and curriculum to be brought in. So, part of our commitment was to work with local libraries to help build this curriculum, run it, and then pass it over to them so they could continue it in subsequent years. If we had pulled back based on our research agenda and said we're going to do this the following year, we would not have followed through on our commitment to the institution from an educational standpoint.

There are quite a few tensions in doing this research and educational work. Carceral logics dictate these rules and structures. This punitive system has come to inform the ways research can happen. The system affects how we are able to learn in these spaces, and the degree to which we were able to have full participatory engagement with the young people involved.

Kristopher Alexander: They call me the Professor of Video Games. My work takes place in three core areas: video game design, e-sports broadcasting, and virtual production.

I'll break this down a little further. When we talk about video game design, we're looking at programs like Unity. Students are building their own experiences to tell their own stories. And one of the core points of both Unreal Engine and Unity is that these are free tools and accessible tools for many, not everyone yet, but for many. For example, there are virtual machines that Epic offers as part of their services for those who do not have machines powerful enough to run the software. The second research area is e-sports broadcasting, one of my favorite things. Some of you may recognize me from Wisecrack, a YouTube Channel with over three million subscribers.

A lot of my work delves into how to use OBS [Open Broadcaster Software] to do things like v-tubing on Twitch. My research looks at the fact that in doctors' simulation and training, many humans feel more comfortable describing ailments to an avatar rather than an actual human being. And the last area we're talking about is virtual production. We are using the Unreal Engine to bring those things to life.

I have over thirty years' experience as a player, professor, and consultant. We've gotten many students jobs at places like Epic Games, Ubisoft, Gameloft, Stitch Media, and Waveform, which is among the top Canadian broadcast e-sports organizations recently purchased by Solotech. And jobs at OverActive media too, which is one of the only franchise-owning organizations in North America.

I'm also a Red Bull–supported scholar. You might say to yourself, wait a second, Red Bull is sponsoring scholars now? Not usually, but if you talk about *Street Fighter*, and you play video games, sometimes! We're working on building a state-of-the-art broadcast facility for students, The Red Bull Gaming Hub, to help them to learn how to stream themselves and monetize their superpowers online and via virtual production.

I'm also a content creator. I'm working on one game called *Bearable*, and another, a typing teaching tutorial involving bread, that I'm building for my daughters. We are also working with organizations like Epic Games to tease out the nuances of virtual production—that is, how you can use tools like your web camera and microphone to make full video games and produce scenes. I also did a study looking at the relationship between performance and engagement in the classroom. We're looking at ways that video game technology can connect you with your learning at the ground level.

We also love to research what equals fun. Nintendo, King, and Activision Blizzard run research studies that use multiple methods of player research to determine what is fun, what will allow people to engage for longer. This is a numbers game of time: how we can captivate and encapsulate your time.

Derritt Mason: Something that compelled me was Dr. Dahya's discussion about institutional barriers. It made me think about barriers to video games and digital text research, and the status of video game studies at the university. Can I invite each of our panelists to say something about your home discipline and how you would describe the status of video game studies or the study of digital texts in that discipline? Are there any barriers to carrying out your research or teaching within the discipline or the institution where you work?

ND: I can go first. I am at the Institute of Communication, Culture, Information and Technology, which is a multidisciplinary space. There are people who do media studies, technology, development, media production, and coding—a mix of things. We do have a video game track; students in the undergraduate program can take courses in video game development.

A few of you here are in English departments, which might not be people's immediate thought as to where you're going to find scholarship in digital media. In my previous experience at the University of Washington, it was also happening there. But it still seems like it is significantly less present compared to coding, web development, data analysis, and other tech skills.

I don't know where the institutional barriers are except to say that so much of the development of those technology programs is about tuition and enrollment, about creating a tunnel that is going to bring students in and get them into what they think will be lucrative jobs. This is a major part of the neoliberal institution we are all a part of—just moving students through. And students also want that because it's an expensive world to live in. People want to make money; they want to have safe and meaningful careers and economic stability. So that is where I see the institutional tensions with regards to certain things growing more than others.

TR: I'm in an English department, and I get students in my classes asking: Why is [video game studies] in an English department? And I just say: it's because I'm here. Humanities departments frequently claim interdisciplinarity and do a lot of different things.

In the English department at UMass, there's a lot of latitude for teaching what you're interested in. But as I said, I really wasn't trained in game studies. I was trained to study popular media, like film and television, and then studying games evolved from that.

I'm also an associate dean, so I'll wear my associate dean hat for a second and think about enrollment in a broader sense. Enrollment numbers in the humanities are declining, and there are a lot of reasons for that, but one of the things we've noticed is that media arts is an area of growth. It's an area of interest, but at UMass it's under realized. The art program and animation programs are solid, but they tend to be small. They have limited studio space and can't serve as many students as we'd like. But there's clear student demand in these areas. Creative writing is also one of those areas that is growing while others are declining.

I've been teaching game studies classes for eleven or twelve years. They have consistently been oversubscribed. I teach a class on dystopias with a theoretical angle. We're reading postmodern theory and studying literary dystopias and comic books, but games are the centerpiece. The course has an analytical thrust. When you look at the content you understand why it's in an English department, but I think the focus on games throws people off. But I like to tell students, hey, you are trained to analyze a variety of types of texts. Yes, there are formal issues and elements that video games are uniquely known for, but the critical skill set that we're proud to cultivate in humanities can apply to a multitude of texts.

I study successful programs in multiple places because I'm trying to get that started here. Usually, they're really interdisciplinary and have folks from all over campus who are doing work in these areas. They have computational literacy and game development, an artistic side, and maybe game studies is a third area that is not as fully integrated into a lot of these programs. But I do think that's changing. The media literacy levels of the public have grown tremendously in the last decade or so. Pop culture discourse has been elevated. People are talking about tropes, conventions, and regressive structures in the popular domain. There's a certain aspect of game studies and popular cultural studies that's already live. I think that the level of popular critical literacy challenges us to do a better job at integrating critical and theoretical studies into game design.

So, I think there is interest and growth in game studies, and we can follow it in a way that isn't just focused on jobs, jobs, jobs, although material and financial stability are important. I approach games by thinking about how they're making citizens. We're making and remaking citizens through our engagement with digital media, so we have a deep responsibility to make that whole project intellectual, creative, and economically accessible to all.

KA: I'm so excited. I believe that video games and e-sports can connect to every single discipline. The trick is finding humans open enough to accept that as a potential reality and to go forward with it.

My background is in media production. I introduced game design in a summer camp at the University of Toronto in 2006 and then realized: oh man, I can teach this stuff. I got all excited. And then I introduced one of the first courses at Toronto Metropolitan University. My excitement is in teasing out the areas that are outside of play. Oftentimes when I'm giving talks, I say to people let's talk about *not* playing and see how far we can take this.

There's one game that I play in my class called *Virginia*. It's one of my favorite titles of all time. You play as a Black woman who is tasked with internally investigating another person of color on the force. When we played this game in front of students, [the protagonist] looked down at her hands for the first time. We paused the game and the students were quiet, and I said: What's going on? They said it was the first time they had looked down with an avatar in a game and seen hands this color. We had a conversation about it. This game is an hour and forty-five minutes of pure joy. This is the world in which I live. You can do this for free, you can learn how to tell your own story, you can publish something. And I think that's where the power is going to come from.

DM: How can instructors use the principles of game design to incorporate gaming elements and create teaching spaces to encourage and support student engagement? And how can we engage students who identify as casual gamers versus those who identify as enthusiasts?

KA: When I teach game design, I have in week two a lecture on persuasion. I invite a student, using a free piece of software called Parsec, to take control of my machine and play *Inside* in front of the entire class as we dissect tunneling, persuasion, analyzation, and repetition. That's how I use video games to engage students in the classroom. I do it by saying to students: "You already know the answers. I'll show you."

And when we play a game, and I say "Pause the game, why did you do that?" They'll say "Well, I had to." "You did? Really? Why did you walk to the right at the beginning?" "Well, because I fell down from the mountain." "Wait a second, you didn't even try to go back?" "Well, it was so high." "That was a programmed experience." So that's one of the ways I engage students. Sixty-one percent of Canadian adults identify as gamers. We know that number is higher within our classroom walls because of the demographic of humans who have the most time to play video games. But I love that statistic and the statistics demonstrating who has enough money and time to play video games. Contrast that with the average age of the full-time faculty member in postsecondary and secondary institutions. If you look at those numbers, the average age is fifty-one.

Generally, there is a disconnect between the average age of those who are immersed in the medium and those who would be excited about integrating OBS and Twitch into classroom instruction. I'm not saying that's not happening, but the slow rollout could have to do with the fact that instructors don't know about *Inside*; they don't know about *Virginia*. They hear anecdotes from peers about *Fortnite* and think that's all it is, not taking into consideration that you can buy Jordans in *Fortnite* and that Ariana Grande and Marshmello performed in *Fortnite*. And that more than 50 percent of players in *Fortnite* right now are creating experiences, rather than playing the game. What does that mean? Humans want to create. They want to use simple tools to tell their own stories.

TR: I'm going to try to tackle the casual versus enthusiast part of that question. We play *Inside* in my classes. Along the lines of persuasion, we talked about proceduralism: how you can make arguments without saying anything; how you can make arguments through [game] mechanics. One of the things we learn about *Inside* right away is the brutality of the world. This is a world where there's mind control and everybody conforms, and you're trying to fight against this very rigid, very troubling system. But the mechanics tell you all you need to know about it.

This question about how you reach different audiences as a teacher and encourage active engagement—whether we're talking about enthusiasts or casual gamers—is a great question. Being in an English department means a lot of times I get people in my classes who are just curious. Many of them are not enthusiasts. I do a couple of different things to address this.

I teach team-based classes, where students work on a project together through the whole semester. I have a survey that students fill out at the beginning of the semester. Sometimes when I'm organizing teams, I put all the enthusiasts in their own teams. It depends on the demographics of the class. If I get a lot of people that describe themselves as hardcore gamers (not terminology I personally use) and if they list more mainstream games, like they're first-person shooter fans, sometimes I put them in their own team. I find they balance each other out, and they're in a space where they won't sort of intimidate the students who are casual gamers. I try to set the tone in my class where we dissolve these artificial hierarchies and play all kinds of games.

But sometimes I find that because the students choose the games that we play in the class, some teams have a certain skill set or certain expectations for what games are, and they can work together in that vein and we can meet them where they are. Whereas students who are more casually involved with the medium might choose a game like *Undertale* that doesn't require a lot of experience playing games.

I also set a tone that says we're going to explore all kinds of things. We're going to get out of our comfort zones. We're going to try a bunch of things and be open minded and explore a game like *Virginia*, which is an excellent game. This semester in my Introduction to Games class we played *Aerial_Knight's Never Yield*, which was so amazing and fun. It has a default setting that allows many casual players to just pick up and play it. It's a runner-style game, and you don't have to ever have played games to enjoy it. So I'll shout that game out—it's a really great, futuristic dystopia, but it's also got so much going on artistically. Another game I'll shout out that we played and that I've written about recently is *Treachery in Beatdown City*, which is Shawn Alexander's totally different kind of fighter game. It's a game that lots of different play styles can enjoy. One of the things that I do is offer a range of games. In the same class we'll play *Fallout 4*, and we will play small and independent games. That way lots of people with different backgrounds can participate, learn, and enjoy.

So those are some of the strategies that I have for being able to create engagement and interactivity and still have everybody get a lot out of the class. We may work in specific teams, but all of us play lots of different types of games. And then I set that tone that says, hey, we're here to dissolve hierarchies and to play promiscuously and broadly.

Catherine Burwell: Dr. Dahya, you talked about the blurred lines that can occur when you enter participatory research as both an educator and a researcher. Could you tell us more about some of those challenges and how you address them or even how they become part of your research?

ND: Thank you for the question. It's an important topic, and I think more and more we see media education researchers who are trying to name these realities and identify where these tensions come up. It suggests a couple of things. One part is about your commitments as a human, not just as an educator or as a researcher, but your ultimate goals of contributing to society. What is it that you really want to do? If, like me, you are working with racialized, marginalized, or vulnerable populations in settings where people are under-resourced and underrepresented, my position is that the net benefit to the community must be the priority. This becomes very difficult when you are a graduate student and/or even a pretenure faculty member, and you feel you have certain pressures that you need to meet in terms of your research agenda. That also comes into tension with funding structures that don't always give you the time you need to build trust and have good relations with the people that you are working with. There isn't always the time to do earnest participatory and community driven work.

But I think you have to figure out how to do it correctly. How do I build good relationships, create meaningful curriculum driven by the community, implement a program on the schedule that is needed by the organization, and respect the values of the young people who are participating? How can I do these things and meet my research requirements? I think you must be strategic to do that well and accept the reality of the conflict of these spaces.

Part of the answer is really thinking about your commitments. Then as you get further along in your career and once you have tenure, I think it becomes about changing the norms as much as you can and taking the steps to say we're going to do this differently, and it's going to take longer.

DM: Two questions from audience members: the first is about resistance to digital learning spaces and how to push back against such resistance. The second question is about the gamification of difficult histories such as slavery, colonialism, and genocide. Generally, we tend to hear about when these games go wrong, but are there "good" examples?

KA: I'll start with the first question about digital classrooms and resistance from faculty. What I've seen is a lot of resistance that may come from a nonaffinity with the technology. I often open myself to teach anybody how to use this piece of free transcription software. One of the issues that I have is that once I explain to people that it's beyond the clicking of an executable [file], I lose them. Captivating humans online is not easy. I'll give you an example right now. Watch this. [He clicks, and the color of his image washes out; the screen is much duller]. This is what my camera actually looks like. But I watch YouTube tutorials to learn how to light and color somebody with my skin complexion because I know that the gaze matters in the classroom. If somebody is interested in going that route, they can. What I'm hoping for is a world where humans who want to do it can say they want to do it. You can't expect everybody to want to do the same thing. So, a lot of the resistance has to do with a disconnect from the technology. I'm like—what do you call yourself, Dr. TreaAndrea?

TR: AfroGeek.

KA: Okay, I love that. I'm like an AfroGeek. The second question about the gamification of difficult histories has to do with who's telling the story. Have you heard of a game called *Venba* that explores Tamil immigration culture? Do y'all know about [adventure game] *Thirsty Suitors*? This game is going to change your lives, folks! Check out the publisher, Annapurna Interactive: these are the games that they specialize in. So, my answer is: those games exist and will continue to exist, but as usual, it depends on who's telling the story.

TR: I can hop in on the first question about the digital or remote classroom. I think that maybe this is one area where teaching games has an advantage. During the pandemic, we used Twitch to play games because normally in my classes we spend the first hour of class playing a game or a sample of a game. We work together to analyze it, and it's a valuable experience to be in person in the same room and play that game. But when we were mostly remote, we were playing the games on Twitch. We had Tuesday and Thursday night sessions for the class. It was even cooler in some ways, because Twitch being Twitch, we also had lots of people who weren't in the class joining us. So, we have that same experience for the class to be able to comment on and analyze a play session, but because it was public play, we also had random people hopping in and giving advice and saying "Oh, this is a class?" We had really good experiences. I know it could have gone badly, but it didn't. Extending that playing into a more public venue worked out well. So, there are some things that maybe translate well to remote teaching or the digital classroom. When it comes to teaching games, that was one positive experience.

As far as the other question, those are great examples from Kris. I don't want to add anything other than maybe a AAA title that I thought did this well, which was *Mafia 3*. I think part of it is having a certain sophistication about the cultural context and history that you're trying to depict. And yes, involving people in the decision-making and the design process who can speak from that background. In *Mafia 3*, the protagonist of color had a very faithful and committed portrayal of that particular character's background. It was detailed enough and worked well. It was almost like a Blaxploitation film. There are definitely some challenges with that genre, but one of the things that is always going to be true is that the protagonists have a particular kind of social, political, African American–specific sense of agency. And that pairs nicely with the Black action film formula, so the action film/game formula can work well.

ND: People can make these games well, but you still have to interact with the gaze—the male gaze, the white gaze, all the oppressive perspectives and views that can be read and imposed upon those artifacts. That doesn't mean they shouldn't be created, but I think we have to recognize that when they are put into the world, they are no longer in your control. Things get taken up in all kinds of ways, and that is why having media education and critical media studies in universities is so important: so that we're able to have these conversations.

DM: Dr. Kris Alexander, Dr. TreaAndrea M. Russworm, and Dr. Negin Dahya: thank you so much for sharing your knowledge, expertise, and enthusiasm with us today.

Works Cited

Aerial_Knight's Never Yield. Headup Publishing, 2021.
Alexander, Shawn. *Treachery in Beatdown City*. NuChallenger, 2020.
Fallout 4. Bethesda Softworks, 2015.
Foucault, Michel. *Discipline and Punish: The Birth of the Prison*. Pantheon Books, 1977.
Inside. Playdead, 2017.
The Last of Us. Sony Computer Entertainment, 2013.
Mafia 3. 2K Games, 2016.
Malkowski, Jennifer, and TreaAndrea M. Russworm, editors. *Gaming Representation: Race, Gender, and Sexuality in Video Games*. Indiana UP, 2017.
Thirsty Suitors. Annapurna Interactive, forthcoming.
Venba. Visai Studios, forthcoming.
Virginia. 505 Games, 2016.

Part III
ALT EPISTEMOLOGY

THE ALT WITHIN
Queerness, Psychoanalysis, and Children's Literature as Enigmatic Signifier

Natasha Hurley

Despite the welcome proliferation of cultural objects for and about queer and trans youth today, there continue to be many stories we don't tell directly to children about sex, gender, and sexuality. In this essay, I seek to understand the sexuality of children's literature not just as a matter of plot, content, or identity, but, building on Jean Laplanche's concept of the "enigmatic signifier," as a constitutive feature of all (not only overt) messages between adults and children. That is to say: the sexuality of text is as much a matter of its *form* as it is of its *content*. The "alt within" allows us to understand what may seem like alternative children's literature as having always been part of children's literature tout court: part of all messaging to children, but a feature whose disavowed presence can erupt in any temporal unfolding of the text's circulation.

How one accesses the unconscious of any message, text, or individual is always a murky matter or sideways engagement. But we can learn a lot about the stories we ostensibly still don't tell to children about sex, gender, and sexuality by attending to examples that expose the existing alternative worlds within children's literature by way of parody. Perhaps you have seen *The Onion*'s widely circulated story announcing The Mapplethorpe Museum for Children. Or maybe your social media feed has acquainted you with online galleries of bad or impossible children's books, like Bob Staake's parodies of Golden Books or similar postings by "Your Childhood Ruined." (Gems include "Polly Paints a Penis," "Bukowski for Kids," "Fido Finds a Dildo," and "The Long and Awkward Walk Home after Disappointing Forest Sex.")[1] Alt children's lit seems to make for good adult humor (as long as you keep your audiences neatly compartmentalized). These parodies shine a light, not on the impossibilities of children's literature but on the impossible aspirations of policing those boundaries of address. Ultimately they reveal what we shelve into our unconscious when it comes to imagining childhood sexuality. The irony works because a child audience/consumer/listener is simultaneously imagined and refused: hovering in that non-place of impossibility or "badness" while clearly inverting the more wholesome understandings of gender and sexuality nestled within the frames of unruined childhoods.

At a time when the cry to affirm a wider range of children's genders and sexualities has never been louder, a new wave of panic has emerged around what this all means. You can't "say gay" in Florida politics, there are more and more restrictions on sex education in many North American schools, and the parents of trans children in Texas are being accused of child abuse for their gender supportive care of their kids. But what those insisting on the affirmative proliferation of queer representations in children's literature and those trying to curtail discussions of gender and sexuality among children share is a common belief in the power of language and literature together to stabilize and affirm particular world views through representation. Such an irony thus invites us to look more carefully at our persistent no-fly zones beyond the narratives we tell about sexuality at the level of manifest content—either in speech or in fiction—so as to consider what is displaced from view in these modes of address to children.

In an effort to explore these matters, I argue for a reading of sexuality that exceeds the representational plots of texts ostensibly about queer sexuality for young people. Impossible addresses to children call attention to the conditions under which we know what we leave out, identifying as they do a hip fantasy whose knowingness inoculates a children's culture that ultimately denies its own self-repressive force. For it subscribes to the fantasy that progressive adults are somehow more at home with sexuality than their "don't say gay" counterparts. Rather than suggest an additive approach where we just need more diverse or sex-positive stories about queer youth for queer youth, I argue for a shift from content to form, form not just of sentences or books but the broader forms that messaging to children takes. Texts for young people are, after all, defined by mode of address, and sexuality itself, as queer theorists have established, is not merely a property of the self but a mode of relationality. I'm not arguing against creating more diverse and sex-positive stories about or for queer youth, but rather that the creation of more content is missing a crucial point about how these stories function first as touchstones for the complex inner life of sexuality that can only be partially grasped through the narrative form we give it, even (especially) in our addresses to children. The stories we refuse to tell children about sexuality can be read instead as a different kind of symptom: a symptom of a sexual unconscious that attends the very act of addressing children regardless of the content of that address. In this sense, there is no alternative children's lit; there is only the alt *within* children's lit. For the stories we tell to children are fully shaped and formed by the stories we do not tell either about them or to them.

In order to understand the stories we do and do not tell about child and youth sexuality to young people themselves, we have to understand these stories beyond their manifest content and treat them as what Laplanche calls "enigmatic signifiers." As such, these explicitly fictional addresses to children both constitute and put into play the force of an unconscious central to the inner life of sexuality for both the adult and the child being addressed. The stories we tell to children about sexuality tell us as much about the demands that narrating childhood sexuality makes on our own adult sexuality—operating as if to secure the coherence of adult sexuality itself—while nonetheless showing the child what is enigmatic about the form of sexuality despite the seeming certainties of narrative content.

If we look to the burgeoning literature for and about queer youth, and think about the enigmatic pathways of sexuality, a related way to imagine an affirmative queer adolescence is as a non-place, a place you pass, innocuously (rather than traumatically), along the way to adulthood. The term "non-place" was first coined by anthropologist Marc Augé, who defines the "non-place" as the banal, often institutionalized spaces (like airports, hospitals, or hallways) through which subjects pass, less traumatically, on their way to somewhere else. In *Non-Places: Introduction to an Anthropology of Supermodernity*, Augé argues that "[s]upermodernity produces non-places, meaning spaces which are not themselves anthropological places" (77). An effect of capitalist intensification and globalization, these spaces are designed to be passed through or consumed rather than appropriated, and they retain little or no trace of our engagement with them. As Augé explains in an interview about his work, "Non-places could be seen . . . as the heirs to everything that has created discomfort or annoyance in the history of human spaces."[2] The non-place is thus the solution to discomfort or annoyance, a response to the complexity of human space. Augé's concept of the non-place vis-à-vis the discomfits of human space might help us also to understand how narratives that foreground banality have become the heirs to the stories historically told about queer youth sexuality. From the vantage point of adults looking in or back on it, queer adolescence is often narrated through the fantasy structure that makes sexuality itself a non-place—a place to pass through to somewhere where/when it allegedly gets better.

What interests me, then, is what we learn in tracking the nonworlds of children's literature (those sites of untold stories), which exist in adjacent internal relation to the worlds we are surer about narrating. In operating beyond the avowed worlds of representation in queer children's literature as such, these non-places of children's literature might be read productively as animating the unconscious or enigmatic signifiers of childhoods rather than managing them or foreclosing them. The queer nonworlds of children's literature invite us to consider the elided sexualities of childhood culture not merely as minoritized, identitarian, and homeostatic forms of being but as perverse psychic realities that subtend all addresses to children, the spaces and unconscious matter which demand ongoing engagement for all subjects, adult and child alike.

If literature for children and young adults might be said to operate as a kind of enigmatic signifier, how, then, might we read its dynamic sexual unconscious? By attending to the forms of sexuality that the genre of children's literature tends to repress or refuse at the level of manifest content, I suggest we might gain some insight for a way of reading the queerness of childhood not merely as representation or identity but as a form of social relationality that continuously unfolds in the aftermath of adult-child encounters with the sexual unconscious. The alt within, in other words, is always emerging and never outside of children's literature.

Seduction and the Compromise Messages of Addresses to Children

Laplanche's concept of the enigmatic signifier provides us with a powerful way to understand the alts within addresses to children as something more than missing content and more like a relational orientation that must take the unconscious seriously. The "enigmatic signifier," as a concept that refuses the identity boundaries that have emerged around queer childworlds, opens up ways of reading adult messages to young people as repositories of a sexual unconscious often projected onto young people, a sexual unconscious that is also often a racialized and colonially taken-for-granted absence at the heart of our thinking about and for young people. According to Laplanche, enigmatic signifiers are the messages a child receives as an infant that are beyond comprehension and thus must be translated later. This translation is complicated not only by the child's inability to comprehend but by the adult's relationship to her own unconscious and the status of the specifically sexual element of the form of address: Laplanche describes this enigmatic signifier and the other-relationality at its heart as follows: "To address someone with no shared interpretive system, in a mainly extraverbal manner: such is the function of adult messages, of those signifiers which I claim are simultaneously indissociably enigmatic and sexual, in so far as they are not transparent to themselves, but compromised by the adult's relation to their own unconscious, by unconscious sexual fantasies set in motion by his relation to the child" (79–80). The adult's own unconscious, which is also always a sexual unconscious, compromises the manifest content of any message (linguistic or symbolic) communicated to the child. The child, Laplanche argues, is seduced into the interpretive system by the adult whose messages (often unconscious even to the adult herself) eventually will be subjected to translation by the child who gradually will decode the mode of relationality they have experienced. What is sexual about the form of address is *precisely not its content*. In the context of a children's literature that explicitly addresses questions of sexuality as content, there may not *necessarily* be any effort to attend to the sexuality of form that Laplanche describes. It is nonetheless conceivable that the form-content dialectic helps to unconceal what has been unconscious about the sexuality of address in an earlier moment.

Equally important to the structural unconscious of the sexual form, in Laplanche's framework, is the fact that what is internalized as the sexual unconscious of form is simultaneously understood in language akin to the alt within. Laplanche calls this "internal alien-ness": an alien-ness that is "maintained, held in place by external alien-ness, in turn, held in place by the enigmatic relation of the other to his own internal alien" (80). In this sense, sexuality can be seen both as a mode of sociability as well as a process unfolding in a vexed time-shape—a nostalgically framed forward-looking search, not an identity fixed by desire and or reducible to a particular original identification. Making sexuality a non-place of adolescence—a place of banality—is precisely a defense against the complexity of sexuality that Laplanche sees at the heart of the adult's address to the child. To see sexuality as a banal, developmental non-place essentially seeks to make sexuality also nonperverse—strangely, and counterintuitively, *de*sexualized at the level of content. It is therefore counterintuitive to stabilize sexuality through affirmative content without understanding fully the ways in which (a) sexuality is a fundamentally destabilizing force, (b) the unconscious is not just the child's but the adult's, and (c) the ways the boundaries between self and other, adult and child are structured psychically by language that is at once racialized and subject to fantasy of sovereignty derived from nationalism and colonialism.

To the first point about sexuality as a fundamentally destabilizing force, Laplanche follows Freud by insisting that perversion finds itself at the heart of all sexuality—just as alt children's lit is not outside of children's lit but central to it, *within* it. Foundational to Laplanche's entire psychoanalytic approach is the status of the other who is central to the scene of primary, or originary, seduction from which the enigmatic signifier emerges. "The *primal* situation," he argues in *New Foundations*, "is one in which a new born child, an infant in the etymological sense of the word (*in-fans*—speechless), is confronted with the adult world. This may even mean that what we call the Oedipus complex is in a sense subject to contingency" (89–90). The confrontation between the adult and the newborn foregrounds for Laplanche the essentially relational nature of psychic development and the establishment of the other as a persistent recursive force tied directly to adult-child modes of address—modes of address that include, but also exceed, linguistic signification per se. "I am," he continues later in the same text, "using the term *primal seduction* to describe a fundamental situation in which an adult proffers to a child verbal, non-verbal, and even behavioral signifiers which are pregnant with unconscious sexual signification" (126). The child, in effect, is hailed into subjectivity through the other, who does not just set in motion the child's internal fantasy life but remains a structural feature of his psychic landscape: a force of subjective decentering within and beyond the child's and the adult's psyches.

This focus on the other's unconscious in addressing the child (the second point following from above) is central to Laplanche's understanding of both sexuality and the conditions of address. Laplanche's intervention is to retain the other at the heart of psychoanalysis, via the structural conditions of seduction, which Laplanche argues Freud discovered but ultimately abandoned.[3] Hence Laplanche and Pontalis's insistence, in "Fantasy and the Origins of Sexuality," that "sexuality literally breaks in from the outside . . . [and] reaches the subject from the *other* where its traces remain unintegrated and encysted" (10). It becomes a life-long project for the child to engage with what Laplanche calls the "compromise message" that comes from the other. As Laplanche puts it in "The Unfinished Copernican Revolution," it is from the adult's engagement with the child that sexuality emerges, precisely in its tie to the conscious and unconscious messages the child receives: "two worlds without communication divide, so to speak: on one side, parental behavior, the experience and content of which are by definition beyond the subject's grasp; and on the other side, the side of the child, a traumatic spectacle, more often glimpsed or guessed than seen, suggested by mere allusion (animal coitus) which the child must then fill out, interpret, symbolize" (78). The seduction at the heart of the primal scene, out of which the enigmatic signifier emerges, thus establishes a model of sexuality that is both other-oriented and very much tied to the unconscious of that other.

Laplanche's model of sexuality disrupts many of our truisms about sexuality more generally, for Laplanche's sexuality is neither autologically generated, nor self-contained as a property of the self. And nowhere in this model of other-oriented psychic engagement does Laplanche distinguish between heterosexual and homosexual enigmas. Further, the kind of seduction that Laplanche has in mind is not necessarily sexual in a genital sense and it is not a message that the adult himself consciously possesses. What Laplanche argues for is a "third domain of reality," reducible neither to psychological reality (where the adult at the scene of seduction is responsible for thinking and apprehending seduction) nor material reality (which is reducible to recognizably sexual gestures) (169). This third domain of reality can begin to be grasped, posits Laplanche, when we ask not whether seduction can be seen to take place through observable sexual gestures (like touching a child's penis) but whether the conditions of seduction are in place through "the gesture of touching the child's big toe" (169). Such an action can be assessed neither according to the pure materiality of the gesture nor to the pure psychology of the protagonist. In the context of adult-child message relay, "we have the reality of the message and the irreducibility of the fact of communication. What psychoanalysis adds," Laplanche argues, "is a fact of its experience, namely that this message is frequently compromised, that it both fails and succeeds at one and the same time. It is opaque to its recipient and its transmitter alike" (169). By calling attention to this opacity of both sender and receiver to the message itself, Laplanche thus describes a model of sexuality that, at its heart, is not just the unconscious but the indeterminacy of sexuality itself. Such a model of sexuality does not renounce sexuality as a form of identity but nonetheless identifies a fundamental indeterminacy at the heart of sexual relationality.

How might the force of the unconscious and this attendant indeterminacy reshape the kinds of messages we interpret in the texts we address to young people? To the extent that the earliest texts for children "address someone with no shared interpretive system," they constitute a subset of "adult messages" for children more generally. The problem of the enigmatic signifier that concerns us thus is not just a problem of delayed translation for the child but a problem of the adult's management of the message system itself. What we take to be the content of such messages is never the only thing being communicated in such an address. The adult's "relation to their own unconscious" combined with "the fantasies set in motion by his relation to the child" distorts any efforts the adults may deploy to clarify the messages themselves. The problem of the enigmatic signifier is not merely one of retroactive reading but of the way the adult's fantasy of the relation to the child sets meaning in motion—and by corollary impedes that very meaning.

Under these conditions, the adult who engages the child is not just "maker, giver, and receiver," as Rose puts it in *The Case of Peter Pan; or, The Impossibility of Children's Fiction* (1–2). The adult is a self divided (divided, that it, from itself), deploying unconscious as well as conscious messages, while encountering another self in the making. The message the child receives is not reducible to the conscious desires or wishes of the other but contains as well the unconscious desires of the other in his engagement with the child:

> In the primal situation we have, then, a child whose ability to adapt is real, but limited, weak and waiting to be perverted, and a deviant adult (deviant with regard to any sexual norms . . . deviant or split with regard to himself) . . . given that the child lives on in the adult, an adult faced with a child is particularly likely to be deviant and inclined to perform bungled or even symbolic actions because he is involved in a relationship with his other self, with the other he once was. The child in front of him brings out the child within him. . . . [W]e have a "Traviata," someone who has been led astray and "seduced." (Laplanche, "Unfinished" 103)

The child's formative interaction with the other is, in other words, not merely an interaction with the manifest content of what the adult wants the child to know and understand: it is also an encounter with the unconscious of the other. It is the force of the unconscious at the scene of the child's seduction by the adult that makes signification enigmatic, and which also constitutes the force that leads both the child and the adult astray. What is enigmatic and sexual about the signifier and its origins in seduction will set in motion a process of engagement with the subjects' unconscious over time. What Freud called *Nachträglichkeit*, but which Laplanche translates as "afterwardness" (rather than deferred effect), thus depends fundamentally on a structural relationship to the "other" (within and beyond the individual psyche) as well as what Freud called a "dynamic unconscious."

Crucial to any understanding of the "alt within" children's literature is the fact that the deferred effect is only possible because messaging to the child installs sexuality within the psyche as a "foreign body." Sexuality is, as Laplanche insists, an incursion of and from the other, foregrounding a fundamental alien-ness central to the very psychic operation of sexuality. (The language here flags directly the ways in which sexuality has always been enmeshed with colonialism, race, and empire). This is not to say that all adult-child relations mimic those of social dominance—only that the ways Laplanche describes it carry that weight. In general, Laplanche believes that the initial encounter between adult and child is not necessarily experienced as either sexual or traumatic. It becomes so, as John Fletcher puts it in his introduction to Laplanche's *Essays on Otherness*, in the interval between the scene of seduction and its reminiscence: "In the interplay between the two scenes, a moment of inscription and a later moment of reinscription or translation[,] . . . there arises a sexual and traumatic representation of a scene that was for the subject neither fully sexual nor traumatic in its happening as an event" (8). This interval is key for Laplanche as he elaborates the central question raised by a "dynamic unconscious": "[H]ow is it that the unconscious can consist of that which is repressed and yet despite this be inexhaustible—be capable, that is, of endlessly slipping away from our grasp?" (70). It is in this oscillation between the becoming-sexual of a foundational seduction moment and its reverberation within the scene of the present that Laplanche locates the play of the enigmatic signifier.

In so doing, Laplanche opens a space not just for the unconscious force of the enigmatic signifier but for a temporal model of sexuality that is not merely archived in the past but is continually unfolding in the present as it engages with the structural enigmas that have been set in motion through an engagement with the other. He answers his own question first by pointing out that "unconscious fantasy is not simply the memory of lived scenes" (70). The unconscious, rather, "has a close link with the past, the past of the individual, *while at the same time abandoning the psychological problematic of memory* with its intentionality aimed at *my* past" (71; emphasis original). Laplanche thus returns to a key insight about hysterics that he claims Freud ultimately neglected: they "suffer not from memories, forgotten or not, but from 'reminiscences.' The term could, of course, be reduced to memory—a memory cut off from its context—but it could equally be allowed to bear the value of *extravagance* which is not lacking in Platonic doctrine: something which returns as if from elsewhere, a pseudo-memory perhaps, coming from . . . the other" (71; emphasis and ellipses original). It is not, then, that the individual returns obsessively to the scene of seduction as traumatic origin in the past. Rather, in the ongoing process of comprehending the sexual message of the enigmatic signifier and the mode of relationality encoded at the scene of seduction, the individual's unconscious encounters the unconscious of the other.

From the standpoint of Laplanche's key investments in the enigmatic signifier, the force of the other's unconscious ensuing the scene of seduction, and the afterwardness of both the scene and its unconscious in reminiscences, we might venture to expand our theories of childhood sexuality and children's literature to consider the following:

1. To the extent that children's literature constitutes an address to the child by the usually adult other, it mobilizes beyond any representational content that affirms or denies particular sexual categories. The forms of sexuality addressed to young people inhere as much in what is shown or even refused at the scene of reading and/or reception as it does in what is told.
2. The scene of seduction for the child is not a scene of explicit sexual initiation in the genital sense but an initiation into other-relationality where the child encounters the unconscious of the other as both a force from the outside and an incursion into her own psyche. This initial incursion is not inherently sexual or traumatic but may come to be either or both through the dynamic force of the unconscious mobilized through reminiscences. To address a child is to mobilize the sexual force of desire through the very act of hailing, even and especially where there is no specific sexual content.
3. The messages communicated via enigmatic signifiers are neither reducible to language alone nor consciously articulated. They set in motion a complex psychic and interpretive dynamic that includes gestures, silences, sounds, shapes, and smells. Sign-forms exceed words and images. By insisting upon the form of the message over the content of language per se, Laplanche argues that the scene of communication between adult and child is a scene of dense meaning-making; the elements of the message acquire what Laplanche calls "the force of signs and this is because, isolated by the sender, they are addressed to the subject" (75). By this logic, even the blandest and most conservative texts for children *no less so* than those most liberal on matters of sexuality constitute enigmatic signifiers. Our understanding of how literature (or any mode of communication or representation) models or shapes sexuality may be tied to the stories we tell to children, but not exclusively to those stories' representational content. The biggest story we don't tell to children about sexuality may well be the story of our own refusal of our implication in the way their sexuality forms.

4. Such an approach to sexuality invites us to consider that forms of sexuality are not divisible into norms and perversions and are themselves both (a) destablizing forces that unfold over time and (b) shaped by other norms of otherness (race, alien-ness, foreignness, sovereignty).
5. These phenomena that seem like modes of otherness are, moreover, not alternative norms but forms of the *alt within*. As Laplanche puts it, "Perversion, rather, is in everyone, as an important component of sexuality" (qtd. in Caruth). Harking back to Freud's "Three Essays on the Theory of Sexuality," he points out that "in every adult's so-called normal sexuality, there is perversion: there is perversion in the means of taking pleasure, in the forepleasure, and also in the fantasies. . . . More sexuality, that is, in the sense that sexuality and perverse sexuality are everywhere in the most 'innocent' relation of parent and child" (qtd. in Caruth). That such an insight makes many squeamish stands perhaps as the best evidence of the unconscious forces at play in the supposed "innocence" of the adult-child relational dynamic.
6. Understanding the *alt within* also calls us to understand a non-developmental mode of unfolding. Laplanche's translation of *Nachträglichkeit* thus positions us to expand our still univocal thinking about the temporal unfolding of both sexuality and what it means to grow up. Such an intervention recalls Kathryn Bond Stockton's discussion of *Nachträglichkeit* in *The Queer Child* and her discussion of growing sideways. The protohomosexual, she argues, "literalizes a concept that Derrida deemed to govern the whole of Freud's thought: *Nachträglichkeit*, loosely translated by a range of critics as 'deferred effect,' 'belated understanding,' 'retro-causality,' and 'afterwardness'" (14)—all of which frame the temporal conditions under which the queer child can be read as such. Laplanche's theory poses no real challenge to Stockton's reading of the queer child as belatedly emergent but would insist that it is not only the child's unconscious that participates in this belatedness. It is also the adult's.
7. In this sense, the enigmatic signifier also constitutes a rejoinder to Jacqueline Rose's insistence on the adult as the primary agent of children's literature. The problem of the enigmatic signifier is precisely the problem of adult-child relations that, for Rose, underwrites the impossibility of children's fiction.
8. To see language acquisition and message-relationality as foundational to subject development is to insist upon the force of language

in all its myriad forms (gestural, spoken, aural, textual, contextual) as an animating force for sexual desire. Adult-child relationships within and beyond the family likewise can be imagined at play. Encountering sexuality in its formative stages in childhood is already doing so outside of the boxes we have built for sexuality in adulthood—it is to encounter it estranged from the forms that breathe political and representational life into it.

The *Alt Within* and Children's Literature's Fundamental Strangeness

In his interview with Cathy Caruth, Laplanche pursues the question of the enigmatic signifier from the vantage point of the child at his smallest who encounters the other, an other whose reality is bound to his absolute strangeness: "How," Laplanche asks, "does the human being, the baby, encounter this strangeness?" (Caruth). The answer to this question inheres for Laplanche in the fundamental strangeness of the messages themselves:

> It is in the fact that the messages [the child] receives are enigmatic. His messages are enigmatic because those messages are strange to themselves. That is, if the other was not himself invaded by his own other, his internal other, that is, the unconscious, the messages wouldn't be strange and enigmatic. So the problem of the other is strictly bound to the fact that the small human being has no unconscious, and he is confronted with messages invaded by the unconscious of the other.

If adult messages to children are essentially enigmatic signifiers that occasion encounters between the unconscious of the adult and the emergent unconscious of the child, the complexity of such addresses would seem to lie as much in the conditions of their articulation and circulation as in the representational content of the message itself.

Such a recognition stands very much at odds with the ways we talk about the politics of children's literature—particularly in the pressure exerted on politically charged texts that precisely concern representations of sexuality itself. What happens if, following Laplanche, we read as if "sexuality cannot be identified with specific forms of perversity, as if it's not just something that can be isolated here and there"? And what might it mean to track the unconscious as a cultural force when this unconscious (memories, fragments of memories, fantasies—it matters little for the moment) consists of scene or fragments of scene, and above all that these scenes are essentially sexual. The significance of this is not merely contingent—why after all is sexuality accorded a primacy over, say, the alimentary or the need for security? Because the primacy of sexuality opens directly onto the question of the other, and in the case of the child, onto the adult other in his or her alien-ness." ("Unfinished" 64)

It's hard not to wonder what might happen were we to dwell in the enigmatic space of sexuality that the child inhabits in the face of the adult's alien-ness. For the inverse of Laplanche's formulation also remains true: the child reflects back to the adult his own unbearable alien-ness. And one solution to that encounter with the child's unconscious is to remediate it, to familiarize it by categorizing and taxonomizing his desires and relationality into recognizable forms.

In so doing, we treat our messages to young people not as enigmatic or as compromised but as (fantasies of) risk management. If only representation in books were a cure for the material risks to youth! Anyone who has a strong relationship to reading knows that addresses to children exert a force in the world, just as most of us understand that risk is as paradoxically essential to self-making as it may be unbearable to the adult in relation to that child. This unbearability—to the extent that it is a conscious phenomenon for the adult—emerges from the nexus of responsibility they hold in both addressing the child and in managing material risk for that child. It also inheres in what is unsaid by the adult—the unspoken, even unconscious phenomena—the *alt within*. Such a intermingling of the stories we do and do not to tell children suggests that what we don't say often keeps the unsaid, unthought, unconscious alive anyway.

And of course, the child herself also participates in this dynamic—it is not the sole domain of the adult. As Adam Phillips writes, "In the taking and making of bodily risks [the adolescent] begins to constitute his own possibility for a benign solitude, reliably alone in the presence of his own body and its thoughts. The world and his body can feel as dangerous to the adolescent, and not only to the adolescent, as the risks he has *failed* to take with them" (32). The risks of attending to the narratives of childhood that seem impossible to narrate to children and young adults and of representing the complexity of being at risk as something not merely to be swerved away from, in themselves, are risks worth taking, at least in the psychic sense.

The enigmas of enigmatic signifiers—encased as they are within seemingly impossible orders of signs, whether the message takes the form of a bad children's book or a homonormative fiction—are paradoxically enough sites of possibility. The conditions under which young people are addressed by books about sexuality encode within themselves attitudes about sexuality. By tracking the narrative forms that seem impossible or laughable, we begin to place alongside each other the tragic naming of queer youth as a social problem and the farcical limits of our own address to those youth. In so doing, perhaps we begin to understand what it means for young people to live *with* and *in* risk— in the space of the focalized *alt* that is as central to children's lit as it seems peripheral to it: to play with possibility rather than learn correct paths, and so to press beyond our own adult fantasies of youth resilience and the remediation of risk. Such an approach invites us to consider not just the contents of our psychic tickle trunks, where childhood self-making may take narrative form as if it were an endless scene of play, but the forms of relationality, seduction, and even aggression that structure our encounter with interpretive content. The unbearable takes a range of shapes as does the courage to see and recognize forms of relationality, sexual experimentation, gendered belonging, and atypical other-relationality that exist among young people and adults alike. Nowhere, we might say, does the force of the enigmatic signifier make its presence more fully known than in the desire for sexuality to be a banal non-place. We may want to think that it is the child's sexuality and their unconscious that are at risk when in fact it may be our own that we cannot bear.

Notes

1. The Staake website has since disappeared, but it used to be located at http://www.bobstaake.com/badchildrensbooks/. See also the webpage www.facebook.com/YourChildhoodRuined.

2. On this point, he differs from someone like Michel de Certeau for whom naming a place makes it a non-place because the name frames and mediates one's encounter with space.

3. Laplanche traces the origins of his seduction theory to Freud while pointing out that Freud abandoned this crucial feature of his own work, begetting a field that ultimately became "auto-centered." The adult other (usually parental) is, for Laplanche, foundational to subject formation, to such an extent that the other remains encased within the subject.

Works Cited

Augé, Marc. *Non-Places: An Introduction to an Anthropology of Supermodernity*. 1992. Translated by John Howe, Verso, 1995.

Caruth, Cathy. "An Interview with Jean LaPlanche." 2001. http://pmc.iath.virginia.edu/text-only/issue.101/11.2caruth.txt. Accessed 2 Jan. 2023.

Laplanche, Jean. "Interpretation Between Determinism and Hermeneutics." 1992. *Essays on Otherness*, edited by John Fletcher, Routledge, 1999, pp. 138–65.

Laplanche, Jean. "The Unfinished Copernican Revolution." 1992. *Essays on Otherness*, edited by John Fletcher, Routledge, 1999, pp. 52–83.
Phillips, Adam. "Narcissism, For and Against." *Promises, Promises: Essays on Literature and Psychoanalysis*, Faber and Faber, 2000, pp. 200–225.
Phillips, Adam. "On Risk and Solitude." *On Kissing, Tickling, and Being Bored: Psychoanalytic Essays on the Unexamined Life*, Harvard UP, 1993, pp. 27–41.
Rose, Jacqueline. *The Case of Peter Pan; or, The Impossibility of Children's Fiction*. 1984. U of Penn P, 1992.
Sedgwick, Eve Kosofsky. "How to Bring Your Kids Up Gay." *Social Text*, vol. 29, 1991, pp. 18–27.
Staake, Bob. "Bad Little Children's Books: A Bob Staake Gallery. Satire, Humor and Visual Parody of Classic Children's Books from the 1940s through 1960s." http://www.bobstaake.com/badchildrensbooks/. Accessed 28 Apr. 2013.
Stockton, Kathryn Bond. *The Queer Child; or, Growing Sideways in the Twentieth Century*. Duke UP, 2009.

"WE'RE AMERICANS TOO!"
Contingencies and Contradictions in Picture Books about Japanese American Incarceration

Gabrielle Atwood Halko

> *Because theories of liberal democracy embrace a universality of citizenship in relation to the rights and freedoms of individuals within a nation-state, there is an inherent assumption that these rights function to equalize individuals, that citizenship is full membership in a community whereby differences become irrelevant to individuals' status as citizens.*
> —T. H. MARSHALL, *Citizenship and Social Class*

Over the past three decades, World War II has become the central defining experience of the United States in the twentieth century. Simultaneously lauded and commodified, the values of the so-called "Greatest Generation"— tireless work ethic, humility, and sacrifice in the service of patriotism—have been heralded as representing the best of America. Literature, including books for young readers, has been a powerful vehicle for reframing and sustaining the significance of World War II in the American consciousness; indeed, children's books are "one of the most significant ways through which we entrust a future generation with the continuing survival of key American cultural memories" (Reeds 384).

Picture books such as Chaconas and Lewin's *Across the Blue Pacific* (2006) and Borden and Parker's *Pennies In a Jar* (2007) reinforce the values of the Greatest Generation; their portrayals of home front experiences during WWII foreground White child protagonists' experiences of patriotism and sacrifice in the service of freedom. In a canny alignment of diverse representation and dominant narrative, a growing body of picture books featuring non-White protagonists such as *Wind Flyers* (2007), *Nim and the War Effort* (1997), and *Chester Nez and the Unbreakable Code* (2018) sustains that story by positioning Black, Chinese, and Navajo characters as patriotic Americans who persevere despite the racism that they endure. In their ultimately positive portrayal of America and its heroic role in defending and preserving freedom, these picture books reify both past and current constructs of citizenship, patriotism, and American identity.

Raiford and Romano note the powerful influence and multiple functions of these dominant historical narratives: "Representations of the past can be mobilized to serve partisan purposes; they can shape a nation's sense of identity, build hegemony, or serve to shore up the political interests of the state; and they can certainly influence the ways in which people understand their world" (xxi). Picture books about Japanese American incarceration occupy a peculiar space in which they both further and resist the collective identity and cultural understanding that Raiford and Romano describe.[1] There is no question that these books attempt to disrupt the hegemonic narratives of unified home front and wartime triumph that the United States continually refreshes in its own mythology. But do they succeed?

Located at the complicated intersection of historical narrative and collective memory, literature about Japanese American incarceration performs critical historical and cultural work.[2] Patricia Wakida calls the story of the incarceration "disturbingly relevant." To study it, she writes, "is not just to explore history, but to use that exploration to understand more deeply the consequences of racial prejudice, to confront more fully the harm that it does and the strengths that it calls forth, and by increasing intellectual and emotional awareness, to help ensure that such events cannot occur again" (xiv). Rachel Endo meanwhile positions Japanese American incarceration literature as work that "surfaces a relatively invisible moment in our nation's history while offering critical counterperspectives about what it means to be 'American'" (4).

In this chapter I examine nine picture books about Japanese American incarceration published from 1993–2013. Each text centers a Japanese American incarceree and makes visible this "relatively invisible" historical moment as it engages explicitly with questions of citizenship and American identity.[3] Through both textual and visual representations, these texts disrupt the popular narrative that the status and privileges of citizenship are granted uniformly to all. In doing so, they interrogate existing ideas of American identity, including the perpetual exclusion of Japanese Americans[4] from claiming it, and the contradictions and caveats that exist within definitions of citizenship. Ultimately, I argue that despite overwhelming displays of loyalty and patriotism by Japanese Americans, these texts illuminate the impossibility of their fully recognized, universal citizenship.

Citizenship, Alt Citizenship, and the Cultural Work of Picture Books

While picture books initially might appear to be ill-matched to the complexity of Japanese American incarceration, they are important sites of exposure and learning. Picture book scholar Lawrence R. Sipe identifies these texts as "the principal format through which young children experience literature" (122). Their importance rests not only in their "firstness" but also in their status as ideologically charged: as Sipe notes, "All art, including literature for children, is saturated with the ideology and worldview of those who produce it. And children's response to literature can either reinscribe or challenge their own ideology and worldview" (124). The role of picture books in ideological construction, including the concepts and practices of patriotism and citizenship, cannot be underestimated.

Some scholars envision possibilities for picture books to move beyond the role of reification of existing majoritarian beliefs and perform crucial cultural work around resistance and counternarrativity. According to Gretchen Papazian, "Picturebooks are . . . taking advantage of specific aspects of their format in order to expose, push against, and even break longstanding forms of social and political oppression" (170). Papazian specifies possibilities beyond ideological reification: "Nowhere is twenty-first-century children's literature making efforts to acknowledge and alter American history's ideological bequests more effectively than in the picturebook format" (169).

But what are the limits of acknowledging those bequests, and what is required to alter them? Noreen Naseem Rodríguez encourages elementary teachers to "use Asian American children's literature as a means to disrupt exclusionary official narratives and dominant notions of white citizenship" (555) though she notes that supplementation with primary sources and additional historical context is necessary. Rodríguez continues, "When teachers adopt a critical stance in the teaching of histories, counternarratives can lead to transformative understandings of the past and present" (556). However, she warns that counterstories can be used in ways that uphold the dominant narrative rather than resist it. In writing about another American moment of crisis, the September 11 attacks, Jo Lampert cautions that nationalistic discourse is difficult for both writers and readers to navigate due to what is privileged and what is subordinated: for example, "a discourse of multiculturalism might be present in a text, yet nullified by a competing discourse of nationalism" (31).

By illuminating an event driven by racism and xenophobia, picture books about Japanese American incarceration necessarily expand and disrupt the story of World War II and more broadly of US history overall.[5] That disruption highlights one of the most intensely contested questions in American history: Who is a citizen? Nearly 250 years after the founding of the US, we continue to grapple with what citizenship means and how (or whether) citizenship can be performed to such a convincing degree that it is considered both unconditional and incontestable.

Despite the fact that "in both social and political terms, one of the most powerful designations one can claim, or be given, is that of citizen," Asian Americans have been excluded from that privilege since their arrival in what is now the United States (Macintosh and Loutzenheiser 95). Rodríguez elaborates: "In the American imagination, to be Asian American means to act according to fundamentally different cultural dictates regardless of legal status or political activity that render individuals unassimilable and immutably foreign" (531). Gilbert C. Park adds that Asian Americans "are faced with the 'authenticity dilemma' as Americans where others consider them to be less than complete Americans" (452). In an analysis of Asian Americans and Constitutional citizenship, Leti Volpp maintains that "the discourse of constitutional citizenship claims that all citizens ought to be treated equally. But there are assumptions about Asian Americans that have forever rendered their presumptive fitness for citizenship suspect" (588). Perhaps the most succinct statement comes from Frank H. Wu: "Ours is citizenship based on consent, not descent" (87).

In twenty-first-century America, the question of citizenship—who is born with rights to claim it and who successfully seeks it—remains a topic both popular and controversial.[6] Amidst this ongoing discussion, picture books are especially important because they engage child readers during the developmental period when they begin to grapple with ideas such as nationhood and citizenship. Lampert predicts, "If children are indeed constituted by what they read, then the books written about major critical events will be an important source of new and competing discourses with respect to identity, culture, race, and citizenship" (3).

Citizenship education is a common component of American school curricula by kindergarten.[7] For American children in elementary grades, good citizenship includes local efforts (being a good neighbor, volunteering) as well as "showing pride in the country" through performative acts such as reciting the Pledge of Allegiance and standing for the national anthem (Dennis). Resources for teaching citizenship are plentiful and diverse, and the ideals of citizenship often appear as desired character traits in picture books.⁸

Yet the nature of citizenship education remains ambiguous. Jennifer Tupper points to the "impossible citizenship" common in schools; this ideal supposes "universal" conditions for citizenship without acknowledging the inequities that exist for many individuals attempting to exercise their rights as citizens (45). This slippage in how we teach children to be citizens is not only significant on its own; in combination with the ideal of "impossible citizenship," it both reflects and shapes cultural expectations of who is American and who is not. That latter group—those deemed not American despite their birthright to citizenship—are driven into a liminal space of alt citizenship because of some perceived deficit in their American identity. Complicating this impossible ideal is that students, regardless of their racial or ethnic identification, commonly equate citizenship with whiteness. In a study of second graders working with Yoshiko Uchida's *The Bracelet* (1993), students "implicitly understood whiteness as the norm in U.S. society and thus equated whiteness with Americanness, and in turn, citizenship" (548). These students recognized whiteness as "the 'natural' state of affairs" and therefore, "to be nonwhite is to be non-American" (548).⁹

It is not entirely surprising, then, that despite the alignment of picture book readership and citizenship education curriculum, the circumstances of the characters in texts about Japanese American incarceration consistently contradict the values of equality, democracy, and fairness that citizenship education centers. The question of how to represent this contradiction is vexing but necessary if we are to convey the incarceration with historical accuracy. Traise Yamamoto summarizes the gap between the ideal of citizenship and the reality of incarceration: "Fully two thirds of those forcibly dislocated and imprisoned were American citizens, putting into crisis the issue and meaning of US citizenship; national, social, and cultural inclusion; and loyalty and group identification. President Roosevelt's signing of Executive Order 9066 signified the extent to which the rights of citizenship and national identity could not be assumed as a consequence of birth but rather were conferred or granted" (99). Emily Roxworthy labels this disconnect "the American myth of performative citizenship." This myth "proclaims that American citizenship is officially and effectively conferred upon any individual, regardless of race or national origin, based simply upon the performance of a codified repertoire of speech acts and embodied acts" (13). Roxworthy notes that this is not exclusively a Japanese American issue: "What this myth obscures is the extent to which citizenship has been officially denied to various racialized groups and, when conferred, has lacked efficacy in terms of the unequal enforcement of its privileges based on proximity to whiteness" (13). As these picture books show, the myth of performative citizenship is powerful and ultimately tragic; characters in the picture books initially express faith that their citizenship will be recognized because they are loyal Americans but ultimately realize that their hopes are futile. Universal citizenship will never be theirs no matter how visibly, performatively American they are; they remain theoretically American, theoretically citizens, trapped in that liminal space.

Early Picture Book Representations

In 1993, three picture books about Japanese American incarceration were published in the United States: Ken Mochizuki and Dom Lee's *Baseball Saved Us*, Yoshiko Uchida and Joanna Yardley's *The Bracelet*, and Marlene Shigekawa and Isao Kikuchi's *Blue Jay in the Desert*. As these texts establish a narrative and visual baseline for picture books about Japanese American incarceration, they simultaneously reveal the tension between resistance and conformity to consensus memory and dominant cultural narratives.[10]

Each picture book features a child protagonist and renders the events of camp life from a child's point of view. While adult characters add context via their comments and communities of various sizes are pictured in each book, it is the protagonists and their immediate families who are foregrounded. The narratives highlight some of the many losses, both individual and collective, that Japanese American incarcerees suffered in the camps: the disintegration of families and cultural traditions in *Baseball Saved Us*; the loss of a treasured keepsake in *The Bracelet*; the adjustment of self-image from majestic eagle to ordinary blue jay in *Blue Jay in the Desert*.

This trio of 1993 texts addresses the concept of citizenship—not only the legalities but also the "belongingness" and state of being American that aligns with so much citizenship education.[11] Uchida includes this passage in the opening scene of *The Bracelet*:

> The government was sending them to a prison camp b/c they were Japanese-Americans. They hadn't done anything wrong. They were being treated like the enemy just because they *looked* like the enemy. The FBI had sent Papa to a prisoner-of-war camp in Montana just because he worked for a Japanese company. It was crazy, Emi thought. They loved America, but America didn't love them back. And it didn't want to trust them. (1)

The language of patriotism, a key element of citizenship, is explicit: "They loved America." The language of betrayal and exclusion, of the failure of the promise of citizenship, is present too: "but America didn't love them back. And it didn't want to trust them." A later passage reinforces Emi's love of country as well as her American citizenship: "The windows were boarded up now, but Emi saw a sign still hanging on the door. It said, WE ARE LOYAL AMERICANS. I am, too, Emi thought. We all are. But the Army didn't seem to think so" (14).

Mochizuki begins *Baseball Saved Us* in a similar way, with overt language of patriotism and claiming of American identity/citizenship: "I asked [Dad] again why we were here. 'Because,' he said, 'America is at war with Japan, and the government thinks that Japanese Americans can't be trusted. But it's wrong that we're here. We're Americans too!'" (2) This text, set on the far right, is paired with a closeup illustration of the protagonist, Shorty, at the far left and his father across the gutter at the right edge of the visual. Behind them, a barbed wire–topped fence stretches across the sepia-toned illustration; a guard tower with an armed guard triangulates the visual. Shorty's acceptance and potential recognition of his Americanness comes at the end of the story when he hits the winning run in a postincarceration baseball game. While that moment is joyful and redemptive for both the protagonist and the reader, it is also fleeting—and there is no promise that Shorty's identity as a "real" American will last beyond the game.

In contrast, Shigekawa chooses more circumspect language and positions it later in the narrative of *Blue Jay in the Desert*. Midway through the story, Grandpa and Junior meet two Mojave men who offer Junior's family a gift of corn for Grandpa's victory garden (19); in writing the Mojave men into the story, Shigekawa highlights both the performative, patriotic citizenship of Junior's grandfather and the often unrecognized, disrespected citizenship of Native Americans. Shigekawa expands the portrayal of incarceration beyond those of *Baseball Saved Us* or *The Bracelet* and acknowledges the reality that some camps, including Gila River and Poston, were built on existing Native American reservations.[12]

In his illustrations, however, Kikuchi breaks from the realism of *The Bracelet* and *Baseball Saved Us* to present cartoonlike characters in an improbably bright color palette. Furthermore, he draws the characters as racially ambiguous; it is the text that does the work of positioning Junior and his family as Japanese Americans. Finally, Kikuchi situates most of his illustrations on a white background; of the eighteen illustrative openings, only five contain explicit visuals of camp life such as barracks, barbed wire, soldiers, or guard towers.

Each of these 1993 picture books showcases performative citizenship in multiple ways—the families portrayed own their homes, run successful businesses, assimilate into White communities, play baseball, and grow victory gardens to aid the war effort despite their own incarceration. The books feature endings that provide resolution to the child protagonists and readers alike; while they are stories of an upsetting history, they are not in and of themselves upsetting (though arguably, Kikuchi's illustrations that depart from realism and remain "unraced" can be interpreted as countering the work of Shigekawa's text and ultimately making the book more palatable for mainstream readers).

The Growth of the Collection

The books that follow this early trio expand possibilities for visual and textual representation of the incarceration as they explicitly address citizenship, patriotism, and belonging. *So Far from the Sea* (1998) depicts a family's 1972 visit to Manzanar. The essential rights imbued in American citizenship and identity underlie this statement by narrator Laura to her father, a former incarceree: "'It wasn't fair,' I say. 'It was the meanest thing in the whole world. You were Americans. Like I am'" (14). The father remembers a moment when performative citizenship failed his family: "'When they came for us, my father said to me, "Koharu! Put on your Cub Scout uniform. That way they will know you are a true American and they will not take you." I put it on. But they took me anyway. They took all of us'" (28). This passage in the text is accompanied by an illustration of the boy in his Cub Scout uniform saluting two armed soldiers.[13] Family photos and an American flag hang on the walls of what appears to be a middle-class home; however, these visual artifacts of American ideals do not spare the family from incarceration.

The 2001 picture book *Flowers from Mariko* also addresses "after" by focusing on postwar repatriation. The story begins on the day that Mariko is set to leave "Camp" after being incarcerated with her family for three years. In the second opening, the visual and textual narrative flash back to the time when "she and her family, along with all the other families of Japanese ancestry she knew, were forced into Camp." Citizenship and belonging remain central: "'Just because I look like the enemy doesn't mean I am,' [Mariko] had told her mother angrily. 'I am American. I was born right here in Los Angeles'" (3). The text also acknowledges the realities of economic loss—Mariko's father has to leave his gardening business and truck in the care of his landlord—and the anti-Japanese racism that continues after the war. While the story ends on a hopeful note, the family is still living at the trailer park, the place for people "who didn't have anywhere else to go" (16).

Repatriation is explored further in *Welcome Home, Swallows*, also published in 2001. This picture book, a second collaboration between Shigekawa and Kikuchi, continues Junior's story after he and his family return home to California. Two of Junior's beloved uncles, one a combat veteran and the other a "no-no boy,"[14] expand the story of Japanese American incarceration and portray contrasting attitudes regarding citizenship and patriotism. Uncle Willie returns home from war as an amputee: "'Why did you go into the Army?' asked Junior.[15] Uncle Willie paused and then said, 'Because I wanted to show everyone that we are loyal Americans. We may look Japanese on the outside, but we're Americans in our hearts'" (26–27). In contrast, Uncle Min has spent the war at Tule Lake Segregation Center "thinking about our family and thinking about the war" (28–29).

The 2006 *A Place Where Sunflowers Grow* by Amy Lee-Tai offers a bilingual textual narrative in Japanese and English. Although citizenship is referenced only obliquely in this picture book, both the text and illustrations are more graphic in their depiction of the incarceration. "Had it only been thirteen months since they were forced to leave? First they had to live in a horse stall that smelled of manure in Tanforan, California. Now they were living in a tarpaper barrack in Topaz, Utah. Everything but her family had been taken from Mari—and she hadn't done anything wrong!" (6) The next opening shows Mari and Papa as small figures set against the rows of barracks that extend towards the guard tower, fence, and mountains on the horizon. The perspective is from a guard tower in the foreground; much of the left page is dominated by the side and roof of the tower. An armed soldier is visible; readers can see his helmet, neck, and back but not his face. The guard holds a gun that is pointed at the camp. The text reads, "They passed beneath watchtowers where military police pointed guns at anyone they feared might escape" (9).

Katie Yamasaki's picture book *Fish for Jimmy* (2013) further expands the portrayal of incarceration both visually and textually, including a scene of Father being taken into FBI custody: "*Bang! Bang! Bang!* Mother answered the door to three men whose badges read FBI. The men told Father that, because he was Japanese, he posed a threat to America. Father tried to explain that he loved living in America. He had a home and a vegetable market and a family here. But the men said he had to go with them" (6). Despite Father's attempts at assimilation through acts of performative citizenship—he is a homeowner, an entrepreneur with a successful business, and devoted to his family and country—he is not viewed as American. Because he is Japanese American, he cannot ever fully belong.

Barbed Wire Baseball, also published in 2013, differs from its predecessors by portraying an adult protagonist, the professional baseball player Kenichi "Zeni" Zenimura and presenting Zeni's story as nonfiction. The jacket blurb is the most direct to date: "Zeni, his wife, and their two sons, along with more than 100,000 other American citizens of Japanese descent, were sent to internment camps in the American Midwest and West. They were imprisoned not for any wrongdoing but simply because of their ancestry." The text offers more details: "120,000 Americans of Japanese descent who lived on the West Coast were forced into ten internment camps. The government considered those Japanese Americans to be possible spies and, without evidence or trial, locked them up—men, women, and children. American citizens, all were treated like prisoners of war, housed in barracks and penned in with barbed wire" (6). Notably, however, this 2013 text still uses the sanitized term "internment" rather than "incarceration"—and the Library of Congress heading for these books remains the infuriatingly benign "Japanese Americans—Evacuation and relocation, 1942–45."

In this story, citizenship is not addressed directly; Zeni's fame and athletic ability, however, mitigate his experience of incarceration to some extent by granting him legitimacy through baseball. As Zeni builds the baseball field that he hopes will offer recreation and respite, he is granted permission to borrow the camp's bulldozer (7). More significantly, despite rules prohibiting leaving the barracks after dark, Zeni and his sons sneak out to gather lumber for the backstop and bleachers; although the camp commander knows about this violation, he tells the guards to "let them go, so long as they [don't] escape" (11). In contrast to Shorty's experience in *Baseball Saved Us*, Zeni is recognized as American throughout his time incarcerated because of his baseball fame and talent, which positioned him as closer to American identity—yet he is still incarcerated as a potential enemy of the state.

Present Stasis, Future Possibilities

Over a twenty-year span, then, picture books about Japanese American incarceration reveal both growth and stasis. The hopeful endings of some early texts give way to more ambivalent and realistic conclusions; as Japanese American incarceration has received more mainstream cultural acknowledgement, writers and artists have presented increasingly complicated narratives.[16] Yet the dual themes of claiming American identity and the precarity of that identity remain consistent. Intentionally or not, citizenship is modeled in these picture books as racialized, unequal status that is conferred conditionally and unequally; in reality, then as now, citizens' rights and privileges align with how closely they conform to contemporary constructs of both "White" and "foreign."

While these picture books appear to convey a message of equality and democracy—of correcting a mistake—they do so while reinforcing US nationalism and a very particular kind of patriotism that simultaneously demands proof while it denies any such evidence. The characters in these stories embody/perform their Americanness in multiple ways: through homeownership, business ownership, and friendships with White classmates. They play baseball, perhaps the most American of sports. They obey Executive Order 9066. They successfully integrate with White communities preincarceration and attempt to do so when repatriated. And yet none of these illustrations of normalcy, loyalty, or belonging matter; Americans or not, they are subjected to the racist dehumanization of removal and incarceration.

In their attempts to broaden the definition of who is American, these picture books paradoxically replicate ideologies of impossible citizenship as well as a construct of childhood that uncritically reproduces norms of racism and exclusion and portrays them as distanced from the present. A congruent concern is that these books help to acculturate young readers to accept inequality and racism as fundamental elements of citizenship and to view citizenship as inextricably tied to Whiteness. In other words, the system that creates and sustains alt citizenship remains undisturbed.

Through their presentation of Japanese American incarceration as a delimited historical moment, the power of picture books about Japanese American incarceration is diluted. Certainly some readers absorb and appreciate the counternarrative that these books create and sustain, and there is anecdotal evidence of this occurring both in informal and classroom settings.[17] Yet the dominant cultural narrative of WWII is so strong and so inextricably tied to our present-day identity as a nation that these books are equally likely to be read and used as a cultural salve—a representation of racism and nationalism as a historical anomaly rather than the inevitable distillation of centuries of anti-Asian racism and resentment. Such a representation decontextualizes Japanese American incarceration from history, distances it from any connection to the present, and relieves readers from any obligation to act or affect any meaningful change.

In picture books about Japanese American incarceration, readers find both constancy and change as the books simultaneously resist and reinscribe ideals of patriotism and citizenship. That they cannot reach a resolution, that their work remains unfinished, is a consequence of their position as counternarrative within the dominant culture. Because these texts must constantly negotiate their existence and significance within the overpowering dominant narrative, including contradictory messages about childhood citizenship, their work remains incomplete.

Notes

1. While this event is still commonly referred to as "internment," that terminology is both factually inaccurate and inappropriately benign. I follow the recommendations of Densho and the Japanese American Citizens League. See "Terminology" and Japanese American Citizens League Power of Words II Committee.

2. See Teorey.

3. I do not include Allen Say's *Home of the Brave* (2002) in this analysis because it does not meet these criteria.

4. This exclusion is not limited to Japanese Americans; it is common for Asian Americans to be constructed as "perpetual foreigners." See Lee; Omi and Winant; Rodríguez; and Wu.

5. The racism that formed the basis of Japanese American incarceration was not a new development in the 1940s. See The Pluralism Project and Waite.

6. Established programs such as DACA, Deferred Action for Childhood Arrivals, came under increased threat during the Trump administration; while this was unsurprising given the overt racism of Trump's campaign and staff, his administration also sought to repeal foundational rights such as birthright citizenship and to strip naturalized citizens of their citizenship status. See "What Is DACA"; East Bay Community Law Center; Gessen; and Lyons.

7. See "Teaching Children How to Be Good Citizens" and "Best Ideas for Teaching Citizenship to Early Learners."

8. For more resources on citizenship education, see Cooper; "Children Are Citizens"; "Kid Nation"; Messier; and Planbook. For an example of local citizenship, see "Children Are Citizens."

9. See also Lee; Park; Volpp; and Wu.

10. See Halko.

11. The publication of three picture books in 1993 is most likely the culmination of many factors, including the redress movement of the 1970s and 1980s, the forming of Congressional committees to study the incarceration, and the eventual apology and reparations payments to survivors. The presses ranged from Asian American–focused Polychrome to mainstream Houghton Mifflin, which suggests that Japanese American incarceration was considered a relevant and marketable topic.

12. See Mastropolo and Trakes.

13. The Scout Oath and Scout Law add context to this illustration with their emphasis on loyalty and duty to country. The Scout Oath goes, "On my honor, I will do my best To do my duty to God and my country and to obey the Scout Law; To help other people at all times; To keep myself physically strong, mentally awake and morally straight." The Scout Law states, "A Scout is: Trustworthy, Loyal, Helpful, Friendly, Courteous, Kind, Obedient, Cheerful, Thrifty, Brave, Clean, and Reverent."

14. For a definition and context for this term, see Niiya.

15. Based on the segregated military that existed during WWII, it is highly likely that Uncle Willie served in the 442nd Regimental Combat Team. See "442nd Regimental Combat Team" and Odo.

16. Examples include the 1992 opening of the Japanese American National Museum in Los Angeles, the 1996 founding of Densho, the 2015 Broadway musical *Allegiance*, and George Takei's 2019 graphic novel *They Called Us Enemy*.

17. See Gariepy; JanBuyer; Pen Name; PWR; Rodríguez; and Youngs.

Works Cited

"442nd Regimental Combat Team." *Go for Broke National Education Center*, goforbroke.org/history/unit-history/442nd-regimental-combat-team. Accessed 20 Dec. 2020.

"Asians and Asian Exclusion." *The Pluralism Project*, pluralism.org/asians-and-asian-exclusion. Accessed 3 Jan. 2021.

"Best Ideas for Teaching Citizenship to Early Learners." *Kids Academy*, 3 Dec. 2018, kidsacademy.mobi/storytime/teaching-citizenship-elementary-students/. Accessed 5 Feb. 2021.

"Boy Scout Oath, Law, Motto and Slogan and the Outdoor Code." *US Scouting Service Project*, usscouts.org/advance/boyscout/bsoathlaw.asp. Accessed 19 Oct. 2021.

Bright Horizons Education Team, "Teaching Children How to Be Good Citizens." *Bright Horizons*, 24 Nov. 2019, brighthorizons.com/family-resources/how-to-be-good-citizen-for-kids. Accessed 5 Feb. 2021.

Chen, Fu-jen, and Su-lin Yu. "Asian North-American Children's Literature about the Internment: Visualizing and Verbalizing the Traumatic *Thing*." *Children's Literature in Education*, vol. 37, 2006, pp. 111–24, DOI 10.1007/s10583-006-9001-9.

"Children Are Citizens." *Project Zero*, Harvard Graduate School of Education, pz.harvard.edu/projects/children-are-citizens. Accessed 5 Feb. 2021.

Ching, Stuart H. D., and Jann Pataray-Ching. "Toward a Socio-Political Framework for Asian American Children's Literature." *The New Advocate*, vol. 16, no. 2, spring 2003, pp. 123–28.

Cooper, Stacy D. "Teaching Citizenship to First Graders." *The Classroom*, theclassroom.com/teaching-citizenship-first-graders-8030550.html. Accessed 5 Feb. 2021.

Dennis, Letise. "How to Teach Your Child to Be a Good Citizen." *K12 Learning Liftoff*, 16 Sept. 2016, learningliftoff.com/teach-child-good-citizen/. Accessed 5 Feb. 2021.

East Bay Community Law Center. "DACA Information." Undocumented Student Program, University of California at Berkeley, 20 Apr. 2022, undocu.berkeley.edu/legal-support-overview/what-is-daca/. Accessed 10 Feb. 2021.

Endo, Rachel. *The Incarceration of Japanese Americans in the 1940s: Literature for the High School Classroom*. NCTE, 2018.

Gariepy, Shonna. Review of *So Far from the Sea*, by Eve Bunting. *Amazon*, 7 Oct. 2006, www.amazon.com/So-Far-Sea-Eve-Bunting/product-reviews/0547237529/ref=cm_cr_dp_d_show_all_btm?ie=UTF8&reviewerType=all_reviews. Accessed 10 Jan. 2021.

Gessen, Masha. "In America, Naturalized Citizens No Longer Have an Assumption of Permanence." *The New Yorker*, 18 June 2018, newyorker.com/news/our-columnists/in-america-naturalized-citizens-no-longer-have-an-assumption-of-permanence.

Halko, Gabrielle Atwood. "Baseball, Blue Jays, Bracelets, and Barbed Wire: Picture Books and the Visual Iconography of Japanese American Incarceration." *Children's Literature Association Quarterly*, vol. 46, no. 4, 2021, pp. 414–31. *Project MUSE*, doi:10.1353/chq.2021.0049.

Harada, Violet H. "Breaking the Silence: Sharing the Japanese American Internment Experience with Adolescent Readers." *Journal of Adolescent and Adult Literacy*, vol. 39, no. 8, May 1996, pp. 630–37.

JanBuyer. Review of *Baseball Saved Us*, by Ken Mochizuki. *Amazon*, 16 Jan. 2012, amazon.com/Baseball-Saved-Us-Ken-Mochizuki/product-reviews/1880000199/ref=cm_cr_getr_d_paging_btm_next_4?ie=UTF8&reviewerType=all_reviews&pageNumber=4. Accessed 10 Feb. 2021.

Japanese American Citizens League Power of Words II Committee. *Power of Words Handbook: A Guide to Language about Japanese Americans in World War II: Understanding Euphemisms and Preferred Terminology*. Japanese American Citizens League, 2013.
"Kid Nation." *Harvard Graduate School of Education*, gse.harvard.edu/news/uk/15/04/kid-nation#sthash.1V23Ubty.dpuf. Accessed 5 Feb. 2021.
Lampert, Jo. *Children's Fiction about 9/11: Ethnic, Heroic, and National Identities*. Routledge, 2010.
Lee, Erika. *The Making of Asian America: A History*. Simon and Schuster, 2015.
Lyons, Patrick J. "Trump Wants to Abolish Birthright Citizenship. Can He Do That?" *The New York Times*, 23 Aug. 2019, nytimes.com/2019/08/22/us/birthright-citizenship-14th-amendment-trump.html.
Macintosh, Lori B., and Lisa W. Loutzenheiser. "Troubling Bodies in Citizenship Education: Queering Citizenship." *Troubling the Canon of Citizenship Education*, edited by George H. Richardson and David W. Blades, Peter Lang, 2006, pp. 95–102.
Marshall, T. H. *Citizenship and Social Class*. Cambridge UP, 1950.
Mastropolo, Frank. "An Internment Camp within an Internment Camp." *ABC News*, 9 Feb. 2009, abcnews.go.com/US/story?id=4310157&page=1.
Messier, Alyssa. "Citizenship and Elementary Education—How Do You Teach That?" *iCivics*, 9 July 2015, icivics.org/news/blog-post/citizenship-and-elementary-education-how-do-you-teach. Accessed 5 Feb. 2021.
Niiya, Brian. "No-no boys." *Densho Encyclopedia*, 15 July 2020, encyclopedia.densho.org/No-no_boys/. Accessed 15 Feb. 2021.
Odo, Franklin. "442nd Regimental Combat Team." *Densho Encyclopedia*, 16 Oct. 2020, encyclopedia.densho.org/442nd_Regimental_Combat_Team/. Accessed 15 Feb. 2021.
Papazian, Gretchen. "Color Multiculturally: Twenty-First-Century Multicultural Picturebooks, Color(ing) beyond the Lines." *Children's Literature*, vol. 46, 2018, p. 169–200. *Project MUSE*, doi:10.1353/chl.2018.0008.
Pen Name. Review of *Baseball Saved Us*, by Ken Mochizuki. *Amazon*, 21 May 2009, amazon.com/Baseball-Saved-Us-Ken-Mochizuki/product-reviews/1880000199/ref=cm_cr_getr_d_paging_btm_prev_1?ie=UTF8&reviewerType=all_reviews&pageNumber=1. Accessed 10 Feb. 2021.
Planbook. "Why Are We Learning This? Teaching Citizenship and Its Value." *Planbook*, blog .planbook.com/teaching-citizenship/. Accessed 5 Feb. 2021.
PWR. Review of *The Bracelet*, by Yoshiko Uchida. *Amazon*, 24 Feb 2006, amazon.com/Bracelet-Yoshiko-Uchida/dp/069811390X/ref=sr_1_1?dchild=1&keywords=the+bracelet&qid=1628536514&sr=8-1#customerReviews. Accessed 10 Feb. 2021.
Reeds, Eleanor. "Representing the Integration of Baseball to a New Generation." *Children's Literature Association Quarterly*, vol. 41, no. 4, 2016, pp. 384–402. doi:10.1353/chq.2016.0045.
Rodríguez, Noreen Naseem. "From Margins to Center: Developing Cultural Citizenship through the Teaching of Asian American History." *Theory and Research in Social Education*, vol. 46, no. 4, 2018, pp. 528–73.
Romano, Renee C., and Leigh Raiford. *The Civil Rights Movement in American Memory*. U of Georgia P, 2006.
Roxworthy, Emily. *The Spectacle of Japanese American Trauma: Racial Performativity and World War II*. U of Hawaii P, 2008.
Sipe, Lawrence R. "Children's Response to Literature: Author, Text, Reader, Context." *Theory Into Practice*, summer 1999, pp. 120–29.
Takei, George, et al. *They Called Us Enemy*. Illustrated by Harmony Becker, Top Shelf Productions, 2019.
Teorey, Matthew. "Untangling Barbed Wire Attitudes: Internment Literature for Young Adults." *Children's Literature Association Quarterly*, vol. 33, no. 3, fall 2008, pp. 227–45. https://doi.org/10.1353/chq.0.0019.

"Terminology." *Densho*, densho.org/terminology/. Accessed 15 Oct. 2021.
Trakes, Wendy. "Arizona Japanese Internment Camps." *Salt River Stories*, saltriverstories.org/items/show/338. Accessed 15 Oct. 2021.
Tupper, Jennifer. "Education and the (Im)Possibilities of Citizenship." *Troubling the Canon of Citizenship Education*, edited by George H. Richardson and David W. Blades. Peter Lang, 2006, pp. 43–54.
Volpp, Leti. "'Obnoxious to Their Very Nature': Asian Americans and Constitutional Citizenship." *Citizenship Studies*, vol. 5, no. 1, 2001, https://ssrn.com/abstract=268790.
Waite, Kevin. "The Bloody History of Anti-Asian Violence in the West." *National Geographic*, 10 May 2021, nationalgeographic.com/history/article/the-bloody-history-of-anti-asian-violence-in-the-west.
Wakida, Patricia. "Preface." *Only What We Could Carry: The Japanese American Internment Experience*, edited by Lawson Fusao Inada, Heyday Books, 2000.
"What Is DACA and Who Are the DREAMers?" *Anti-Defamation League*. 11 Sep. 2017, updated Aug. 2021. adl.org/education/resources/tools-and-strategies/table-talk/what-is-daca-and-who-are-the-dreamers. Accessed 10 Feb. 2021.
Wu, Frank H. *Yellow: Race in America Beyond Black and White*. Basic Books, 2002.
Yamamoto, Traise. "Reaching across the Barbed Wire: Interracial Friendships in Young Adult Japanese American Incarceration Literature." *Growing Up Asian American in Young Adult Fiction*, edited by Ymitri Mathison, UP of Mississippi, 2018.
Youngs, Suzette. "Understanding History through the Visual Images in Historical Fiction." *Language Arts*, vol. 89, no. 6, July 2012, pp. 379–95, jstor.org/stable/41804361.

Picture Books

Borden, Louise W. *Across the Blue Pacific*. Illustrated by Robert Andrew Parker, Houghton Mifflin, 2006.
Bruchac, Joseph. *Chester Nez and the Unbreakable Code*. Illustrated by Liz Amini-Holmes, Albert Whitman, 2018.
Bunting, Eve. *So Far from the Sea*. Illustrated by Chris Sontpiet, Sandpiper/Houghton Mifflin, 1998.
Chaconas, Dori J. *Pennies in a Jar*. Illustrated by Ted Lewin, Peachtree, 2007.
Johnson, Angela. *Wind Flyers*. Illustrated by Loren Long, Simon and Schuster, 2007.
Lee, Milly. *Nim and the War Effort*. Illustrated by Yangsook Choi, Farrar, Straus and Giroux, 1997.
Lee-Tai, Amy. *A Place Where Sunflowers Grow*. Illustrated by Felicia Hoshino, Children's Book Press, 2006.
Mochizuki, Ken. *Baseball Saved Us*. Illustrated by Dom Lee, Lee, and Low, 1993.
Moss, Marissa. *Barbed Wire Baseball*. Illustrated by Yoko Shimizu, Abrams, 2013.
Noguchi, Rick, and Deneen Jenks. *Flowers from Mariko*. Illustrated by Michelle Reiko Kumata, Lee, and Low, 2001
Shigekawa, Marlene. *Blue Jay in the Desert*. Illustrated by Isao Kikuchi, Polychrome, 1993.
Shigekawa, Marlene. *Welcome Home, Swallows*. Illustrated by Isao Kikuchi, Polychrome, 2001.
Uchida, Yoshiko. *The Bracelet*. Illustrated by Joanna Yardley, Philomel Books, 1993.
Yamasaki, Katie. *Fish for Jimmy*. Holiday House, 2013.

RETOMANDO EL DÍA DE LOS MUERTOS
Death, Life, and Latinx Epistemology in Children's Literature

Cristina Rhodes

> *Though we tremble before uncertain futures may we meet illness, death and adversity with strength; may we dance in the face of our fears.*
> —GLORIA ANZALDÚA, *This Bridge We Call Home*

Death isn't something children's and young adult (YA) literature eschews. In fact, children's literature is full of dead parents and grandparents, dying pets, and friends and love interests who pass tragically—all, ostensibly, in service of teaching the main character something about the world or themselves. Particularly in books for younger children, death's inclusion is a didactic tool, meant to socialize children into the appropriate responses and motions in the wake of loss and trauma.[1] Scholars of children's literature acknowledge as much through research framed around such questions as: "How is it best to introduce a child through literature to the idea of death?" (Butler 120) and "Why is death so difficult to read and write about?" (Gibson and Zaidman 233). Ultimately, though, scholars tend to agree that by "presenting death within a controlled environment . . . literature can offer a space within which the fears and questions death prompts can be explored" (Carroll 74). The implication here is death is otherwise impossibly scary—an unknowable and unquantifiable entity. Children's literature can help children explore and make sense of death, the logic runs, but it's still something to overcome.

At the same time, however, contemporary children's literature and media is fascinated with el Día de los Muertos, the Latinx holiday that, with its roots in Indigenous religious and agricultural practice, views death not as an end but as part of the cycle of life. While children's books by white authors and for white audiences about el Día de los Muertos appear to serve similar purposes to other children's books about death in that they impart some kind of lesson, that lesson isn't necessarily about coping with death—instead, that lesson is often xenophobia.² In *Maria Molina and the Days of the Dead*, for instance, Kathleen Krull calls el Día de los Muertos "ghoulish," reinforcing the attitude that death should be feared rather than embraced. In such books young white readers find white supremacy alongside the exoticization of Latinx people. White people are much less likely to die young or from preventable causes than are Black and Brown people,³ which makes white fear of death all the more perverse, perhaps.

In keeping with this volume's emphasis on alternative epistemologies of children's literature, I center my analyses of el Día de los Muertos not on whiteness, but on Latinidad. There are tensions, of course, between this Latinx epistemology of death and the necropolitical machinations that mean that Latinx youth experience greater violence and higher mortality than non-Latinx peoples. A 2019 NBC News article opens with the shocking statement: "At least seven children are known to have died in immigration custody since last year, after almost a decade in which no child reportedly died while in the custody of US Customs and Border Protection" (Acevedo para. 1). More and more Latinx children are dying in US custody at the border. Black and Brown peoples are those most deeply affected in the US by the COVID-19 pandemic in 2020. I say this not to contend that we need to rationalize these deaths for young readers or turn them into a teachable moment. These deaths are atrocious and preventable. They are a stain on humanity. How, then, can we celebrate death when it is leveraged against us through racialized and ethnic violence? My goal is to not ignore these lived realities but to assert that Latinx epistemologies of death are already rooted in transformation and empowerment, not just as a response to white supremacy but predating and undermining it.

El Día de los Muertos

Most, if not all, of the existing scholarship on this holiday examines how el Día de los Muertos is packaged for hegemonic consumption.⁴ But much Latinx children's literature delivers death for a distinctly Latinx audience. So, what if we look at death from that vantage point? Octavio Paz's typical Mexican in *The Labyrinth of Solitude* "is familiar with death, jokes about it, caresses it, sleeps with it, celebrates it; it is one of his favorite toys and his most steadfast love" (57). In this light, then, I ground my analysis in Latinx books that explore el Día de los Muertos or that use it as a motif within a Latinx ideology that holds death as revelatory. In this tradition, death can be a future, a possibility, a transformation. As such, we can regard el Día de los Muertos and adjacent themes in Latinx children's and YA literature as revolutionary. I utilize this chapter to reclaim el Día de los Muertos and to assert that understanding the relationships between the living and the dead in Latinx children's literature is vital to providing a more inclusive image of Latinxs in children's and YA literature. To that end, I first theorize that death can be imagined as an ideological construct, one that is full of possibility and transformation;[5] I then provide case studies of two young adult novels that innovate on el Día de los Muertos, Aiden Thomas's *Cemetery Boys* (2020) and Zoraida Córdova's *Labyrinth Lost* (2016), to demonstrate that transformational power of death (or its adjacent motifs).

Before examining these texts, I do want to note that they aren't the only titles for young people to work this way. Indeed, the transformational power of death is a key conceit in two hit animated features about el Día de los Muertos: 20th Century Fox's *The Book of Life* (2014) and Disney/Pixar's *Coco* (2017). In *The Book of Life*, the aspiring musician Manolo is killed and must impress the gods to be returned to the living and to his beloved, María. In *Coco*, Miguel steals a guitar from a crypt and unwittingly links himself to the Land of the Dead. Trapped there, Miguel must seek the blessing of a family member to be able to return to his life. Like the books I discuss in this chapter, these films frame death as neither fear inspiring nor infinite. As my examples show, Latinx epistemologies about and celebrations of death in children's and young adult literature are rooted in a verve for life. For Latinx youth, especially those living in or travelling to the US, death seems almost inevitable given entrenched traditions of racism and racist persecution. But even in this context of violence, books such as these recast death to allow Latinx youth to take control of their narratives and to reassert the celebratory dimensions of death and life.

Paz isn't necessarily wrong when he claims that Mexicans regard death as a novelty, but he's not entirely right, either. In Indigenous Mexica tradition, "Death was glorified because it was conceived as a necessity for the continuity of the universe and of life cycles" (Arredondo and Capistrán-López 299). However, modern Mexicans' "attitudes toward death . . . vary not only individually but also by class, ethnicity, and region" (Brandes 132). Further, "celebrations of el Día de los Muertos reflect this diversity" (Aguilar Montes de Oca 98). It is important, then, when discussing el Día de los Muertos and Latin American ideologies of death, that we do not erase the contours of diversity in and among Latin American subjects. For example, "Mexico and Central-American countries are known for the worshipping of Santa Muerte, the saint of death. In Brazil, Suriname and other areas where Afro-American populations are numerous, rituals are based on celebrations of the continued presence of the dead in daily life" (Klaufus 103). My goal in discussing death as an ideology is not to overgeneralize, nor to pinpoint exactly what Mexicans, Latin Americans, or Latinxs believe about death (opinions being wide and varied), but rather to use Indigenous Mesoamerican rituals and ideologies to conceptualize death as a transitory event. Within many Indigenous South and Central American traditions, death is a transition from one plane of life to another, and this permeability between life and death is clear in Latinx children's literature and media centering el Día de los Muertos.

According to Paz, "The opposition between life and death was not so absolute to the ancient Mexicans as it is to us. Life extended into death, and vice versa. Death was not the natural end of life but one phase of an infinite cycle" (54). Adelina Arredondo and Carlos Capistrán-López further explain, "Death coexists with life along a continuum, in a dialectic that allows us to understand that the one is contained within the other" (319). That formulation blurs the lines between what is typically conceived as alive and dead. Biological death seems an ending, but, within this ideology, it is another moment in the span of many moments in one's existence. Within the contexts of el Día de los Muertos, Denise Davila notes, "The celebration[,] . . . in contrast to dominant ideology, commemorates death as an inseparable part of life; death is not an end, but rather a transition in the life cycle" (16). Likewise, death or el Día de los Muertos motifs in Thomas's *Cemetery Boys* and Córdova's *Labyrinth Lost* are malleable, permeable, and transformative. As these titles suggest, the inclusion of death/el Día de los Muertos in Latinx children's and YA literature can signal a reordering of life cycles and suggest how young people can take ownership over their lives by also owning death.

Rituals of Death

Within these two novels, death is ritualized. The syncretic holiday of el Día de los Muertos maintains specific and often regional rituals, like curating ofrendas or cleaning graveyards. Stanley Brandes hypothesizes that "the Day of the Dead became ritualistically elaborate in Mexico as a by-product of the enormous loss of life during the sixteenth and seventeenth centuries" (289). The effects of colonization and the massive genocide of Indigenous peoples necessitated the preservation of the Indigenous components of el Día de los

Muertos. Due to the dominant influence of Catholicism, the Indigenous elements of el Día de los Muertos that survived European colonization have undergone significant transformation—both to become more palatable to colonial Catholicism and to stand the test of time. In *Cemetery Boys* and *Labyrinth Lost*, the ritualized nature of death connects to deeply-held and sacred rites of passage. In both *Cemetery Boys* and *Labyrinth Lost* a birthday celebration marks the young characters' moves from childhood into adulthood. The celebrations' connections with death highlight the interconnectedness between life and death within the Latinx imagination. More than that, though, these celebrations also provide the perfect opportunity for the young, Latinx characters to demonstrate their ownership of their life cycles.

Zoraida Córdova's *Labyrinth Lost* follows Alex, a reluctant bruja, as she approaches her "Deathday: a bruja's coming-of-age ceremony" (17). Alex, somewhat tongue-in-cheek, explains: "While some girls are having their bat mitzvahs, sweet sixteens, or quinceañeras, brujas get their Deathday. There's no cut-off age, but puberty is when our magic develops. . . . Over the years, modern brujas like to have Deathdays line up with birthdays to have even bigger celebrations. Nothing says 'happy birthday' like summoning the spirits of your dead relatives" (Córdova 17). But, Alex doesn't *want* a Deathday. She doesn't want her magic period. She asks herself, "What *do* I want? To stop my Deathday? That's only half the problem. I'd still have this magic inside me" (Córdova 34, emphasis in original). Alex's trepidation about her magic is born from the ways it has torn her family apart. Her father has gone missing, ostensibly because of the magic, and she has seen the ways it hurt her other relatives. Magic can be good, but also destructive, and Alex is worried that her magic as an encantrix, one of the most powerful types of bruja, will be too much to handle. At the urging of Nova, a young man with his own problems, Alex resolves to abort the ritual. During her Deathday ceremony, Alex seemingly participates, but when it comes time to bind her magic, she goes off script. She invokes "'Lady de la Muerte,'" and asks, "'Protect me from my living. Protect me from my dead'" (Córdova 54). Rejecting the cycle of life and death massively backfires for Alex. Her family disappears, ostensibly spirited away to Los Lagos, realm of the Deos, or the gods of the brujos. In interrupting the cycle between life and death, Alex disrupts familiar patterns and refuses tradition.

Unlike Alex, Yadriel, the main character in Aiden Thomas's *Cemetery Boys*, longs for his own ritual to become a brujo. Yad "wanted to be like the other brujos, to find lost spirits and help them pass to the afterlife. . . . Hell, he'd even spend hours pulling weeds and painting tombs if it meant being accepted by his people as a brujo" (Thomas 9). Denied the ceremony because he is transgender, Yad secrets himself away to perform the ritual with only his cousin Maritza in attendance. He reasons, "If he could summon a spirit and release it to the afterlife, then he would finally prove himself to everyone.... They would see him as he was. A boy and a brujo" (Thomas 16). Unlike Alex, whose ceremony isn't tied to a specific age, Yad's fifteenth birthday, the traditional time for brujxs to come into their own, comes and goes without fanfare. Thomas solemnly explains, "[Yadriel's] quinces had been postponed indefinitely" (10). Like Alex, however, Yad takes his fate into his own hands when he performs the ritual on his own. "In order to show his family what he was, *who* he was, Yadriel needed to go through with his own quinces ceremony—with or without their blessings. His father and the rest of the brujx hadn't left him a choice" (Thomas 10, emphasis in original). Yadriel's attempt to prove himself is ultimately successful; he is able to activate his portaje, a dagger "required to sever the golden thread that bound a spirit to their earthly tether. By cutting that tie, brujos were able to release spirits to the afterlife" (Thomas 10). But, like Alex's ritual, Yadriel's is not without its mishaps. While Yadriel is performing his ceremony, his cousin Miguel is murdered and the other brujxs, including Yadriel, feel the loss as a physical pain. Yadriel and his family are devastated by this event and seek in vain to find the culprit as well as Miguel's missing body. While looking, Yad unwittingly finds the ghost of his classmate, Julian, who has been killed by the same perpetrator. Yadriel, seeing his opportunity to cement the ritual by releasing Julian's soul to the afterlife, attempts to complete his transition to brujo but, for reasons unknown, cannot release Julian and instead is stuck with an undead sidekick.

It is significant that both Alex and Yadriel try to take control of their rituals, even if neither action goes exactly as planned. In fact, the obstacles that they must face when those rituals are disrupted underlines the mutability of life and death. Rites of passage for adolescents and death rites equally address significant life transitions. These ceremonies in *Labyrinth Lost* and *Cemetery Boys* are like "quinces ... not just *any* rituals but 'rites of passage' ... [that] provide magnificent *ventanas*, or windows ... into how these groups demarcate and assign meaning to different stages of life" (Rodriguez 5, emphasis and italics in original). Likewise, death and rituals associated with it serve to mark another stage of life. What's more, the el Día de los Muertos "ritual [serves] as a medium of ... reconciling feelings of social and cultural displacement, fragmentation, and negation" (Marchi 1). Both Alex and Yadriel are out of place within their communities—Alex because of her rejection of her magic and Yad because of his gender identity—and their reclamation and transformation of their communities' rigid rituals connecting to life and death allows them to find balance and to actualize new selves.

Death as Transition

In finding those new identities through rewritten rites of passage, Alex and Yadriel establish new ways of being and new knowledges connected to death. This intervention is even more significant given that Yadriel is a transgender character. Sara Ahmed's work on queer fatalism illuminates the ways that characters who inhabit subject positions like Yad's are often maneuvered as cautionary tales against queerness. Ahmed explains, "Queer deaths are often framed as a consequence of queerness; queer fatalism = queer as fatal" (para. 1). In Ahmed's configuration of queer fatalism, death may be an inevitability but it also pushes us to look for spaces that disrupt. Ahmed further explains "[q]ueer happiness as world making" (para. 40)—in other words, the counternarrative of queer fatalism is queer happiness, which is rooted in creating and bringing about a new world in which queer happiness can thrive. Likewise, el Día de los Muertos is all about rewriting the narrative, allowing individuals to speak from beyond the grave. Alex and Yadriel thus can speak from within the liminal and transitory spaces they occupy as they defy and remake tradition. As young characters who interact with the dead, Alex and Yad occupy a sort of third world, one that offers numerous possibilities for transformation. Gloria Anzaldúa theorizes this space as "[n]epantla," an Indigenous concept that "is the midway point between the conscious and the unconscious, the place where transformations are enacted" (56). Within nepantla, Alex and Yad (and ostensibly other characters who interact with death) remix understandings of life cycles. They take control of their own rites of passage and blur the lines between the living and the dead.

The changes they individually undergo through this alteration of ritual also signal a larger communal or institutional shift. In *Labyrinth Lost*, the journey through Los Lagos intimately changes Alex. Rather than rejecting her magic, she embraces it and wields it to bring about a future of her own design. She explains, "My magic is linked to everything—the infinity of time, the rapid snuff of death, the sprinkle of stardust, and the released sigh of freedom" (Córdova 177). It takes Alex's realization that her magic is an asset not a liability to set in motion the salvation of Alex's family. Importantly, however, Alex does not act alone. While Alex is perceived as "the girl who destroyed the Devourer of Los Lagos," what "[t]hey don't mention [is she] was partly responsible for banishing [her] family there or that four hundred generations of both ghosts and the living helped right [her] wrong" (Córdova 180). Alex's communion with the dead brings about a resolution to her problems.

Likewise, Yadriel must work with Julian, his classmate-turned-ghost, to solve both of their tempestuous situations. Yadriel's inability to send Julian to the afterlife and subsequent inability to complete his ritual coming of age is compounded by the spirits who haven't passed becoming increasingly violent. And, even if he could release Julian, Yadriel doesn't want to lose him, whom he has come to love. Even so, Yadriel knows that "keeping Julian meant he'd be trapped between the worlds of the living and the dead" (Thomas 287). What Yadriel doesn't know is that Julian is already trapped. The reason Yadriel cannot release him to the afterlife is because Julian's body is still alive, but just dead enough that his spirit has become untethered. Julian is quite literally trapped in the liminal space between life and death. Nevertheless, Yadriel unwittingly continues with the ritual to unbind Julian's soul from the mortal plane, incanting: "'Te libero a *la otra vida*'" (Thomas 288; emphasis added). This release to "another life" rather than to a fixed death or a specific afterlife is significant—it allows for the permeability of death. The brujxs' role as mediators means that they act as sort of toll collectors or road maintenance, rather than gatekeepers. The brujxs' most important time of the year is el Día de los Muertos, when the spirits they have released may return. Yadriel, while being preoccupied with Julian and his cousin's death, is also worried about the first el Día de los Muertos following his mother's death. He's anxious because her spirit, which has been released, will return for the celebration. She was one of the few people in his life who affirmed and supported his gender identity and the opportunity to demonstrate to her that he has become a full-fledged brujo is not just appealing but necessary to his full self-actualization. The validation that Yadriel receives from the dead situates his own liminality and solidifies his power to evoke the transitional nature of life and death.

Indeed, Yadriel's relationship with Julian, who has grown from undead nuisance to burgeoning love interest by the end of the novel, allows him to solve Miguel's murder and to abort a dangerous ritual being enacted by Yadriel's wayward uncle. His uncle, much like Yadriel, was never given a ceremonial coming of age, not because of his gender identity like Yad but because he lacks the magic to release the dead. Yadriel seizes control of the narrative surrounding his own identity and utilizes his proximity to the dead to effect change. However, his uncle instead grows bitter and attempts to unleash destruction upon the world of the brujxs by unleashing the ancient god Bahlam from Xibalba, the otherworld. Bahlam requires human sacrifices, among them Yadriel's cousin Miguel and Julian. Were Bahlam to be released by Yadriel's tío's ritual, he would reclaim the souls of brujxs passed on, including Yadriel's mother, and "'trap them [in Xibalba] for all eternity'" (Thomas 299). But this ceremony, unlike the reclaimed ones exacted by Alex and Yad, is not meant to be changed or even undertaken. Bahlam instead claims Yadriel's uncle's soul and drags it back to Xibalba before the ritual can be completed. Even though the ritual does not come to fruition, Julian is left half-dead and Yadriel is at a loss. At the urging of La Santa Muerte, who granted him his brujo powers at the beginning of the novel, Yadriel vows he "would let himself die, gladly, if it meant saving [those] who had been so viciously and carelessly sacrificed" (Thomas 314). He attempts to exchange his life for Julian's, incurring the same wounds as Julian's body is healed. But Maritza, who has been present throughout the book and helps to support Yadriel, heals him. By slighting death in more ways than one, Yadriel claims the ultimate power over life cycles. He is able to understand, more intimately than anyone, the interwoven and cyclical nature of life and death.

So, too, does Alex's vanquishing of the Devourer elide the link between life and death. "For days" after her return from defeating the Devourer, Alex "[dreamed] of Los Lagos" (Córdova 177). This plane of the afterlife is ingrained in Alex's very being. It is a part of her, just as it will serve as a resting place when she transitions away from the land of the living. Thanks to her intervention in Los Lagos, the place is now primed for regrowth; even "[t]he Wastelands show signs of growth, new buds that bloom like starflowers" (Córdova 177). Alex's intimate connection to Los Lagos, like Yadriel's own brush with death, delinks the familiar sequence of living and then dead. These characters are able to transition between life and death in ways that defy biology and Western coding of life cycles. And it's not just Alex and Yadriel who can move between these spaces—Julian exists in *Cemetery Boys* as both a pseudo-ghost and a living teenager, and Rishi, Alex's best friend/girlfriend in *Labyrinth Lost*, travels to Los Lagos to aid Alex. That other characters, and not just the protagonists, can transition between life and death in these noncircular ways is significant. In this way, the permeability of the border between life and death for these young characters demonstrates that childhood and adolescence act as the perfect location for death to aid in self-actualization.

Transformative Actions

In *Cemetery Boys*, following his recovery from the battle, Yadriel is accepted by his family and community as a true brujo because of his interventions between the living and the dead. As a fully-fledged brujo, Yadriel attends his family's el Día de los Muertos celebration and reunites with his mother on her first Día as a released spirit. Just as Yadriel is able to transform his harrowing journey between life and death into a celebration, Alex gets a second Deathday ceremony in the wake of her family's rescue at the end of *Labyrinth Lost*. According to Alex, "The second party was better than the first . . . because *we're alive and it's a beautiful thing*" (Córdova 181, emphasis added). Despite this emphasis on life, death is still present within both celebrations. It is, after all, Alex's Deathday and Yadriel is celebrating el Día de los Muertos. Death's presence is necessary and important because of its intimate connections to both protagonists. In contrast to the didactic and othering function of death for white audiences, in Latinx contexts death illuminates the beauty of life and allows readers to regard death as just another part of existence. The two are, after all, sides of the same coin. For Alex and Yad, that coin is ever turning, flipping in the air as if suspended mid-toss. What's more, the almost queered nature of death here connects to both Alex's and Yad's own queerness. Yadriel's trans identity, in particular, fuels his potential for queer fatalism but also poses his transformation as radical. Such transformation and reclamation of agency helps to rewrite dominant scripts.[6]

Returning to Anzaldúa's foundational thinking about transformation, I have previously explained, "Transformation is a discursive process and one that children are intimately familiar with, given that childhood is a time of continuous transformation from infant, to toddler, to child, and beyond" (475). Alex, Yadriel, and other characters in el Día de los Muertos books for young readers model this kind of transformation. Using the foundations laid in these fictional portrayals, we can redress the ways that death is ignored, brushed aside, and Othered when it concerns young Latinxs. In denying the Western cycle of life and death, the narratives I consider here help us to see a world that prioritizes Latinx views of death as a transition both independent of whiteness and in response to white supremacy.[7] And, importantly, this trend extends beyond *Labyrinth Lost* and *Cemetery Boys*. While I do not discuss picture books, middle grade, or graphic novels here, many of these books also redress death.[8] When Latinx authors engage their cultural knowledge and pose death as a transformative process, they reorient epistemologies of trauma and fear to those of change and agency.

These books take us not to death's terrifying doorstep, as it were, but to a place where the living and the dead coexist and realize the wisdom they can offer one another. The transformative and ameliorative nature of death allows for such relationships. Books like *Cemetery Boys* and *Labyrinth Lost* that demonstrate the power of Latinx youth and the necessity of Latinx epistemologies of death provide a counternarrative to redress dominant notions that exoticize and Other Latinxs. Though they are less circulated than white-authored and white-audienced narratives that exoticize el Día de los Muertos, children's and YA literature *by* Latinx authors, *for* Latinx audiences, and *about* real Latinx epistemologies dispels dominant notions of death and of the incapabilities of Latinx youth. In these books, as it should be in our own epistemologies, Latinx youth have the ability to transform themselves and the world. When Latinx youth and their stories speak for themselves, we see their complexities and the vital knowledge they offer us that helps us better understand life—and death.

Notes

1. For further reading on representations of death in children's literature, particularly for Western audiences, see Brown; Gutiérrez et al.; James; Maguth et al.; Poling and Hupp; Tribunella; and Wiseman.

2. Denise Davila asserts that books about the Day of the Dead "[position] readers as mainstream American tourists" thus, "[undermining] the objectives for fostering a pluralistic society" (24). Vargas and Rodríguez further warn, "El Día de Muertos es una manifestación cultural muy frágil al encontrarse inmersa en un proceso de sobre-explotación turística, comercialización y pérdida de identidad familiar por una identidad globalizada" (171).

3. See Centers for Disease Control and Prevention, "Disparities in COVID-19 Deaths."

4. For further reading on representations of el Día de los Muertos for Western/white consumption, see Castro; Davila; Loza and González; Roberts; Verela; and Wax-Edwards.

5. I focus more here on non-Western epistemologies of death. There are, of course, important works on Western conceptions of death, such as Philippe Ariès's *Western Attitudes toward Death: From the Middle Ages to the Present*, in which three conceptions of death throughout the ages are discussed. Ariès explains, in the concluding chapter, "Death, so omnipresent in the past that it was familiar, would be effaced, would disappear. It would become shameful and forbidden" (85).

6. In *Old Futures: Speculative Fiction and Queer Possibility*, Alexis Lothian explains, "Speculative fictions by radical people of color have grown in popularity in recent years among readers who see them as hopeful articulations of radical political possibility" (101).

7. See Regina M. Marchi's *Day of the Dead in the USA: The Migration and Transformation of a Cultural Phenomenon* for a more nuanced look at modern Mexican conceptions of death and el Día de los Muertos.

8. Some books that utilize el Día de los Muertos or motifs associated with death in this way are: *Just a Minute* and *Just in Case*, by Yuyi Morales; *Funny Bones*, by Duncan Tonatiuh; the *Love, Sugar, Magic* series, by Anna Meriano; *The First Rule of Punk*, by Celia C. Pérez; and *Ghost Squad*, by Claribel Ortega.

Works Cited

Acevedo, Nicole. "Why Are Migrant Children Dying in US Custody?" *NBC News*, 29 May 2019, www.nbcnews.com/news/latino/why-are-migrant-children-dying-u-s-custody-n1010316.

Aguilar Montes de Oca, Rosa Isela. "The Day of the Dead: One Ritual, New Folk Costumes, and Old Identities." *Folklore: Electronic Journal of Folklore*, vol. 66, 2016, pp. 95–114. *MLA International Bibliography*, https://www.folklore.ee/folklore/vol66/aguilar.pdf.

Ahmed, Sara. "Queer Fatalism." *feministkilljoy*, 13 Jan. 2017. feministkilljoys.com/2017/01/13/queer-fatalism/. Accessed 2 Dec. 2021.

Anzaldúa, Gloria. *Light in the Dark/Luz en lo oscuro: Rewriting Identity, Spirituality, Reality*. Duke UP, 2015.

Ariès, Philippe. *Western Attitudes toward Death: From the Middle Ages to the Present*. Translated by Patricia M. Ranum, Johns Hopkins UP, 1974.

Arredondo, Adelina, and Carlos Capistrán-López. "Pedagogy of Death in Popular Traditions and in the Institutionalization of the Day of the Dead in México." *History of Education and Children's Literature*, vol. 12, no. 1, Jan. 2017, pp. 297–319. *Historical Abstracts with Full Text*, https://www.researchgate.net/publication/318091206.

Brandes, Stanley. "Is There a Mexican View of Death?" *Ethos*, vol. 31, no. 1, 2003, pp. 127–44. *JSTOR*, www.jstor.org/stable/3651867.

Browne, Katelyn R. "Reimagining Queer Death in Young Adult Fiction." *Research on Diversity in Youth Literature*, vol. 2, no. 2, 2020, pp. 1–25. https://sophia.stkate.edu/rdyl/vol2/iss2/3.

Butler, Francelia. "Death in Children's Literature." *Children's Literature*, vol. 1, 1972, p. 104–24. *Project MUSE*, doi:10.1353/chl.0.0649.

Carroll, Jane Suzanne. "Death and the Landscape in *The Dark Is Rising* and Its Adaptations." *What Do We Tell the Children? Critical Essays on Children's Literature*, edited by Ciara Ni Bhroin and Patricia Kennon, Cambridge Scholars Publishing, 2012, pp. 74–89.

Castro, Elizabeth. "When Coco Feels like Home: Film as Homenaje." *Harvard Journal of Hispanic Policy*, 2018, p. 33. *Gale General OneFile*, https://www.proquest.com/docview/2187897395.

Centers for Disease Control and Prevention. "Disparities in COVID-19 Deaths." *CDC*, 10 Dec. 2020, www.cdc.gov/coronavirus/2019-ncov/community/health-equity/racial-ethnic-disparities/disparities-deaths.html. Accessed 2 Dec. 2021.

Coco. Directed by Lee Unkrich, Walt Disney Studios, 2017.

Córdova, Zoraida. *Labyrinth Lost*. e-Book ed., Sourcebooks, 2016.

Davila, Denise. "In Search of the Ideal Reader for Nonfiction Children's Books about El Día de Los Muertos." *Journal of Children's Literature*, vol. 38, no. 1, spring 2012, pp. 16–26. *Education Source*, https://eric.ed.gov/?id=EJ984591.

Gibson, Lois Rauch, and Laura M. Zaidman. "Death in Children's Literature: Taboo or Not Taboo?" *Children's Literature Association Quarterly*, vol. 16, no. 4, 1991, p. 232–34. *Project MUSE*, doi:10.1353/chq.0.0855.

Gutiérrez, Isabel T., et al. "Affective Dimensions of Death: Children's Books, Questions, and Understandings." *Monographs of the Society for Research in Child Development*, vol. 79, no. 1, 2014, p. 43. doi:10.1111/mono.12078.

James, Kathryn. *Death, Gender and Sexuality in Contemporary Adolescent Literature*. Routledge, 2008.

Klaufus, Christien. "Deathscapes in Latin America's Metropolises: Urban Land Use, Funerary Transformations, and Daily Inconveniences." *European Review of Latin American and Caribbean Studies / Revista Europea de Estudios Latinoamericanos y Del Caribe*, no. 96, 2014, pp. 99–111. *JSTOR*, www.jstor.org/stable/23722437.

Krull, Kathleen. *Maria Molina and the Days of the Dead*. Simon and Schuster, 1994.

Lothian, Alexis. *Old Futures: Speculative Fiction and Queer Possibility*. New York UP, 2018.

Loza, Roxana, and Tanya González. "A Bone to Pick: Día de los Muertos in Children's Literature." *Voices of Resistance: Interdisciplinary Approaches to Chican@ Children's Literature*, edited by Laura Alamillo et al., Rowman and Littlefield, 2017, pp. 33–46.

Maguth, Brad M., et al. "Grappling with Death and Loss through Children's Literature in the Social Studies." *Social Studies Research and Practice*, vol. 10, no. 3, 2015, pp. 80–87. *Education Source*, https://www.researchgate.net/publication/319143185.

Marchi, Regina M. *Day of the Dead in the USA: The Migration and Transformation of a Cultural Phenomenon*. Rutgers UP, 2009.

Paz, Octavio. *The Labyrinth of Solitude: Life and Thought in Mexico*. Translated by Lysander Kemp, Grove Press, 1961.

Poling, Devereaux A., and Julie M. Hupp. "Death Sentences: A Content Analysis of Children's Death Literature." *Journal of Genetic Psychology*, vol. 169, no. 2, 2008, pp. 165–76. *Sociological Connection*, doi:10.3200/GNTP.169.2.165–76.

Rhodes, Cristina. "Processes of Transformation: Theorizing Activism and Change Through Gloria Anzaldúa's Picture Books." *Children's Literature in Education*, 2020, pp. 464–77. doi.org/10.1007/s10583-020-09429-2.

Rodriguez, Evelyn Ibatan. *Celebrating Debutantes and Quinceañeras: Coming of Age in American Ethnic Communities*, Temple UP, 2013.

The Book of Life. Directed by Jorge R. Gutierrez, 20th Century Fox, 2014.

Thomas, Aiden. *Cemetery Boys*. Swoon Reads, 2020.

Tribunella, Eric L. *Melancholia and Maturation: The Use of Trauma in American Children's Literature*. Tennessee UP, 2010.

Vargas, Mauricio Piñón, and José Sánchez Rodríguez. "El Día de Muertos en los textos de primaria de México / The Day of the Dead in Elementary School Textbooks in Mexico." *Revista Electrónica de Investigación Educativa*, vol. 18, no. 2, 2016, pp. 170–79. redie.uabc.mx/redie/article/view/612.

Verela, Sandra L. López. "Approaching Pixar's *Coco* during the Trump Era." *iMex. México Interdisciplinario. Interdisciplinary Mexico*, vol. 9, no. 18, 2020, pp. 130–44. doi: 10.23692/iMex.18.9.

Wax-Edwards, Jessica. "Re-animating Mexicanidad: Mexican Cultural Representations in *The Book of Life* (2014) and *Coco* (2017)." *iMex. México Interdisciplinario. Interdisciplinary Mexico*, vol. 9, no. 18, 2020, pp. 112–29. doi: 10.23692/iMex.18.

Wiseman, Angela M. "Summer's End and Sad Goodbyes: Children's Picturebooks about Death and Dying." *Children's Literature in Education: An International Quarterly*, vol. 44, no. 1, 2013, pp. 1–14. *MLA International Bibliography*, doi:10.1007/s10583-012-9174-3.

REIMAGINING THE "ALTERNATIVE"
Sustaining Representation of Indigenous People and People of Color through Speculative Fiction in *The Marrow Thieves* and *Mañanaland*

Erica Law-Montes and Cristina Rivera

Speculative fiction (SF) historically privileges White[1] childhood experiences. One consequence is that speculative fiction featuring non-White or otherwise diverse characters is constructed as "alternative" in some form or fashion. This positionality is complicated, as it shows and also threatens to naturalize the disenfranchisement of marginalized people. In this essay, we consider two recent speculative novels for young adults that decenter Whiteness and dramatize the realities of colonialist and racist persecution. *The Marrow Thieves* (2017), by Cherie Dimaline, takes place in a postapocalyptic future, where Indigenous peoples are the last humans capable of dreaming and are thus hunted. Through this reaping, Dimaline exposes the realistic sediments of White privilege. Speculative fiction here elucidates modern Indigenous struggles and reimagines the survival of Indigenous people. Pam Muños Ryan's *Mañanaland* (2020), meanwhile, tells the story of a twelve-year-old boy who discovers that the lore of his community is actually true—"guardians" are helping oppressed women escape to Mañanaland. Ryan's novel uses the metaphorical Underground Railroad, exposing the realities of immigration and the uncertain promise of a better future on the other side of the border. These texts provide new understandings of "alternative" spaces and figurations that push against more traditional themes and storylines in realistic fiction.

Our investigation draws upon Ebony Elizabeth Thomas's *The Dark Fantastic: Race and the Imagination from Harry Potter to the Hunger Games*. Using the term "imagination gap," Thomas theorizes that "the diversity crisis in children's and young adult media" is reflected in the "empathy, opportunities, and technology" for disenfranchised youth (5–6). To combat this issue of self-actualization through imagination, she uses the term "the dark fantastic"[2] to explain "the role that racial difference plays in our fantastically storied imaginations" (7). *The Marrow Thieves* and *Mañanaland* represent how the "dark fantastic" diversifies modalities of language through magic, fantasy, and imaginative realms.

Examining the storyworlds of these two novels and their mediation of sociopolitical realities, we show how *The Marrow Thieves* and *Mañanaland* challenge dominant norms in standard language practices and institutionalized racism more generally. We investigate modalities of culturally sustaining language usage in the novels and evaluate their disruption of dominant narrative standards, taking up Django Paris and H. Samy Alim's discussion of culturally sustaining pedagogies. Ultimately, we ask: If speculative fiction creates a future in which Indigenous people are bled for their dreams (*Marrow Thieves*) and young people south of the US border are left questioning their familial and cultural pasts (*Mañanaland*), what potential is there for the genre to offer empowering perspectives for youth through literature? We suggest that *The Marrow Thieves* and *Mañanaland* constitute narrative spaces through which readers from any community can experience fictionalized yet realistic social and political inequalities.

Defining the "Alternative" in Discussions of Race in Standard Language Practices

The relationship between the public/private education system and lack of non-White characters in SF speaks to the prevention of social mobility for marginalized youths because they most often see themselves characterized primarily through representations of disenfranchisement. It is more common for non-White youth to see themselves in literature and media being hindered by society, leaving them without avenues for empowerment and agency. We see this in recent popular titles dealing with topics such as police brutality in *The Hate U Give* (2017), teen pregnancy in *With the Fire on High* (2019), and stereotyping, abuse, and other difficulties as Native women in fictional and nonfictional stories within *#Notyourprincess: Stories of Native American Women* (2017). As Thomas argues, "The problem of the diversity gap extends far beyond the mere lack of representation of characters of color in children's publishing and media" (5). Thus, the internalization of non-White youth in CYA mirrors the disparities taking place in the US by images of suppression rather than subverting assumptions of marginalized positions and impoverished communities.

Thomas's latest work, *The Dark Fantastic*, aligns with the academic call for cultural sustaining pedagogies in regard to language reinforced by educational institutions. Asao B. Inoue spoke to this disparity in his 2019 CCCC keynote speech. Touching on ways that academics (perhaps inadvertently) carry racism, he stated: "My colleagues of color[,] . . . [w]e will break the steel cage of White supremacy, of White racial bias, of the many bars, like the physical bars of the jails and prisons. . . . We academics of color . . . have many things in common with the US prison population, one being the steel cage of racism" (2–3). For Inoue, elucidating language is an economic system. Considering that educational resources are not distributed equally in the US, White language situates itself as the dominant maker of achievement and disadvantages those who do not master it or even use it. Thus, language that the publishing industry continues to value and distribute perpetuates this economic imbalance and even rewards participation in the dominant language or mastery of Standard American English. Inoue argues, "[Y]ou always are implicated and circulate in market economies that dictate the nature of the cage around you. . . . You are always beholden to the market. The market I call your attention to today is the market of White language preferences in schools, although it is also not hard to find the connections between it and the flows of Capital." Therefore, because White discourses control, produce, and market CYA media, literature is one known tool to challenge these oppressive cages.

Inoue's and Thomas's discussion of what is missing for youth today acknowledges that there is more work to be done due to ever-present White, dominant standardization of writing practices from education to publication. While many CYA authors and scholars agree that the landscape is changing in favor of more non-White representation, producers of CYA and literary critics of color and Indigenous backgrounds continue to challenge the factors that go into how we are represented. In an interview, Daniel Jose Older explains that while the publishing industry self-claims a gold star for producing more diverse texts—it is not enough. Older highlights that "[t]he next step, then, is to build characters that are true to life. To write these characters not as tropes, but as living, breathing beings. . . . It's an entire ecosystem shift that the literary world requires—not simple tolerance of alternative narratives" (Simand). Thus, we return to the "alternate" with quotes, implying otherness and marking empowering non-White discourses.

The way that these novels include their respective cultural languages demonstrates the written "alternative" and challenges the language standards in contemporary CYA publishing. In not italicizing Spanish or Indigenous words, these novels subvert dominant, White-language publishing practices, presenting "alternate" languages as a synchronous dominant form; they would otherwise look "othered" through italics. Older challenges this common publishing trope, stating, "The function of language is to communicate things clearly. The function of grammar and rules around language are to facilitate that communication—that's it. . . . You know when you should italicize another language, when there is emphasis on it, just like with any other word that you would italicize" (YouTube 2014). Dimaline makes exactly this point in *The Marrow Thieves*. For example, Rose explains to Frenchie, "'As a matter of fact, being with Minerva is pretty nishin.' [Frenchie] narrowed her eyes. Uh-oh. 'Nishin? What the hell is that?' 'Oh nothing, just a little of the language.' I jumped up. 'Bullshit!.' . . . 'Not bullshit. Real shit.'" (Dimaline 38). Dimaline doesn't italicize nor directly tell the reader what nishin (good) means. The protagonist deduces nishin's meaning upon hearing it and feels connected to the word. Dimaline continuously normalizes Indigenous language by not italicizing it. Similarly, in *Mañanaland*, words like fútbol (soccer's original term) and Buelo (short for abuelo, meaning grandfather) are not italicized.

The Dark Fantastic also emphasizes that publishing norms replicate the racist perpetuation of oppression and continue to go unchallenged. Thomas writes, "[T]he number of Latinx, Asian, Arab, and Native American youth [media] . . . certainly does not reflect their numbers in United States schools, neighborhoods, and society" (136). Through this disproportionate reality we also find the physical and metaphorical cages hindering social freedom and upward economic mobility. Thomas uses Rudine Sims Bishop's framework, asserting that "[the] metaphor of the mirrors, windows, and doors of children's literature also applies to what is necessary to reconcile dark fantastic crises in infinite storyworlds. Restorying fantastic traditions is one solution; an emancipatory dark fantastic is another" (167–68). This framework implies that Indigenous and POC characters "alternatively" replace those of their White counterparts in spaces that typically do not belong to them, and because these texts narrate adversely, they remain "alternative."

Figuring the Non-White Child as Still "Alternative"

Before evaluating the novels' "alternative" thematic underpinnings and marginalizing tropes in CYA, we explore the child as a figure, position, and identity. Claudia Castañeda's *Figurations: Child, Bodies, and Worlds* explores the hegemonic creation and maintenance of the child, calling attention to it as a constructed identity. Castañeda asks, "What is the child but a human in an incomplete form, which must acquire the necessary traits and skills to live as an adult?" and argues that in challenging common assumptions of the child "is a conceptualization [of] . . . a potentiality rather than an actuality, a becoming rather than a being: an entity in the making" (1). Castañeda semiotically breaks down the child as a liminal figure that transforms over stages. Here, the White child figure comparatively sheds light on the "alternative" child form. However, since the child is "never complete in itself" but manifests rather sets of transitioning figurations (2), is there a way for the non-White or diverse figurations to access power through this inevitable transformation process?

Dimaline and Ryan both represent their respective cultures narratively in using CYA SF and world-making-based narratives that have rarely included minorities. In doing so, these novels produce avenues that feel like equality. The protagonists are, as most child characters, learning about the world around them to grow into more mature figures through their environments. Because the "alternative" child character can't be separated from the growth/maturation process, the novels contain transformative paths by focusing on the achievement of selfhood in the SF storyworld.

Growth and power for the "alternative" occurs where the fantastic grants access to elitist discourse through alternate/speculative narrative spaces. It is in spaces of imagined futures that both *The Marrow Thieves* and *Mañanaland* give readers environments to speculate "alternative" ways of being. *The Marrow Thieves* places emphasis on genocide through its futuristic society that is not far off from the literal history of North American Indigenous lands but primarily focuses on Frenchie's self-discovery. *Mañanaland* ends not with Isadora making it across the border but with Max achieving his dream of being on Santa Maria's fútbol team. As both narratives focus on characters' transformations, they also lessen the "alternative" figurations (specific qualities of non-White difference) and therefore overcome the common narrativizing of adversity or othered positionality. In other words, SF makes room for an "alternative" vision of who participates in future societies, and it does not need to highlight the realities of disenfranchisement regular fiction most often focuses on.

Yet, this vision is not so clear-cut—it cannot be representation for the sake of representation. Publishing these stories complicates the opportunity for overcoming conformity to social stratification that keeps our "alternative" still marked. As Older explains on writing fantasy in *Art of the Matter: Interviews with Latino/a Children's and Young Adult Fiction Authors,*

That is why I include in my fiction issues of patriarchy, colorism, and violence within our community. Because these topics have been used by the mainstream to negatively portray us and to keep us down . . . we have to check ourselves, too. Writing overly affirmative, glorious, magical versions of who we are is a lie; it's still not getting at the complex truth of who we are as human beings. (qtd. in Aldama 18)

Therefore, normalization is not easily obtained, but potential remains in CYA when SF redirects the focal point of the narrative from the typical overcoming or dealing with disenfranchisement.

The Marrow Thieves: Futurism and Reimagining Histories

In *The Marrow Thieves*, speculative worldbuilding supersedes the typical character representation of Indigenous identities today by looking past self-actualizing non-White disparity. Dimaline breaks conventional time, devising an "alternative" way of experiencing Indigenous stories. The reader imagines a futuristic genocide of Indigenous people—a cyclical representation of what has happened in the historic past. After Frenchie, a young Indigenous (Metis)[3] adolescent loses his biological family, his story foregrounds an amalgamation of multiple Indigenous Nations, providing an authentic Indigenous diasporic experience. Recurrent migration is necessary for surviving against an oppressive regime that connotes the privileging of White over Indigenous lives. To survive in this futuristic world, the recruiters (suggested colonizers) harvest bone marrow from Indigenous people. In depicting Indigenous peoples' marrow as the cure to regain dreams and stay alive, the novel recreates Indigenous histories of being stolen from their lands, murdered, displaced, and traumatized. Specifically, by creating a speculative setting for Indigenous genocide, Dimaline provides readers a glimpse of the actual racial disparities put in place by White colonialism.

The "alternate" voice in Dimaline's novel changes the "collective consciousness" by placing emphasis on a resurgence of Indigenous culture and traditions. Frenchie provides the reader with an "alternate" figuration of Indigenous identity through SF. His story reimagines past, present, and future for Indigenous people, imparting readers' access to this minoritized perspective through a parallel to reality. Looking through the lens of "Native American Futurisms," the novel establishes the "alternative" as the figure connecting imagined futures for Indigenous peoples. De Vos explores Grace L. Dillon (Anishnaabe)'s groundbreaking term and states that "Native

American Futurisms [are] 'based on the existing "Afrofuturism"'" (4). Dillon describes Afrofuturism as "'weav[ing] in traditional knowledge and culture with futuristic ideas and settings'" (qtd. in Muzyka), and De Vos points out that "Indigenous futurism is centrally about bringing traditional knowledges into faraway futures, privileging traditional values like sustainable, balanced relationality over so-called progress" (4). These futurisms exist within the novel, through the continuation of traditional knowledge within the diasporic experience. This view of diaspora, thus, reclaims power and strength for Indigenous people by reimagining the world it takes place in. Dillon further explains that "Indigenous Futurisms are not the product of a victimized people's wishful amelioration of their past, but instead a continuation of a spiritual and cultural path that remains unbroken by genocide and war" (2). Ultimately, Dillon emphasizes the future of Indigenous people when deconstructing time and altering progress within imagined possibilities. *The Marrow Thieves* thus becomes an example of an "alternative" reclamation of what Indigenous futures could be and, therefore, can reshape the "collective consciousness" of Indigenous identity.

Dimaline's novel draws upon the historical displacement of Indigenous peoples through futuristic worldbuilding. This representation of Indigenous peoples' pasts aligns with Frenchie's experiences within this reimagined futuristic world, allowing the "alternative" to prevail. Throughout *The Marrow Thieves*, Frenchie and his reconstructed family go on a northward journey to find safety and other Indigenous peoples along the way. They constantly uproot their lives to stay one step ahead of the recruiters. Through Frenchie's perspective, readers experience migration and diaspora because of a White mindset privileging genocide—a retelling of the Trail of Tears, a time in history where Indigenous peoples were forced out of their homes and Tribal regions. In *An Indigenous Peoples' History of the United States*, Dunbar-Ortiz explains, "The takeover of Native American homelands did not end with the removal of Eastern tribes.... Every Native American Nation on the continent eventually dealt with settlers who ... were bent on its destruction, removal, or assimilation" (121). Thus, Frenchie's futuristic journey acts as a metaphor for displacements of Native peoples—historically and currently.

The Marrow Thieves also invites readers to internalize the Indigenous experience and the horrors of settler-colonialism. As Leanne Betasamosake Simpson (Michi Saagiig Nishnaabeg) explains in *As We Have Always Done*,

> When colonialism could not eliminate grounded normativity, it tried to contain it so that it exists only to the degree that it does not impede land acquisition,

settlement, and resource extraction. It is this situation, the dispossession of Indigenous peoples from our grounded normativities through the process of colonialism and now settler colonialism, that has set up the circumstances that require a radical Indigenous resurgence as a mechanism for our continuance as Indigenous peoples. (25)

Through SF, however, we can challenge the "othering" through consideration of the "alternate," while still commenting on colonization itself and recreating Indigenous struggles for readers. Miigwans, an elder in the novel, remembers settler-colonialism, explaining that "they [colonizers] opened the first schools. We suffered there. We almost lost our languages. Many lost their innocence, their laughter, their lives" (Dimaline 23–24). Thus, colonialism depicts a loss of culture through the education system, which mimics the establishment of Boarding Schools in the US and Canada and Indigenous children being ripped from their homes and forced to become an assimilated colonized figuration. It is again through SF that the novel grants readers of all backgrounds access into authentic historic hardships. In other words, this "alternative" setting calls on audiences to digest a traumatic past that carries colonial discourses into the contemporary real world.

Much of Indigenous culture is deeply rooted in a connection to the land on which Indigenous peoples live. There is an investment in the continuation and preservation of the natural world. The novel depicts this custom, as Miigwans explains, "America reached up and started sipping on our lakes with a great metal straw. And where were the freshest lakes and the cleanest rivers? On our lands, of course" (Dimaline 24). In this illusory future, as has been in the past, readers witness Indigenous respect and care for the lands that provide for them. However, as Marcus Briggs-Cloud states, "Indigenous relationships to land were deeply altered by adoption of settler-colonial ideology that views land as a commodity" (274). What Briggs-Cloud's quote implies is that colonialism replaced traditional ideologies of those who were originally there. But, through this imagined future, *The Marrow Thieves* challenges the prominent narrativized evil of settler-colonialism that permeates the Indigenous community. Rejection of settler-colonial ideology sweeps the Indigenous faction, bringing on a resurgence of Indigenous culture, showing readers an "alternative" way of Indigenous cultural connection through living harmoniously with nature.

While the natural world is a fundamental part of Indigenous culture, so were nomadic traditions. However, there came a point when these traditions turned into forced migrations, scattering people from their homelands. This trope is evident in *The Marrow Thieves* as Frenchie and his reconstructed family aren't able to define one place as "home." His story demonstrates the physical and emotional effects of forced migration on Indigenous peoples and their communities. The "recruiters" make it impossible for Frenchie and his family to settle or return "home." Diaspora becomes the only safety they have. However, the diasporic narrative also presents an "alternate," more positive, view of migration for Frenchie and his community as the Indigenous population create a larger community welcome to all Tribes and Nations.

The "alternate" finds its resolution in a new, all-encompassing Indigenous community that not only survives but also thrives. Mandy Suhr-Sytsma asserts in *Self-Determined Stories: The Indigenous Reinvention of Young Adult Literature* that SF novels that discuss Indigenous characters "illuminate how the alternative Indigenous hybridities they depict can support Native people's efforts to confront the ongoing manifestations of colonialism that freewheeling hybridity, like multiculturalism, too often elides and that speculative fiction too often reinscribes" (207–8). SF allows the "alternate" voice to imagine "alternative" futures so that the represented demographic can see themselves heroically within the literature. *The Marrow Thieves* provides a simultaneous realistic and fantastical outlet to discuss issues within the Indigenous community, authentically. Furthermore, books such as *Mañanaland* and *The Marrow Thieves* demonstrate how futurisms "alter" narratives of minoritized protagonists that give disenfranchised youth new ways of imagining tomorrow.

Decolonizing Speculative Lore in *Mañanaland*

Pam Muños Ryan is a respected name in the CYA community and known for her unique Latinx storyworlds that sit between realism and fantasy. *Mañanaland*'s "alternate" perspective confirms Alexis Lothian's observation in *Old Futures: Speculative Fiction and Queer Possibility* that "[f]ictional speculation often opens up alternative potentialities only to close them down into futures that are all too predictable according to dominant ideologies" (20). In situating Max's story as an "alternative" to traditional Latinx narratives of immigration and Latinx youth, Ryan transcribes Latinidad through SF, leaving the future of belonging up to the reader's imagination. In doing so, readers must create their own perspectives regarding hardships Latinx immigrants face outside of political debates and governmental policies. Through this "alternative" narrative, SF in *Mañanaland* cultivates a space in CYA where the child figure reclaims power and agency within the dominant, colonizing culture.

Mañanaland also gives readers an "alternative" way of imagining diasporic realities for those needing a better tomorrow. The novel takes place in the fictional city of Santa Maria, where citizens circulate tales of guardians helping the "hidden ones" move unnoticed beyond the city's borders. There are two versions of the tale: some believed the guardians were heroes and others viewed them as criminals helping other criminals escape. But, when this lore becomes Max's actual reality, the novel "alternatively" exposes the brutal reality of women and girls escaping human trafficking south of the border. This "alternate" narrative also juxtaposes common assumptions of why individuals cross the US border before obtaining required documentation. Max's youthful agency—as he takes up the quest to help Isadora flee, becoming a guardian himself—provides a safe platform for audiences to learn alongside his character about immigrant realities, rather than being taught at. SF in *Mañanaland* captures a multitude of past and present racial disparities: the historic Underground Railroad, modern day traumas of human trafficking, and unguaranteed safety on the other side of the US border for immigrants.

Mañanaland, like *The Marrow Thieves*, fictionalizes lived traumas to combat hegemonic ideologies by establishing these realities in its own storyworld's lore. The lore narratively challenges readers to understand immigration in an "alternative" way. Arguing among his peers, Max disputes the correct story of the "hidden ones'" reasons for fleeing from Abismo (a neighboring city) guided by "Los Guarduanes" (the guardians). After Max tells his grandfather's rendition of the lore, the version that correlates the guardians to heroism, another of the boys interjects:

> "Stop!" said Ortiz. " . . . Want to know the real truth?" . . . "My parents said the hidden ones were dangerous—murderers and thieves—the worst of the worst. Why do you think they were cast out of their own country? You don't see any of them living in Santa Maria, do you? That's because if they'd shown their face, they would have been driven out of town." (17–18)

These two definitions of the hidden ones—criminalizing versus liberating—echo contemporary debates around US immigration. In "Disposable Strangers: Mexican American, Latinxs, and the Ethnic Label 'Hispanic' in the Twenty-First Century," Suzanne Obolder unpacks the discrimination of Mexican/Mexican Americans in the US after reminding us that Mexicans south of the US border really return to once Mexico lands (Arizona, California, Colorado, Nevada, New Mexico, Texas, and Utah). Citing Nuñez, Obolder states that unlike the Black community in the US, who now hold secure citizenship, "the mobility and displacement forced by globalization had instead led Latinxs to fix their eyes and hopes on the future. It is a pact that emphasizes their 'work ethic' and other similar values as contributing to their worth as workers in an exploitative and highly racializing context that reinforces their status as disposable strangers, permanently excluded from the national community" (75). A 2001 study published in *Hispanic Journal of Behavioral Science* examined the lasting effects of the 1994 California Proposition 187,[4] finding that "prejudice toward people of Hispanic descent may be rooted in gut-level affective reactions derived from childhood socialization" (Lee 431). Nineteen years later, NBC shed light on the "all time high" number of hate crimes against Latinx folk in 2020. These statements reinforce the idea that representations of Indigenous and POC in media for young people are more valuable than ever.

Lore in *Mañanaland* functions as an important "alternate" narrative tool, giving readers access to authentic representations of Latinx identity. Utilizing SF, the novel mythifies present prejudices through youthful eyes. The incomplete/influx child figure familiarizes readers with othered identities. Even though Max is only twelve, he is faced with danger on his journey to the next Guarduanes safehouse. Barely escaping from a man who recognizes Isadora as a hidden one, Max consoles her by relating to her struggle:

> "You know, Isadora, *I* want to get to the next safe place, too. And do you know why? Because I have a big secret." . . . "Are you running away?" she asked. "Do you live with someone awful who scares you?" . . . Max hesitated. Should he tell her? Maybe it would make her feel better, knowing that his mother was from Abismo, too, and that he had struggles, in spite of all the good things in his life. (172–73)

Max's innocent search for his mother indicates immigration not as a desirable option but rather as the only option for some.

Isadora's child-aged character and need to escape educates readers on the realistic dangers that exist even for children south of the border. She explains that after her parents died, she was brought to a "very important" man's house, where they could stay if they cleaned. She tells Max, "'He promised to let us go to school. But he never did. I begged every day. He didn't like that. One day he grabbed my hand to make me stop asking . . . and twisted it.' She winced. 'It broke'" (Ryan 177). Her innocence emphasizes the dehumanizing assumptions dominant, White ideologies place on undocumented individuals. Such a character "allows us to see the fallacy of measuring ourselves and the young people in our communities solely against White middle-class norms of knowing and being that continue to dominate notions of education achievement"

(Paris and Alim 2). Ryan's authoring of tragedy as part of the story but not the focal point again interjects the subversive power of SF for readers to experience what schools continuously fail to teach. Since the figuration of childhood is a part of the collective imagination, using the normalized persona of the child along with the "alternate" perspective and voice introduces authentic racialized disparities in familiar storytelling modes. Tropes of discrimination, danger for a community, and finding agency in SF allow readers to imagine realities outside of prescribed norms.

The novel's inclusion of Spanish words also performs "alternative" voice within the colonial repertoire of CYA publishing. Samia Mehrez's "Radical Bilingualism in North African Literature" conceptualizes the "bilingual postcolonial writer" and suggests that a colonial presence will always exist for authors who come from once colonized backgrounds (258). Thus, the presence of Spanish words "alternatively" constructs the narrative but still alludes to the ever-present colonial influence within the current CYA publishing culture. Django Paris and H. Samy Alim, in *Culturally Sustaining Pedagogies: Teaching and Learning for Justice in a Changing World*, ask the right question in regards to the possibility of "alternative" modes of languaging, particularly in educational settings. They explore the idea that "[t]he purpose of the state-sanctioned schooling has been to forward the largely assimilationist and often violent White imperial project, with students and families being asked to lose or deny their languages, literacies, cultures, and histories in order to achieve in schools" (1). We also see this presence in the publishing industry standards, as aforementioned, where arguably the primary audience is seemingly always White, and those who are not must adjust their imaginations to fit into categories that continue to marginalize and suppress. The main purpose for Paris and Alim's work is to decenter diverse cultural backgrounds as deficit and recenter those mindsets as "critically enriching strengths" (1). These qualities also find viability in the way CYA literature and media work as hopeful subversive means.

Using Spanish artistically rather than as a trademark for Latinx identity in *Mañanaland* highlights this potential. For example, "Solo mañana sabe. Only the place we know as tomorrow holds the answers" (Ryan 29), indirectly translates—the literal translation is "only tomorrow know." Assuming that misleading non-Spanish-speaking audiences is not the goal, the loose translation still captures the essence of what tomorrow really means for refuge seeking migrants. Not only does the ambiguity of the phrase itself provide room for interpretation, but it also subverts the monolithic language and, therefore, assumptions about Latinx immigrants. Here texts like *Mañanaland* sustain diversity rather than merely acknowledge and value it.

While Mehrez focuses on North African literature, CYA needs examination through a postcolonial lens considering that publishing companies have profited and grown without accountability in representing the diverse population that consumes it. Mehrez writes, "[D]ecolonization has been, and continues to be, an active confrontation with a hegemonic system of thought and hence a process of the contestation of all dominant forms and structures whether they be linguistic, discursive, or ideological" (258). This process of decolonization in literature is continuously burdened by structures of dominant writing culture and speaks to Inoue's argument for inclusive writing practices. If these novels, like other speculative novels, are published by mainstream presses and contribute to mainstream press profits, this decolonial project matters because institutional racism continues. Yet, no matter the assertive critique afforded by novels like these, a significant challenge remains that still must be worked past.

Looking through this [de]colonial lens, *Mañanaland* challenges the popular imagination and erects "alternative" places to minimize the "imagination gap." In the final section, titled "Tomorrow," a spirit-like presence guides Max on a meditative journey after the reader learns that "Mañanaland is not a destination. It's a . . . way of thinking" (Ryan 211). As the voice explains, "*Unanswered questions don't always mean a closed door. The challenge is to find a flicker, a spark . . .*" (224; italics original). This didactic message gives audiences the opportunity to discover that walls and uncertainty—like for those crossing the US border—even if metaphorically. A spark of the "alternative" mindset helps ameliorate diverse spaces.

The novel also refocuses migration on the act of leaving rather than on where one is heading. In "Diaspora, Transnationalism, and the Decolonial Project," Walcott writes, "To 'leave' one must have a destination in mind. Of course, one could rush out the door with no destination in mind, but to 'rush' or 'to leave' would suggest some self-possession; rushing would suggest a purpose, a purpose with some urgency, some reason" (343). Walcott goes on to argue for a "*pure decolonial project*" and states:

> To refuse such a "romance story" is not to deny history, but rather to account for the ways in which history might offer us a better calculation of how to alter the human yet again in our time. Such an alter-native will require the production of 'new indigenisms' of our globe, and those new indigenisms will require us to have conversations, debates, politics, and maybe even policies that are centered in the "catastrophic culture" that has brought us together. (356)

Novels like *Mañanaland* and *The Marrow Thieves* do not take history for granted; rather, they move us toward the decolonial project envisioned by Walcott.

"Altering" for the Future

In his introduction to *The Bounds of Race: Perspectives on Hegemony and Resistance*, Dominick LaCapra explores the ideological concept of race. He writes: "Here the broader issue is how to avoid racial stereotyping or uncontrolled mythologizing and come to terms with race critically and transformatively without denying the historical and political need for people of color to find effective voices and to work out necessary subject-positions" (1–2). Both Dimaline and Ryan take up this call by representing their respective groups and communities imaginatively. Because ideology is always recycled through unquestioned authorship, it maintains dominant discourses, reaffirming the very need for more Indigenous and POC characters in works of SF.

Mañanaland and *The Marrow Thieves* both highlight the importance of home and hope. They manifest and achieve these goals in different ways, but ultimately both represent shared struggles and accomplishments in non-White communities. Although the novels' stories are different, they both provide readers with a sense of hope. Furthermore, the novels enable the "alternate" within society to see themselves through a "sliding glass door" (Bishop 1) because of the imagined possibilities in SF. As Thomas suggests, "A reader or viewer of the fantastic can enter a portal and go on a quest. He or she can be immediately immersed within the fantasy world. . . . The fantastic can intrude upon the world the reader knows, or the reader can choose to remain in the liminal space between real and the unreal" (18). These particular novels also demonstrate how readers can gaze through an "alternative" lens. By pushing the boundaries of stories for characters like Frenchie, Isadora, and Max through SF, diverse youth become the heroes and the champions of endless possibility. *As they should be.*

Notes

1. A June 2020 article in *The Atlantic* by Kwame Anthony Appiah, entitled "The Case for Capitalizing the 'B' in Black" asserts that the capitalization of White is defined from the American Psychological Association's style rules, stating "We believe that it is important to call attention to White as a race as a way to understand and give voice to how Whiteness functions in our social and political institutions and our communities. Moreover, the detachment of 'White' as a proper noun allows White people to sit out of conversations about race and removes accountability from White people's and White institutions' involvement in racism."

2. "Emancipating the dark fantastic requires decolonizing our fantasies and dreams. It means liberating magic itself" (Thomas 169).

3. "The Metis nation emerged during the colonization of Canada and traces its origin to communities first formed by the offspring of First Nations and European settlers (primarily the French). The term is also sometimes used to describe all Aboriginal persons of mixed descent" (Mundy 139).

4. This proposition allowed for any POC to be racially profiled by police and asked for proof of nationality.

Works Cited

Aldama, Frederick Luis. *The Art of the Matter: Interviews with Latino/a Children's and Young Adult Fiction Authors*. U of Pittsburgh P, 2018.

Appiah, Kwame Anthony. "The Case for Capitalizing the 'B' in Black." *The Atlantic*, 2 June 2021, www.theatlantic.com/ideas/archive/2020/06/time-to-capitalize-blackand-white/613159/.

Bishop, Rudine Sims. "Mirrors, Windows, and Sliding Glass Doors." *Perspectives: Choosing and Using Books for the Classroom*, vol. 6, no. 3, summer 1990, pp. ix–xi.

Castañeda, Claudia. *Figurations: Child, Bodies, Worlds*. Duke UP, 2003.

De Vos, Laura Maria. "Spiralic Temporality and Cultural Continuity for Native American Sovereignty: Idle No More and *The Marrow Thieves*." *Transmotion*, vol. 6, no. 2, 2020, pp. 1–42.

Dillon, Grace L. "Native American Futurisms, Bimaashi Biidaas Mose, Flying and Walking towards You." *Extrapolation*, vol. 57, no. 1/2, 2016, pp. 1–6.

Dimaline, Cherie. *The Marrow Thieves*. Cormorant Books, 2017.

Dunbar-Ortiz, Roxanne. *An Indigenous Peoples' History of the United States for Young People*. Adapted by Jean Mendoza and Debbie Reese, Penguin Random House Canada, 2019.

Gamboa, Suzanne, and Associated Press. "Rise in Reports of Hate Crimes against Latinos Pushes Overall Number to 11-Year High." *CBS News*, 16 Nov. 2020, https://www.nbcnews.com/news/latino/rise-hate-crimes-against-latinos-pushes-overall-number-highest-over-n1247932.

Hintz, Carrie, and Eric Tribunella. *Reading Children's Literature: A Critical Introduction*. Bedford St. Martin's, 2013.

Inoue, Asao B. "How Do We Language So People Stop Killing Each Other, Or What Do We Do about White Language Supremacy?" Chair's Address. Conference on College Composition and Communication, Annual Convention, 14 Mar. 2019, tinyurl.com/4C19ChairAddress.

King, Tiffany Lethabo, et al. *Otherwise Worlds: Against Settler Colonialism and Anti-Blackness*. Duke UP, 2020.

LaCapora, Dominick. Introduction. *The Bounds of Race: Perspectives on Hegemony and Resistance*, edited by LaCapra, Cornell UP, 1991, pp. 1–16.

Lee, Yueh-Ting, et al. "Attitudes Toward 'Illegal' Immigration into the United States: California Proposition 187." *Hispanic Journal of Behavioral Sciences*, vol. 23, no. 4, 2001, p. 430.

Lothian, Alexis. *Old Futures: Speculative Fiction and Queer Possibility*. New York UP, 2018.

Mehrez, Samia. "Radical Bilingualism in North African Literature." *The Bounds of Race: Perspectives on Hegemony and Resistance*, edited by Dominick LaCapra, Cornell UP, 1991, pp. 255–77.

Mundy, Karen. "The *Binti* Series and *The Marrow Thieves*." *Comparative Education Review*, vol. 644, no. 1, Feb. 2020, pp. 139–42. https://doi.org/10.1086/706848.

Muzyka, Kyle. "From Growing Medicine to Space Rockets: What Is Indigenous Futurism?" *CBC Unreserved*, 8 Mar. 2019. https://www.cbc.ca/radio/unreserved/looking-towards-the-future-indigenous-futurism-in-literature-music-film-and-fashion-1.5036479/from-growing-medicine-to-space-rockets-what-is-indigenous-futurism-1.5036480.

Nuñez, Gabriela. "The Latino Pastoral Narrative: Backstretch Workers in Kentucky." *Latino Studies*, vol. 10, nos. 1–2, 2012, pp. 107–27.

Paris, Django, and H. Samy Slim. *Culturally Sustaining Pedagogies: Teaching and Learning for Justice in a Changing World*. Teachers College Press, Columbia U, 2017.

Ryan, Pam Muñoz, and Jiménez Alberto Rioja. *Mañanaland*. Scholastic, 2020.

Simpson, Leanne Betasamosake. *As We Have Always Done: Indigenous Freedom through Radical Resistance*. U of Minnesota P, 2020.

Suhr-Systma, Mandy. *Self-Determined Stories: The Indigenous Reinvention of Young Adult Literature*. Michigan State UP, 2018.

Thomas, Ebony Elizabeth. *The Dark Fantastic: Race and the Imagination from Harry Potter to the Hunger Games*. New York UP, 2020.

Walcott, Rinaldo. "Diaspora, Transnationalism, and the Decolonial Project." *Otherwise Worlds: Against Settler Colonialism and Anti-Blackness*, edited by Tiffany Lethabo King, Jenell Navarro, and Andrea Smith, Duke UP, 2020, pp. 343–61.

"Why We Don't Italicize Spanish." *YouTube*, uploaded by Daniel J. Older, 4 Aug. 2014, http://www.youtube.com/watch?v=24gCI3Ur7FM. Accessed 1 May 2021.

SILKPUNK AND AGENDER CHILDHOODS IN NEON YANG'S *TENSORATE* UNIVERSE

Shuyin Yu

The first child introduced in Neon Yang's 2017 silkpunk novella *The Black Tides of Heaven* is "Sanao Sonami, the [then] youngest of Protector Sanao's [then] six children" (16). Sonami, with their "genderfree tunic of a child, their hair cropped to a small square at the top of their head and gathered into a bun" is no more confined to a gender than the "squarish, silk draped" floating cart they stood next to (16). In the fantastical world of Ea that Yang has built, Asian inspiration and genderqueerness are inseparable, with the world influencing the culture, culture influencing the language, and, as a result, the language reflecting the world of the narrative. Yang's worldbuilding is a direct challenge to concepts of gender identity, normative sexuality, and compulsory sexuality in children. In the world of Ea, not only do children not need gender when they are young, they arguably thrive without it; children who are ready to choose and be certain about their genders are able to assert their identities, while those who are not are able to wait until they have a sense of who they may want to be.

I focus on two related threads in *The Black Tides of Heaven*. First, I examine how specifically the Asian influences in silkpunk help establish the *Tensorate* universe and how these epistemologies lend themselves to alternate worldviews that make agender childhood possible. I contrast this radical reinterpretation of childhood with conventional understandings of childhood in nonspeculative literature, arguing that the boundaries imposed on children in more realistic genres are tied to hegemonic structures and oppressive systems. Second, I examine how gender and sexuality are depicted in *The Black Tides of Heaven* and how this representation complicates the narrative of queer child development. I emphasize how the agender child's act of negation (refusal to grow upwards, sideways, or in any direction) further complicates the identity of queer children. I look at the agender child and the world they live in not as solutions for contemporary childhood issues resulting from superimposed gender binaries but rather as a kind of alternative potentiality for thinking about how children are able to recognize and come into their genders if they choose to identify with them. Following the novel itself, I refer to children who have not yet confirmed their gender with "they/them" pronouns and use gendered pronouns once they have been confirmed as adults, substituting gendered third-person pronouns as necessary (partially because English lacks gendered first-person pronouns, unlike languages such as Japanese). It is also important to note that while I privilege traditional Asian epistemologies and ontologies as foundational to Yang's worldbuilding, I do not want to superimpose a fantastical and hypothetical reinterpretation of Asian knowledge bases as uncritical solutions for the real world. Rather, I acknowledge the embedded hegemonic structural issues inherited with those paradigms, balancing (to borrow terms from Eve Kosofsky Sedgwick) a "reparative reading" of the potential solutions within the *Tensorate* series with a "paranoid reading" that is critical of the problems embedded when fictional worlds import real-world ideas.

The goal in framing *The Black Tides of Heaven* in the context of the silkpunk is to challenge familiar Western understandings of worldbuilding and metaphysics, and assumptions about binary childhoods and gendered children. If steampunk, as Roger Whitson explains, anachronistically recombines information about the Victorian industrial revolution in order to create "alternate forms of history and technology" (3) foundational to contemporary Western understandings of technological and social advancements, then it is possible to imagine silkpunk as one of many newer multicultural and postcolonial approaches that focus on "discrete elements [that] are decontextualized, remixed, remade, appropriated, and otherwise transformed" (7) in the context of the "specific materials and cultures interacting with them" (79). Even the name "silkpunk" hints at how multicultural techniques in steampunk reimagine alternative histories and cultures, specifically those of Asia. Silk, being an organic but strong and tensile material that was invented in China, becomes emblematic of non-Western knowledge; combined with the countercultural implications of the punk genre, silkpunk doesn't only look toward futures of high technology but toward an often-ignored past as origins of alternative forms of knowledge with applications in the present and the future. If "[s]teampunk explores the pastness of the future, or the futurity of the past" (Whitson 12), silkpunk reexamines temporality as a "multilayered production" that exists in racialized and marginalized identities (25). Silkpunk challenges hegemonic thoughts found in contemporary Western society and social structures, and instead reorients the worldview around Asian epistemologies and metaphysics. The reimagined silkpunk world thus becomes a way to "understand technological history as an emergent ontology constantly branching into various possible alternate directions" and a way to "conceptualize alternate cultural techniques" (Whitson 77).

In his essay "'Silkpunk': Redefining Technology for 'The Grace of Kings,'" Ken Liu describes how "the technological vocabulary and grammar of steampunk are based on chrome, glass and steam, and on mechanical precision and rigidity" whereas "the vocabulary and grammar of silkpunk are based on organic materials and biomechanics" (*LiveScience*). In a later interview with Gizmodo, Liu "crib[s]" from his own answer and expands on how the "silkpunk technology vocabulary is based on organic materials historically important to East Asia (bamboo, paper, silk) and seafaring cultures of the Pacific (coconut, feathers, coral), and the technology grammar follows biomechanical principles. . . . The overall aesthetic is one of suppleness and flexibility, expressive of the cultures that inhabit the islands" (Misra). Silkpunk's technology vocabulary and grammar also reflect the alternate universes' metaphysics and social constructs, which means that the genre "emphasizes the way different materials construct different forms of cultural experience and—by extension—different forms of political subjectivity" (Whitson 79–80). Through this reorientation toward Eastern knowledge bases, silkpunk reimagines alternative histories that foreground the complexities and intra-Asian dynamics rather than Asia's and Asian literature's historical relationship with the West.

Silkpunk is not meant to be antithetical to steampunk (the same way the East/the Orient is not actually meant to be antithetical to the West/the Occident). While "variations of that premodern-hypermodern dynamic in speculative visions of Asia and Asians have been recycled numerous times" (Roh et al. 1), the "phenomenon of imagining Asia and Asians in hypo- or hypertechnological terms in cultural productions and political discourse" often falls into Techno-Orientalist territory (2). Like many theories that build on Edward Said's theories on Orientalism as "a style of thought based upon an ontological and epistemological distinction" between the Orient and the Occident and a "Western style for dominating, restructuring, and having authority over the Orient" (2–3), silkpunk as a genre is meant to challenge Techno-Orientalist assumptions by presenting alternative histories that privilege Eastern knowledge not as Other but rather as a comparative partner whose knowledges and epistemologies are worthy of ontological consideration.

Yang's novellas in the *Tensorate* series follow in the silkpunk tradition of reimaging how the world can be, and thus Yang has managed to create a fantastical agender childhood that is what George Mann might call "'an alternative to a history that is too often seen as immutable'" (qtd. in Whitson 4). Much of the subversion in the *Tensorate* universe comes from this interplay of Classical Chinese metaphysics and alternative queer potential in terms of gender and attraction. Yang's foregrounding of Asian epistemologies and histories is not only the foundation for the fantastical worldbuilding but also the internal logic of the technologies and interactivity in the world. *The Black Tides of Heaven* and *The Red Threads of Fortune* follow Sonami's younger siblings, the twins Akeha and Mokoya, as they grow up in the Protectorate in Ea. This paper focuses on *The Black Tides of Heaven*, which is divided into four parts, paralleling each section of Akeha's growth. "Part One: Mokoya" is about Akeha's childhood and their relationship with their sibling Mokoya. Before the series began, climate catastrophe had brought on riots, rationing, and discontent, and the Protectorate had put down the rebellions (14). In order to put down the rebellions, Sonami's mother, the Protector Sanao, enlisted the help of Head Abbot Sung of the Grand Monastery, promising him one of her children as a future apprentice. Head Abbott Sung had hoped for Sonami, with their elegant slackcraft (the manipulation of the five elements that make up the foundation of their world) and their desire to be admitted to the monastery, to join him and perhaps one day replace him as Head Abbot.

The story begins when Head Abbot Sung approaches the Great High Palace of the Protectorate, and Protector Sanao offers him two newborn infants to "'settle [their] debt from last summer'" (21). It is then revealed the birth of twins was "'an accident'" (23) and Sonami comments that "'[t]he fortunes didn't give Mother twins for no reason. That means that if there's a plan, she's not the one controlling it'" (24). "Part One: Mokoya" thus follows the twins when they are children at the monastery and explores the codependency Akeha shares with their sibling. When Mokoya's visions of the future begins, the Protector calls for Mokoya's return, and the Head Abbot allows them to return together, even though he was within his rights to keep one of the children as his successor, because separating the two children "'would clearly be an unthinkable cruelty'" (65).

"Part Two: Thennjay" is about Akeha's adolescence and discovering themself as a man; the narrative picks up years later when the twins are teens and explores their divergence from each other, driven by their differing gender identities and their mutual attraction to Thennjay, a Gauri circus doctor who would replace Head Abbot Sung. While the stirrings of civil unrest appear in the background of Part One, Part Two makes it clear that there are tensions and social strife tearing at the Protectorate, which often leads to sectarian violence that falls along ethnic and social lines. At the end of Part Two, after stealing a kiss from Thennjay, Akeha leaves the Kuanjin capital of Chengbee, leaving behind his sister Mokoya, who would eventually marry Thennjay. "Part Three: Yongcheow" is about Akeha's adulthood and spans from when an adult Akeha rescues Yongcheow and becomes further entangled in a rebellion that pits him against his sister, until "Part Four: Mother" when an adult Akeha returns to Chengbee after a tragedy strikes Mokoya and her young family. The novella concludes with Akeha recognizing himself and separating from his twin, even as he is willing to give up parts of his body to save her after the climax of story.

The books in the *Tensorate* series are not marketed as "young adult fiction" because the majority of the series follows adult characters, but *The Black Tides of Heaven* is unique in that it follows Akeha through their childhood, adolescence, and all the way to his adulthood. While generalizations separate the entwicklungsroman from the bildungsroman by the age the protagonists reach by the end of the story—i.e., a text can be classified as an "*Entwicklungsroman* because the protagonist has grown or as a *Bildungsroman* because the protagonist reaches adulthood by the novel's end" (Trites 16)—the age restrictions of such categorizations do not fully capture the nuance with which childhood decisions have repercussions that extend into adulthood. *The Black Tides of Heaven*, like many young adult and liminal texts, has a much more nuanced position on growth and progress. The four sections of *The Black Tides of Heaven* are concerned with "participat[ing] in a mythology of cultural legitimization" or having Akeha's "narrative of growth" be processed as "an acceptance of one's cultural habitat rather than serving as a narrative about transcendence or separation" (Trites 18). More than just growing up, Akeha grows into himself, differing from his twin not only because of his gender but because his choices and agency juxtapose against Mokoya's visions of the future and prophecies.

While *The Black Tides of Heaven* does contain a "home-away-home" pattern that is often indicative of the bildungsroman (Trites 10), Akeha's journey is about reconciling with the world within which he exists and has never left. Like many texts focused on adolescence, *The Black Tides of Heaven* is primarily concerned with Akeha finding out where they/he belongs and the role that they/he will play as they/he grows up. Unlike Mokoya, with their/her heterochromia and visions of the future as the first "prophet recorded in the Protectorate for hundreds of years" (Yang 39), Akeha, who is skilled in slackcraft, struggles with their/his existence as a spare or a "mistake" (163) when compared to their/his sibling/sister because Akeha had been an unexpected twin. Part of the way Akeha asserts themself as being different from his sibling is by choosing to be confirmed as a man, differentiating himself not only from Mokoya but also from the Protector's other children because "[i]t has been a long time since [she's] had a son'" (121). Because Akeha had never been "part of [the Protector's] plans" (121), he would fall outside of the confinements she has placed on his siblings. Akeha's assertion of his agency is tied to layers of decisions interconnected with the world in which he lives.

Akeha's ability to choose his gender is pivotal to both the plot and themes of the novella. The *Tensorate* world allows children to make their own decisions and will delay the process until children are able to decide—which sometimes involves visiting the doctors and masters of forest-nature who reform their physical bodies into gendered bodies (Yang 148). Until then, these children are "agender"—both etymologically in the sense that they are "without a gender" and also building on precedents set by asexuality/aromantic/agender studies that differentiate the "a-" prefix as different from the "de-" prefix and separate from identities like "nonbinary" and/or "gender nonconforming." Critiques of "children's desexualization" often "[insist] instead on the child's right to sexual agency, sexual subjecthood" without being "sanitized" (Przybylo 90). A "persistent slippage in queer and nonqueer work alike between the terms 'asexuality' and 'desexualization'" occurs, Ela Przybylo explains, when asexuality is often "subsumed into the negative force of desexualization" (93). In reality, Przybylo continues, "asexuality is not an elaboration of something lost or denied; it is, quite conversely, a marker of something found and understood about oneself, a site of self-meaning, a welcome term in the process of self-understanding" (93). This is certainly the case with children's identities in the *Tensorate* series, since the child characters do not have adults superimpose artificial confines or denial on their identities. Instead, their agender identity is how they understand themselves until they choose to decide their gender identities.

This space of existence without external pressures (at least until one is able to assert one's agency) is meant to complicate the theories Kathryn Bond Stockton presents in *The Queer Child*. Instead of sideways growth, which still prescribes a direction, agender childhood instead proposes that there is no direction in which a child needs to grow at all—which is to suggest that growth itself is unnecessary. By taking the concept of "delayed, deferred" queer childhood (Stockton 4) to the extreme, and proposing that not having a gender isn't a delay or deferral at all, the agender childhoods in Yang's *Tensorate* series represent a starting point where children are neither defined nor limited by external extrapolations of their gender identity. As a result, children can choose to grow in any direction, or to not grow in any direction at all (both figuratively and literally). Instead of growing upwards, like a line segment with two predetermined points and limited direction, the development of the agender child is more like a ray, with a starting point but no limitation on where it might go. Likewise, the agender child is not limited by gendered constraints before they are ready to confirm their identities. This agender child thus becomes a challenge to generalized assumptions about children's identities, forcing gendered adults to confront these assumptions until the children are ready to acknowledge their own genders.

Instead of debating between the "child's right to sexual purity, sexual innocence" and "the child's right to sexual agency, sexual subjecthood" (Przybylo 89–90), agender childhood in Yang's story acknowledges children's agency in the construction of their own subjectivity based on their individual timelines as long there is a world that is able to accommodate them and their choices. By keeping most children agender until they can decide for themselves, while leaving them open to explore their potential identities, the Protectorate engages in what Pzybylo might describe as "erotic childhood and intergenerational desires without succumbing to a sexual presumption" (91). In her critique of "models of asexuality as a 'stunting' or 'arrest'" (93), Przybylo points out that these ideas are often "entangled in whiteness and ability that ground proper development as necessitating sex" (93), tying ideas of sexual innocence (and thus untouched gender) with concepts and discourses surrounding "racial innocence" as explained by Robin Bernstein. By removing binary gender outside of the usual assumed social constraints and turning gender identification into a decision, being agender is not an indecision any more than a dot is not a direction; instead, agender is a state that is able to exist simultaneously with, as an origin for, and/or as an alternative to genders. Stockton describes how growth "has been relentlessly figured as vertical movement ward (hence, 'growing up')" (4). But the world of the *Tensorate* challenges such linearity by shifting where children begin.

Like most people in the Protectorate, Akeha and Mokoya are genderless while they are young, referred to with gender neutral pronouns, with the expectation that they would eventually get "confirmed" with a gender. The twins are confirmed "the week of their seventeenth birthday" (Yang 125), with Mokoya getting confirmed as a woman and Akeha as a man; the narration highlights the pivotal importance of this date as the "week their lives would start anew" (125). But the world of the Protectorate doesn't make the confirmation of gender a strict deadline, and there is a wide range of opinions, reactions, and realities that reflect the way gender and its confirmation are understood and experienced. Yang thereby makes space in the *Tensorate* universe for those who do not want to confirm their gender at a particular time that shifts from (and thus separates) agender childhood to gendered adulthood. When the twins were six, they made a promise that they would never get confirmed, an idea that Akeha held onto even as they grew up to be a teen and Mokoya had left behind as the first twin to consider being confirmed. Rather than "notions of the horizontal—what spreads sideways—or sideways and backwards—more than a simple thrust toward height and forward time" (Stockton 4), the agender children of the Protectorate are able to grow in any direction that suits them. Akeha and Mokoya, who are "'identical twins'" (Yang 216), thus arguably starting from the same origin point, grow in radically different directions.

The freedom from traditional gender assignations in the novel also means there is a huge range for when people choose and confirm their gender. Most people in the *Tensorate* world choose not to "[jump] from undeclared gender straight to confirmation. They'd take a few years to be sure" (Yang 74). The narration, told from Akeha's perspective as a teen, generalized it to "[n]obody ... [u]nless they were Sonami" (Yang 74). However, Yang nevertheless makes space in the *Tensorate* universe for those who do not want to confirm their gender at a particular time that shifts from (and thus separates) agender childhood to gendered adulthood. As it progresses, the story nuances the generalization by recognizing that there are children who come into awareness of their gender earlier. For instance, at the age of three, Akeha's niece Eien "had told her mother she was a girl, and had not changed her mind thereafter" (Yang 205), demonstrating how individual children are able to come into their own sexual and gender subjectivity at their own time. The reaction of the adults in the *Tensorate* series is to treat her choice and validate her gender as if she had chosen it later in life, and their constant affirmation of her chosen subjectivity through the use of her pronouns recognizes her agency as both a child and as a person.

Akeha's partner, Yongcheow, on the other hand, demonstrates that gender confirmation doesn't always lead to physical conformation—because while he was confirmed, he does not visit those doctors and masters who would transform his physical body (Yang 148). While Yongcheow identifies with a gender, he had never conformed physically to that gender. When Akeha presses Yongcheow on this choice, Yongcheow explains he "just didn't do it because it didn't feel right" (Yang 163), once again foregrounding the importance of choice and agency in regards to gender in the Protectorate. In the world of the *Tensorate* series, there are those who believe in Fortune and the inescapability of Fate, and those who believe in "'the black tides of heaven [that] direct the courses of human lives [but] as with all waters, one can swim against the tide'" (Yang 166). Yongcheow, who is an Obedient and believer in how the "Almighty decides our circumstances [but] doesn't decide our actions" (Yang 166), enacts his free will not only in his politics and rebellion but in his very physical existence by choosing to not conform after his confirmation. Agender characters (or, at least, those who refuse to conform to gender norms) regain control when they are able to reject expectations and maintain their agender status from childhood into adulthood. As Kristina Gupta points out, while sexual interest could be seen as a way to gain power, "norms about sexual interest function as a system of social control" (132). The *Tensorate* universe is not immune from reinforcing hegemonic structures; however, there are still ways for individuals within that universe to regain control outside of the expected systems through subversion, rejection, or conversion. Thus, I argue *The Black Tides of Heaven* models a reparative approach to the compulsory sexuality of childhood by demonstrating how space can be created for children to place themselves on the scale of "sexual purity, sexual innocence" to "sexual agency, sexual subjecthood" (Przybylo 89–90).

Because the children in the *Tensorate* series literally have no gender, they are simultaneously desexualized (by the society they live in) and asexualized (by their own concept of childhood sexuality). For most children in the *Tensorate* universe, their pivot from childhood into adulthood is the moment they "confirmed [and thus conformed to] their gender" (117), leading to what Przybylo calls "sexuality's centralizing energy" (92). This agency granted to the agender child to decide their own future and their relationship to gender is subversive in its own right. Stockton describes how children often "cannot, according to our concepts, advance to adulthood until we [the adults] say it's time" (6); by putting the power into the hands of the child, adulthood is not just "when full stature (or reproduction) is achieved" (11) but when the child is cognitively able to process their own identity. As Roberta Seelinger Trites points out, often "[s]exual potency is a common metaphor for empowerment in adolescent literature" (84). If, "for many characters in YA novels, experiencing sexuality marks a rite of passage that helps them define themselves as having left childhood behind" (Trites 84), then the *Tensorate* universe takes this actualization from a metaphorical to a literal level, as their lives would literally "start anew" (Yang 125) with a new body now that "the masters of forest-nature" would no longer "ke[ep] the markers of adulthood at bay" (117) and the doctors "[reshape] hips" and "[shift] bone" (127). The characters' sexual and social actualization, tied to their concept of the self and the pronouns that they use, marks their subjectivity and existence. The way Yang has sculpted the world of Ea and the metaphysics of the *Tensorate* universe is thus pivotal to this kind of self-actualization.

Because the silkpunk genre is set in worlds influenced by Asian histories, metaphysics, cultures, and linguistics, the genre also helps to curate spaces that allow for a full exploration of the fantastical alternative potentiality. For example, while many existing languages have gendered pronouns, they are bound to preconceptions of gendered children, whereas *The Black Tides of Heaven* is able to explore how gendered pronouns help shape the ways characters conceptualize themselves and how they serve as a narrative tool. Thus, Yang uses gender neutral pronouns for the agender children, assumed to be a unique pronoun in the world of the novel, but written as they/them because English doesn't have a gender-neutral equivalent widely in use. This usage of the gender-neutral pronoun used to describe the twins both individually and collectively as "they" means the "they/them" pronouns adapt to being singular and plural as the narrative demands. Yang also takes advantage of this word's fluidity and ambiguity, leaving lines like "[t]hey could pretend that nothing had happened" (40) open to interpretation. This inability to determine if the narrative is referring to one or both twins opens up the interpretation to readers, who can then assign the projection of ignorance depending on how they understand the uncertainty and ambiguity in the narrative. This flexibility is what scholars like Bernhard Siegert call "the recursive nature of cultural techniques," emphasizing how "cultural techniques [are] chains of operations focused on a processual understanding of culture and technology rather than a static one" (Whitson 87). Yang draws semiotic inspiration from languages like Japanese, which has multiple pronouns, and Chinese, which has homophonous pronouns, to purposefully defamiliarize English readers from the *Tensorate* universe through the usage of language.

The reason that agender childhoods can exist within the *Tensorate* universe is that the very foundations of the world (and the resulting ontologies and epistemologies) allow for nonbinary ways of thinking. Within the *Tensorate* universe, where "*[t]he Slack is all, and all is the Slack*" (Yang 37), the agender child makes sense because the world is fundamentally opposed to binaries. Many cultures think of four elements: water, earth, fire, and air, which exist in opposition to keep each other in check; water and fire cancel each other out, and earth and air are opposites. Yet, when Akeha recites to themself a "better, shorter" version of the "First Sutra," they summarize the foundations of their world as "Earth, for gravity; Water, for motion; Fire, for hot and cold; Forest, for flesh and blood; Metal, for electricity; Everything else is extra" (Yang 37).

The five natures not only reflect the literal foundations of the world of the Protectorate but also the metaphysical understandings of the universe. The Slack is based on the Classical Chinese understanding of the elements or *wuxing*. In *wuxing*, the elements are always in conversation with each other, flowing into each other in cycles: forests feeds fire, the fire creates earth (ash), the earth bears metal, the metal enriches water, the water nourishes forests. These elements also keep each other in check: forests breaking through the earth, the earth absorbing water, water extinguishing fire, fire melting metal, metal cutting through forests. Like the more popular yin-yang theory, *wuxing* is all about balance and continuous movement; the difference is that instead of having diametrically opposed sides, the five elements are never in true opposition but rather constantly in flux, with the ability to adapt and change when necessary and constantly feeding into each other. Without dividing the world into opposing sides, the *Tensorate* universe has no need to reinforce gender binaries because the worldview (and everything from medicine to technology to even bodies) is built upon the cyclical Slack. The *Tensorate* universe's "counterfactual speculation is . . . about understanding how [ideas] could have taken a different shape under different technological and cultural conditions" (Whitson 71). Instead, Yang's world creates what Whitson describes as "recursive, anachronistic, and counterfactual history—providing us with conjectural alternatives to our present" (12). The agender child, then, is the perfect embodiment of silkpunk's capacity to "understand technological history as an emergent ontology constantly branching into various possible alternate directions" and "conceptualize alternate cultural techniques" (Whitson 77). In this respect, silkpunk models how children's and young adult literature might likewise move in alternative directions or provide alternatives to our present.

The world of Ea (the very name hinting at the acronyms for "East Asia" and punning on "Asia") (24) that Yang has created presents clear inspirations from and coding of Asia and Asian elements. In her review in *The Straits Times*, Ong Sor Fern describes the books as akin to "rojak—a local [Singaporean] salad of fruit and vegetables—it is a surprisingly delicious blend of unexpected flavours." With names like Kuanjin, Katau Kebang, Tiguman, and Gaur Antam, and the fictional Gusai Desert resting on the map of the Protectorate where one might expect the Gobi or Arabian deserts, the geography is coded to evoke understandings of Asia as well as diverse, multicultural Asian cities like Singapore (such cities sometimes resemble microcosms of Asia in their own right). The description of "spiced tea and fruit on sticks" (Yang 76), meant to evoke images of chai and tanghulu, speaks to existing cultures and the ways they intersect in multicultural cities (both inside and outside of Asia).

While Yang's worldbuilding allows for the imagination of an agender child, the text is also wary of presenting the Protectorate as a queer utopic ideal; instead, Yang's positionality as a queer and nonbinary Singaporean writer means they are hyperaware that the Protectorate could be subject to what George Mann calls a "nostalgia for what never was" (Whitson 4). Once one of the most important ports in Southeast Asia and settled by a largely Chinese diasporic population, and intimately tied with Malaysia, Singapore continues to be a central financial hub that reflects the complexities of an intra-Asian history and culture (both connected with and also independent of Western influences). Yang's description of "children in varying shades of brown" (76) highlights how, even outside of the contexts of Eurocentric and Western lenses, there is still complex intracontinental Asian history with many layers of ethnic and colorist tensions. The conflicts in the *Tensorate* universe are ultimately a reflection of the complex geopolitical history that also includes settler-colonialism independent of Western imperialism. The East Asian privilege in Singapore is thus reflected in Yang's novel through characters that are heavily coded as Japanese and Chinese oppressing characters who are coded as South Asian. In fact, the novel begins with Head Abbott Sung describing Protector Sanao (Mokoya and Akeha's mother) as "a descendent of foreign invaders into this land" (20), making Sanao's Japanese-coded name a gesture towards a history of Japanese imperialism that is still part of living memory for much of Asia.

Outside of a Western context, any privileged group can take on the position of power; this is especially true in Singapore, whose history is intimately tied with multiple layers and intersections of colonialism, imperialism, and diaspora. There are still layers of hegemonic powers and structural problems that shape the world of the *Tensorate* series as greatly as the alternative epistemologies do. Or, as Whitson puts it in a reflection of James Ng's interview on *Steamcast*, the point of "counterfactual speculation is not about idealizing other cultures, but about understanding how industrialization could have taken a different shape under different technological and cultural conditions" (71); silkpunk, like all genres, is influenced by social constructs and social constraints, which means that recognizing and acknowledging the possible alternatives and the potential spaces depends on acknowledging and working with those social constructs and social constraints.

After all, even though the first time Head Abbot Sung met Sanao Sonami, Sonami's "features [were] still cushioned by the fat of innocence" (Yang 25) and they were still an agender child, Sonami would exit a cart five years later as "a graceful figure wrapped in a light silk dress the colour of chrysanthemums and jade" because "[s]he had chosen her gender the same year the twins were born and had grown well into that role" (Yang 28). Sonami had not made their/her decisions in a vacuum, and they/she is as influenced by the political and social confines of the world as much as she is influenced by the metaphysical structures. In order to "look after [the twins] [them/her]self" (Yang 24), Sonami needed to make "'concessions'" and provide her mother, the Protector, with grandchildren (Yang 31). Like with the real world, the world of the *Tensorate* series associates Sonami's parental impulses with maternity, and Sonami ultimately ended up embracing a particular kind of femininity. Even though Sonami as an agender child had, theoretically, been able to grow in any direction, they/she had nevertheless been pressured to develop in a particular direction (and, as an older sibling, been forced to grow up). While the histories and semiotics in the *Tensorate* universe provide alternative ways of existing outside of the binaries of gender, the progression from agender child to an adult with gender doesn't exist in a utopic idealized space but with the structures that force individuals to negotiate their existence with expectations. Sedgwick's careful balance between "paranoid and reparative critical practice, not as theoretical ideologies (and certainly not as stable personality types of critics), but as changing heterogeneous relational stances" (8) works particularly well in the context of silkpunk children's and young adult literature because both critical practices help to curate a multiplicity of ways to engage with the potentialities and possibilities in both fictional and real worlds. Agender childhoods are embodied in a variety of ways in the *Tensorate* series, including an example wherein the child actively chose to have a gender; in this context, Sonami's decision, to borrow from Sedgwick, is "profoundly painful [and] profoundly relieving" as "the past, in turn, could have happened differently from the way it actually did" (24). Sonami's decision, that is, remains but one of many possibilities that children (agender or not) could end up taking.

Works Cited

Bernstein, Robin. *Racial Innocence: Performing American Childhood from Slavery to Civil Rights*. New York UP, 2011.

Fern, Ong Sor. "J. Y. Yang's Two Novellas Are like Rojak, a Surprisingly Delicious Blend of Unexpected Flavours." *The Straits Times*, 25 Sept. 2017, www.straitstimes.com/lifestyle/arts/fantastical-world-rooted-in-the-east.

Gupta, Kristina. "Compulsory Sexuality: Evaluating an Emerging Concept." *Signs*, vol. 41, no. 1, 2015, pp. 131–54.

Liu, Ken. "'Silkpunk': Redefining Technology for 'the Grace of Kings.'" *LiveScience*, 7 Apr. 2015, https://www.livescience.com/50403-defining-silkpunk-technology-in-novel-grace-of-kings.html.

Misra, Ria. "Author Ken Liu Explains 'Silkpunk' to Us." *Gizmodo*, 16 Dec. 2015, i09.gizmodo.com/author-ken-liu-explains-silkpunk-to-us-1717812714.

Przybylo, Ela. *Asexual Erotics: Intimate Readings of Compulsory Sexuality*. The Ohio State UP, 2019.

Roh, David S., et al. *Techno-Orientalism: Imagining Asia in Speculative Fiction, History, and Media*. Rutgers UP, 2015.

Said, Edward. *Orientalism*. Pantheon Books, 1978.

Sedgwick, Eve Kosofsky. "Paranoid Reading and Reparative Reading; or, You're So Paranoid, You Probably Think This Introduction Is about You." *Novel Gazing: Queer Readings in Fiction*. Duke UP, 1997, pp. 1–37.

Stockton, Kathryn Bond. *The Queer Child; or, Growing Sideways in the Twentieth Century*. Duke UP, 2009.

Trites, Roberta Seelinger. *Disturbing the Universe: Power and Repression in Adolescent Literature*. U of Iowa P, 1998.

Whitson, Roger. *Steampunk and Nineteenth-Century Digital Humanities: Literary Retrofuturisms, Media Archaeologies, Alternate Histories*. Routledge, 2017.

Yang, Neon. *The Black Tides of Heaven*. Tom Doherty Associates, 2017.

Yang, Neon. *The Red Threads of Fortune*. Tom Doherty Associates, 2017.

ALT PUBLISHING FOR YOUNG PEOPLE
An Interview with Vivek Shraya

Vivek Shraya and Derritt Mason

Vivek Shraya is a celebrated multidisciplinary artist whose impressive body of work features children's and young adult books, literary fiction and nonfiction, poetry, a play, several photo projects and films, and albums that include *Baby, You're Projecting* (2023) and the Polaris Prize–nominated *Part-Time Woman* (2017). She also has her own imprint, VS. Books, which offers mentorship and publishing opportunities to BIPOC writers. Recently, Shraya released a ten-year anniversary edition of *God Loves Hair*—a book of illustrated short stories that she originally self-published in 2010—as well as her second children's picture book, *Revenge of the Raccoons* (2022). Shraya's work challenges and provokes, pushes at the boundaries of genre and form, and often invites audiences to consider how childhood and adolescence are shaped so profoundly by the intersectionality of race, religion, sexuality, and gender. In our conversation, Shraya details *God Loves Hair*'s unusual publication trajectory; her artistic agenda as a queer, trans, and racialized author of children's books; the challenges and benefits of Canadian publishing; the importance of visual elements to her storytelling; and why it was so hard to publish a book about raccoons set in Toronto.

Derritt Mason: *God Loves Hair* is such a unique book on many levels, including its unusual shape. You could call it an illustrated collection of short stories, but that seems somehow reductive. It is a picture book, but smaller than a traditional picture book, and its content is more mature than we might expect from a picture book. How would you describe it?

Vivek Shraya: The illustrated stories in *God Loves Hair* are based on my experience growing up in Edmonton [Canada] as a gender nonconforming child of Hindu immigrants. The original idea was for it to be a picture book, but when I started working on it, I realized that if I limited it to a traditionally young picture book audience, then the narrative would also have to be limited. The book's protagonist moves from being two or three years old to about fifteen or sixteen. And if I had stuck to the idea of it being a children's picture book, I would have had to lose a lot of the later stories in the book.

When I decided that the format didn't really work for me, I was excited about how I might create something that has a children's picture book feel. I wanted it to be the kind of object that I did not have access to growing up in Edmonton, and that didn't seem to exist in the world of children's picture books. I grew up devouring picture books at the Edmonton Public Library, and they never had an Indian aesthetic or characters with brown skin or brown faces, so I really wanted to preserve that intention. I can't remember why we settled into the postcard format of the book. I think part of it is because it's not like a picture book. Picture books tend to measure around eight by ten, whereas this book is more of a four by six.

Additionally, there was something so tender and precious about the stories themselves but also the act of writing and self-publishing my first book. It was a totally different world that I had never tapped into before, and I didn't really know what I was doing, so I think there was something like a lack of confidence, where I felt that this was just a little gesture into the book world. I think that the size conveys the ways that the endeavor and its contents were, at the time, very precious to me.

The book I published right after *God Loves Hair* is called *What I LOVE about being QUEER*, and that's my largest book. It's an interesting juxtaposition that *God Loves Hair* is sort of this weird, tender, small size and then I go from that to an ostentatious, bold title with capitalized letters, a twelve-by-twelve bright yellow book. I do think that there is this element of confidence, or lack thereof, that was at play in the first book.

DM: Is there anything else about your experience with picture books or young adult literature that inspired you to tell the stories of *God Loves Hair* in this format?

VS: I think of myself now as a very intentional artist. Even with *God Loves Hair* I was so intentional about the font and paper size, but I think there were a lot of choices that were also kind of innocent. I hate saying this because people just assume that people of color are ripping pages out of their diary [when telling stories], but the truth is that *God Loves Hair* did start out, I would say, as journalesque entries. The book began from this idea of thinking about the ways that gender and sexuality aren't innate. What are stories or incidences through which I could map out the ways in which my sexuality and gender were socially created, or socially enhanced, or socially facilitated? And when I shared these journal entries with friends, they were like, "Oh, maybe there's a book here!"

At the time, too, I was taking a break from my pop music career. And pop music revels in short format. Songs are about three minutes long. It's an efficient format, and so I think similarly it doesn't surprise me that in some ways *God Loves Hair* is like a very long album.

It wasn't until years later that I heard the word microfiction to describe very short stories: one or two pages long; very, very, short. In a lot of ways, they feel more like pop song lyrics not in their structure but in their size.

DM: When you were working on *God Loves Hair*, did you have an audience in mind?

VS: Initially I wasn't thinking of an audience, but once I had this idea that I wanted it to be illustrated, it felt very clear to me that the audience included the other brown, queer, gender nonconforming kids in Edmonton or in small towns who could benefit from a resource like this. I had just read *Stone Butch Blues*, which was such a transformative book for me. But I also started thinking about the differences with the book, like its white protagonist. Given the impact that *Stone Butch Blues* had on me, I was curious: Could I write something that could also have an impact, but for people who weren't necessarily white?

DM: Can you describe the publication history of *God Loves Hair*?

VS: Thanks, this is a fun question! So, iteration one: May 2010, a thousand copies, self-published, thank you VISA. Prior to publishing I had reached out to Brian Francis, who wrote a fantastic book called *Fruit*, which was a CBC Canada Reads finalist. And in February of 2010 he blurbed *God Loves Hair*, and he said: don't underestimate the book, let me do an intro for you, you should send it out to publishers. I had been chasing the legitimacy that I thought would come from a record deal for ten years prior to this. When I got a record deal, I found out that, actually, that path didn't lead to success for me. I didn't want to make the same mistake with *God Loves Hair*, so I agreed to submit it to publishers, and if I heard back before it went to print, which had already been scheduled, then I would literally stop the presses and see. But if I didn't hear back, I'd move on, and that way I wouldn't be waiting for publishers to take note. So we reached out, and sure enough we didn't hear back for six months to a year from people who said: thanks so much for your submission, our calendar is already full of titles until 2013. This was in July and the book had already been out, and I was already touring it, so I was glad that I had just done it on my own.

But then the book was relatively successful. I sold a thousand copies in a year, which was significant for a self-published first-time author. The book was nominated for a Lambda Literary Award, and I had done readings in India, and so I approached publishers again with a little bit more confidence and was like hey, I have this like successful product, would you be interested in doing a second edition? Same thing, not interested. I wondered, do I publish another iteration of this book? One of my friends, Farzana Doctor, an amazing queer author, said that I had to make more copies and keep this in print.

So, I ran up my VISA again. And this is the funny thing about self-publishing: I dumped so much money into the first one, which technically I made back, but because I was constantly putting money back into touring or publishing another iteration, it never felt like I was making money. Anyway, in March or April of 2012, I self-published the second edition of *God Loves Hair*, and that also sold out relatively quickly. During this time I was starting to move away from *God Loves Hair*, and I was working on my first novel, *She of the Mountains*, and I pitched that to Arsenal Pulp Press in 2013.

After about six months, Arsenal got back to me and said: we'd love to publish *She of the Mountains*, and if you still have *God Loves Hair* kicking around, we'd love to do a third iteration of that book. So, in 2014 they published both *She of the Mountains* and a third edition of *God Loves Hair*. One of the things I loved about working with Arsenal is that the first question I asked was: Can we maintain the same cover and font and overall design? They agreed, which was one of the reasons why I decided to sign with them. Not that I had a ton of options. But I felt so attached to the choices I made about that book. I was really happy to hear that they were open to letting me preserve that. We did add a new story, just as I had for the second version.

The most recent iteration is a ten-year anniversary edition. My publisher emailed me in 2019 saying, you know, your book is sold out, we're looking at doing another run, are there any corrections or anything you want to change? And I pointed out that 2020 was going to be the book's ten-year anniversary. I said I'd love to do a special edition, because it's such a milestone project for me in my career. He agreed. So, in 2020, we put out a new version of *God Loves Hair*. The fourth iteration includes a new story, new illustrations, an illustrated preface that I wrote, and a foreword by Cherie Dimaline, the amazing author of *The Marrow Thieves*.

And so *God Loves Hair* keeps growing in this weird way. From version one to version four there are about four new illustrations and three or four new stories, and now a foreword and a preface. The new edition is also in hardcover with a new cover illustration. It'll be interesting to see ten years from now how much bigger the book is.

DM: What was it like returning to your first book ten years later? Did the new story feel like an organic addition to the book?

VS: In the second book I included a story called "Suicide Jeans," which was written new for that book. Suicidal ideation was one of the things that I wanted to address in the first book that I just didn't get into; maybe it's because I was busy talking about masturbation and sexual violence. Book two felt like a meaningful opportunity to add this layer.

In the latest edition, the new story is called "Garden Hose," and it's a B-side. There were three or four stories that got cut out of the very first version, and when we decided to publish this new anniversary edition, I didn't want to write something new because *God Loves Hair* still feels precious to me. There's something about that initial outing and the impact that it had on my artistic career.

I'm now a quote-unquote "writer," largely because of that book, so it feels like I don't want to touch it too much; I don't want to mess with the recipe. It felt more organic to use a B-side as opposed to writing something new for it at this point.

I probably wouldn't make a lot of the same choices now, but that's less interesting to me than just being proud of the choices I made back then. I'm proud that, for example, the second story, "Bed Humper," is about masturbation, and to me that feels great.

I'm also really moved by the ways in which the book holds as more of a trans narrative now than it did at the time. I write about this in the preface: people started reading it as a trans narrative, even when I wasn't trans, and I remember being really moved by that. But at the time, I wasn't identifying as trans, so I didn't want to appropriate that narrative. So now being trans, I was like, oh, is this an instance where the art was ahead of me, where the art revealed something that I wasn't able to tap into? Or where I felt more comfortable circling around something in art than I did in reality?

The ten-year anniversary edition of *God Loves Hair* also came out around the same time that I put out my first play, *How to Fail as a Popstar*. I think in a lot of ways [*Popstar*] is the closest project to *God Loves Hair* in its references to my religion, to junior high, to my mom. This is such a weird thing to say, but I sort of feel like I knew ten years ago that I was going to write a story about my pop career.

DM: Speaking of your play, you tend to work across genre and form quite a bit. You've published poetry, a play, novels, and you've recorded albums, but children's and young adult literature is something that you return to every few years. First you published *God Loves Hair*, then *The Boy & the Bindi* in 2016, and now your brand-new picture book *Revenge of the Raccoons*. What makes you come back to children's literature?

VS: One of the things I've seen time and time again with *God Loves Hair* and *The Boy & the Bindi* is how children's books can be mobilized to get people to think differently about a range of social issues. This happens in ways that I haven't seen to be as effective in other forms. I've heard so many stories from brown parents, from white parents, from a range of parents who have engaged with *The Boy & the Bindi* and have described the impact of seeing a gender nonconforming dark-skinned brown child be curious about his mom's Bindi. The impact the book has had on their child and on them feels so singular to me, especially because there's such a simplicity, or a seeming simplicity, in children's books. A lot of craft goes into making an agenda seem covert. I think for me it feels exciting to do that.

Also, for years and years I did positive space training for a college in Toronto, which was about how to be an ally in the workplace. I often found myself wishing this training could take place when people are a lot younger. That's not to say that people don't have the capacity for change or to think differently as adults. I think they do, but there's just so much more baggage and often a lot more resistance. Overall, I find children to be much more receptive to conversations about gender nonconformity, or racism, or the lived experiences of prejudice. For me, the picture book feels like an efficient, powerful, and magical way to do a lot of the things that feel like part of my artistic agenda, which is to inspire change and growth, to challenge, and to encourage people to think critically. These things can happen so beautifully through a picture book.

DM: Can you say more about your experience publishing *The Boy & the Bindi*?

VS: The book was inspired by a panel I sat on in 2015. We were supposed to evaluate the merit of children's books released that year by various publishers in certain regions. I remember being so disheartened. So often in the positive space workshops I ran, one of the most common forms of resistance was the claim: "but things are getting so much better, have you seen children's books lately?"

As someone who's not a parent and who admittedly didn't spend a lot of time with children's books, I just took their word for it and assumed that children's books must have changed. Being on this jury, however, confirmed that so many of the books were by white authors, and if they featured BIPOC children they were still written by white authors. I was so frustrated that during the lunch break I did what J. K. Rowling did and wrote the *Boy & the Bindi* on a napkin. I felt like I had to do it myself. That's always been my motivation:

seeing something and being frustrated and wondering how I could do this differently, what my contribution could be to make a shift.

So, I put together a pitch. I got good advice from Cory Silverberg who has published wonderful children's books including *What Makes a Baby* and *Sex Is a Funny Word*. He advised me that the worst thing you can tell a publisher is that your book is original; what you need to tell them is how your book is just like all these other books that are selling well. So, I came up with a comparative title list and put Robert Munsch on there. Aim high! I said that *The Boy & the Bindi* is basically like *Love You Forever*, which is also a story about a boy and his mom. And then I just pitched it directly to Arsenal Pulp Press. At this point in my career, Arsenal had done the third edition of *God Loves Hair*, and they'd published *She of the Mountains*, my first novel, which was also illustrated. I felt like they had a history of supporting what the publishing industry would deem unusual books. However, they had never published a picture book.

As part of my pitch, I hired Rajni Perera to create three sketches, two characters and a panel. Six months later, I heard from the press that they'd do it, and it was super exciting. It was their first picture book in forty years, and it's been exciting to see their children's portfolio expand since *The Boy & the Bindi*.

Because it was the first children's book for me and for the press, I felt like I got to have a lot of say. It felt similar to *God Loves Hair* in that I chose the illustrator, Rajni; she and I chose the paper, the shape of the book, and the fonts, and I was a big part of the illustration process. It was wonderful working together.

DM: Earlier, you alluded to thematic repetition between your works. However, your latest picture book, *Revenge of the Raccoons*, is thematically different from anything else you've produced. I know you had some challenges bringing this book to press. Can you describe what that process was like, what obstacles you encountered, and why you worked with a different press on this?

VS: It's so funny to me because, in many ways, *Revenge of the Raccoons* feels like the most basic thing I've done in my entire art career. It's a children's picture book about raccoons. Yet, when I think about the time it took from pitch to publication, it's been the longest journey. We started pitching the book in 2018, and it will come out this fall [2022], so it will have been almost five years. For some people, this is a short amount of time. For me, someone who's a very reactive writer, that's a very, very long time, and that's because it was very hard to get published.

I was really surprised, especially because I thought that I'd finally made something accessible. And this speaks to my naivete around accessibility.

Any time I think I've made work that will be accessible to a mass market, I'm always wrong. It's sometimes a very painful thing. But it's also kind of a beautiful thing, because it means that a desire for success isn't the driving force of the project. It also speaks to a big divide between, even after all these years, what I make and what institutions think will sell. I've had so much experience, I have my own publishing imprint, and yet: ask me what a publisher thinks will sell, and I just cannot tell you.

With *Raccoons*, publishers wanted me to supply them with a children's book about gender. I was really frustrated because I'd already done that with *The Boy & the Bindi*. Also, I think it speaks to the limitations that are often put on marginalized artists. If you are seen as someone who creates a particular kind of work, then that is how you will be forever seen. I have often referred to this as a kind of trap that I didn't realize I was deliberately casting myself into, especially when I wrote *God Loves Hair*, because it was the first time that I was openly talking about identity: queerness, gender, religion, race. I didn't know that by writing about those things that suddenly those would be the only things I get to write about.

I have a range of interests that expand beyond those things. That's not to say, though, that an intersectional lens isn't applied to *Raccoons*, which I would argue is rooted in a kind of social consciousness or social awareness. One could make ties to colonization, urban displacement, climate change. But because it's not *The Boy & the Bindi*, the Boy and Doing-Something-Gender-Nonconforming, publishers just didn't know what to do with it.

It has felt really, really frustrating. But I'm thrilled that Owlkids Books has come on board, especially since I grew up reading *Chickadee* magazine in the Edmonton Public Library. And even being able to reference that with my parents and recall when we used to read *Chickadee* magazine together—they're now publishing my book. For me, this is really meaningful. It's also interesting to work with a children's publisher because they have a very different approach—children's books are their wheelhouse.

I'm working with Juliana [Neufeld] who is the illustrator of *God Loves Hair*, so we have a great relationship. One of the things that I have found to be very different working with a children's press is that I've learned you don't typically engage with the illustrator. With *The Boy & the Bindi*, *God Loves Hair*, and *She of the Mountains*, I had constant exchanges with the illustrator. With *God Loves Hair*, Juliana would send the illustrations to me, I would approve, we would go back and forth, and Arsenal Pulp Press didn't see anything until it was done. Same with *The Boy & the Bindi*. Whereas, in the case of *Raccoons*, Juliana does the illustration and sends it to Owl, Owl provides notes, I get a version from Owl with their notes, they ask me for any additional notes, and then everything goes back to Juliana. It's a very different process. But in many ways it's exciting because I hadn't realized just how much work the illustration and illustration management processes can be. It's been nice to just be the writer.

DM: You've mentioned that a number of your works are illustrated. We tend to associate illustrations with children's genres and forms, like comics and picture books. But you've published a comic book, *Death Threat*, which is not necessarily a child-oriented topic. You have an illustrated novel, *She of the Mountains*—a bisexual love story. Why has it been important to you to work with illustrations across your projects?

VS: I feel like I am a kind of illustrator with very few skills. I have a strong visual sense and aesthetic, but I have zero skills in that arena. I'm drawn to illustrations because I tend to conceive of things visually. Illustrations feel like a way to extend what I'm not able to do. For example, I imagined *God Loves Hair* not as a collection of short stories, but as an illustrated collection of short stories. That was always the vision for the project.

I think that illustrations also allow me to push a kind of an agenda around representation. Being able to feature queer representation in *She of the Mountains* or racialized representation—a dark skinned, brown, gender non-conforming person in *the Boy & the Bindi*—and trans representation in *Death Threat*. I think illustrations can do that in a powerful way.

I have a short attention span and I love the idea of inviting people into art in as many ways as possible. If the story is boring, then you get to look at some pictures for a while. There's something about using illustrations as an opportunity to amplify what's in the text, to transcend what's beyond the text, but also bring the reader into the text in moments where the text maybe isn't that interesting.

DM: Do you see yourself returning again and again to children's and young adult literature? Are these genres permanent parts of your artistic career?

VS: I love the picture book medium so much. I really hope that it is the kind of format that I can return to because it's just so joyful. A lot of my work can just feel so heavy, especially because I'm drawn to like themes like misogyny and racism. *The Boy & the Bindi* in many ways was such a joy to make, and *Raccoons* was challenging to publish but it's been a joy to put together.

And I'm really moved by the impact of these books. I partnered with a school in Calgary that recorded a reading of *Revenge of the Raccoons*. Seeing the book brought to life by children—there's just so much joy there that I don't get to access otherwise.

As for young adult literature: I don't know. My next novel, *The Hystericals*, is arguably YA. It's told from the perspective of a high school senior, but in many ways the intended audience is wider. I'm always drawn to the limitations of form, as opposed to what a form offers, and with YA I often wonder: how do you talk about emotion, how do you talk about perspective and experience when you don't have the freedom to use a certain vocabulary? That's not to say that YA doesn't use a large vocabulary. But it's interesting that I have once again returned to YA in a way.

With YA, I struggle because we so often get stories about young people in school. With *The Hystericals*, I really wanted to avoid the school setting: we've just seen it so much. It's not interesting to me. And I think that's my difficulty with YA as a consumer. Maybe it's because I'm an old lady, but I am less and less interested in "kids at school" as a narrative. So, with *The Hystericals* it's been a fun challenge. It all takes place during summer break. Spoiler.

DM: Can you describe the difference between the Canadian and American publishing landscapes, in the context of the type of work you want to put into the world?

VS: I don't know. I think one of the things I am fascinated by in the US is how often first-time writers get large publishing contracts. In Canada it always just seems like people who get published are making waves; they have some sort of digital footprint or buzz around them. The American market seems to be so much more saturated. The Canadian market feels very small, at times, like a small and sometimes unhealthy workplace. Whereas I feel like in the US, there's probably no way to know all your colleagues in the workplace, so that to me feels kind of exciting. I wonder about what it means to get to write your work more anonymously and produce your work in a more anonymous atmosphere versus creating work that you know your colleagues are going to potentially have access to or read or have feelings about.

DM: Would you say there are advantages associated with the Canadian publishing context?

VS: The other thing that's not an advantage is that in the US the money is, I want to say, sometimes like three or four times as much as the Canadian numbers I have seen. There was recently a "publishing paid me" hashtag, and seeing what authors in the US were getting paid was bananas to me. I'll just be transparent about it: for my book of poetry [*even this page is white*], for instance, my advance was $700, and this was in 2016.

The book was longlisted for Canada Reads, but that stuff ultimately doesn't pay. I have a friend in the US who had signed a deal for her debut poetry book. She was complaining because she'd gotten what she called a "shitty" advance from her publisher and she disclosed that it was fifteen thousand dollars. In her defense, fifteen thousand dollars from what I have seen in the US for advances is probably small.

So, are there advantages to Canadian publishing? I think about my relationship with Arsenal Pulp Press, which I'm so grateful for. They became familiar with my work through their other authors, like Amber Dawn and Rae Spoon. I think I had access to them because it's a smaller community. I don't know what my publishing trajectory could have looked like in the US, if it would have taken longer for me to get "officially" published. I don't know, but a benefit of being in the Canadian industry is that it's small enough that people can start to take notice, and I do feel like when I self-published *God Loves Hair*, people did start to take notice. Even though I was just a self-published author at the time, I was asked to be on the jury of the Dayne Ogilvie Prize for LGBTQ2S+ Emerging Writers. Again, I think that could only happen because the industry so small.

DM: Some of your books are very deliberately set in Canadian cities: both *Raccoons* and *The Subtweet* feature Toronto quite prominently, for example. I understand that your book-in-progress, *The Hystericals*, is set in the US. How do you determine where your stories will be set?

VS: Alberta comes up a lot in my work, too, because that's where I'm from. *Raccoons* and *The Subtweet* were the hardest books for me to get published, and I do think some of that is because I so specifically and emphatically set them in Toronto. Feedback on both books from different editors claimed they were too Toronto-centric, too Canadian. I can't imagine US authors having an equivalent problem. I'm thankful that the publishers who picked up these books saw Toronto as an asset.

With *Raccoons* it just made sense. Raccoons are what we're known for. When I lived in Toronto, the city was known as the "trash panda" capital of the world. So why not lean into it? And how come leaning into a Canadian setting is seen as something that won't sell books? I wonder if this is true for audiences, or if it's just the industry's perception?

With my new book, *The Hystericals*, I've often thought about [author] Zoe Whittall. She has spoken publicly about *The Best Kind of People*—one of her most successful books, if not the most successful. She made a deliberate choice after years and years of not quite getting the reach or success that she wanted. As an experiment, she decided to write a book that did not center queer characters and is set in Connecticut. And it ended up paying off for her in terms of awards and sales and future book deals. I'm curious about these choices as well. So, *The Hystericals* takes place in an unnamed American city. There is no queer storyline and no racialized storyline. One of the things that was really fun, oddly, about writing *The Hystericals*, was writing something white and straight and American. I'm looking forward to my $15,000 advance.

DM: Finally, are there any children's and young adult books that have been particularly influential to you, or anything you've read recently that you would recommend?

VS: Robert Munsch was a huge fave. Dr. Seuss, too. It's interesting: both *Bindi* and *Raccoons* feature a rhyme structure, which I was advised against. When I originally submitted *The Boy & the Bindi* to a different publisher, they came back and said they felt like the story was not a children's book. Part of the problem I've heard about rhyme structures in kids' books is that it limits their ability to be translated. But there's a rich history of rhyming children's books. Clearly, people have found a way to translate Dr. Seuss.

Some of the most innovative children's books I've read recently include B. J. Novak's *The Book with No Pictures*. I was just so excited by it. It felt so different. What a creative way to engage children; he's turning the form upside down. There's also Sesame Street's *The Monster at the End of the Book*. Really creative. I found it so innovative; I was so moved. Both books took the picture book format and did something totally new with it.

An exciting book that I like to shout out, which is probably very inappropriate but on-brand for me, is one that I bought in Japan: Sato Shin and Nishimura Toshio's *Unko!*. It's about this little poo that looks like a poop emoji. We see its trajectory—it gets rejected by its maker and then it feels abandoned. It tries to find itself. It's like the identity story of poo. Spoiler: it ends up finding its home in a farm where it becomes this helpful fertilizer. It's such a wacky story, a children's book about poo. It's just so silly, but it was just so well done. It was actually moving.

DM: Bowel-moving, if you will.

VS: Exactly. I just admired how it took something kind of disgusting and turned it into a story about rejection, acceptance, and belonging, like where do you fit in as a poo in the world? So, I of course bought it and I'm obsessed with it.

DM: Thank you so much for this and all of your comments, Vivek! I really appreciate it, and I know our readers will too.

Works Cited

Dimaline, Cherie. *The Marrow Thieves*. Cormorant Books, 2017.
Feinberg, Leslie. *Stone Butch Blues*. Firebrand Books, 1993.
Francis, Brian. *Fruit*. ECW Press, 2004.
Munsch, Robert. *Love You Forever*. Illustrated by Sheila McGraw, Firefly Books, 1986.
Novak, B. J. *The Book with No Pictures*. Dial Books, 2014.
Shin, Sato, and Nishimura Toshio. *Unko!* Bunkeidō, 2009.
Shraya, Vivek. *The Boy & the Bindi*. Illustrated by Rajni Perera, Arsenal Pulp Press, 2016.
Shraya, Vivek. *Death Threat*. Illustrated by Ness Lee, Arsenal Pulp Press, 2019.
Shraya, Vivek. *even this page is white*. Arsenal Pulp Press, 2016.
Shraya, Vivek. *God Loves Hair: 10th Anniversary Edition*. Illustrated by Juliana Neufeld, Arsenal Pulp Press, 2020.
Shraya, Vivek. *How to Fail as a Popstar: A Play*. Arsenal Pulp Press, 2021.
Shraya, Vivek. *Revenge of the Raccoons*. Illustrated by Juliana Neufeld, Owlkids Books, 2022.
Shraya, Vivek. *She of the Mountains*. Illustrated by Raymond Biesinger, Arsenal Pulp Press, 2014.
Shraya, Vivek. *The Subtweet*. ECW Press, 2020.
Shraya, Vivek. *What I LOVE about being QUEER*. George Brown College, 2013.
Silverberg, Cory, and Fiona Smyth. *Sex Is a Funny Word*. Seven Stories Press, 2015.
Silverberg, Cory, and Fiona Smyth. *What Makes a Baby*. Seven Stories Press, 2013.
Stone, Jon. *The Monster at the End of This Book*. Illustrated by Michael Smollin, Sesame Street, 1971.
Whittall, Zoe. *The Best Kind of People*. Penguin Random House, 2016.

CONTRIBUTORS

Kristopher Alexander is an assistant professor of media production at Toronto Metropolitan University. His research focuses on how video game design provides a model for developing active engagement within higher education. Most recently, Dr. Alexander has undertaken research-creation in the area of e-sports, where he developed curricula for video game engine architecture and helped build e-sports infrastructure via two training facilities and eight collegiate e-sport teams. At the time of this writing, Dr. Alexander is the #1 Canadian *Lightseekers*™ player, was formerly globally ranked #17th in *Street Fighter 3: Third Strike Online Edition*, and is a video game streamer, known as "PhDigi."

Amanda K. Allen is professor of children's literature at Eastern Michigan University. Her research focuses on postwar adolescent romance novels (known as junior novels) and the midcentury network of professional women who produced and distributed them. Her current book project constructs a revised history of twentieth-century young adult literature that incorporates histories of women's employment in publishing, librarianship, and education. She has also published articles on fan and fandom studies, and she is currently the YA section editor of the *Journal of Popular Romance Studies*.

Brianna Anderson is a Marion L. Brittain Postdoctoral Fellow at the Georgia Institute of Technology. She is currently working on a book-length project on representations of environmental disasters and youth activism in children's and young adult comics. Her research interests include comics studies, digital humanities, ecohorror, girlhood studies, and zines. Her work has recently appeared in *Children's Literature in Education*, *The Lion and the Unicorn*, and *Studies in Comics*. She received her PhD in English from the University of Florida.

Catherine Burwell is an associate professor in the Werklund School of Education at the University of Calgary. Her research and teaching are situated in the areas of literacy, language arts and media education. Catherine is particularly interested in exploring the pedagogical implications of youth digital culture. Before joining the University of Calgary, Catherine worked as a secondary school English and media studies teacher with the Toronto District School Board for more than ten years.

Katharine Capshaw is professor of English and Africana studies affiliate at the University of Connecticut. Her work focuses on Black youth culture and social justice, with particular emphases on visual arts, drama, and sequential narrative. Her books include *Civil Rights Childhood: Picturing Liberation in African American Photobooks*, *Children's Literature of the Harlem Renaissance*, and the coedited *Who Writes for Black Children? African American Children's Literature before 1900*.

Negin Dahya is an assistant professor at The Institute of Communication, Culture, Information, and Technology (ICCIT) at University of Toronto. She is the appointed special advisor for Equity, Diversity and Inclusion, Office of the Dean, University of Toronto Mississauga. Dahya's research focuses on race and gender equity among girls and women of color, with a focus on media education and media production. Dahya also conducts research with refugee communities in resettlement in North America and in refugee camps, exploring the roles and relationships between education and technology in their lives. Dahya has published in *Learning, Media and Technology*; *Journal of Documentation*; *Comparative Education*; and *Information, Communication and Society*, among other venues. More information about her work can be found at www.negindahya.ca.

Gabriel Duckels is an Early Career Research Fellow at Fitzwilliam College, University of Cambridge. His research has been published in various journals including the *Children's Literature Association Quarterly*; *Jeunesse: Young People, Texts, Cultures*; and the *European Journal of Cultural Studies*.

Paige Gray is professor of liberal arts and writing at the Savannah College of Art and Design. She's the author of *Cub Reporters: American Children's Literature and Journalism in the Golden Age* (SUNY Press). Her work has appeared in academic journals such as *Children's Literature* and *Children's Literature Association Quarterly*, as well as media outlets including *Time*.

com, *Chicago Tribune*, and *The Conversation*, among others. She's currently researching ideas of childhood, thingness, and American puppetry. Her second monograph, *Children of the Black Press: How Youth Helped Create an African American Youth Literature,* is forthcoming from The Ohio State University Press.

Gabrielle Atwood Halko teaches about representation, race, and visibility in children's and young adult literature. Her research addresses questions of voice and power in the creation of cultural memory and the ways that national and childhood innocence shape historical narrative. She cofounded and served as inaugural coeditor of the peer-reviewed journal, *Research on Diversity in Youth Literature.* More of Dr. Halko's work is available on her website, *War Stories*, www.kidsandwar.com.

Natasha Hurley is dean of humanities and social sciences and professor of English at Memorial University in St John's, Newfoundland. She was previously an associate professor in the Department of English and Film Studies at the University of Alberta in Edmonton. She is the author of *Circulating Queerness: Before the Gay and Lesbian Novel* (University of Minnesota Press 2018), editor of a special double issue of *ESC: English Studies in Canada* on "Childhood and Its Discontents," and coeditor (with Steven Bruhm) of *Curiouser: On the Queerness of Children* (University of Minnesota Press 2004). She has been winner of the Hennig-Cohen Prize from the Melville Society (2018) and the Priestley Prize from the Association of Canadian College and University Teachers of English (2012). Her contribution to this volume is drawn from "Kidless Lit: Children, Childhood, and Minor Kinship Forms," a research project funded by the Social Sciences and Humanities Research Council of Canada.

Kenneth B. Kidd is professor of English at the University of Florida. He is the author of three books, most recently *Theory for Beginners: Children's Literature as Critical Thought* (Fordham University Press), and coeditor of four essay collections, most recently (also with Derritt Mason) *Queer as Camp: Essays on Summer, Style, and Sexuality* (Fordham University Press).

Erica Law-Montes is a PhD candidate at The Ohio State University. She is tribally enrolled at the Cheyenne River Sioux tribe. She has taught writing and literature courses and now works for a nonprofit organization in Columbus, Ohio.

Derritt Mason is an associate professor of English at the University of Calgary, which is situated on the traditional territories of the people of the Treaty Seven region in Southern Alberta. They are the author of *Queer Anxieties of Young Adult Literature and Culture* (University Press of Mississippi, 2021) and coeditor, with Kenneth B. Kidd, of *Queer as Camp: Essays on Summer, Style, and Sexuality* (Fordham University Press, 2019), which won the 2021 Children's Literature Association Edited Book Award.

Brandon Murakami is a PhD candidate in English at the University of Florida. His interests lie at the intersection of cultural studies, children's literature/culture, and media studies, old and new, with a particular emphasis on race and representation in transnational popular culture.

Tehmina Pirzada is an assistant professor of English at Texas A&M University at Qatar. Her research focuses on girlhood studies, youth cultures, and the visual and popular cultures of South Asia. Her work has appeared in *Bookbird: A Journal of International Children's Literature*; *South Asian Popular Culture*; *Girlhood Studies: An Interdisciplinary Journal*; *South Asian Review*; and the *Journal of Language, Literature, and Culture*.

Cristina Rhodes is an assistant professor of multiethnic American literature at Shippensburg University of Pennsylvania. She has published multiple academic articles on Latinx children's literature, particularly thinking about how the Latinx youth body engages in changing the world. In addition to her scholarly writing, she is a regular contributor to *Latinxs in Kid Lit*, publishing reviews and original articles for teachers, librarians, and other consumers. She is also a book review coeditor for the academic journal *Research on Diversity in Youth Literature*.

Cristina Rivera is a PhD candidate at The Ohio State University. She researches and publishes on Latinx representation in children and young adult literature and media. She has taught literature and writing courses on race, culture, and identity in the United States through literature and media for young people. She was a high school hub coordinator for OSU's LASER: Latinx Space for Enrichment and Research and also worked on integrating more culturally sustaining pedagogies with the Writing Across the Curriculum program at OSU.

Jakob Rosendal is a postdoctoral researcher in the Department of Art History, Aesthetics & Culture, and Museology at Aarhus University, Denmark.

His research focuses on pictures of children and the theoretical and methodological relevance of psychoanalysis for image studies. More particularly, his research explores the repetition and/or repression of girl pictures in Western art and visual culture since the latter half of the eighteenth century. This research interest has entailed an expansion of his work into the fields of children's literature and drawings. He is currently working on a project that explores the icon as a phenomenon of visual culture through the recent iconization of Greta Thunberg.

TreaAndrea M. Russworm is professsor in the Interactive Media & Games Division at the University of Southern California. She is book series editor of *Power Play: Games, Politics, Culture* (Duke University Press) and associate editor for Outreach and Equity for the *Journal of Cinema and Media Studies*. With research expertise in digital media, popular culture, and African American studies, Russworm is also the founder of Radical Play, a public humanities initiative and afterschool program in Springfield, Massachusetts, and she is the author or editor of three books: *Blackness is Burning: Civil Rights, Popular Culture, and the Problem of Recognition*; *Gaming Representation: Race, Gender, and Sexuality in Video Games*; and *From Madea to Media Mogul: Theorizing Tyler Perry*.

Vivek Shraya is an artist whose body of work crosses the boundaries of music, literature, visual art, theater, and film. Her album *Part-Time Woman* was nominated for the Polaris Music Prize, and her best-selling book *I'm Afraid of Men* was heralded by *Vanity Fair* as "cultural rocket fuel." She is also the founder of the award-winning publishing imprint VS. Books, which supports emerging BIPOC writers. A seven-time Lambda Literary Award finalist, Vivek was a Pride Toronto grand marshal and has been a brand ambassador for MAC Cosmetics and Pantene. She is a director on the board of the Tegan and Sara Foundation, and her debut play, *How to Fail as a Popstar*, has been adapted for television with the support of the Canadian Broadcasting Corporation (CBC).

Victoria Ford Smith is an associate professor of English at the University of Connecticut, where she specializes in childhood and British literature and culture of the nineteenth and twentieth centuries. Her book *Between Generations: Collaborative Authorship in the Golden Age of Children's Literature* (University Press of Mississippi, 2017) won the Children's Literature Association Book Award. She is currently working on a project about child artists, vision, and modernism.

Joshua Whitehead is an Oji-nêhiyaw, Two-Spirit member of Peguis First Nation (Treaty One). Whitehead is the author of *full-metal indigiqueer*, *Jonny Appleseed*, and *Making Love with the Land*. He is also the editor of *Love after the End: An Anthology of Two-Spirit and Indigiqueer Speculative Fiction*. Currently, Whitehead is an assistant professor at the University of Calgary where he teaches in both the English and International Indigenous Studies Departments.

Shuyin Yu is a PhD candidate in the Department of English at the University of Calgary. Her research interests are East Asian diaspora studies, asexuality studies, and food studies in children's and young adult literature and media. She received her HBA from the University of Toronto and her MA from the University of Calgary.

INDEX

Italicized page numbers indicate illustrations and photographs.

Abate, Michelle Ann, 6, 158
accessibility, 109, 266–67
Across the Blue Pacific (Chaconas and Lewin), 202
activism, 79–80
addresses to children, 190, 194, 196, 199
adult anxieties, 143, 158
Aerial_Knight's Never Yield (game), 180
aetonormativity, 66, 71, 72, 73, 75, 77n14
affinity spaces (Gee), 9, 66, 72–74
African identity, 36, 38
Afrocentrism, 38
Afrofuturism, 236
age, genre and, 115, 117–18
agency of children, 8, 20–21, 25–26; adults and, 47
agender, 14, 246, 249, 251–54, 255, 258
Ahmed, Sara, 223
AIDS: compared to COVID-19 pandemic, 100–101; emergency education and, 100; fear and ignorance about, 100–101; Otherness and, 101; picture books and, 10, 101–5
Ainak Wala Jinn (television show), 11, 142, 143, 144–45, 148–52, 153
Alex, the Kid with AIDS (Girard), 103–4
Alexander, Kristopher: biography, 273; in panel discussion on video games and digital cultures, 175–76, 178, 179, 181–82; referenced, 12
Alice in Wonderland (Carroll), 162
Alif Laila (television show), 11, 142, 143, 144, 145–47, 151, 152

Alim, H. Samy, 231, 240–41
Allbe, James G., 19
Allen, Amanda K.: biography, 273; chapter by, 65–78; referenced, 9
Allison, Anne, 134
Allison, Rachel Hope, 80
alt: as term, 3–4, 6, 7, 33; alt within (Hurley), 197, 199; futurity and, 243; racial discussions and, 231–33; scholarly frameworks, 6
Americanness, 132–33, 205, 208, 212
Anderson, Brianna: biography, 273; chapter by, 79–98; referenced, 9–10
anime, 127–28, 129. *See also* shōnen anime
Annapurna Interactive, 182
antirealism, 70–71
Anzaldúa, Gloria, 217, 223, 226
Appiah, Kwame Anthony, 243n1
Aragon, Cecilia, 75n2, 76n6
archives, 34, 35–36, 100, 104
argumentation, 179–80
Ariès, Philippe, 227n5
Arredondo, Adelina, 220
Arsenal Pulp Press, 117, 263, 266, 267, 270
artifice, 164
Asian American identity, 204, 205, 213n4
Attack on Titan (Isayama), 131
Augé, Marc, 12, 189
authenticity, 205
Awful Library Books (website), 103

Baby, You're Projecting (Shraya), 260
Baird, Bil, 160
Banaji, Shakuntala, 143

279

Bann, Jennifer, 28
Banner of Light (periodical), 19
Baraka, Amiri, 34
Barbed Wire Baseball (Moss), 211
Barnestreger—Køn og seksualitet i børns tegninger (exhibition), 45, 46, 49, 50, 51
Barr, David, 4
Barzilai, Shuli, 62n10
Baseball Saved Us (Mochizuki and Lee), 207, 208, 211
Batman, 85
Bearable (video game), 176
Beauvais, Clémentine, 29, 67, 74
Belcourt, Billy-Ray, 123
Bell, John, 160
Benjamin, Ruha, 173
Benjamin, Walter, 61n6
Berndt, Jaqueline, 138n5
Bernstein, Robin, 5, 22, 101–2, 110–11, 252
Best Kind of People, The (Whittall), 270–71
Bildungsroman conventions, 10, 115–16, 250
Bishop, Rudine Sims, 41, 233
Black, Rebecca, 72, 73
Black Arts Movement, 36, 37
Black children's literature as alt, 32–33
Black culture, 8, 32
#BlackLivesMatter Movement, 91
Blackness in (white) archives, 32
Black Tides of Heaven, The (Yang), 246–47, 249–58
Blue Jay in the Desert (Shigekawa and Kukuchi), 207, 208
Blumenreich, Megan, 102, 103
Blumenthal, Eileen, 160, 167
Book of Life, The (Gutiérrez), 219
Book with No Pictures, The (Novak), 271
Borden, Louise W., 202
Boruto: Naruto Next Generations (series), 130
Bouissou, Jean-Marie, 138n7
Bowie, David, 158
Boy & the Bindi, The (Shraya), 265, 267, 268, 271
Bracelet, The (Uchida and Yardley), 206, 207–8
Brandes, Stanley, 220
Braude, Anne, 23–24, 25
Brewer, Brad, 34
Briggs-Cloud, Marcus, 237
Britten, Emma Hardinge, 24
Brothers Grimm, 48
Brown, Michael, 96

Brownies' Book, The (magazine), 32, 33
Bullins, Ed, 34
Burwell, Catherine: biography, 274; in panel discussion on video games and digital cultures, 181
Busse, Kristina, 70–71
Butler, Catherine, 127
Butler, Francelia, 217

Canby, Vincent, 161
Can We Play Now? (Polsky), 106
Capistrán-López, Carlos, 220
capitalism, 82
Capshaw, Kate: biography, 274; chapter by, 32–43; referenced, 4, 5, 8, 14
carceral logics, 173, 175
Carrier Dove (periodical), 19
Carroll, Jane Suzanne, 217
Carroll, Lewis, 11, 161–62
Caruth, Cathy, 198
Castañeda, Claudia, 233–34
catechisms, 24, 25–26
Catholic Church, 30n5, 221
Cemetery Boys (Thomas), 13, 219, 220, 221–22, 225–27
Chaconas, Dori J., 202
Chandler, Karen, 32
Chester Nez and the Unbreakable Code (Bruchac), 203
Chickadee (magazine), 267
child-adult relationship: collaboration between, 73–74; hierarchies of relationship, 22–23, 26–27, 71–72, 92–93; kinship, 5, 6, 9; otherness to each other, 67, 191–92, 193–94; unconscious and, 194, 197, 199
childhood: agender, 14, 246, 249, 251–54, 255, 258; compulsory sexuality of, 254; construction of, 5; kinship model, 47, 66, 67, 72; queer possibility and, 157–58; romanticism for, 19–20, 28; threshold model, 9, 45–51, 61
child mediums, 8, 19–29
children: agency of, 8, 20–21; as construct, 20–21, 30n3; CYA by, 80; desexualization, 251; formation, 45–47, 234, 240, 251–52; as passive, 25; skepticism towards, 22; taking seriously, 45
Children's Literature Association Quarterly, 127
children's media as Western, 11

Childress, Alice, 8, 34, 34–41, 35, 39, 40–41, 42n4, 42n5. *See also* "Sea Island Song"
Christensen, Nina, 21, 22
citizenship, 205–12, 239–40
Clark, Beverly Lyon, 7
Clifton, Jennifer, 156
Coco (Molina and Unkrich), 219
co-creation, 173
collaboration, 5–6, 91–93
collage, 93
collective memory, 203
colonialism, 119–20
coloring books, 109, 110
comic books, 268
conjuncture (Rustin), 105–6
Conrad, Rachel, 6, 21
consciousness, 171
consent, 69, 76n10, 174–75
content creation, 176
Cook, Florence, 28, 30n5
Cook, Siân, 100, 104
Cooperative Children's Book Center, 5
Córdova, Zoraida, 221. See also *Labyrinth Lost*
Corner, John, 129–30
COVID-19 pandemic, 218; affect and experience of, 99; compared to HIV/AIDS, 100–101; enscription and, 105–11; impacts, 134; picture books and, 10, 99–101, 106–12; television shows and, 145
Craig, David, 100–101
Cree language, 116
crip time, 106
criticality, 171
Crozier, Lorna, 122
CRYTC (Centre for Research in Young People's Texts and Cultures), 6
cultural memory, 152, 202
CYA (children's and young adult literature): as affinity space, 73; anime and, 127; Black, 32–33; by children, 80; cultural memory and, 202; death in, 102, 217; decolonization, 242; environmental, 80; fanfiction as, 9; genre conventions, 117–18, 120–21; as humor for adults, 187–88; imagetext and visual media, 10–12; nonwhite representation, 231–32; scholarship in, generally, 5–7; as scriptive (Bernstein), 102; sex and sexuality in, 118–19; white privilege and, 4, 5
cyborgs, 163

DACA (Deferred Action for Childhood Arrivals), 213n6
Dahlen, Sarah Park, 4–5
Dahya, Negin: biography, 274; in panel discussion on video games and digital cultures, 172–77, 181, 183; referenced, 12
Dark Crystal, The (Henson), 156–67
Davenport, Reuben Briggs, 22
Davila, Denise, 220, 227n2
Davis, Andrew Jackson, 27
Davis, Katie, 75n2, 76n6
Dawn, Amber, 270
death: in CYA, 102, 217; el Día de los Muertos, 217–21, 223, 224, 225–26; epistemologies of, 13; life cycle and, 13; Mexican traditions, 219; as possibility, 219, 220; rituals, 220–23; suicidal ideation, 264; as transition, 223–25. *See also* el Día de los Muertos
Death Threat (Shraya), 268
de Certeau, Michel, 200n2
decolonization, 242
Dennis, Letise, 206
Derby, Doris, 33
Derrida, Jacques, 197
desire and lack, 55
De Vos, Laura Maria, 235–36
Día de los Muertos, el, 217–21, 223, 224, 225–26
Diaz, Natalie, 121
digital literacy, 106
digital technology, pedagogical potential of, 12
Dillon, Grace L., 235–36
Dimaline, Cherie, 234, 235, 237, 243, 263. See also *Marrow Thieves, The*
disabilities, 106, 145
Disintegrate/Dissociate (Twist), 123
Disney, 128
Disneyfication, 151–52
Doctor, Farzana, 263
Doordarshan (television channel), 141–42, 147
drama, literature on, 40–41
drawing, 8–9; analyzing, 48–50, 90; conceptually, 44; as inspiration, 162; narrative and, 48; nonfigurative, 58; psychoanalysis and, 51–59, 62n7; scholarship on, 61n1; violence in, 50, 51. See also *Little Red Riding Hood*; *World War 3*
dreaming, 121
Du Bois, W. E. B., 33

Duckels, Gabriel: biography, 274; chapter by, 99–113; referenced, 10, 105, 106–7
Dunbar-Ortiz, Roxanne, 236
Duncombe, Stephen, 81, 82, 88, 90

Eastwood, Jemima, 90
Echterling, Clare, 80
Edelman, Lee, 70, 131
el Día de los Muertos, 217–21, 223, 224, 225–26
ELM (Educated Little Monsters), 92–93
Elman, Julia Passanante, 6
emergency education, 99–100
Endo, Rachel, 203
English language: literature challenging, 120; in *My Hero Academia*, 133
enigmatic signifiers (Laplanche), 187, 189, 190–91, 193, 195, 196, 197; enigmas of, 199–200; strangeness and, 198
enscription, 102, 105–11
environmental crises, 9–10, 79, 81–88, 91
ephemeral cultural production, 32, 34
Epic Games, 176
epistemologies of death, 13
Eurocentrism, 10, 116, 131
even this page is white (Shraya), 269–70
excrement, 271

Facebook groups, 154n3, 156–57, 158, 167
fairy tales, 11, 162
Fallout 4 (game), 180
fandom for *Dark Crystal*, 11, 166–67
fanfiction: community surrounding, 72–73; as CYA, 9; demographics, 75n6; Harry Potter, 9; parents on children writing, 65; scholarly significance, 65
Fauset, Jessie, 33
female sexuality, 148
Fern, Ong Sor, 256
Finch, Christopher, 161
Fire Song (Jones), 115, 123
Fish for Jimmy (Yamasaki), 210
Fleming, Julius B., 41
Fletcher, John, 195
flowers, 55
Flowers from Mariko (Noguchi and Jenks), 209
Flynn, Richard, 21
formal limitations, 269
Forsgren, La Donna, 33–34
Fortnite (game), 179

Foucault, Michel, 173
Fox, Ferdy, 19
Fox, Kate, 22
Fox, Margaret, 22, 28–29
Francis, Brian, 262
Freire, Paolo, 10, 81
French, Jess, 80
Freud, Sigmund, 53, 164, 192, 194, 197, 200n3
Froud, Brian, 164, 167
Fruit (Francis), 262
Full-Metal Indigiqueer (Whitehead), 114, 115, 116, 120
futurism, 88, 234, 235–36, 238; Afrofuturism, 236; reproductive, 70

Galland, Antoine, 146
Galvan, Margaret, 80, 96
games, pedagogical potential of, 12, 179
game studies, 170
gamification, 181, 182
gaze, 183
Gee, James Paul, 9, 66, 72
gender: genderqueerness, 246; identity, 222–23; mediumship and, 24; nonconforming expressions, 246, 260–61; pronouns, 247, 252, 255; roles, 26, 148, 151
genre: age and, 115, 117–18; "alt" sensibilities and, 143; conventions, 145–52; Eurocentric understandings, 10, 116, 131; picture books as, 260–61; as term, 129–30; work across, 264–65. *See also* shōnen anime
gentrification, 91–95, 94
George, Elizabeth, 42n3
Gibson, Louis Rauch, 217
Girard, Linda, 103–4
Giroux, Henry, 106, 107, 109
globalization, 143, 189, 240
Glynne, Andy, 103, 105
God Loves Hair (Shraya), 14, 260–64, 265, 266, 267
Goldin, Rebecca, 88, 89
Gray, Paige: biography, 274–75; chapter by, 156–69; referenced, 11
Great Realisation, The, 108–9
Gripsrud, Jostein, 146
Gubar, Marah, 5–6, 9, 21, 47, 61n6, 66, 67, 72; on approaching children's literature, 74–75
Gullah culture, 35–36, 37, 39
Gupta, Kristina, 254

Haberkorn, Gideon, 162–63
Hager, Lisa, 127
Halberstam, Jack, 164
Halko, Gabrielle Atwood: biography, 275; chapter by, 202–16; referenced, 13
Hameed, Abdul, 143, 144–45, 149
Haraway, Donna, 163, 166
Harde, Roxanne, 162
Harry Potter fandom, 157; SS/HG fanfiction, 9, 66–73, 75n3, 75n5, 76n6, 76n11
Hate U Give, The (Thomas), 231
Hello Hello (Wenzel), 80
Hemmann, Kathryn, 138n8
Henson, Cheryl, 163–64, 165
Henson, Jim, 160, 163. See also *Dark Crystal, The*; *Labyrinth*
hero's journey, 161
heteronormativity, 119, 158
History of My Brief Body, A (Belcourt), 123
HIV/AIDS: compared to COVID-19 pandemic, 100–101; emergency education and, 100; fear and ignorance about, 100–101; Otherness and, 101; picture books and, 10, 101–5
HIV Graphic Communication (archive), 100, 104
home: formations of, 116, 143; homelessness, 100
"home-away-home" narratives, 115, 116, 250
Horikoshi Kohei, 11, 128, 132–37, 138n4
Houghton Mifflin (press), 213n11
How to Fail as a Popstar (Shraya), 264–65
Hu, Frank H., 205
humor, 149–50, 187–88
Hurley, Natasha: biography, 275; chapter by, 187–201; referenced, 12–13, 74
Hurricane Katrina, 109
Huyck, David, 4–5
Hystericals, The (Shraya), 269, 270–71

identification, 53
identity: African, 38; Asian American, 204, 205; "enigmatic signifier" as challenging, 190; Latinx, 240; Otherkin, 166; queer children, 247
immigration, 182, 218, 231, 239, 240
I'm Not a Plastic Bag (Allison), 80
Indigenous peoples: displacement, 236, 237–38; genocide of, 220–21; Indigeneity, 115, 121–22; in *The Marrow Thieves*, 230, 235–36; speculative fiction and, 231, 235
innocence, cultural capital of, 27–28
Inoue, Asao B., 232, 242
Inside (game), 179
institutional barriers, 176–77, 181–82
Isayama Hajime, 131
It's Clinic Day (Stevens), 100, 103, 104

Jahju, Muntu, 81–84, 83
Jalal, Ayesha, 151
James, Adrian, 79
James, Allison, 79
Japan, politics with US, 128, 132–33, 134
Japanese American incarceration, 13, 202–14
Jaques, Zoe, 158
Jencken, Kate Fox, 19
jewelry, 156–57
Jiménez Garcia, Marilisa, 5, 112n1
*jinn*s, 152–53
Johns Island, 36, 37, 38
Johnson, Derek, 77n15
Johnson, Richard, 146
Jones, Adam Garnet, 115, 123
Jones, Brian Jay, 161
Jonny Appleseed (Whitehead), 10, 114–22
Justice, Daniel Heath, 121

Kaliyaan (Farooq), 142
Kawahara Reki, 131
Kazi, Taha, 143
Kendall, George W., 20
Kerr, Ted, 100
Kersey, H. A., 24
Kidd, Kenneth B.: biography, 275; referenced, 62nn6–7, 158, 162
kid lit, as term, 7
Kikuchi, Isao, 207, 208, 209, 210
Kincaid, James, 20, 30n3, 71, 77n13
King, Katie, 30n5
Kini, Sashank, 142
Kishimoto Masashi, 130
Kitabna (charity), 109–10
kitsch, 149
Kitson, Alfred, 24
Kittredge, Katharine, 127
Klaufus, Christien, 220
Kleinman, Jake, 128
Konsmo, Erin, 117

Krull, Kathleen, 218
Kuilan, Alejandro, 84–85, *85*, *86–87*
Kümmerling-Meibauer, Bettina, 137n2, 138n5
Kuper, Peter, 81
Kusama, Yayoi, 55
Kustritz, Anne, 76n8

Labyrinth (Henson), 158
Labyrinth Lost (Córdova), 13, 219, 220, 221, 223–25, 226–27
Lacan, Jacques, 54
LaCapra, Dominick, 243
Lampert, Jo, 204–5
land ownership, 42n5, 208, 237
language: as alternative voice, 241; "correctness," 142; politics of, 153n1; pronouns, 247, 252, 255; Punjabi, 150; sexual desire and, 198; signification beyond, 196; Spanish, 241; translation, 146; Urdu, 142; whiteness and, 232–33
Laplanche, Jean, 12, 55–56, 187, 190–91, 192, 193, 194, 196, 197; on strangeness, 198; on the unconscious, 199
Larrick, Nancy, 5
Latinx people, 13, 218, 238
Laurence, Margaret, 122
Law-Montes, Erica: biography, 275; chapter by (with Rivera), 230–45; referenced, 13–14
Lawson, Donovan, 96
Laycock, Joseph, 166
Lee, Dom, 207
Lee-Tai, Amy, 210
Lesnik-Oberstein, Karín, 74
Levin, Kelly, 82
Lewin, Ted, 202
libraries, 100, 103, 172–73, 175, 261, 267
literacy, digital, 106
literary awards, 114, 116, 118, 120, 262, 263, 270
Little Red Riding Hood, 9; children's drawings, *49, 50, 51, 53, 54, 55, 57, 58, 59, 60*; editions, 44, 50, 52; gender in interpretations, 51–52, 58; variant versions, 47–48, 52, 58–59
Liu, Ken, 248
Lorde, Audre, 119
lore, 240
Lorenzo, Ronald, 138n4
Lothian, Alexis, 227n6, 238
Loutzenheiser, Lisa W., 205
Love after the End (Whitehead), 114, 120, 121
Lyceum Manual, The, 24–25

MacCormack, Patricia, 164
Macintosh, Lori B., 205
Mafia 3 (game), 183
magic, 164–67, 221, 223
Making Love with the Land (Whitehead), 114, 122
Mañanaland (Ryan), 230, 231, 233, 234, 238–43
manga: scholarship on, 127–28; as term, 127, 129. *See also* shōnen anime
Mann, George, 249
Maria Molina and the Days of the Dead (Krull), 218
Marrow Thieves, The (Dimaline), 230, 231, 233, 234, 235–38, 239
Marshall, T. H., 202
masculinity: *Little Red Riding Hood* and, 52; toxic, 119
Mason, Derritt: biography, 276; interview with Shraya, 260–71; interview with Whitehead, 114–23; in panel discussion on video games and digital cultures, 176, 179, 181, 183; referenced, 10, 14, 143
mass culture, 85, 88, 101, 131
masturbation, 264
material culture, 91
Matie, Spirit, 19
McAllister, Matthew P., 104
McAra, Catriona, 163
McLuhan, Marshall, 90
McRuer, Robert, 102
media mix (Steinberg), 129
mediumship, 19, 22, 23, 27, 30n5
Mehrez, Samia, 241, 242
Melissa's Story (Glynne), 103, 105
melodrama, 143, 145–46, 148
memory: collective, 203; cultural, 152, 202
Message from Corona, A (Tedder), 108
methodology, 172–75
Metis nation, 244n3
MMIWG (Missing and Murdered Indigenous Women and Girls), 119
Mochizuki, Ken, 207, 208
Moore, Rebecca, 75n5
Mortensen, Karen Vibeke, 61n1
Moten, Fred, 40
Mughal, Raees Ahmed, 145
Munsch, Robert, 266, 271
Muppet franchise, 11

Murakami, Brandon: biography, 276; chapter by, 127–40; referenced, 10–11
music from Sea Islands, 39
My Camp Is Closed (Polsky), 106
My Hero Academia (anime series), 11, 128, 132–37, 138n4
My Hero Is You (Patuck), 99–100, 109, 110, 112
My School Is Closed Today (Polsky), 106
My School Is Still Closed (Polsky), 106
mythology, 144, 145, 152–53, 164–67, 206–7

Nachträglichkeit (afterwardness/deferred effect), 194, 197
Nagano Tadashi, 130
Nairn, Karen, 84
Napier, Susan, 128
narratives: disruption of dominant, 231; of heroification, 107; hero's journey, 161; "home-away-home," 115, 116, 250; as impossible and laughable, 200; shōnen, 131; visual, 79–80, 85, 88, 93, 104, 107
Naruto (series), 130
National Child Traumatic Stress Network, 109
nationalism, 205, 212
Native American land, 208, 236
Native American peoples. *See* Indigenous peoples
Neale, Stephen, 129
negation, 247
neoliberalism, 107, 132, 134, 135, 138n7, 177
nepantla, 223
Neufeld, Juliana, 267–68
newsgroups, 3
Ng, James, 257
Nicholas, S. B., 27
Nikolajeva, Maria, 71, 77n14
Nim and the War Effort (Lee), 203
Nodelman, Perry, 25, 26
nonhuman life, 159, 166
Nora Ray the Child-Medium, 23
normalization, 68–69, 235
normative behavior, 60
#Notyourprincess: Voices of Native American Women, 231
Novak, B. J., 271
Nuñez, Gabriela, 239–40
nursery rhymes, 34

objectification, 37, 40
Obolder, Suzanne, 239–40
OBS (Open Broadcaster Software), 175–76, 179
Oda Eiichirō, 130–31
Older, Daniel Jose, 232, 234–35
Once Upon a Time in Zaatari and Azraq (Al-Sayyah and Patuck), 109
One Piece (series), 130–31
op de Beeck, Nathalie, 91
oral culture, 116, 142
Orenstein, Claudia, 160
Orientalism, 14, 248
Otherness: child-adult relationship, 67, 191, 192, 194; in *The Dark Crystal*, 159; death and, 226; desire for Other (Lacan), 54; HIV/AIDS and, 101; sexuality and, 194–95; speculative fiction and, 237
Owlkids Books, 267
Oz, Frank, 158

Pakistani culture, 145
Papa Legba (spirit), 39
Papazian, Gretchen, 204
paranoid reading (Sedgwick), 247, 258
parental consent, 174–75
Paris, Django, 231, 240–41
Park, Gilbert C., 205
Parker, Robert Andrew, 202
parody, 187–88
Part-Time Woman (Shraya), 260
Patuck, Helen, 99–100, 109, 110, 112
Paz, Octavio, 218, 219, 220
pedagogy: for Black children, 40; critical approaches to history, 204; games and digital technology and, 12; of hope (Freire), 81, 88; of pandemics, 109; video games and, 171, 179–80
pedophilia, 30n3, 71
Pennies in a Jar (Borden and Parker), 202
Perera, Rajni, 266
Perloff, Marjorie, 93
persuasion, 179
perversion, 197
Peters, Leonard, 35
Phillips, Adam, 199
Phoenix Gets Great (Wilson-Trudeau and Wilson), 123
Pico, Tommy, 121

picture books: alt citizenship cultivation and, 13; COVID-19 pandemic and, 99–101, 106–12; as genre, 260–61, 271; HIV/AIDS and, 101–5; ideological construction and, 204; on Japanese American incarceration, 203; vs. zines, 91
Piepmeier, Alison, 81, 85, 90, 96
Pigozzi, Mary Joy, 100
Piplo Productions, 109–10, 112
Pirzada, Tehmina: biography, 276; chapter by, 141–55; referenced, 11
place: importance of, 122; non-place, 189, 200n2
Place Where Sunflowers Grow, A (Lee-Tai), 210
poetry, 118, 120, 153
police brutality, 93–96, 231
Polsky, Meredith, 106–7
Polychrome (press), 213n11
pop culture discourse, 178
Pope, Alexander, 146
Posner, Jasmine, 90
posthumanism, 158, 163–64
prairie landscape, 116, 122–23
privatization, 142
proceduralism, 179–80
Przybylo, Ela, 251, 252, 254
psychoanalysis, 51–59, 193
publishing industry: acquisitions, 262, 266; Arsenal Pulp Press, 117, 263, 266, 267, 270; in Canada vs. US, 121, 269–70; children's plays, 34; environmental degradation and, 91; Owlkids Books, 267; race and economic imbalances, 232, 241; Second Story Press, 123; self-publishing, 261, 263
Punjabi language, 150, 151
puppetry, 34, 142, 157, 159–61, 165
Pyle, Kevin, 81

Qaiser, Farooq, 142
queer, as term, 158
queerness: *The Dark Crystal* and, 157–58; death and, 223
queer theory, 6, 164

racial disparities, 239
racial empathy, 12
Radical Play (community engagement program), 12, 171–72

Radway, Janice, 85
Raiford, Leigh, 203
Ramayan (Sagar), 144
Ramayana, 154n2
Reay, Emma Joy, 11–12
redress movement, 213n11
Red Threads of Fortune, The (Yang), 249
Reed, Rex, 157, 161
Reid, Raziel, 116, 117, 118
Reid-Walsh, Jacqueline, 111
Reitan, Richard, 138n7
remix culture, 85
reparative reading (Sedgwick), 247, 258
repatriation, 209–10
representation, 170, 174, 268
reproductive futurism, 70
Reservation Dogs (television series), 123
resistance, 181–82
responsiveness, 33, 34
Revenge of the Raccoons (Shraya), 260, 265, 266, 267–68, 270
Reynolds, Kimberley, 9
Rhodes, Cristina: biography, 276; chapter by, 217–29; referenced, 13
Riot grrrl movement, 81
rituals, 220–23
Rivera, Cristina: biography, 276; chapter by (with Law-Montes), 230–45; referenced, 13–14
Robbins, Trina, 81
Robert Mapplethorpe Museum for Children, 12, 187
Rodriguez, Clemencia, 92
Rodríguez, José Sánchez, 227n2
Rodríguez, Noreen Naseem, 204, 205
Romano, Renee C., 203
Roosevelt, Franklin D., 206
Rose, Jacqueline, 6, 21, 47, 194
Rosenberg, Charles, 107–8
Rosendal, Jakob: biography, 276–77; chapter by, 44–64; referenced, 8–9
Roxworthy, Emily, 206–7
Rudd, David, 74
Russworm, TreaAndrea M.: biography, 277; in panel discussion on video games and digital cultures, 170–72, 177–78, 179–81, 182–83; referenced, 12, 174
Rustin, Michael, 105–6

Ryan, Pam Muños, 234, 238, 243. See also *Mañanaland*
Ryder, Amy, 105, 106–7

Sagar, Ramanand, 144, 147
Said, Edward, 248
Samuels, Ellen, 106
Sánchez-Eppler, Karen, 47
Sanchez, Sonia, 34
Sanders, Joe Sutliff, 5
Sargent, Epes, 30n5
Schodt, Frederik L., 129
Schwebel, Sarah, 21
scriptive thing (Bernstein), 101
Sea Islands, 35, 36, 37, 39–40
"Sea Island Song" (Childress), 34–41, 42n4
Second Story Press, 123
Sedgwick, Eve Kosofsky, 247
seduction, 52–59, 193, 195, 196, 200n3
self, the, 194, 200, 231, 254–55
Sendlor, Charles, 75n6
September 11 attacks, 204–5
sex education, 147–48, 188
Sex Is a Funny Word (Silverberg), 266
sexuality: asexuality, 251; of childhood, 254; as destabilizing, 192, 193; of form, 187, 191, 197; gendered expectations, 148; *Little Red Riding Hood* and, 44, 56; as non-place, 189–90; otherness and, 194–95; as relationality, 188
sexual violence, 68, 70–71, 76n9, 118, 264
Shavit, Zohar, 76n12
She of the Mountains (Shraya), 263, 266, 267, 268
Shepard, Louisa, 25–26
Shigekawa, Marlene, 207, 208, 210
shōnen anime, 10–11, 127–38; approaches to, 128; audience for, 129; characteristics, 130, 137; as genre, 129; publications, 130; scholarship on, 138n4, 138n5
Shraya, Vivek: biography, 277; interview with, 260–71. See also *Baby, You're Projecting*; *Boy & the Bindi, The*; *Death Threat*; *even this page is white*; *God Loves Hair*; *How to Fail as a Popstar*; *Hystericals, The*; *Part-Time Woman*; *Revenge of the Raccoons*; *She of the Mountains*; *Subtweet, The*; *What I LOVE about being QUEER*

Sibii, Razvan, 142
Siegel, Marjorie, 102, 103
Siegert, Bernhard, 255
Sigley, Alek, 138n4
signification, linguistic, 192
silkpunk, 14, 246, 247–48, 255, 256, 257
Silverberg, Cory, 266
Simpson, Leanne Betasamosake, 236–37
Singapore, 257
Sipe, Lawrence R., 204
Smith, Isabella, 23
Smith, Victoria Ford: biography, 277; chapter by, 19–31; referenced, 5, 8
social authority, 69
socialization, 47
societal commentary, 81–82
So Far from the Sea (Bunting), 209
songs and singing: on Gullah culture, 35; in Pakistan, 143; Shraya's musical career, 262
spaces: affinity (Gee), 9, 66, 72–74; non-places, 189
speculative fiction, 230–44; whiteness and, 13, 230, 231
Spiritualism, 8, 19, 22, 25–28
sponsorship, 176
Spoon, Rae, 270
Staake, Bob, 187, 200n1
steampunk, 14, 247, 248
Steinberg, Marc, 129
Stevens, Ruth, 100, 103, 104
Stockton, Kathryn Bond, 61, 158, 197, 251, 252, 253
Stone Butch Blues (Feinberg), 262
Story of Grandmother, The, 47–48
storytelling, 116, 144, 153. See also narratives
streaming services, 128
Subtweet, The (Shraya), 270
Suhr-Sytsma, Mandy, 6, 13, 238
Suzuki Takaaki, 134
Sword Art Online (series), 131

taboos, 68–71
Tahir, Hafeez, 144–45
Tarbox, Gwen Athene, 127
Tedder, Charity, 108
television, 11, 141, 142, 144, 147
Temple, Nellie, 19, 27–28

temporality, 67, 69, 129; crip time, 106; futurity, 131, 234; timelessness, 147
Thighpen, Jim, 35, 41n2
Thirsty Suitors (game), 182
Thomas, Aiden, 13, 219, 220, 221–22, 225–27
Thomas, Ebony Elizabeth, 13, 230–31, 233, 243
Thompson, Jason, 130
Thunberg, Greta, 10, 29, 79, 84
Tides That Bind, The (Radical Play), 172
Time for In-Person School (Polsky), 106
Tomfoolery (author), 108–9
Tosenberger, Catherine, 9, 65, 67
transformation, 226
translation, 146
trauma, 144, 239
Treachery in Beatdown City (game), 180
Trench, Mikael, 165
Tribunella, Eric, 74
Trinka and Sam (series), 109, 110–11, 112
Trites, Roberta Seelinger, 254
Trump, Donald, 213n6
Tubman, Harriet, 34
Tupper, Jennifer, 206
Twist, Arielle, 123
Twitch, 175, 179, 182

Uchida, Yoshiko, 206, 207–8
Ulfelder, Isabella, 88
uncanniness, 163–64
unconscious, 191, 193, 194, 197, 199, 223
Undertale (game), 180
United States, politics with Japan, 128, 132–33, 134
University of Minnesota Press, 121
Urdu language, 142, 145, 149–50, 154n3

Vargas, Mauricio Piñón, 227n2
Varnelis, Kazys, 107
Venba (game), 182
Verniero, Joan C., 103
video games, 11–12, 171, 175, 176
violence in drawing, 50, 51
Virginia (game), 178, 179, 180
virtual reality, 172–73, 174
visual narrative, 79–80, 85, 88, 93, 104, 107
Volpp, Leti, 205
VS. Books, 260

Walcott, Rinaldo, 242–43
Wald, Priscilla, 108

Walker, Alice, 38
Waller, Alison, 6
Warner, Michael, 158
Washington, Mary Helen, 36
Wasylak, Katarzyna, 127
Weekly Shōnen Jump (magazine), 130
Welcome Home, Swallows (Shigekawa), 210
#WeNeedDiverseBooks, 5
#WeNeedDiverseScholars, 5
Wenzel, Brendan, 80
What a Waste! (French), 80
What I LOVE about being QUEER (Shraya), 261
What Makes a Baby (Silverberg), 266
Wheeler, Elizabeth, 6
When Everything Like the Movies (Reid), 116, 117, 118
Whitehead, Joshua: biography, 278; interview with, 114–23; referenced, 10. See also *Full-Metal Indigiqueer*; *Jonny Appleseed*; *Love after the End*; *Making Love with the Land*
whiteness, 119, 206, 230, 243n1, 252; speculative fiction and, 13, 230, 231
white privilege, CYA and, 4, 5
white supremacy, 33, 218, 232
Whitson, Roger, 247–48, 255, 256, 257
Whittall, Zoe, 270
Wilson, Brent, 92
Wilson, Phoenix, 123
Wilson-Trudeau, Marty, 123
Wind Flyers (Johnson), 203
With the Fire on High (Acevedo), 231
Wizard of Oz, The, 88
Woodard, Nathan, 34, 39
worldbuilding, 109, 130, 131, 134, 235, 236, 246, 247, 249, 257; Asian epistemologies and, 247, 256–57, 258; futuristic, 236; queer happiness as, 223; silkpunk, 14; speculative, 235
World War 3, 9, 10, 80–82, 83, 85–88, 86, 87, 89, 96–97
World War II, 202–3, 212. See also Japanese American incarceration
wuxing, 256

xenophobia, 13, 108, 205, 218

Yamamoto, Traise, 206
Yamasaki, Katie, 210
Yang, Neon, 249, 257. See also *Black Tides of Heaven, The*

Yardley, Joanna, 207
yin-yang theory, 256
You Can Call Me Willy (Verniero), 103
youth literature (Jiménez Garcia), 5, 7
Yu, Shuyin: biography, 278; chapter by, 246–59; referenced, 13, 14

Zaidman, Laura M., 217
zine culture, 9–10, 80–81, 85, 88, 90, 92–93

www.ingramcontent.com/pod-product-compliance
Lightning Source LLC
Chambersburg PA
CBHW021959220426
43663CB00007B/887